Gender Politics and Post-Communism

REFLECTIONS FROM EASTERN EUROPE AND THE FORMER SOVIET UNION

EDITED BY NANETTE FUNK AND MAGDA MUELLER

INTRODUCTION BY NANETTE FUNK

D0060754

ROUTLEDGE　New York　London

Published in 1993 by

Routledge
29 West 35th Street
New York, NY 10001

Published in Great Britain by

Routledge
11 New Fetter Lane
London EC4P 4EE

Library of Congress Cataloging-in-Publication Data

Gender politics and post-communism / edited by Nanette Funk and Magda Mueller.
    p. cm. — (Thinking gender)
  Includes bibliographical references.
  ISBN 0-415-90477-3 (hard).—ISBN 0-415-90478-1 (pbk.)
    1. Women—Europe, Eastern. 2. Women—Former Soviet republics.
  3. Feminism—Europe, Eastern. 4. Feminism—Former Soviet republics.
  5. Post-communism—Europe, Eastern. 6. Post-communism—Former
Soviet republics.   I. Funk, Nanette. II. Mueller, Magda.
  III. Series.
  HQ1590.7.G46 1993
  305.42′0947—dc20   92-36334
                               CIP

British Library Cataloguing-in-Publication Data also available.

Contents

Acknowledgments   ix

Introduction: Women and Post-Communism   1

Bulgaria

1. Thinking Gender: Bulgarian Women's Im/possibilities   15
   Rossica Panova, Raina Gavrilova, and Cornelia Merdzanska
2. The Winding Road to Emancipation in Bulgaria   22
   Dimitrina Petrova
3. The Bulgarian Case: Women's Issues or Feminist Issues?   30
   Maria Todorova

Romania

4. Women in Romania   39
   Doina Pasca Harsanyi
5. Women in Romania: Before and After the Collapse   53
   Mariana Hausleitner

Czech and Slovak Republics

6. A Few Prefeminist Thoughts   62
   Hana Havelková
7. Are Women in Central and Eastern Europe Conservative?   74
   Jiřina Šiklová
8. The Emancipation of Women: A Concept that Failed   84
   Zuzana Kiczková and Etela Farkašová

9. The Impact of the Transition from Communism on the Status of
Women in the Czech and Slovak Republics   95
Alena Heitlinger

Former Yugoslavia

10. Women and Nationalism in the Former Yugoslavia   109
Andjelka Milić
11. Women and the New Democracy in the Former Yugoslavia   123
Slavenka Drakulić
12. Women's Time in the Former Yugoslavia   131
Daša Duhaček

Former German Democratic Republic

13. Women in the German Democratic Republic and in the
New Federal States: Looking Backward and Forward (Five Theses)   138
Hildegard Maria Nickel
14. The Women's Question as a Democratic Question:
In Search of Civil Society   151
Tatiana Böhm
15. Lesbians and Their Emancipation in the Former German
Democratic Republic: Past and Future   160
Christina Schenk
16. "But the Pictures Stay the Same . . ." The Image of Women
in the Journal *Für Dich* Before and After the "Turning Point"   168
Irene Dölling
17. The Organized Women's Movement in the Collapse of the GDR:
The Independent Women's Association (UFV)   180
Anne Hampele
18. Abortion and German Unification   194
Nanette Funk

Hungary

19. "Totalitarian Lib": The Legacy of Communism for
Hungarian Women   201
Enikö Bollobás
20. Feminism and Hungary   207
Maria Adamik
21. No Envy, No Pity   213
Olga Tóth
22. Gender Politics in Hungary: Autonomy and Antifeminism   224
Joanna Goven

Poland

23. Abortion and the Formation of the Public Sphere in Poland   241
    Małgorzata Fuszara
24. Political Change in Poland: Cause, Modifier, or Barrier to
    Gender Equality?   253
    Anna Titkow
25. Feminism in the Interstices of Politics and Culture:
    Poland in Transition   257
    Ewa Hauser, Barbara Heyns, and Jane Mansbridge

Former USSR-Commonwealth of Independent States

26. Soviet Women at the Crossroads of Perestroika   274
    Larissa Lissyutkina
27. Finding a Voice: The Emergence of a Women's Movement   287
    Elizabeth Waters

Reflections from Outside

28. Eastern European Male Democracies: A Problem of
    Unequal Equality   303
    Zillah Eisenstein
29. Feminism East and West   318
    Nanette Funk

Contributors   331

Index   337

Acknowledgments

We would like to thank the series editor, Linda Nicholson, for her generous support and for her extremely intelligent and timely cooperation. Her insightful suggestions on the Introduction are deeply appreciated. Above all, we want to thank her for making this book possible and for having seen, early on, the importance of such a project. We also want to thank our editor, Maureen MacGrogan, for her great help in facilitating this project—for her support, cooperative manner, and helpful suggestions.

Ann Snitow and Sonia Robbins and the Network of East-West Women (NEEW) provided indispensable solidarity, made available the names of many active post-communist women and provided innumerable opportunities for many personal meetings between East-West women. We want to thank Krisztina Mänicke-Gyöngyösi, Siegrid Meuschel, Herta Nagl-Docekal, Alison Jaggar, Rayna Rapp, Susan Buck-Morss, Gail Kligman, Martha Lampland, Gail Lapidus, and Agnes Heller, all of whom helped put us on the trail of women currently writing in this area. We thank Manuela Dobos for sharing her knowledge of the region and its many languages. It was only though the cooperative sharing of information that this book became possible. Most important, we want to thank the many wonderful women from Eastern Europe whose cooperation, energy, knowledge, intelligence, and commitment were so important to this project.

We are grateful to Lucy Komisar for her technical support and for broadening the editors' technological horizons, without which this book would not have been possible. Her generosity is deeply appreciated.

Nanette Funk also wishes to thank Robert Roth for his intellectual support, friendship, and encouragement when it was particularly needed, and for his insightful suggestions and comments at various stages in this project. She also wants to thank Jack Feder for his ongoing support and Matthias Weiss for his help in understanding the changes under way in Germany.

She would also like to thank the staff of the Computer Center of Brooklyn

College and Tony Chambers and Raul Morales of the MicroLab at the CUNY Computer Center. She is grateful to the PSC-Cuny Research Foundation for their support during 1991–92.

Magda Mueller also wishes to thank Pat Herminghouse, Ruth-Ellen Boetcher-Joeres, Heidrun Suhr, and Silvia Schlenstedt for intellectual support and advice.

We are grateful for permission to reprint the following:

—Hildegard Maria Nickel, "Frauen auf dem Sprung in die Marktwirtschaft," *Ypsilon*, no. 2 (1990), published in English in *German Politics and Society* no. 24-25 (Winter 1991–92).

—The photograph on p. 173, by Jens Hübner of Berlin.

—"Eastern European Male Democracies: A Problem of Unequal Equality," which appears as part of Zillah Eisenstein, *Reclaiming Democracy: Sex, Race and Rights* (University of California Press).

Finally, Nanette Funk dedicates this book to her parents, grandparents, and their parents, etc., who were scattered throughout the lands of Eastern Europe and the Soviet Union.

Introduction: Women and Post-Communism

This collection is a joint venture of women from post-communist countries and Western feminists. The essays, mainly by post-communist women, discuss the gender politics of the turbulent transformation to post-communism and help to make sense of the transformation as a whole. The discussions offer Western readers a sense of the extremely different philosophical and cultural as well as economic and political context in which these changes are taking place. The essays will hopefully forestall Western and U.S. misunderstanding and further divisions among feminists East and West, such as those that have surfaced between East and West German women. These essays may also help alleviate the difficulty women in post-communist countries experience in creating a public discourse about women, one shaped by women themselves and committed to helping women become subjects on their own behalf.

There is a striking contrast between the development of post-communist women's activities and the second wave of the U.S. women's movement in the 1960s and 1970s. Whereas in the United States the totality changed through the transformation of the particular (women, blacks, gays, etc.), in Eastern and Central Europe and the former USSR, it was the transformation of the totality that created the possibility for a transformation by the particular. Whereas the Western women's movement grappled with the role of capitalism in women's oppression and looked to socialist theory for new insights, the reverse has often been the case in post-communism. In addition, post-communist women are responding to their own, very distinct conditions, both material and cultural. Such conditions include the fact that these societies hailed the equality of women as a *fait accompli* which served to legitimate socialism (Petrova [Bulgaria]; Havelková [Czechoslovakia]. Finally, post-communist women's writings and activities arise in the context of, and in response to, Western feminism. Their writing is often stimulated and based on knowledge of Western feminist literature and direct contact with Western feminists, whose concerns and discourse they appropriate, reject, or transform. The Western feminist inheritance is a mixed blessing; its dangers and difficulties as well as importance is a major theme explored in the essays by Šiklová, Havelková, and Heitlinger of the Czech and Slovak Republics, as well as by Duhaček (ex-Yugoslavia) and Lissyutkina (ex-USSR.)

But post-communist women's activities, in contrast to U.S. second-wave feminism, are also taking place in the context of a fully elaborated and sometimes hegemonic antifeminist ideology—an antifeminism preceding feminism, as Goven makes clear in her detailed discussion of antifeminist discourse in Hungary. As Posadskaya (in Waters, ex-USSR) and Eisenstein (United States) discuss, antifeminism was also part of perestroika in the ex-USSR and exists in Bulgaria (Petrova) as well. It arose, in part, as men's response to women's full employment in paid work, and as a "preventive reaction" to 1960s and 1970s Western feminism, but it has also been a response by women to their "triple burden," as in Petrova (Bulgaria).

The role of women is absolutely crucial, both economically and symbolically, in the transformation under way. Women's interests are being sacrificed to the transformation. Returning women to the "private sphere" is a central mechanism for transformation from a "full employment" economic-political system to a quasi-capitalist system. The control and regulation of women's bodies indicates male hostility to women's sexuality (Goven) and a desire for the subordination of women, but it also functions to implement the socioeconomic transformation. Restriction of the right to abortion is part of a fight over the role of women in society, ties women even more strongly to the role of mother, eases women out of the paid workforce, reduces competition with men for jobs, and reduces official unemployment figures. The right to abortion for women and women's full participation in paid employment outside the home have been viewed as symbols of state socialism (Funk). Reassertion of control over women's bodies and returning women to the home signifies men's regaining control over what is "theirs," a reappropriation of (male) collective identity and a symbol of having wrestled control away from a dead state socialism. It similarly signifies the reinstituted power of the church. At the same time, the symbol of woman as mother is a useful instrument in nationalist conflicts.

Post-communist women's heritage includes having received extensive benefits from state socialism and an inheritance of a Marxist intellectual discourse. The benefits were of mixed value, however, and were threaded through authoritarian structures that denied the worth of the individual. The process of sorting out this heritage ranges from outright rejection of anything in that heritage to a nostalgia for that past (Petrova [Bulgaria]; Hampele [ex-GDR]; Lissyutkina [ex-USSR]).

It is in this context that women, primarily from post-communist countries, were invited to write on the philosophical, ideological, historical, cultural, economic, and sociological dimensions of feminism and of women's situation in their countries. Owing to the lateness of developments in Albania we were unable to include an author from that country. This collection is not intended to prove or disprove that "socialism liberates women," a debate that assumes a fixed and stable conception of "socialism." Rather, it is a dialogue within feminism, confronting such questions as: What will be the face of feminism in post-communist societies? What are the issues, problems, and obstacles facing women in post-communism? What is their relationship to Western feminism? In short, feminism here confronts yet another difference, the difference of political system.

The authors write explicitly for a Western audience. Havelková (Czech and Slovak Republics) and Duhaček (ex-Yugoslavia) discuss the risks inherent in such a starting point and concern themselves with the often erroneous image Western women have held of women in "really existing socialist societies," as do Bollobás and Tóth of Hungary and Šiklová (Czech and Slovak Republics). The issues to be dealt with were originally posed by the editors within the philosophical and theoretical categories of Western feminism, raising topics that post-communist women might not have raised themselves. There was a dialogue in which all could pose and challenge the questions themselves. Authors rejected some topics as appropriate or relevant, and suggested their own. For such cooperation to take place, this process had to be predicated on a commitment to trust and respect, to understand each other, to let others speak, coupled with an awareness that at each step there will very likely be misunderstanding, as well as disagreement. Only then could we attempt to bridge the gaps of experience, language, culture, and political system.

In the editing process, as well as in the posing of topics, there was a risk of imposing a new system of thought control on women who had long been silenced. Where to draw the line in editing, when to challenge claims and arguments that seemed implausible to a Western feminist and when to let them stand, were difficult issues. Editorial decisions led to asking for elaboration on some issues, but also accepting essays with positions Western feminists might find difficult to support, and essays evincing some tension between those women living or writing in the context of Western feminism and those who are not. There had to be a sensitivity to, and recognition of the implicit inequalities and underlying power relations of this joint venture. In effect, we entered a dialogue, stunted as it was by the practical difficulties of long-distance communication, even in this age of faxes and modems.

Difficulties arose from differences in native language, although these were the least of the problems. Many authors wrote in English or German, which were not their first language. But this problem was overshadowed by differences in the meaning of concepts, such as "socialist feminism" or "full employment" (Bollobás [Hungary], and the absence of certain categories and concepts taken for granted in Western feminist discourse. Harsanyi (Romania) discusses these problems at length.

The most important source of misunderstandings between East and West, however, arises from words existing in both cultures, but with very different meanings. The concepts "left," "emancipation," "politics," "solidarity," "social-ism," and even "women's equality" are not used normatively by post-communist women, but as descriptive terms appropriated by an authoritarian, repressive socialism, referring to disturbing realities imposed by that system. "Quotas" are associated with the selection of powerless women as spokespersons for the existing system (Šiklová [Czech and Slovak Republics]; Lissyutkina [ex-USSR]). "Feminism" itself has a completely different set of associations, and is often regarded with hostility, as many authors discuss. Indeed, not only abstract con-cepts are misunderstood, but banal and yet extremely important terms such as "restaurant," "day care," "shopping," and "housework," which Harsanyi dis-cusses for Romania.

This also became a problem of translation. Should one translate a foreign term as a "problem of gender identity" when the word "gender" does not even exist in the original language, thereby obscuring the problem of the absence of the concept? The significance of the concept of gender is discussed by Šiklová (Czech and Slovak Republics) and Todorova (Bulgaria).

These problems of communication are just a microcosm of the problems in any meeting or dialogue between Eastern and Western women (Funk, United States). It has already become a source of serious tension in the relationships of East and West German women, resulting in hostilities that are seriously handicapping cooperation.

I. Women's Turning Point

A misconception exploded by many of the authors is that 1989 was the transition year for women in state socialism, when restrictions on abortion were first proposed, women first removed from employment, and an anti-feminist discourse introduced. The authors reveal that much of this began long before, in the 1980s—a growing neo-conservatism in Bulgaria (Petrova) and in Romania (Harsanyi), in the former Yugoslavia (Drakulić) with its attempt to restrict reproductive rights in Serbia, in the ex-GDR (Nickel), with changes in women's employment, in the Czech and Slovak Republics (Heitlinger) and Poland (Hauser, Heyns, and Mansbridge) and in the growing antifeminist discourse in Hungary (Goven). On the other side, some women's activities had also started in the 1970s and 1980s, as in the ex-GDR (Hampele), in the former Yugoslavia (Drakulić, Duhaček), and in glimmerings in the ex-USSR (Waters).

II. Philosophical Issues

A philosophical, ethical, normative, cultural transformation as much as an economic and political one is taking place. A moral crisis is occurring, due partly to the moral deterioration of the past. Bollobás (Hungary), Havelková and Heitlinger (Czech and Slovak Republics), and Lissyutkina (ex-USSR) discuss these battles between conflicting value systems, while Nickel (ex-GDR) refers to the moral confusions of the past system. Duhaček (Yugoslavia), as well as Havelková and Kiczková and Farkašová (Czech and Slovak Republics), discuss the philosophical transformations of 1989: their normative and metaphysical dimensions, and their meaning for women. The very conception of time itself has changed and is explored by Duhaček (ex-Yugoslavia) and Kiczková and Farkašová (Czech and Slovak Republics).

Feminist theorists in the West have discussed the public/private dichotomy in relation to women. Havelková (Czech and Slovak Republics); Hauser, Heyns, and Mansbridge (Poland); Nickel (ex-GDR); and Goven (Hungary) reveal how the operative dichotomy in state socialism was not that of public/private but of state/family, in which the family was itself an ersatz public sphere (Havelková), representing the anti-state and freedom.

Philosophy under state socialism was, to varying degrees, part of the state ideology of Marxist-Leninism, severely circumscribing what could be studied. The very notion of "political philosophy"—research on the conception of the individual, contract theory, and rights—did not exist, and there was certainly no feminist philosophy. In contrast to Western feminism, predicated on individualism, the philosophical context, social structure, and reality of state socialism was holistic and collectivist, with no emphasis on the individual and her or his rights. Havelková (Czech and Slovak Republics) and Harsanyi (Romania) discuss how universalism and the lack of recognition of subjectivity under state socialism resulted in an absence of feminism. Schenk (ex-GDR) suggests the role of universalist assumptions in a lack of attention to lesbians. Petrova (Bulgaria) argues that the instrumental rationality on which communist rationalization was predicated was intrinsically hostile to women. Kiczková and Farkašová (Czech and Slovak Republics); Hauser, Heyns, and Mansbridge (Poland); and Harsanyi (Romania) discuss the role of these philosophical presuppositions in justifications of the social order and women's position in it, contrasting these justifications to individualist-based arguments predicated on freedom, self-development, and individual rights. Fuszara (Poland) reveals how nonindividualist assumptions play a role in arguments about abortion, both pro and con; Harsanyi's discussion of required gynecological examinations in Romania and Bollobás' brief discussion of pornography in Hungary are similarly illustrative, revealing assumptions about privacy.

Theory as well as social reality was predicated under state socialism on a productivism that saw liberation only in terms of paid employment and class struggle, leaving no room for feminism. Reflections on these philosophical presuppositions, their relevance to women in state socialism, and to the development of women's own discourse and practice, have begun. Funk (United States) discusses and rejects the claim that all these differences dictate a relativism of feminist principles. But the development of a post-communist philosophical and feminist discourse, as well as reflections on Western feminism, will take time. In each country there is a small group of women familiar in varying degrees with the writings of Western feminism, but the overwhelming majority of women, including intellectual women, are not.

Harsanyi (Romania), Havelková (Czech and Slovak Republics), Tóth (Hungary), and Nickel (ex-GDR) reveal the paradox between this collectivist theoretical, structural, and practical subordination of the individual to the whole, and the individualism and orientation to the family and lack of civic consciousness it produced in practice. Western feminists will be surprised by the form women's moves toward individuality and resistance to collectivism took (Harsanyi [Romania), forms that could readily be misunderstood by Western feminists and that are important to the question of whether women want to work (Posadskaya, cited in Waters; Havelková [Czech and Slovak Republics]; Funk [United States]).

The necessity for an ideological deconstruction of state socialist interpretations of the nature and meaning of equality is great, an issue raised by Heitlinger and Havelková (Czech and Slovak Republics) and Eisenstein (United States). "Equality," for reasons discussed by Harsanyi (Romania) and others, was associated with contempt and disrespect for women, rather than commitment to women's dignity and equal worth as persons. The resentment by Eastern women of the androgynous conception of equality that had been imposed on them (Duhaček [ex-Yugoslavia]; Lissyutkina [ex-USSR]), the misunderstanding concerning whether they were equal or not, the relationship of emancipation and work, are all discussed by Siklová, Heitlinger, Havelková, and Kiczková and Farkašová (Czech and Slovak Republics) Harsanyi (Romania), Bollobás (Hungary), Panova, Gavrilova and Merdzanska (Bulgaria), Lissyutkina (ex-USSR), and Funk (United States). Eisenstein (United States) discusses how the conception of sexual equality in post-communism must reject an identification of equality with sameness of treatment, and recognize differences.

In several countries, such as Bulgaria (Petrova) and the former USSR, one response to state socialist conditions for women has been a strong essentialism: a position that women are, by nature, different from men, a difference the previous system failed to acknowledge. A related issue is whether there was a different conception of gender identity in state socialism, and whether a change in women's identity has accompanied the transformation to post-communism. Dölling (ex-GDR) analyzes images of women in *Für Dich,* the only women's magazine in the GDR, discussing them with respect to sexuality, domination/subordination, the new role of woman as consumer, and the role of work in women's identity. Harsanyi (Romania) and Havelková (Czech and Slovak Republics) discuss the lack of recognition of subjectivity in the post-communist countries. That lack reveals itself in the practical, material problems of contraception, modern household technology (Harsanyi), and housing construction.

Precisely because philosophy and ideology played such central roles in state socialism and were used to deny social realities, there exists a deep suspicion of any organized body of belief, including feminism (Lissyutkina [ex-USSR]; Havelková [Czech and Slovak Republics]). It is widely believed that imposing another foreign theory, such as feminism, would not differ much from the previous imposition of a socioeconomic "ism" (Harsanyi) [Romania].

III. Socioeconomic Commonalities

Reducing women's paid work is a major instrument of economic quasi-privatization and the integration of post-communist societies into a capitalist market system. Past gender segregation of the work force under state socialism, in conjunction with new Western-style sex discrimination, help along that process.

Socioeconomic circumstances both past and present are discussed by the authors in each country. The striking similarities among all state socialist societies discussed by these authors deserves to be mentioned in advance: the extremely high participation of women in the paid work force, largely determined by economic and demographic policies and family necessity; the gender segregation of the work force, in which women worked overwhelmingly in feminized fields (textiles, office work, health and education) and in low-paid positions of little authority; and extensive maternity benefits and sick leave benefits for women, which while enabling women to work also served to reinforce women's traditional role in the home, legitimize gender inequality and discrimination in employment, and were a means of removing women from the labor force (Milić [ex-Yugoslavia]; Heitlinger [Czech and Slovak Republics]; Posadskaya [in Waters, ex-USSR], Tóth [Hungary]). Jointly, these conditions of "patriarchal emancipation" helped create women's "double" or "triple" burden. Nickel discusses in detail the gender hierarchy in paid employment in the ex-GDR, discussing the probable impact of the new market system. The issue of modernization and women is discussed by Hausleitner in the case of Romania.

One of the most serious and urgent issues is women's increasing share in the growing unemployment—about 60 percent of the unemployed in Poland (Hauser, Heyns, and Mansbridge), Bulgaria (Todorova, Petrova) and the ex-GDR (Nickel, Schenk), perhaps more (Posadskaya, in Waters) in the former USSR. Women also have lower unemployment benefits than men (Adamik [Hungary]). That women are frequently doing worse than men in the transition must be noted in the context of evidence offered by Hauser, Heyns, and Mansbridge (Poland) and Nickel (ex-GDR) revealing that women in the labor force are in some ways better situated than men to benefit from the restructuring of the economy, by having a higher level of general education than men (Tóth [Hungary]).

The deterioration in women's economic position is encouraged by challenges to the old norms of state socialism concerning how much paid work is "fitting" for women, and whether day care is or is not good for children (Schenk [ex-GDR]). These challenges trigger women's own ambivalences, discussed by Tóth (Hungary), Petrova (Bulgaria), Harsanyi (Romania), Hauser, Heyns, and Mansbridge (Poland), and Lissyutkina (ex-USSR). Women's role in work bears on the question of whether there was a different gender identity under state socialism (Nickel, Dölling, Schenk [ex-GDR]) than in capitalist societies.

The central role, both political and economic, of the family in state socialism must be understood if Western feminists are to avoid simple moralizing attitudes toward post-communist women. Tóth discusses the special role of children in the family and differences in day care in Hungary. The traditional role of the woman in the family and high marriage rates are just as typical of state socialism as the notoriously heavy "double burden." The family also plays an absolutely central role in the transformation, both practically and symbolically (Nickel [ex-GDR]); Tóth and Goven [Hungary]; Lissyutkina [ex-USSR]; Havelková [Czech and Slovak Republics]).

Reductions in day care, questions of the form in which it will continue (as an entitlement or means-tested, discussed by Hauser et al. on Poland), and its cost to parents are issues that loom large in every country and have direct bearing on the possibility of women's employment. No less important are women's and children's ambivalent attitudes toward day-care (Adamik [Hungary]; Lissyutkina [ex-USSR]) and the conditions of day care. Previously, all these issues had been officially taboo subjects (Nickel [ex-GDR]). Women's paid employment will also be influenced by the extent to which women will be called on to substitute for reduced day care and care for the aged (Adamik [Hungary]; Drakulić [ex-Yugoslavia]).

IV. Differences

Yet in spite of the universality of some conditions in post-communist countries, these essays are deliberately organized according to country. One cannot overestimate the enormous cultural and historical differences between countries and the different degrees of political freedom, openness to the West, economic development, degrees of modernization, and openness to market practices and standards of living, etc. All these differences mean different social positions of women, and differing concerns. Havelková (Czech Slovak) discusses the importance of forestalling an oversimplifying analysis of "women in post-communism." To do so would be another universalizing injustice to women, imitating the injustices of authoritarian socialism and would result in ignoring the distinctive character of, and difficulties for, a potential women's movement in each country. Havelková raises this issue to a theoretical level in her discussion of the distinction between social integration and system. This distinction frames the issue of the conflict between the traditional culture, with its own normative assumptions, and the imposed socioeconomic system. Conflicts between system and social integration differ significantly in each country. The particular historical context is the subject for both Todorova and Panova, Gavrilova, and Merdzanska (Bulgaria), and is briefly discussed by Lissyutkina (ex-USSR). Todorova (Bulgaria) and Harsanyi (Romania) discuss the peasant tradition's strong influence on gender relations even today, or the lack of a chivalrous tradition in Russia (Lissyutkina). This is quite different from the former-GDR or the Czech and Slovak Republics.

The presence or absence of collective social and political actors also differs by country and will influence the development of women's movements in particular. Poland, a country with a broad-based political movement, Solidarity, is certainly more likely to develop a strong women's movement than Bulgaria, Romania, or Hungary. The church plays a very different social and political role in post-communist countries, ranging from its central role in Poland to its minor role in Romania. Hauser, Heyns, and Mansbridge discuss in detail the significance of the church for women's activities and the possibility of feminism in Poland, drawing fascinating analogies between the church, the communist party, and Solidarity.

Significant differences exist in methods used to instrumentalize and control women's bodies, from offers of enabling entitlements in the ex-GDR or Hungary to encourage women to have children, to legal coercion in Romania and economic sanctions for too many children in the former Yugoslavia (Drakulić). Significant differences exist between the ex-GDR, in which lesbian groups already existed before 1989 (Schenk), and countries in which there was a blanket denial of the existence of lesbians. In some countries particular issues became major sources of hostility toward women, such as divorce in Hungary (Goven, Adamik, Tóth), whereas these same issues are hardly mentioned in others. While inattention to female-headed families is virtually universal, the percentage of female-headed single-parent families varies tremendously from about 30 percent in the ex-GDR to 10 percent in Hungary (Adamik), while statistics are unknown for many countries. Circumstances of women within each country also vary as a result of ethnic, religious, and national differences, as in the case of Gypsy women in Hungary (Adamik), Muslim women in Serbia, and the various nationalities peopling ex-Yugoslavia or the Commonwealth of Independent States (ex-USSR). The economic approaches to women's present conditions vary from moderate social welfare methods in the ex-GDR under conditions of massive unemployment of women, and even some funding for women's centers, to utter inattention to women's situation in others.

Compounding all of these differences is a tremendous difference in the extent of women's organization, tentative and preliminary as it may be in all post-communist countries. In the ex-GDR, even in the 1980s, one could see the beginnings of autonomous women's groups, as was also true in Yugoslavia; now, one finds increasing women's activity in Poland and the Czech and Slovak Republics, yet still very little in Romania or Bulgaria. Where relevant, and within the limits of space, we have included authors from different republics, such as from each of the Czech and Slovak Republics and from Croatia and Serbia in ex-Yugoslavia. However, it was simply not possible to include adequate representation from the diverse republics of the former USSR.

V. Collective Identity and Culture

The elimination of communism has created peoples in search of a collective identity, trying to distinguish what is their own from what is a contribution of their sometimes premodern, traditionalist, presocialist culture, what they regard as part of their identity and what only a forced imposition of state communism (Havelková [Czech and Slovak Republics]; Panova, Gavrilova, and Merdzanska [Bulgaria]; Lissyutkina [ex-USSR]). After forty-five years (seventy-five in the ex-USSR), answers to such questions are none too clear. This is especially complicated in those traditional cultures that were themselves very mixed, as Panova et al. discuss in the case of Bulgaria. The authors discuss the experience of having their culture stripped away by the state and the deep sense of lack of respect this expressed.

Interestingly, the pull toward the premodern coming from the traditional culture represents a vantage point for a criticism of modernist culture very different from the postmodernist critique of the West. The authors begin to appropriate their own distinctive histories as women, recalling women's activities prior to 1945 in Bulgaria (Todorova) Romania (Harsanyi), and the pre-Stalinist USSR (Posadskaya, in Waters, and Lissyutkina). The positive effects for women's liberation of World War II, of antifascist and national liberation struggles, are discussed by Milić and Duhaček (ex-Yugoslavia). Similar phenomena occurred in Albania. Women's activities in their own countries during communism, both on behalf of women as well as on other issues, are discussed by Bollobás (Hungary) and by Šiklová (Czech and Slovak Republics), a very active dissident, as well as by Posadskaya, Waters, and Lissyutkina (ex-USSR).

The deeply disturbing and sometimes horrifying struggles over nationalism which occupy center stage in some post-communist countries, sometimes taking on neo-fascist qualities, must be understood in the context of a tradition of collectivism and universalism and the search for a new collective identity which Milić discusses regarding the former Yugoslavia. In the attempt to forge new, collective identities, cultures, and families, that are inextricably multicultural are being ripped apart, destroying people's identities as much, if not more than creating them. While discussions of nationalism often refer to the restrictions placed on women, Milić shows how the erosion of women's rights itself sets the stage for the possibility of the growth of nationalism. Tóth (Hungary) and Drakulić (ex-Yugoslavia) further discuss how nationalism played a role in natality policies.

The search for new collective identities will have a deep impact on the role of women and the possibility for women's movements and the tensions between women. A return to the pre-communist role of women is often symbolic of a reappropriation of identity and culture, as with the Slavophil tradition in Russia. This issue is discussed in reference to Bulgaria (Todorova), Romania (Harsanyi), and the former USSR (Lissyutkina). This important reflection on what was, the need to articulate one's own experience and to understand one's own identity, is the theme of Panova et al. (Bulgaria) and Kiczková and Farkašová (Czech and Slovak Republics).

VI. Sexual Politics and Women's Bodies: Sexuality, Abortion, Lesbianism

Puritanism that placed a taboo on discussion or even recognition of sexuality was a striking trademark of state socialism, although there are differences between the East Central states (the ex-GDR, Czech and Slovak Republics, Poland, and Hungary), Eastern Europe (Romania and Bulgaria), Southeastern Europe (the former Yugoslavia), and the ex-USSR. There had to various degrees been an instrumentalization of women's bodies as well, most horrifyingly in Romania (Hausleitner, Harsanyi). In some countries there is now an incipient "sexual revolution" and an apparent recognition of the body (Lissyutkina [ex-USSR]), but also a new eroticization of domination in the explosion of pornography. Repression of sexuality, and the absence of even a language in which to discuss it, is examined by Hausleitner and Harsanyi (Romania) and Heitlinger (Czech and Slovak Republics). Lissyutkina (ex-USSR) discusses the role of the prostitute as a symbol of the sexual and the anti-ascetic.

Abortion rights are threatened in virtually every post-communist country, where abortion is a highly contested and intense political issue—with the exception, at least for the time being, of Romania, where women were previously brutalized by the prohibition on abortion. Fuszara examines in detail the abortion debates in Poland and discusses the history and status of abortion there. She reveals how the debate differs from those in the West, as does Heitlinger for the Czech and Slovak Republics. The roles of the major institutions, including the church, the Communist Party, and Solidarity in Poland, are discussed by Hauser, Heyns, and Mansbridge and by Fuszara. Funk discusses how abortion debates almost blocked the unification of Germany in 1990. The issue of reproductive rights includes not only questions of the legality of abortion, its increasing costs and the conditions under which it is performed (Heitlinger [Czech and Slovak Republics]), but also birth control and sex education. Women in Bulgaria, Romania, and the ex-USSR have virtually no access to the pill, but it is the main form of contraception in Hungary and the ex-GDR.

In most state socialist countries there had been total denial of lesbianism (Hauser et al., [Poland]; Adamik [Hungary]; somewhat less so in the ex-GDR (Schenk). This situation is beginning to change. There was a small lesbian meeting in Russia in the summer of 1991. Schenk discusses the development of a lesbian movement and the politicization of lesbian groups in the GDR prior to 1989. She describes the strong presence, as well as recognition, of lesbians in the Independent Women's Association in the ex-GDR.

The sexual exploitation of post-communist women by the West, whether in prostitution, the hiring of surrogate mothers, or as a source of children for adoption and even for sale are discussed by Heitlinger (Czech and Slovak Republics) and

Hausleitner (Romania). Prostitution by very young girls is a growing problem in Albania. A major issue for women's organizing, as well as feminist theory, will be women's health and infertility and ecology and the environment, all issues that are deeply linked (Harsanyi [Romania]; Heitlinger [Czech and Slovak Republics]; Petrova [Bulgaria], and Posadskaya (in Waters, ex-USSR)].

VII. Democracy, Civil Society and the State

"Post-communism" does not refer to a fixed social form, but to an ongoing process, in part political, that includes the writing of new constitutions and laws and the forging of new economic policies. In many drafts of new constitutions women's abortion rights are being threatened (Drakulić). The outcomes are far from clear, but it is clear that democracy without women's participation is no democracy. Given the dialectics of the new public sphere and the quasi-privatization of the economy, women will have to struggle to participate in the political process, in parties, and in public discourse. This issue is discussed by Böhm (ex-GDR), Šiklová (Czech and Slovak Republics), Waters (ex-USSR), and Petrova (Bulgaria). Eisenstein (United States) argues that democratization itself requires the democratization of the family. Böhm discusses the Round Table in the ex-GDR in which she participated. Böhm's and Hausleitner's (Romania) discussion of women's actual political practices raise the question if there is a distinctive form, style, and content for women's politics.

The remarkable inattention paid to women's issues other than abortion in post-communism and in elections in particular is noted by Lissyutkina (ex-USSR). Milić (ex-Yugoslavia) notes the lack of interest even in women's voting patterns. Eisenstein discusses Václav Havel's and Mikhail Gorbachev's lack of recognition of gender and feminist issues, even as they argued for democracy. Women's lack of participation in elections and the substantial drop in the number of women in parliament and political parties from the obligatory 25 to 30 percent of the communist period, and the significance of this change, is discussed by Hauser et al. (Poland), Petrova (Bulgaria), Drakulić and Milić (ex-Yugoslavia), and Heitlinger (Czech and Slovak Republics).

Active women nevertheless realize the importance of being coparticipants in democratic institutions and the new public sphere, and in the molding of the new economy. This realization is evidenced by mottos such as that from a meeting of some Soviet women in Dubna, Russia, in March 1991—"Democracy minus women is no democracy"—and of the Independent Women's Organization in the ex-GDR—"You can't make a state without women." A political transformation is not only an institutional change but also the creation of a political culture. To the extent that women participate in the public sphere by building women's organizations, they will have the opportunity to be part of that new democratic culture. Only then will they unlearn the many small forms of authoritarian political practice and the ingrained political passivity of letting "father-state" do it all, and have an opportunity to influence the very nature of the public sphere.

There is a necessarily strong orientation toward institutional politics among active women in these countries, in contrast to the alternative and cultural orientation typical of second-wave Western feminism twenty or thirty years ago. The formation of tentative women's parties, women's lobbies, and women's parliamentary and nonparliamentary groups in Poland is discussed by Hauser, Heyns, and Mansbridge and by Fuszara; by Milić and Drakulić for ex-Yugoslavia; and by Waters for the ex-USSR. The development and objectives of feminist and women's organizations and activities are discussed by Šiklová for the Czech and Slovak Republics and by Petrova and Panova, Gavrilova, and Merdzanska for Bulgaria. The difficulties autonomous women's organization face, such as lack of support even among professional women and negative experiences with the media, are discussed by Adamik (Hungary). Schenk, Böhm, and Hampele discuss the Independent Women's Association (UFV) of the ex-GDR, the first explicitly feminist independent national women's group in post-communism and a major player in the political transition of fall 1989. They discuss the difficulties the UFV faced both in its parliamentary and nonparliamentary activity. Hampele explores how it was possible for such an organization to develop in the former GDR.

Women in state socialism grew up with the now discredited official communist party women's organizations. To distinguish themselves from these groups, new women's groups frequently call themselves "independent" (Hampele [ex-GDR]). Šiklová (Czech and Slovak Republics), Hauser et al. (Poland), Harsanyi (Romania), Milić (ex-Yugoslavia), Bollobás (Hungary), and Posadskaya (in Waters, ex-Soviet Union) discuss women's present negative attitudes toward politics. The issue of women's participation in politics both as dissidents and in the present is discussed by Hausleitner (Romania) and Šiklová (Czech and Slovak Republics). Šiklová explores the fascinating hypothesis that the distinctive female experience in state socialism, including the much more minor role women had in the security police (a tremendously powerful issue in every post-communist country) should be a political asset for women in post-communism.

The transformation of the state in 1989 and the opening up of a political public sphere, initiated in 1987 by Gorbachev, was conceptualized in Eastern Europe and by proponents in the United States as the creation of "civil society." Goven and Funk discuss the problematic nature of this category for women both conceptually and practically. The new public sphere made possible the formation of women's studies departments and women's centers, battered women's shelters, rape crisis centers, and actions against anti-abortion legislation. Negatively, it has also led to the formation of anti-abortion groups.

The relationship of other organizations—the church, the Communist Party, and "anti-politics" groups—to women and women's issues are discussed by Hauser, Heyns, and Mansbridge for Poland. They discuss Solidarity's position on abortion, pay inequity, and protective legislation. Similar issues are discussed by Posadskaya and Waters (ex-USSR) and Adamik (Hungary). Hauser, Heyns, and Mansbridge offer a fascinating analysis of the church and the Communist Party, the major institutions of Poland, considering their philosophical assumptions and organizational nature and the bearing of these on women's activities. Attempted restrictions on abortion in Poland (Fuszara) and the emergence of nationalism and militarism in ex-Yugoslavia (Milić, Drakulić, Duhaček) have strongly stimulated women's organizing efforts. Women have been the major peace activists in the former Yugoslavia.

The role of the media both pre- and post-1989 with respect to women is discussed by Dölling (ex-GDR), Milić and Drakulić (ex-Yugoslavia), and Waters (ex-USSR). Dölling's analysis of the magazine *Für Dich* shows how it reinforced traditional gender ideology, both pre- and post-1989, despite depicting women at work. The general anti-woman stance of the media is discussed by Adamik (Hungary) and Drakulić (ex-Yugoslavia).

Conclusion

The women's activities and feminism that develop in post-communism will not be univocal. They will range from Western feminist to traditionalist and Slavophil versions, some of which will be very strange to the West. (Posadskaya, in Waters [ex-USSR]).

The importance of the international community in securing women's rights and well-being cannot be ignored. The laws of the European Community coupled with the strong desire of post-communist countries to join Europe (Bollobás, Hauser et al., Heitlinger) and the influential identification of certain practices as "European" can affect such issues as labor laws for women. At the same time, the integration of Eastern and Central Europe and the ex-USSR into the West can challenge the problematic norms of women's employment and insufficient day care in the West. The political and theoretical developments advanced by women in post-communism may provide new insights and correctives to Western feminism. Women in the European Community, in both Western member countries and Eastern countries seeking to join, will be deeply influenced by the developments for women in post-communism.

The transformations to post-communism must be predicated on a feminist commitment to the equal worth and dignity of women's lives, East and West. Western feminism must raise its voice loudly, make its presence felt, share its knowledge, and aid and abet the development of post-communist feminism and women's independent organizations. We must also be open to understanding and learning from post-communist women.

Nanette Funk
August, 1992

1

Thinking Gender: Bulgarian Women's Im/possibilities

Rossica Panova, Raina Gavrilova, and Cornelia Merdzanska

Who is the Bulgarian woman? Overburdened and overexploited, she hardly has time to look at herself, to think about her identity, which depends so much on social mirroring: the way in which others—the family, the group, community, and society—see her. Historical patriarchy is still omnipotent in Bulgarian ways of thinking, reacting, and living, which the Bulgarian woman has internalized. This constrains her search for identity. The contemporary Bulgarian woman has inherited three different models and traditions of women's roles: the Oriental, the patriarchal Eastern Orthodox, and the totalitarian-socialist. She is a strange hybrid of idiosyncratic features, influences, and world views, hence the difficulty she finds in identifying, defining, and accepting herself, even at the end of the twentieth century.

The Bulgarian language abounds in gynophobic expressions about women and a specific usage of the gender category very similar to that found in English, with a strong pejorative connotation. Such English concepts and phrases as "women's sicknesses" (for minor diseases), "women's poetry" (sentimental, low-quality work), "women's fears" (stupid, groundless fears), or "women's talk," might not be found word for word in Bulgarian, but the connotations of inferiority, underestimation, and vulgar simplification remain. If we compare the words "bachelor" and "spinster" (even "old maid") in the two languages, we see that they are not simply equivalent, gender-marked members of a binary opposition such as that between "married" and "single." In both languages one might well say, "Nellie hopes to meet an eligible bachelor," while rarely asserting that "Robert hopes to meet an eligible spinster." In Bulgarian one finds the same jokes about women drivers, the same centuries-old stereotypes of women as overemotional, passive, and instinctive while men are viewed as rational, active, and intellectual.

In order to understand the contemporary woman in Bulgaria, however, one must recognize that the legacy she has received is a conflicted one. The Slav and Protobulgarian traditions, which form the basis for contemporary Bulgarian society, did not emphasize sexual differences, and, as far as we can tell, regarded the two sexes more or less equally. The Christianization imposed in the ninth century did not seriously affect the structures of everyday life and social roles. Yet while the blame placed on women for committing the primordial sin never really motivated social behavior, Christianity encouraged a set of presumptions and attitudes that definitely assigned women an inferior place and sacralized a paternalistic attitude.

After Bulgarian lands were conquered by the Ottoman Turks in 1396, the Islamic religion, though adopted by only a small percentage of the Bulgarian population, enormously influenced gender roles and relations for all. Women, regarded by Islam as inferiors subject to countless restrictions, were confined to the house. In the streets, they were exposed to shouted obscenities, sexual insinuations, and open advances. Even Christian women dared not leave their neighborhood unattended. For a woman to appear in the bazaar was unthinkable; the only public place she was permitted to visit was the church. There, the Christian religion furthered discrimination, assigning women to the second-floor gallery of the church, separated from the men by a screen.

Only in the last few decades before the liberation in 1878, with its deep changes and increased openness, did women gain access to some public institutions: public schools, lecture rooms, associations of their own. Even then, the family and household remained the only generally accepted and approved spheres for women. No women ever served on the board of a public institution or governing body. Public activities and appearances of women, even the expression of opinion, were considered highly inappropriate. The few professional women and schoolmistresses, despite the recognition of their usefulness, were easy prey to gossip, and almost all fell victim to nasty rumors. Immediately after marriage, they quit teaching and joined the silent and obedient group of housewives.

Yet in the "private" sphere, both in town and country, Bulgarian women were held in high respect. Their judgment on household affairs, marriage of children, and child rearing was unchallenged. They had a strong say in the family economy, as many of them earned additional income in domestic industries. In customary law peasant women held the right to inherit and possess land, which their dowry usually included; after divorce they were permitted to take back their possessions. In large families where more than two generations lived together, when the husband died his role was assumed by his wife, not the eldest son.

After World War II, however, a new model of social development was introduced and forced upon the Bulgarian people—the alien, transplanted model of totalitarian socialist thinking, which, while claiming to liberate women, imposed new limitations on her. The totalitarian system established the cult of the collective and denied the individual. Yet the male figure turned out to be the personification, the embodiment of the totalitarian code, which under the officially proclaimed ideal of freedom and equality silenced and suppressed any public sphere or the possibility of alternative decisions and dialogue.

Ideological bigotry strongly affected the family, women's professional groups, and the overall gender framework of society. The gravest effects resulted from the so-called "liberation of women from the chains of capitalism." According to socialist ideology, the Bulgarian woman was to rise out of the darkness of her uneducated slavery and servitude to her husband, father-in-law, the family, and children. But where did she come to? She became trapped in the double slavery of both her traditional role of wife and mother and her new role as a member of the paid labor force. Women, according to the taxonomy of totalitarianism, were incorporated into a family structure conceived as the "smallest cell of socialist society" in the newspeak of communism; the traditional and proud responsibility of women to raise their children was altered.

Bulgarian society came to be built on vertical and horizontal structures that rendered it more readily controlled and governed. Children between seven and nine years old were organized in schools in *Chavdar* organizations, named after a revolutionary communist antifascist brigade from the resistance movement in 1943–44. Nine- to fourteen-year-olds were automatically transferred to the Pioneers, named after George Dimitrov, the hero of the Leipzig trial in 1933 and leader of the Comintern. At high school, at age fourteen, they became members of Comsomol, the Young Communist League. All of these groups were extremely hierarchical organizations with very strict rules, strong discipline, and elaborate rituals, slogans, emblems, uniforms, hymns, oaths, charters, and constitutions. Every member of the family was expected to join other "organizations": professional groups, ad hoc groups, amateur and sports groups.

What were the bounds of im/possibility for the Bulgarian woman? She was allowed, and even assigned, to bear and raise children, to keep house, and to do the shopping, which meant lining up for at least two hours daily. Like an ant, she carried huge shopping bags to work and back home. She was also awarded the "honor" of doing the cleaning, cooking, and ironing, teaching the children the alphabet, doing arithmetic and homework with them, playing with them, and, of course, regularly entertaining guests, usually her husband's friends. There were also great possibilities—to make sacrifices and compromises to keep the marriage together "for the sake of the children." All these activities, and many others, too, were performed free of charge in the woman's "free" time—sixteen hours a day plus forty-eight hours on Saturdays and Sundays, again in the name of the husband and the children.

But the greatest "possibility" for 90 percent of Bulgarian women was the right to work outside the family, the exercise of their so-called labor rights eight and a half hours a day. Unfortunately, this human right turned into a burden, a compulsion, for most women had to work out of necessity; the men could not earn enough money to make ends meet.

What has been within the bounds of *im*possibility, then? For the Bulgarian woman, it has been impossible to have the economic, moral, and cultural opportunities to enjoy life, to enjoy herself, to betray her husband, to go out for a spree, to have hobbies and interests, to get a rest. In public life, except for a tiny group of intellectuals, these women have no means of being properly appreciated, of making a career, of earning scientific titles and ranks, awards, and prestigious positions. The majority of the Bulgarian women take their pride in cooking, in the shining bathroom, the nursery, the bedroom, and the success of their children. According to statistics, about 90 percent of employed Bulgarian women work as kindergarten and primary school teachers, nurses, low-level office workers, sales attendants, and manual workers. The figures from 1988 are as follows:

34.6% of women work in industry
18.3% of women work in agriculture
11.8% of women work in service trades
10.2% of women work in education
7.7% of women work in health service.[1]

Only 1.6 percent work in management, decision-making, and administrative spheres. Males control access to institutional power and have molded ideology, economics, philosophy, culture, art, and politics to suit their needs.

Even in the newly elected Parliament only 32 of 400 members are women. There is only one woman leader of a political party among over fifty officially registered political parties in Bulgaria. It is not difficult to reach the conclusion that the ex-socialist Bulgarian society, even in the 1990s, is still a flawless patriarchy, despite the claim of a "victorious socialism" and despite the democratic changes begun in 1989. All power—political, financial, institutional, social, scientific—is entirely in male hands. The myth of the emancipated working socialist woman has already been debunked. The Bulgarian woman was sent to work and enmeshed in the system of building socialism, in which one is above all not a person but human building material, a working hand, a cheap work force, a cog in the huge mechanism of the system at work. For the past forty-five years the Bulgarian woman has been perceived primarily as a working woman, a toiler in all the spheres of manual labor and dirty drudgery. The women most highly praised for their contribution to the building of socialism have usually been those who milk cows, who are weavers, spinners, kolhoz and peasant women. The history textbooks were filled with the names of eminent weavers putting into practice the methods of Mr. X. This was the way in which history presented women, and these groups of women were given appreciation in the form of medals and speeches—a stunning example of a hypocritical strategy to institutionalize inequality as well as a general miserable standard of living.

What was the actual state of affairs? According to statistical data there are more women than men in Bulgaria: 4,516,000 women vs. 4,433,000 men in

1985.[2] Yet women are treated as a "minority group," or as a subgroup of men. Women's longevity exceeds men's—74.39 years vs. 68.17 years (1986)[3]—but this just gives women a longer time in harness, a longer life of drudgery.

At the same time, because of being a worker first, and then a mother, the Bulgarian woman does not have the time or financial opportunities to fulfill successfully her "reproductive" role. Over the past ten years there has been a marked decrease in population. Inquiries have demonstrated that regardless of mental or manual work, Bulgarian women rarely give birth to more than two children. A breakdown of who has a third child is as follows:

   3.1% among intellectual women
  10.2% among women doing mechanized physical work
  16.3% among women manual workers.[4]

Similar results are seen if one compares the educational level of mothers. Women with only a primary-school education have an average of 1.98 children, while those with secondary education have 1.57 and those with higher education 1.47 (1985).[5]

It is more than obvious that the prestige and well-being of the Bulgarian socialist "emancipated" woman is a sham. On the contrary, she is not free, she is exploited twice, at home and at work, twice muted, twice excluded from history, politics, and social life. The best example to illustrate the hypocrisy is in the myth of March 8th, International Women's Day, and how it has been observed. This single day is intended to make amends for the rest of the 364 days of humiliation throughout the year. The holiday is celebrated with flowers, presents, speeches, even seats offered to women on the bus. Usually women dress up, have their hair done, and in general act the part of the perfect object of sexual desire. This seems a most disgusting possibility for women's advancement, but many women get trapped, smile, and laugh—probably to keep from crying.

Worst of all, the Bulgarian woman has taken for granted and internalized even the condescending male look at her; she rarely aims for self-awareness, let alone self- fulfillment. Her identity is in many ways double. Her body is both a decorative object and a draught animal, her consciousness both that of mother and wife and that of wage earner and intellectual, her free will submitted both to family interests and state chains. Small wonder that she is a split personality; her two halves belong to different spheres, and therefore she can be happy and satisfied neither at work nor at home. She is very often hypersensitive, hypertense, and cantankerous. If this extreme situation is called the "superwoman syndrome" in the United States, then in Bulgaria 90 percent of our women are superwomen, or rather, super-toiling pseudo-emancipated women. A woman's constant effort to define her real place and identity is sabotaged by layers of tradition, ambiguous at its very roots. The controversy between the denial, for centuries, of her civil rights in public, and the high respect she enjoyed at home, between the deprecatory attitude of Islam and the strong erotic appreciation in a previous semi-oriental society—the clash between possibilities and reality, between propaganda and facts, has added up to more confusion than most women have to endure.

Bulgarian women realize that the right to work and to be financially independent and self-sufficient is an irreversible human right, but within the framework of totalitarian socialism, this right was also a compulsion. Socialism kept some of its promises, and a woman's job is guaranteed for three consecutive years while she brings up her child; in addition, women have the right to divorce and retain custody of the children. If a woman wants to return to work earlier, the father has the right to take a paid paternity leave, although this never happens. If women are not legally discriminated against, if they have been granted essential human rights, what then is the catch? First, if they go to work, they can hardly make a career; they would rarely be appointed to decision-making positions. Second, although they get paid, the small salary cannot guarantee financial independence, especially in the case of divorce, in which case mothers must find another person to help. In this case a woman has two options: she may go back to her parents or, if living on her own, accept money and help from them. Or she may remarry immediately. Alimony does not exist and child support is ridiculously low. The first alternative, however, besides being the prevailing trend, is generally accepted, as in a patriarchal society connections of blood matter a great deal. Third, while the law does not criminalize homosexuality, lesbianism, or pre- and extramarital sexual relations (except when minors are involved) such deviations from the norm are considered reprehensible and tend to be held up to public and personal opprobrium.

Thus, the Bulgarian woman is a slave of patriarchal traditions, backward modes of thinking, pseudo-socialism, and a low standard of living. What could offer a way out? With the breakdown of ideological and state boundaries and the Iron Curtain, great possibilities arise for new ideas and models to come into Bulgaria, for new contacts with women from all over the world. The process of democratic changes within our society will probably also bring about women's spiritual liberation, the unveiling of their thoughts and dreams, their hidden selves. The first symptoms of this new awareness are already on the way: Fragile and isolated women's rights groups have appeared here and there, mostly in professional circles. In spring 1991, a Workshop of University Women initiated by a group of young professors held its first meetings; a similar interest group exists for women journalists. The real challenge for a women's awareness movement will come from the difficulty of spreading ideas beyond the narrow circle of educated women, to office workers, manual workers, and peasant women. The resistance of the totalitarian system may have crumbled, but the Chinese Wall of their own traditionalism—an enemy of Bulgarian women—will remain for a long time to come. The old totalitarian Women's Union and its carefully camouflaged off-spring, the Democratic Union of Women, inspired and manipulated by the reborn communists socialists, will certainly be able to do much harm in urging the need to stick to the "old values" of the house, the husband, and the children. These groups' generous funding, their sophisticated and widely read newspapers and magazines are serious weapons in the struggle for the souls of Bulgarian women.

Through the transformation from invisibility to visibility, through the discovery of our own identity, and a social identity based on that self-determination, we will find our way out. In this struggle we will grapple with the question whose answer will resolve a major problem for the Bulgarian woman: Who is the Bulgarian woman? The more conscious we are of our cultural, personal, and gender history, the greater our freedom. A higher living standard and better economic status will provide for the possibility of, and act as a catalyst to, further moral, economic, and cultural advancement for Bulgarian women. Only then will the Bulgarian woman cease to be an "understudy," one who learns the part of another and waits, prepared to appear only as a substitute, and come upon the life stage to act her own part—her own self. Only then will her impossibility become a possibility.

Notes

1. *Statisticeski Godisnik* (Statistical Annual) (Sofia: Central Statistics Office, 1988), pp. 62–63. Serious doubts could be raised about the credibility of the data, but there is no more reliable source. We feel that since the annual lists numbers from the census, population figures and ratios are fairly accurate.

2. *Statisticeski Godisnik* (1986), p. 22.

3. Ibid., p. 29.

4. Ibid., p. 29.

5. Ibid., p. 27.

2

The Winding Road to Emancipation in Bulgaria

Dimitrina Petrova

I. Femina Socialisticus

The official ideology of former Eastern European societies was to Marxism as these societies themselves were to "the realm of freedom": a superficial imitation masking an incompatibility. Exploitation, lifelong vertical division of labor, social stratification, and alienated labor were fully in place; only the concrete forms of their manifestation were new. The state ownership of the means of production could not change the nature of society and render it "socialist."

Eastern European communist societies neither avoided elites and hierarchical decision making in which ordinary people had no say, nor did they transcend patriarchy. Official ideology contained in its *corpus immobile* the ideas of the emancipation of women, equality, and full development of women's personality. The lesson of 45 years of communist rule, however, is that those ideas work ambiguously when materialized in an inadequate social setting. The everyday life of women was furrowed with ripples of formal equality and emancipation in a seemingly endless patriarchal ocean.

In Bulgaria, there was a serious attempt made to emancipate women formally through the machinery of male supremacist institutions. On paper, women were entitled to equal rights—political, civil, economic, social, and cultural. Reproductive rights were protected through monthly payments and paid leave for child care, free medical assistance, free medicine for children, and so on. But all these achievements, which the official communist women functionaries advertised at international women's conferences, had their dark sides. In theory, nothing prevented women from being equal with men. In reality, despite being as educated and qualified as men and accounting for close to 50 percent of the labor force, Bulgarian women were unequal on the labor market in terms of employment opportunity, pay, and promotion. They were unequal in all other spheres, too, due to an official "Marxist" ideology that was ambivalent about women's emancipation. Official Soviet-style Marxism harbored a tension between calls for the equality and emancipation of women and a cultural immaturity about basic values—a tension between content and form. Values like "equality of women" and "all-around personal fulfillment of women" were not internalized and remained foreign to the "socialist" lifeworld. Women themselves did not realize that law in itself could not exclude the numerous forms of discrimination against women that resulted in such gender-specific stratification as lower-paying jobs. Despite informal women's quotas of no more than 15 percent of official party and state bodies, women in government never reached even those levels. The whole atmosphere was discouraging, for women who opted for a professional career simply were not taken seriously.

In *The Death of Nature,*[1] Carolyn Merchant argued that the progress of scientific rationality during the Renaissance, when the current mechanical world view took shape, was at the same time a crusade against the irrational, the mystical, and the feminine. Communist modernization of society rested on very similar standards of scientific rationality and the "scientific" management of society, thereby omitting and distorting the Marxian categories of "emancipation" and "equality." Still less was it possible for meanings originating in the non-Marxist libertarian socialist tradition to be incorporated into the official ideology.

The result of this imposition of a quasi-Marxist ideology on a Soviet-style state capitalism was negative for women. Formally equal with men, they were expected to "function" in three social roles ("struggle on three fronts"): mother and wife, good worker or competent professional, and social activist. Society recognized women as complete personalities only when all three roles were duly performed. The model "socialist" woman featured by the women's magazines was a creature hardly ever found in real life, one who fulfilled this triple role. Ordinary women responded to this official image with the complaint that it was very difficult and hazardous "to carry three watermelons under one arm." Generally, women saw this impossibility not as the result of low living standards, a backward cultural context, or an exploitative social structure, but increasingly as inherent in the very goal of the triple role.

In addition, women realized with bitterness the demographic imperative behind favorable state reproduction policies. Over 15 percent of Bulgarians are Turkish and Gypsy minorities, whose birth rate has been much higher than that of ethnic Bulgarians. The Communist government has tried to encourage ethnic Bulgarian women to have more children (the average Bulgarian family has no more than two), with such tactics as restrictions on the right to abortion. Until 1990, legal abortion was not available to married women with fewer than two children. Abortion was available for other women, but because abortion and coitus interruptus served as the two main forms of contraception, most women had had three or more abortions by the time they reached menopause.[2] Occasionally, one or two kinds of the pill, IUD, or condoms could be found on the market, but women were reluctant or afraid to use them, both because of prejudice (a cult of "naturalness") and medical warnings. Women were permitted abortion by choice during the first trimester, but at a later stage of pregnancy only on medical grounds, requiring a decision made by a commission of three doctors. Those two categories of women who did not enjoy the right to abortion often resorted to illegal abortions outside the clinic, with all the attendant hazards.

II. The Failure of the "Socialist Promise"

Sometimes changes in Eastern Europe with respect to women are presented as if women had been victims of a doctrine of forced emancipation until 1989, which was immediately replaced by a liberating doctrine after the "revolutions" of the fall of that year. This is far from the truth. During the late 1970s and early 1980s the official "socialist" indoctrination of women had already changed, overtaken by a more conservative, basically antifeminist ideology of essentialist inspiration. The new official position recognized that the early socialist promise to women had been inadequate and utopian, and therefore in need of serious reconsideration. The following piece of journalism, representative of the ongoing new indoctrination and the dominant tone of women's periodicals, reveals this well:

> It took us too long to realize that we have irreversibly confused our ideas of equal rights. It took us too long to sense how perfectly it suits men to ignore women's intellect and capacities—in order to use them without a guilty conscience. It took us too long . . .
>
> And see: our homes are not the comfortable havens where we can forget our concerns; our children are not well bred and educated; our husbands do not provide the support we need. No one has given us the right to complain. The women's little dodges that were so helpful to our grandmothers are left far behind too. We looked around and saw that we had turned nature upside down. We've pulled on the jeans and shirts (they suit us well, too), we are holding a cigarette (to stop the trembling of our fingers) . . .
>
> Despite all efforts, we shall never reach men's self-confidence. The likeness that we seek, the endeavor to prove by both appearance and brains our real qualities and independence are doomed to failure. . . .
>
> And if our shoulders are bent with exhaustion, if our eyes don't smile, if our lips are tightly set—it is because we lack recognition. It is because behind our backs we are reproached—for the emancipation that we ourselves fabricated. And that we cherished. To the point of being today less feminine, less admired, less appreciated. Just contrary to what we once wanted.
>
> It will take some time before we suppress protest in ourselves. We shall scatter, each of us taking her own path. Different. Filled with children's laughter. Inspired by men's love. Enjoying many profes-

sional victories. To each according to what is like her. The world cannot do without us. But the world certainly has had enough of seeing us in jeans and shirts, dragging kids along to the kindergarten, running to catch trams and trolleys, loaded down with shopping bags, rushing into the workplace the last minute, choked with embarrassment: what to do first?

We don't like ourselves this way. At least, we can admit this.[3]

The practical conclusion was that women would be wise to return to their "authentic nature": to make home a priority, to give their time to the children, to the kitchen, to knitting, sewing, and cosmetics, thus meeting the inborn needs of their sex. The official women's organization, an auxiliary to the ruling Communist Party, implemented this new ideology. It was the Communist women functionaries, leaders of a nonexistent women's movement, motivated, perhaps, by a sincere concern for women, who betrayed women's long-term interests as well as the "socialist promise."

The very concepts of emancipation and equality were meant ironically. The media created the caricature of the "emancipated woman": smoking a cigarette, extravagantly dressed, sitting in cafés for hours, neglecting her children, promiscuous, abusing cosmetics; or else ugly and unattractive, heroically struggling on all three fronts of women's fulfillment and left with nothing at the end. The emancipated woman was pictured as a self-mutilated creature, one who had deprived herself of her own femininity. Rejecting the idea of emancipation implied above all voluntarily giving up competition with men, although not competition with women in the struggle for men's attention. The unarticulated message was that our natural enemy is the other woman who is the threat to our happiness. Regrettably, everyday life provided abundant material as illustration.

The ideological turn to conservative antifeminism in the late 1970s was part of the developing legitimation crisis. It prepared the general preconditions for the right-wing boom in value orientation that we have been witnessing since the 1989 "revolution" in Bulgaria. The major women's organization, the Democratic Union of Women, is definitely on the right by Western standards. It supports the death penalty. It publishes a sexist journal in which half of the authors are men, and in which interviewees often end their remarks by expressing the hope that they don't sound like feminists. Love is exalted in edifying tones as the most important thing in a woman's life. I think that progress in the status of women in post-communist society would mean retaining all the formal, legislative achievements and then struggling for equal opportunity, planning for equality, by drawing from the experience of Western women: in other words, standing on the firm ground of "socialist" achievement and building on it. The betrayal of the "socialist promise" dismissed this favorable opportunity. It helped along the process of restoring the pre-"socialist" status of women.

III. Out of the Frying Pan into the Fire

In 1990, women accounted for 50.7 percent of the total population of Bulgaria. Of these, 68.1 percent lived in urban areas. Of all women, 43.3 percent were at their most active age (15–49 years); 33 percent were over 50.[4] Women are likely to suffer disproportionately more than men in the transition to a market economy. Today, unemployment rates grow faster among women than among men; female unemployment is 20 percent higher than men's. Women's jobs are located mainly at the lower levels of the firms' hierarchies. State protection of women's rights is threatened, countered by a gender-segregated labor market increasingly hostile to women's career options. In an opinion poll by the Center for the Study of Democracy of October 1991, and representative of the whole Bulgarian population, only 8.1 percent of the women polled expected a rise in their living standards over the following year, compared to 13.1 percent of the men. 43.1 percent of the women express fear that they will lose their jobs, compared to 38.5 percent of the men. 46.6 percent of the women definitely prefer to work in a state-owned enterprise, while 22.3 percent prefer a private firm; the respective figures for men are 40.9 percent and 33.8 percent. 42.7 percent of the women had neither the intention nor the desire to start a private business, compared to 35.8 percent of the men. Women's lower self-esteem is demonstrated by the fact that 32 percent of the women say they cannot influence the course of their life, compared to 25.7 percent of the men. And only 16.9 percent of the women think that their life is now full of new opportunities, compared to 26.7 percent of the men. Bulgarian women compensate for this lack of optimism with a stronger belief in an afterlife. 43.7 percent of women believe in God, compared to 29 percent of the men.[5] In 1990, of all registered private firms, only 5.5 percent were started by women. The legal protection of employment of pregnant women and mothers of young children is considered good and necessary by 64 percent of women; the rest think this protection is not strong enough and must be improved, as by longer maternity leave, currently providing for up to three years following birth.

Bulgarian women have entered the post-communist epoch with a very positive attitude to working. Only one-fifth of women, compared to one-third of men, think that women should stay at home and not work. And only 16 percent of the working women would agree to stay at home and devote themselves fully to the family if they lost their jobs.

Even were they fully secure financially, 70 percent of working women would still prefer to work full-time. Women in Bulgaria want to work, but opinion polls demonstrate that they still do not want to govern. The sweep of free elections has reduced women's political participation and increased the gender gap in the public sphere. In June 1990, only thirty-four women were elected to the first free parliament (8.5 percent of the seats). The following months showed clearly that the elections were won by men and lost by women. The second free parliamentary election in October 1991 did not alter this proportion.

It remains very uncertain whether newly emerging parliamentary democracy can in itself guarantee women's rights and freedoms. Under the specific Balkan conditions, the societal transformation does not imply a reduction of arrogance, discrimination, and neglect with respect to women: quite the contrary. Changes in the social system also mean substantial changes in the structure of everyday life. The traditional family pattern—the breadwinner/housewife arrangement, which was to a certain degree eroded under communism though never seriously challenged—is now reinforced. This is due mostly to the growing unemployment and the drop in living standards. Accordingly, the number of divorces is decreasing, as the crisis mobilizes the family for survival. The economic factors that stabilize the traditional family patterns are accompanied by the regressive reorientation of women's attitudes to gender. The so-called invisibility of women in the public sphere is expanding, with the "help" of the male-dominated media. The different forms of eroticization of women's oppression, pornography in particular, are flooding everyday life, while real women suffer and are ill. The number of gynecological patients is close to the highest in Europe, due largely to irresponsible environmental pollution, as well as the effects of the Chernobyl disaster.[6] In 1990, the birth rate reached its lowest point ever (10.5 per thousand). According to the UNICEF report for the first three months of 1990, 80 percent of Bulgarian children live on the poverty line or beneath it. 11.4 percent of births are extramarital. Every second single mother regrets having given birth, and two-thirds of the extramarital children are delivered for adoption by their mothers. The network of kindergartens is large enough to include almost all children between three and six years of age, but it is quite inadequate in quality. Violence against women is reportedly much higher as compared to the past decade, in accordance with the dramatic general growth of crime.

In the past communist decades, changes in male patriarchal behavior took place as a result of official egalitarian formalism. After November 1989 this shaky achievement by Bulgarian women was drowned in the upsurge of a strong conservative ideology, prepared by the two decades of essentialist propaganda. The early socialist promise of emancipation is now being energetically dismissed as utopian. On the whole, women will probably come off losers in many respects: the "revolution" of 1989 left the patriarchal system of power intact, transforming its more superficial manifestations from bad to worse.

IV. Once the Blind See Again, They See Through Stone[7]

Bulgarian women's vision of the other woman has been blurry for a long time. Not only the idea but the feeling of sisterhood is absent from our society. For the Bulgarian woman, the other woman is not a possible friend, client, or partner. Under communism, the precondition of a woman's well-being was the absence of the other woman. Objectively, the relations between women were determined by competition, as between commodities on the market. The "goal" of such a competition was not only men's benevolence but small achievements on the level of everyday life, owing to the misery and hardship of reproducing the household routine. Without the other woman, queues would be shorter, and there would be more space in the tram. There, in the queues and crowded trams, the Bulgarian woman's positive attitude to other women was systematically ruined and degraded. The other woman was the person who would "steal my husband" or at least shake her carpets out on her terrace over my washing just hung out at the lower story of the odious "socialist" block of flats.

The structural expression of this lack of sisterhood is the lack of spontaneous grassroots women's activities, the lack of elements of a civil society. The Democratic Union of Women is, regrettably, no more than a holdover of the Communist official state-controlled organization, and continues to play a conservative role. If there are any other women's organizations, they are not covered by the media.[8] Building civil society at the grass roots is the priority for the women's movement in Eastern Europe. This process might be fostered by institutionalizing women's studies, a field that has up until now been unknown. The issues most likely to mobilize women at present are women's unemployment and women's health. The women's movement, which is now at its formative stage in Bulgaria, should choose a strategy of mutual amplification of civil society and pragmatic politics. A small official democratic lobby won't make a difference unless, parallel with parliamentarian and governmental steps, a broader grass roots movement of great moral vigor provides a constant voice from below. Some women will certainly try the institutional, democratic way of empowerment; others will take the long road of local activism outside the official political sphere. The women's movement as a whole should opt for both.

Notes

1. Carolyn Merchant, *The Death of Nature: Women, Ecology and the Scientific Revolution* (New York: Harper and Row, 1979).

2. With a population of about eight million, Bulgaria has a high number of abortions— about 145,000 per year, as against 120,000 births annually over the past few years.

3. Silvia Rakhova, "Nai-Posle" (At Last), *Zhenata Dnes* (Woman Today), special issue (April 1991). Rakhova has played an important part in the women's press over many years. She is very concerned about women's problems and is one of the most progressive journalists. But she also transmitted the message addressed to Bulgarian women in the 1980s. The ideas expressed in this article had been expressed for at least ten years.

4. *Statisticheski Godisnik* (Statistical Annual) (Sofia: Central Statistics Office, 1991).

5. Opinion polls of the Center for the Study of Democracy, October 1991. Excerpts of the data have been published in the Bulgarian press.

6. The Bulgarian population seriously suffered from the effects of Chernobyl. Four days after the accident, the radioactive cloud, moving southward, was above Bulgarian

land, and a heavy rain all over the country intensified its action (May 1, 1986). The government kept lying in the media, saying that everything was "normal" in order to avoid mass panic and to remain loyal to Moscow. Mothers were instructed to feed children as usual, etc. (The disgusting thing was that at the same time some proper safety measures were taken, through special instruction, within the top nomenklatura.) This was condemned by the environmental organization ECOGLASNOST as an "environmental crime."

There is no reliable data proving a direct connection between women's health and environmental pollution. But most people believe in its existence. Over the past five years the number of miscarriages, stillbirths, and deformed infants has grown unprecedently, and the Chernobyl accident has been publicly identified as the source by doctors and researchers. But the problem still invites a large-scale quantitative investigation.

7. Bulgarian proverb.

8. The only organizations I know of are: 1) the Bulgarian Association of University Women (about 100 members), to which I belong; 2) a group calling itself the "Free Feminist Group," which unites a dozen women, does not want to be registered in court, and has no leader, being based on the principle of rotation; 3) within the Union of Democratic Forces, the umbrella coalition that is the main political opponent of the Bulgarian Socialist (former Communist) party, a women's organization formed in 1990 called Nadezhda (Hope), which virtually disappeared in the later transformations of the political spectrum; 4) A feminist group called Osvobozzhdenie (Liberation), which sent me a few letters written in the spirit of radical feminism while I was a member of Parliament, but the letters did not contain contacts. I am sure many attempts are made at forming women's groups that receive no attention from the media.

3

The Bulgarian Case: Women's Issues or Feminist Issues?

Maria Todorova

Elena Bonner, an outstanding leader of the radical democratic movement, spelled out without a trace of irony the beliefs and illusions characteristic of the vast majority of women and men in the USSR and other countries of Eastern Europe. When asked, after delivering an address to the University of California, Berkeley, in March 1990, what role women and women's organizations have played in the struggle in the Soviet Union, she replied, "You know, our country is on such a low socioeconomic level, that at the moment we cannot afford to divide ourselves into 'us women' and 'us men.' We share a common struggle for democracy, a struggle to feed the country."[1]

This paradigmatic statement precludes any discussion of the problems of feminism and of its place and contribution to social life in Eastern Europe. The first illusion contained in Bonner's statement is the postulate that feminism can develop only when economic and social stability have been established. Even if this were true of the women's movements in Europe and the United States, which is questionable, it does not follow that it will be true of other countries. To think so is to adopt another version of economic determinism. It is ironic that Bonner's dictum was spelled out in the jargon of Marxist revolutionary discourse, against which she and others are fighting. If we assume that conditions are not "ripe" for a feminist movement because of the low socioeconomic level, what makes them ripe for democracy? One could argue that democracy also presupposes stability.

We come, then, to the second belief (or illusion) about the priority of different types of struggle. Feminism, in this hierarchy, stands apart from democracy, and falls far lower on the value scale. The illusion is that once democracy is achieved, women, as part of the body politic, will automatically benefit. This framework recalls classical socialist theory: once socialism is installed, it is said, women will be automatically emancipated.

This article examines some specific characteristics of women's situation in Bulgaria by exploring the country's historical and social background, particularly the changing social structure and its implications for women; the nature and role of traditional women's organizations; the character of the discourse on women's issues, and, finally, the problems of continuity and discontinuity.

I. Problems of Social Structure and Mentality

It has been widely asserted that socialism imposed a double burden on women. But we must ask whether the period after 1945 in Bulgaria saw such a drastic transformation and deterioration in the position of women. Do we blame the system for what it has done, or for what it has not done?

On the eve of World War II, over 85 percent of Bulgaria's population worked in agriculture. The sociological, statistical, agricultural, and ethnographical literature of the nineteenth and early twentieth centuries unanimously reveal women's active part in the mainstream of agricultural labor.[2] Ninety percent of agricultural farms in Bulgaria in the interwar period have been classified as small (70 percent) and medium-sized (20 percent), for they could not afford to hire agricultural laborers, relying instead on the family.[3] In fact, the statistics of the period show that women did 50 percent of agricultural work.[4] The descriptions of village women by agronomists, sociologists, ethnographers, and folklorists attest to the fact that women's role and status were functions of being perceived first and foremost as producers, partners in the labor process.[5]

Foreign observers also singled out the uniqueness of the role of Bulgarian women compared to their more home-bound subordinate Balkan counterparts. I ascribe the contrast to a rural milieu of small and poor land holdings, uninfluenced by a hegemonic urban culture.[6] Bulgarian peasant women already had a double burden which resulted in very high mortality rates and low life expectancy.[7] At the same time, however, it secured women a place of respect in both their immediate and extended families, in the kinship network, and in the labor process.

This relative independence and freedom of action for women should not suggest that the village society was not still male-oriented and male-dominated.

Women's life in the Bulgarian village might be compared to Martine Segalen's account of nineteenth-century women in rural France. There, too, by sharing the functions of production, men and women to a great extent integrated their activities.[8] Yet in Western European countries, including Victorian England, the disappearance of women's productive functions finally confined them to the home. The role of the bourgeois wife became identified with that of the mother, producing an influential and oppressive role model. Professional activity was not needed to establish feminine status, but was instead considered to divert women from their primary functions and fulfillment.

The bourgeoisie in Bulgaria emulated this ideal, but given its very recent formation as a class and its relative weakness, it did not provide an overarching role model for other social strata. Still, with the secession of Bulgaria from the Ottoman Empire and the creation of the modern Bulgarian state, modeled on

Western Europe, after 1878, women's socializing roles, their roles as transmitters of tradition, began to be transferred to the state. The new legal code superseded customary law, institutionalizing and legitimizing the secondary and subordinate position of women.

Significantly, women represented a large share of the intelligentsia in Bulgaria.[9] From 1878 through 1944, the intelligentsia was recruited not from the middle class or aristocratic elites as in Western Europe, but from the lower middle class, well-to-do peasants, and quite often the poor peasantry and the working class.[10] This was only natural given the large peasantry, lack of aristocracy, and emerging bourgeoisie and working class. Women reflected this tradition within their new social milieu. Considering that at the turn of the century fewer than 14 percent of Bulgarian women were literate, the rise by 1946 to 21 percent among the specialists with higher education and close to 40 percent among the specialists with high-school education is quite remarkable.[11] Most were represented in the so-called feminized professions, and as teachers, pharmacists, and dentists, their positions were far less stable than those of males, and their salaries were lower. Nonetheless, women were perceived as active participants in the labor process— by families, who educated their daughters, and by husbands, who preferred to keep their wives out of the labor force but could not afford to do so.

The industrial revolution of the 1950s and 1960s was accompanied by a dramatic flow of the labor force from the countryside to the cities, a movement common to all East European countries, but greatest and quickest in Bulgaria. The combined effects of extremely rapid industrialization and miserable overpopulation in the countryside between the wars, alongside the administrative push through the collectivization program, resulted in drastic changes in the rural urban ratio: from 24.7 percent in 1946, the urban population almost doubled by 1965 (46.5 percent), to reach 66.4 percent in 1987.[12] The depletion of the numbers of agricultural workers went hand in hand with a swelling of the ranks of industrial, construction, and transportation workers.[13]

Women had formed an important part of the industrial working force from the outset, and their numbers grew throughout the first half of the century; comprising 22 percent of the industrial laborers in 1909, they reached 36 percent by 1944. During the postwar period not only did their place as industrial laborers stabilize, but they entered en masse into industries that had either been nonexistent before or had been reserved exclusively for men, such as machine construction and metallurgy.

Before the war, the first-generation Bulgarian working-class woman had brought many aspects of peasant culture to the city without encountering much competition and denigration from a hegemonic bourgeois culture. After the war this culture was, for all practical purposes, eradicated. Throughout this period and later, Bulgarian society preserved the practice of virtually universal nuptiality, in contrast to Northern and Western Europe. In 1975, for example, 93 percent of women in the labor force were married, and only 7.4 percent had no children.

Women are both laborers and mothers, a combination often unbearable but not mutually exclusive. Women's "double burden" must be approached from the point of view of a cultural tradition, deeply embedded in rural life, in which women already served this double function, and where an alternative model was, for all practical purposes, nonexistent. Bulgarian women did not, as a group, experience entire periods based on the "cult of domesticity," the "feminine mystique," or the "beauty myth."

The interesting question, thus, is how many women, if conditions permit, will voluntarily shed the double burden and step into the imagined paradise of domesticity promised to them by the popular press, and how many will have internalized the idea, or the myth, of the emancipatory functions of labor. The long history of Bulgarian women's participation in the labor process, though it did facilitate legal and economic recognition of women, has not been equivalent to equal status. It did, however, shape women's activities.

II. Traditional Women's Organizations and Feminism

Women's organizations were first established in Bulgaria during the last decades of Ottoman rule in the 1860s and 1870s. This period marked the end of an era widely known as the National Revival, which left its imprint on the character of women's associations.[14] One of the central aspects of the National Revival during the nineteenth century, both preceding and concommitant with the struggle for church independence and political liberation, was the movement for secular education. This resulted in the formation of a thin layer of educated males, which by the 1870s comprised hardly half of 1 percent of the total population of about 4.5 million. Although education was extended to women only a few years after the establishment of modern secular schools, it produced even more modest results in the numbers of educated women; it is rather a tribute to the modernizing consciousness of the new educators, and their awareness and consideration of the so-called "woman question."

But the few women pioneers and driving forces of women's organizations made contributions to national liberation disproportionate to their numbers. Their associations, which set themselves educational and benevolent tasks, were inspired by the passionate nationalism characteristic of the epoch. Women active in the women's groups were almost exclusively the wives, daughters, or mothers of educated male political and cultural activists. Thus, the initiative for women's organizations came from the thin crust of educated women from the new middle class, usually in small-town settings. This social background and the "modern," "Europeanized" character of education determined the main goals of these organizations: the education and enlightenment of women for the sake of attaining their highest goal, motherhood, and the extension of their maternal duties to the public sphere.

Following the liberation of the country in 1878, women's organizations proliferated, especially after the foundation and under the auspices of the Bulgarian Women's Union (Bulgarski Zhenski Suyuz), founded in 1901 at a time when women were forced by economic transformations to work outside the home, although new protective legislation limited women's work and access to higher education. This problem became the focus of women's efforts in the 1890s and culminated in the creation of a national organization that by 1931 had 77 local units and a membership of close to 8400. This second phase in the development of women's organizations (1878–1944) was almost exclusively an urban phenomenon. Of the 77 constituent associations in 1931 only 10 were located in some of the more developed and enlightened villages, and these associations comprised only slightly over 300 members. It is no surprise that one of the most important goals of the organization was to extend its activities among peasant women.

Of greater interest for our purposes is the public debate, mainly in 1902 and 1903, concerning the goals of the national women's organization. The two main currents in the movement were defined by a contemporary as the "social democratic" and the "purely feminist."[15] The first current argued that the social development of the country was leading to the proletarianization of both men and women, and that, consequently, the organization should focus on class issues. This view also insisted on the adoption of the formula of "complete equality of rights" with men.

The other side insisted that the organization should have a purely feminist and not a class character. It would aim not to enlighten the members of particular classes but "the members of this army which is called the female sex, and which has been subjected throughout the centuries." Realizing that "complete equality of rights" was a need still not internalized by the majority of their followers, and that it was interpreted as a social-democratic slogan, the "purely feminist" leaders formulated and managed to pass as the dominant resolution of the women's congress that its central goal was "to work for the intellectual and moral enlightenment of woman and the improvement of her situation in all respects."

It took until 1921—almost another two decades—to transform the term "improvement" to "equal rights," while still insisting on the purely feminist "supraparty" and "supra-class" character of the organization. While never reaching the terminological and theoretical sophistication of the controversy between socialist feminism and liberal feminism in the postwar United States, the debate between these two currents of the Bulgarian women's movement at the beginning of the twentieth century is quite reminiscent of it.[16] This debate also explains why, once the social-democratic view, with its inability to recognize the autonomy of gender issues from class, became dominant after the war, there was a deep suspicion of "pure feminism" as a conservative and opportunist bourgeois ideology. It should not be forgotten that Bulgarian women were enfranchised only in 1946, after the Communist takeover.[17]

After 1944 the women's movement became an extension of the Communist party. The Committee of Bulgarian Women, which operated unrivaled until 1990 as the country's sole women's organization, was supposed to perpetuate the party's view of feminism and women's issues. While it certainly postured as the official organization, it was expected to be and used a Marxist vocabulary, and while it was completely redundant as an organization of women operating in a totalitarian one-party regime, its organ, the journal *Zhenata dnes* (Woman Today) displayed some refreshing qualities and enjoyed tremendous popularity among women and men alike. The reasons for this were twofold: the party leadership with typical patriarchal condescension tolerated a publication that addressed everyday issues in an everyday language, and the public, saturated by ideologized discourse, basked in the light of the resulting treatment of the "real" issues of life. This explains why a journal written in a popular and unpretentious manner, and intellectually midway between a romance and a cookbook, could for a considerable period of time maintain the reputation of being liberal.

In the aftermath of the 1989 changes[18] a new organization was set up in March 1990 as a splinter group from the old committee: the Women's Democratic Union. Its language displayed a strong commitment to the new democratic ideals, as is typical of practically all political and mass organizations at a time when the discourse of democracy has become the new religion of the public sphere. Alongside the general goals shared with its mother organization, such as improving the position of women and family, raising women's awareness, and championing advanced legislation for women, as well as the specific rhetoric of doing away with the communist aberrations, contributing to the peaceful transformation to democracy, and building a pluralist society, there are also some original messages, chief among them being the emphasis on motherhood, the home, the family, and the personal world of women: the rebirth of the "domesticity" syndrome. This latter is even more explicit in the few declarations coming from the new Christian Women's Movement, which is stressing women's roles in preserving Christian traditions and virtues, and fostering love to the fatherland and the family.[19]

It is too soon to know how these traditional organizations or other future women's groups are going to cope with newly emerging problems such as unemployment, which already disproportionately affects women. It has been reported that 62 percent of the 178,000 registered unemployed as of 1991, were women,[20] even before the drastic reductions in the labor force expected to accompany the privatization of industry.

The discourse of feminism as it has been known in Western Europe and the United States since World War II is practically absent. Issues such as those of the differentiation between gender and class and between sex and gender have not been raised; in fact, the proper terminology for sex-gender problems will have to be coined and introduced. The old Marxist-feminism has made strong contributions, but has shown no signs of overcoming the tendency to give priority to issues such as democracy, revolution, peace, class, and legal and economic struggle over problems of sex and gender. The very word feminism evokes a sneer, and is being avoided even by women who are otherwise well versed in feminist language and theory, and who would describe themselves as feminists off the record.

III. Conclusion: Problems of Continuity and Discontinuity

In 1992, with a transformation only half accomplished and a tumultuous political life fermenting with ideologies, it is too early to assess, let alone predict, the prospects for feminism and the particular forms it may attain.

Appearances indicate a clear trend toward neoconservatism. The euphoria over the market goes hand in hand with, and is explicitly articulated in terms of, happy middle-class visions of well-paid men and well-coiffed women meeting at the porches of their suburban houses. For the consumer somewhat lower on the social ladder there is blunt pornography. All this is the normal reaction of the pendulum swinging in the opposite direction after the ascetic and predictable daily life of the communist decades. The question to be asked is whether the observed neoconservative trend is of a short-term or a longer duration.

So far, only women have been discussed in this article: their social physiognomy, their traditions of labor and their mentality, their receptiveness or resistance to feminist ideas. For the future of women's issues, however, the attitude of men, their political, social, and sexual culture, is extremely important, without necessarily being crucial. The same rural tradition that contributed to women accepting the "double burden" as "natural" was also internalized by men. Most men are ready to accept women as partners only as long as they conform to the traditional image. This is reinforced by first-generation urbanites' typical suspicion of everything radical and intellectual.

In the present political process women at least physically coexist with men, albeit as a minority. The parliamentary elections in October 1991 gave women close to 12 percent of the seats in Parliament. These women are bitterly divided along party lines, however, and a feminist agenda is not even being mentioned, let alone in the making. The only woman in the cabinet, serving in the ministry of culture, is also a token political figure.

Women are completely absent from political discourse. Except for a few articles by women that publicized the creation of the new splinter Women's Democratic Union in the winter of 1990, women's issues are not mentioned in the press, in other mass media, or in political forums, even in the most traditional terms. The political language is lopsidedly male-specific. Such headlines as "What we need are professional political men" and "The country is in need of strong and honest men" proliferate. This is all the more unpardonable since, unlike in English where *man* has assumed the encompassing meaning of *humanity,* Bulgarian keeps the strict distinction between *chovek* or *khora,* meaning human being, and *muzh,* meaning man.

Although growing unemployment can be expected to continue to affect women disproportionately, it is unlikely that the economy will be able to afford only male labor once it stabilizes. It is also unlikely that there will be a serious legal reversal in women's rights. The democratic discourse, at least in words, reaffirms these rights as part of basic human and minority rights in the new constitution of July 1991.

As far as the right to abortion, Bulgaria is not even remotely facing the problems of a Catholic Poland. For the moment, the country does not even have a problem with church and religion. The largest group reported to be religious is the Orthodox, whose estimate ranges in polls from 27 percent to 40 percent. A much smaller percentage are Muslims, while the majority reports being atheist.[21] Although such polls are seriously open to question, at the moment it does not appear that the Orthodox or any other church will be a decisive political force. I do not speak of another trend: the frightening, but also expected, explosion of interest in esoteric phenomena and mysticism.

Coming out of 1989 has not placed Bulgaria, or the rest of Eastern Europe, in the dreamed-of postindustrial bliss. Much will depend on where and how the East European economies will develop in the next few years. The prospects for a "Mexicanization" are open and, it seems, quite probable. Much will also depend on whether these societies will be able to become truly pluralist, another important precondition for a successful feminist movement. Historical traditions will also play, as I have been trying to insist, an important role.

At least one important change will surely leave its imprint: the possibility for real exchange with the world outside. A new generation of men is growing accustomed to the new roles and new status, or demands for a new status, of women. A new generation of women is coming that will at least have been exposed to information about feminism. Already, two things are becoming clear: feminism has to be fought for, and no women's movement, whether feminist or not, can rely on male ideologies, not even the most radical and emancipatory, for its rationale and program.

Notes

1. "On Gorbachev," *The New York Review of Books,* May 17, 1990.

2. Maria Dinkova, *Sotsialen portret na bulgarskata zhena* (Sofia: Profizdat, 1980).

3. Lyuben Berov, "Sotsialna struktura na seloto v balkanskite strani prez perioda mezhdu dvete svetovni voini," *Trudove na V.I.I. "Karl Marx"* 4 (1977): 43–76.

4. T. Stanchev, "Statisticheska kharakteristika na bulgarskoto zemedelsko stopanstvo, ch. 2: Trudut v zemedelskoto stopanstvo," *Zemedelsko-stopanski vuprosi* 2 (1940).

5. See, among others, Irwin T. Sanders, *Balkan Village* (Lexington: University of Kentucky Press, 1948).

6. See, for example, Lucy Garnett, *Balkan Home-Life* (New York: 1917): 177–178.

7. Maria Todorova, "Population Structure, Marriage Patterns, Family and Household

(According to Ottoman Documentary Material from Northeast Bulgaria in the 1860s)," *Etudes Balkaniques* 19, no. 1 (1983): 59–72.

8. Martine Segalen, *Love and Power in the Peasant Family: Rural France in the Nineteenth Century* (Chicago: University of Chicago Press, 1983).

9. By "intelligentsia" in the prewar context is understood the specialists with higher university or high school education.

10. Dinkova, p. 59.

11. Ibid., pp. 59–60.

12. Robert N. Taafe, "Population Structure," in *Bulgaria: Handbook on Southeastern Europe, Vol. VI,* ed. K.-D. Grothusen (Göttingen: Vandenhoeck & Ruprecht, 1990), p. 445.

13. Roger Whitaker, "Social Structure," in *Bulgaria,* pp. 463–464.

14. On women's organizations in this period see Virdzhinia Paskaleva, *Bulgarkata prez Vuzrazhdaneto* (Sofia: Oechestren front, 1964); in English, see Linda Nelson, "Transitional Institutions: Bulgarian Women's Associations from 1856 to 1878," paper presented at the Annual Conference of the American Association of Slavic Studies, Washington, D.C., October 1990, which is part of the author's dissertation in progress.

15. *Bulgarski Zhenski Suyuz (po sluchay 30-godishninata ot negovoto osnovavane, 1901–1931)* (Sofia: 1931), pp. 15–17.

16. Elizabeth Fox-Genovese, "Socialist-Feminist American Women's History," *Journal of Women's History* 1, no. 3 (Winter 1990): 181–210.

17. Sharon L. Wolchik and Alfred G. Meyer, eds. *Women, State, and Party in Eastern Europe.* (Durham: Duke University Press, 1985), p. 34.

18. On the changes of 1989 in Bulgaria see Maria Todorova, "Improbable Maverick or Typical Conformist? Seven Thoughts on the New Bulgaria," *Eastern Europe in Revolution* (Ithaca: Cornell University Press, 1991).

19. *Duma,* June 8, 1991; June 11, 1991. As of October 1992, the number of unemployed is close to 500,000.

20. *Duma,* May 9, 1991; *Vecherni novini,* March 29, 1991.

21. *Los Angeles Times,* May 19, 1991.

4

Women in Romania

Doina Pasca Harsanyi

Before becoming a member of the socialist bloc, Romania was a rural country with a strong peasant culture. In 1938 the agricultural sector employed 80 percent of the working population, providing the most important economic output. Even the "exiles"—the educated urban elites—regarded the peasant culture as the only "pure," sane, and uncorrupted system. In order to understand women's condition in Romania today, one cannot underestimate the importance of the enduring and deeply entrenched peasant culture, which provided the traditions, values, and moral standards for the whole country. This culture, combined with the Bolshevik political system and culture, accounts for the position of women in Romania today.

Romania had been regarded as one of the Balkan countries, a land of many secret charms, "at the gates of the Orient." Its substantial rural population gave it the dignity of well-preserved tradition, while its flamboyant aristocracy combined the appealing mystery of a "wild" land with the sophistication of the Occidental urban culture. In 1918, as a result of the Trianon Treaty, Romania became "Great Romania," home to many nationalities and cultures, the most significant being the Hungarians and the Germans in Transylvania and Banat, and the Serbians in Banat. All shared a patriarchal way of life. These values inform present gender relations.

Women and Peasant Culture

Men's and women's roles and values in peasant culture are strictly defined. A woman moves from being the girl in her father's house to wife and daughter-in-law, then mother, then mother-in-law and grandmother. She is always subordinate to at least one man, and as a daughter-in-law she submits to the mother-in-law's authority as well. Men's domination and women's submissiveness are seen as rooted in a natural and religious order beyond human judgment. The woman is responsible for work in the home, the bearing and raising of children. The man is the provider whose main work lies outside the home; his authority over his wife and children is unquestionable. Occasionally, it can turn into acts of abuse against women and children, which although not fully approved by the community are less frowned upon than any sign of "weakness" shown by a man toward his wife and children.

An authoritarian woman married to a weak man is regarded as unnatural and disruptive of the social order. A man cannot let his family have its own way, since this would be equated with the degradation of a wife holding superior authority. Many popular sayings sanction this attitude: "In this house the rooster sings, not the hen." A man is considered intellectually superior, naturally suited to making decisions, aggressive, emotionally independent, and sexually demanding; any sign of sexual weakness or passivity is instantly ridiculed as a shameful abnormality. The ideal woman is nurturing and loving, but also passive, enduring, and obedient. Emotionally weaker, she is naturally inclined toward the "non-rational." All circumstances requiring an emotional involvement—birth, baptism, wedding, bringing up children, illness, death—are under the direct supervision of women. The smooth functioning of the household and the "peace of the home" depend largely on women. This physical and emotional work at home provides women with a kind of power through participation in decision making.

Yet gender communication is strictly codified; sexuality, being morally questionable, is subject to rigid regulations. Women's virtue is linked to their sexual passivity, for women are not supposed to enjoy making love. These roles and identities, which make the intimacy of a couple quite difficult, are further exacerbated by the lack of privacy of the patrilocal household. Routinely a single room is shared by the whole family—often three generations. Once married, a young woman is not supposed to be beautiful and desirable; husband and wife are not supposed to call each other by name and in general cannot exhibit any inadvertent passion for each other. The resulting frustration and repression influenced social norms and women became accustomed to seeing their lives as a long series of sacrifices, taking comfort in the Virgin Mary's example. Men are allowed to step out of line; drunkenness, adultery, and violence are tolerated as long as the man continues to provide for his family. It is important to recognize that virtually all these attitudes and practices are fully intact today.

Urban Life

Until as late as 1948, Romanian towns were extraordinarily "provincial" and preserved as many rural values as possible. Bucharest, the capital, and two or three other towns mixed urban sophistication, village memories and orientalism. For a long time, the towns in Transylvania carried on the traditions and ways of the Biedermeier culture, inherited from the Austro-Hungarian empire.[1] The incipient industry brought into being a rather scant working class, in which women held roles similar to those of the peasant household. Even home life was not different, for working people generally lived on the outskirts of towns and kept small vegetable gardens and fowl. Patriarchal family traditions were also embodied in working-class culture.

Yet one of the most significant modifications following the rise of the new bourgeoisie at the beginning of the twentieth century had been the diversification of the roles available to women. Keeping at least one servant was the norm for any respectable middle-class family during the interwar period. Even a modest family of teachers or low-level clerks held such servants—all save gardeners and coachmen, women laborers. As such, they freed bourgeois women from some, or all, of the burden of housework. But the wife was still responsible for domestic affairs, and her status depended on making her home as pleasant as possible. Her physical appearance and art of making herself desirable became more positive values the higher she climbed among the Western-educated urban elites, where sexuality was purged of its negative connotations. Upper-class and aristocratic women, such as Elena Vacarescu, Marta Mibescu, and Queen Maria (1876–1938), used their intelligence, education, culture, talents, and beauty with great success.[2] But women could exercise power only through men, hence their acquiring the virtues of "Queens, concubines, and wives," as the title of a recent study suggests.[3]

During the first decades of the twentieth century, and especially during the interwar period, a significant number of self-reliant, educated middle-class women appeared. Usually they worked as teachers, nurses, or office clerks, but some went to medical, law, or engineering schools. More women writers and artists came to national prominence.

Post-1948: The Communist Era

The Communists grabbed power soon after the war ended and immediately installed the "dictatorship of the proletariat." Dictatorship was not exactly news for the Romanians; they had just emerged from the royal and then Marshall Antonescu's dictatorships. But this new brand of dictatorship aimed at upsetting the whole social order. There was a speeded-up modernization, a new ideology of egalitarianism supposedly expressed by the proletariat, which hardly existed in Romania. All the old and familiar rural values were termed outdated, subversive, perverse, and unwanted by the new order. The new ideology declared women equal to men and sought to eliminate patriarchy. In practical terms, this meant that women's previous raison d'êtrre, embedded in the all-important peasant culture, was rejected all at once. Equality did not imply equal affirmation of, and respect for, different values for men and women, but treating women like men. Most women's tasks were regarded as meaningless, legitimizing the inferiority of women; only paid work deserved respect. Giving birth was to be done on the side, for the renewal of the work force, and was viewed as a fatal interruption of productive work, meaningless in itself. There was to be no sharing of housework and child rearing between men and women, but networks of public nurseries and eating places. The very idea of "home" was thrown overboard. The country was to become a euphoric work camp devoted to communist doctrine.

In Romania, the embodiment of the new ideal woman was Ana Pauker, chief of the Communist party (1948–1953) and the first woman to accede to power by herself. She was one of the most detested and feared women in Romanian history, her very name making her "subjects" freeze in fear. She exercised power without "eternal feminine" strategies, and had the determined, severe look of a generic asexual Soviet Commissar—a far cry from the versatile, submissive, compassionate, lovely, and lovable Queen Maria.

In towns, the former political, social, economic, and artistic elites were eliminated, as harmful for the new order. The men were usually executed or imprisoned, while their female relatives were humiliated and forced to live in poverty. As a result, curious new groups of working women appeared: educated and mannered, most often dressed in their once-fashionable clothes, they faced the necessity of making a living for the first time in their lives. They often turned their education into an occupation, selling their knowledge of arts, music, and languages, but their social and moral beliefs remained unchanged. Their role of maintaining the happiness and sanity of the family under such hostile circumstances only increased.

The working-class women continued to work as hard as before at "women's jobs." Most dramatically hurt was the peasantry, whose idealized Romanian culture communism tried to break completely, using aggressive propaganda, physical elimination, and seizure of lands. The whole axiological system was turned upside down, and the most intimate aspects of everyday life were brutally declared out of date. About 80,000 peasants were jailed and more than 10,000 killed by the time collectivization was reportedly accomplished in 1962.[4] The women in the villages were treated as stereotypes and objects, to be remolded into another stereotype. Communism regarded peasant women's lives as oppression from which they needed liberation. Yet although from a modern point of view there was little to be fond of in the harsh, limiting, and brutal world of an archaic and isolated village, it at least formed a coherent world for its inhabitants. With their land and values removed, the world for these peasants simply ceased to make sense.

The party propaganda showed cheerful peasant girls liberating themselves from the despotic ancestral law by going to work in a factory or driving tractors. This served to speed up industrialization. But the values, norms, and strategies of the traditional rural culture dominated the makeshift urban life spawned by industrialization. The growing number of factories and plants generated large numbers of commuters, but the rapid industrialization led to the ruralization of the town rather than to the urbanization of the village.[5] The extended families kept their traditional values, changing only their tactics.[6] Grandparents or other relatives were brought in from the villages to care for the children and help with the household tasks.

Contemporary Life and Women's Issues

The circumstances of daily life created serious difficulties for women. Day care and some sickly looking fast food were available, but these services were so poor and doubtful that one would rather avoid them. In the child-care centers, which provided assistance to children through the age of six, the teacher/child ratio was one to twenty or more, which made it difficult to properly monitor children's development. Most of the facilities were poorly equipped with toys, books, playgrounds, and other educational devices. In the last years children suffered from the shortages of fuel, which left many day-care centers cold and dark; the food hardly met children's needs for vitamins, proteins, and calcium, not to mention the virtually total absence of sweets. Many parents resented the heavy ideologization of their children's education. All preschool children were enrolled in an organization called "The Falcons of the Homeland," had to wear uniforms, were taught "patriotic" songs and poems featuring Elena and Nicolae Ceausescu as their spiritual parents, etc.

When one speaks of restaurants, dining out, fast food, or even pizza or a sandwich, we enter the realm of linguistics. The same words have completely different referents, and thus different meanings, for someone in Romania compared to a Westerner or American. The difference derives from a total absence of respect for the consumer. What might be called fast-food outlets offered a very limited choice of low-quality products, chiefly made out of surrogates. A blend of bone-meal, water, and ground pork, spleen, or lungs stood for bologna, a mix of half-decayed potatoes and greasy mayonnaise for French salad, etc. Dairy products and fresh vegetable or fruit salads were almost nonexistent, as was the very notion of "health food." As a consequence, many families tried to find individual solutions dependent on extended families. Women stood in exhausting hours-long lines in the stores; this was shopping in Romania. Some of these same old women, dressed in peasant clothes, gathered pitifully in front of the concrete-panel apartment buildings in the evening, trying to relive remnants of their previous normal lives. Rural family members provided scarce food, and town relatives managed to provide equally scarce industrial goods.

Symbols of the peasant culture became signifiers in a language of ideological propaganda. For many years, one of the most popular songs, aired thousands of times on the radio and television, was "Little Peasant Girl," which glorified the exemplary life of a woman dedicated exclusively to her family. The Bolshevik dream of community services replacing housework did not come true—not because the rulers hesitated to invade the people's private lives, but because it was too costly in a system openly disinterested in consumption and living standards. The new regime used the old tradition to promote the ideal of "the woman in the home" as a natural feature of women's condition; the difference was that now women had the opportunity to achieve "full humanity" by working in the state-run economy as well. This led to the double or triple burden—work, housework, and children. Women's burden was aggravated by shortages and the lack of time-saving devices. People had to live at the modern pace proper to an industrial society, but without its technical aids. Many household tools and machines were not available or very difficult to obtain. A vacuum cleaner or refrigerator was such a luxury, with long waiting lists to buy one; even so, the joy of finally acquiring such a machine was tempered by the thought that they were not meant to last forever, and if they broke, spare parts were an enormous problem. Washing machines were a great privilege, and dishwashers unheard of. Even smaller things, such as special brushes, sponges, scrubs, and decent detergents, were sold only on the black market at ridiculously high prices. Consequently, in Romania housework required infinitely more time and effort than in an average Western industrialized country, although the majority of women held industrial jobs. Schools and other institutions urged husbands and sons to be kind and help, but this request was not couched in terms of an obligation to do their fair share or to do half of the work. Girls were still taught cooking and embroidery in schools, while boys learned woodcarving and metalwork. This changed in the 1980s, when girls were sent to the shop floor too, but it was out of the question to put boys in the kitchens.

Starting with the 1950s, teenage girls were educated to become "all-purpose" creatures—to learn a practical trade while being good wives and mothers in the traditional sense. This led to semivoluntary work segregation, and many young women sought work in the health-care system or in the textile industry, both perceived as more feminine sectors. Most school teachers, office clerks, salespersons, and administrative workers were women. Although female enrollment in traditionally male schools such as engineering increased each year, the great majority of women graduates worked in environments deemed more "suitable" for women.[7] In fact, the strong norms governing what men and women were to do engendered a curious discrimination against men, which backfired by strengthening the idea of male superiority. Beginning in the 1980s, young men were not even allowed to train to become waiters, barbers, cooks, or jewelers. These were light jobs, good enough for women; the men were needed in the steel and mining industry—which were quite brutal and Dickensian, not fit for women—and what mattered were the needs of the socialist economy.

All these legal and ideological intricacies resulted in new forms of male domination, which became entrenched in most families. It was generally accepted that in a typical family where both spouses worked, the man should have some superiority—more education, a higher or more prestigious professional position, a higher income, or a more difficult and time-consuming job. This justified the demand for women to do the housework; it reinforced the unchanged expectation that women supply all the patient understanding and nurturing a family needed.

The disintegration of the patriarchal peasant society caused a troublesome dissolution of traditional boundaries between men and women, making men and women alike insecure about their roles. Most people still tried to live in accordance with the peasant culture, but adapted it to the new urban life.

Romanian women worked outside the home not only out of necessity but out of boredom. The Romanian socialist society was even more boring and colorless than that of its socialist neighbors. A woman faced a situation of practically no TV, no decent places to go and have a chat with a friend, no women's magazines, no opportunities to do volunteer work or independent study or to start a small business, and practically no possibility of changing careers. It was almost impossible to go back to school and such services as retraining and counseling are still not provided. A job outside the home was a place to meet people, discuss various personal problems, display a new dress, etc. A sociological investigation I carried out semiclandestinely in 1988, interviewing 250 textile workers of all ages, revealed that these women's jobs made their family lives very stressful and left them with no leisure time at all.[8] At that time only Sundays were holidays in Romania, and workers were often summoned to work even on Sundays to fill the requirements of the central plan. After work women headed straight home to do their housework. From spring to late autumn the "holidays" were often spent making preserves, since the Romanian stores did not provide any. But all the women I talked to preferred the situation to being home alone. The workplace was as much a place to socialize as a means to make money. Given shortages, corruption, and the large-scale black market, which with its sophisticated system of connections shaped a curious second barter economy, a job in the state economy guaranteed a precious source of otherwise unavailable goods and services. From railroad tickets to basic foods, from vacuum cleaners or refrigerators to medicines, not to mention "extras" like hygienic tampons or makeup, everything was either in short supply or unknown to ordinary people. Few families could afford to halve their chances to participate in this underground economy by allowing one member to stay home.

Curiously enough, the most sophisticated and elegant women in Romania's big cities were not executives or professionals who had to comply with the numerous rigid rules and stereotypes imposed by the state, but private child-care providers and couturiers. These were the women "dropouts," as in the Soviet Union.[9] Among the most uninhibited and open women in Romania, they were trying to get the state out of their private lives and to control their own lives. Working at home allowed them more opportunities to keep their children around and to educate them as they pleased, minimizing exposure to the state ideology.

The proletarian revolution and the reality of women working outside the home did not bring about sexual liberation. Gone were the times when one member of the brilliant Romanian interwar surrealist school, Gherasim Luca, recommended the liberation of the proletariat through sexual liberation. The ideologues preferred to ignore sexuality just as they preferred to ignore the psyche, for the rigidity of the socialist structures could not come to terms with unpredictable and politically unruly psychosexual anxieties. Communist leaders adopted the attitudes of the Orthodox Church and the peasant culture and eliminated sex from public discourse. The short-lived "spring"[10] of the late sixties and early seventies froze in the late seventies and eighties.

An antiabortion law was passed in 1966 to ensure that the economy would not be short of workers during its intensive industrialization.[11] Every year this law became tougher, augmented by a variety of additional measures, such as compulsory periodical gynecological examinations to detect early pregnancies and the criminalization of contraceptive pills and devices. In 1986 President Ceausescu proclaimed the fetus "the socialist property of the whole society. Giving birth is a patriotic duty . . . Those who refuse to have children are deserters, escaping the law of natural continuity."[12] In the same year, the access to legal abortion was restricted to women over forty-five years of age, having five children under the age of eighteen. Under such circumstances there could be no right to privacy in one's body; state control over women's bodies was overt and brutal. Large factories employing many women were likely to be required to hold gynecological examinations in order to immediately register and subsequently follow up all early pregnancies. These examinations were announced a day before and were performed after work—the state would not stop production for this—so a woman who did not want to be examined had to find a pretext for not stopping by the doctor's office, stay home that day, or sneak out immediately after work. The feeling of being constantly spied and cheated on, of being used as raw material in the achievement of some nebulous "national goals" were harder to take even than these examinations. All medical exams for women started with a gynecological exam, for the same reason. Self-induced abortions, when discovered, were punishable either by imprisonment from six months to two years, or by a fine. Abortionists were punished by one year of imprisonment. Doctors sometimes covered up or tried to help women, although cautiously, since they were supervised in their turn. If a woman refused to divulge the name of the abortionist, she risked being left to bleed to death, physicians being prevented from assisting her until she confessed the identity of the person who had helped her. Every obstetrical-gynecological clinic had a prosecutor in residence who saw that these draconian regulations were strictly implemented. As a result, by 1989 there were 159 maternal deaths per 100,000 live births (the highest figure in Europe) and around one million women became infertile due to unsafe self-induced abortions.[13] A report of the Society for Contraception and Sexual Education (SCSE), formed in 1990, showed that this demographic policy had led to "a biological disaster for women's health, with powerful social implications, and to the diminishing of the newest generation's vitality."[14] Women felt constantly vulnerable and at risk, especially since it was they, never their sexual partners, who were punished if an abortion was discovered by the police.

At the same time, the authorities tried to prevent people from having sex unless they were married, even though women were to bring as many children as they could into the world. Unmarried couples could not share a hotel room or even a berth in a sleeping car. Police routinely checked hotel rooms at six o'clock in the morning to check for illicit sexual activity. A woman so discovered was given a criminal record for prostitution, while the man walked out of the room unscathed.

Given the housing shortages, most young men and women had to live with their parents until they married, and often even after. Very few parents would accept their unmarried offspring's having sex under their roof, and once they were married they were subject to the lack of privacy of overcrowded apartments. Typically, parents and children shared the same bedroom—the state housing policy established that only a family of four was entitled to two rooms, meaning a one-bedroom apartment. Very often three generations lived in a small two- or three-room apartment. This aggravated the psychological stress caused by the constant fear of an unwanted pregnancy, and obviously the private life of people suffered.

The general reaction to this was similar to the traditional rural responses: women saw their lives as naturally rooted in sacrifice, and men indulged in drunkenness, violence, and occasional adultery that were accepted as reasonable and understandable. The pseudo-puritanical atmosphere was reinforced by a socialist reinterpretation of the peasant tradition of female modesty. Little by little, all signs and images of feminine beauty or desirability disappeared, being proclaimed harmful and indecent. Movies were censored so that not even a kiss or a bare arm could be shown; fashion pictures were similarly censored; women entertainers in TV shows had to wear long skirts and long-sleeved blouses buttoned to the neck, without any jewelry. Girls were educated to fear men, avoid pleasure, and see sex as a "necessary evil," accepted only for the sake of establishing a family. But nothing changed in the boys' traditional education; they were still to be tough and emotionally independent, to protect women while dominating them. All this led to the increased prestige of the petty bourgeois family ideal.

Modifications of gender practices, roles, and models are never easily made, particularly when imposed and controlled from the top. Since sociological and psychological investigations were either banned or subject to numerous ideological and political limitations, no scientific survey can show how women actually coped with the changes. Many personal problems were doubtlessly similar to those described in Western studies; women faced the dilemma of either renouncing their identity as women or submitting to male domination, for equality of women was identified with being like men. Women had to neglect their own needs for nurturing but were expected to provide nurturing for others, to neglect their own sexual needs while being expected to show sexual submission.[15]

In the generally oppressive and airless atmosphere of Romania's socialism, the multiple pressures women had to cope with were severely aggravated by the absence of public debate, which was replaced by stiff official stereotypes pretending that everybody was fine and happy. There was no choice between different images of a woman; the ideal woman was depicted as an improbable cross between an ideologically distorted peasant model and a stereotypical Stakhanovite worker—the Bolshevik ideal combined with the traditional peasant one. Both are tyrannical and unattractive, to say the least. This robot-portrait was the standard by which women were officially judged. In real life, the degree of true emancipation consisted in the extent one was able to distance oneself from the official standard. Yet the strict observance of this model was a prerequisite of political and professional promotion. Such a promotion was linked less to the professional abilities of the subject than to her political obedience and moral standards. The Securitate, the infamous secret police, played a decisive role in any promotion. Single women, divorced women, even childless married women, not to mention single mothers, could forget about promotion, regardless of their professional capacity and training. A woman was usually dismissed from a leading position if she got divorced, regardless of how well she performed her job. These rules were even harsher for nomenklatura women, official political women who were supposed to be role models. Women officials had to comply with the party ideal of the exemplary woman, and had to look the part too. They could not dress fashionably, wear makeup, or look attractive in any way. Anyone who looks at pictures of the most prominent female nomenklatura, forced to imitate the generic and asexual communist "comrade," will understand the lack of appeal for young women.

Elena Ceausescu, the dictator's wife, and regarded as having power in her own right, was the model, her official biography a *bildungsroman* in which the central character—Elena, a poor textile worker—while still young joined the righteous struggle of the proletariat, dedicated herself to the "cause" of the working class, and finally rose to an international scientific reputation by means of hard work and special intellectual abilities. A personality cult surrounded her as much as her husband. The stronger the cult became, the more disliked Elena was; people learned from the "bush telephone," which in any dictatorship replaces the tabloids, that her entire "scientific" career was a fake. She was regarded as some sort of wicked witch. She was even more hated than Ceausescu himself and was believed to be behind the most unpopular and oppressive rules and laws, beginning with the antiabortion law. The insistence of the Ceausescu regime on the promotion of women in political life was constantly connected with Elena's rise to leadership and held all the negative connotations associated with the latter.[16] For example, the quotas set for women in leadership positions increased as Elena accumulated yet more positions in the national political bodies.

Official political activity was highly unpopular. It required obedience, and anyone who engaged in political activity was expected to do his or her best to maintain the status quo, to refrain from and to discourage others from thinking differently. The nomenklatura were despised as a bunch of cynical profiteers who profited at ordinary people's expense in a disastrous regime. The fact that every year more women occupied political or leadership positions meant only that women's quotas were being filled to illustrate the equality preached by the regime.

These women had to follow orders or be replaced with less recalcitrant women.[17] The official women's organization, the National Organization of Women, neither represented nor served women, and often worked against women's interests and rights, always following orders. The achievement of the state was to leave women, as a social group, totally disorganized, and to severely damage and tarnish the image of the politically engaged woman.

The 1989 revolution, the execution of the Ceausescu couple, and the collapse of the communist order had the effect of taking the lid off a long-simmering stew; all the frustrations exploded at once. In Timisoara, the town that was a week ahead of the uprising in Bucharest, and that declared itself a free town on December 20, 1989, gynecologists nullified the antiabortion law the same day and began performing abortions for free. A week later, one of the first decrees of the new provisional government, the self-appointed National Salvation Front, declared absolute freedom of abortion. This made the Front's popularity soar. In 1990 more than one million abortions were performed[18] in a country of twenty-three million after two decades of clandestine suffering, the memory of which makes all official or religious bodies keep a low profile on this matter. Education is now needed to encourage women to use other contraceptive methods. Despite the resurgent popularity and influence of the church, the unconditional freedom of abortion goes completely unchallenged. A "pro-life" group is for the time being out of the question.

Similarly, the nauseating puritanical propaganda of the Ceausescu era produced a rush for all the earlier forbidden and sinful subjects. Eager to satisfy a hungry public, dozens of illustrated magazines have appeared—directed to both women and the general public—discussing feminine strategies, eroticism, sex, cosmetics, beauty, and fashion. These magazines, like all media, bypass such "boring" subjects as emancipation, equality, and the advancement of women, fearing, and rightly so, that the use of such concepts, so distorted by former propaganda, might sound too socialist to readers fed up with ideological arguments. Beauty contests and fashion parades merrily replace the Stakhanovite competitions of the past years. The first and most successful small businesses have been the cosmetic and designer clothes boutiques. Western feminists' concern regarding the commercialization of women's bodies and the pressure exerted on women by the "beauty myth" have no place in today's Romania, for both commerce and beauty were clandestine for more than half a century.

The low involvement of women in politics is a response to their previously forced and manipulated involvement.[19] Significantly, during the first free electoral campaign in more than fifty years, women's issues were missing from the agenda of most major parties. The only party to declare women's issues as a specific goal was the National Salvation Front, but the strong neocommunist flavor of its discourse actually stirred more resentment than appreciation. The NSF itself dropped the issue altogether after achieving electoral victory. Very few women went into the spotlight. As of the end of 1992 there were 10 women in the

Chamber of Deputies (out of 328 members), three woman in the Senate (out of 143 members) and very few women in the government. In the 1992 local elections very few women ran for office and no women were elected in the major towns. Women's issues were not mentioned in the campaign, even by the Western-oriented candidates. Women are half of the journalists, but there is no feminist perspective. Women in office do not try to promote women's power or women's issues and the electorate is not aware of distinct issues for women. The wives of the politicians make no public appearances or statements, in order to avoid any comparison with the Ceausescu couple, and the media ignore them anyway, with a veiled superiority. Even those women invested with power and prestige seldom raise specific women's issues. The sole progress one may speak of is that women are left alone to solve their own problems, with no more compulsory standards hanging over their heads. There is a general feeling that things should go "back to normal" in order to make people feel comfortable. This is understood to mean a full restoration of the lost traditions—which were only distorted, not really questioned by the socialist intermezzo—including the roles and values assigned to women in a patriarchal society. As recently as August 1990 Andrei Codrescu noticed that, with very few exceptions, the college-educated wives of his college-educated friends did not sit down to talk after dinner, but got busy in the kitchen.[20] Even scholarly women become elegaic while praising the ancestral wisdom of Romanian women who know how to keep life going through endless adversity, without demanding any compensation for themselves.[21]

Conclusion

In fact, an actual return to the prewar patriarchal order is not possible anymore. In spite of the rampant nationalism, the triad women-mother-nation is absent from the Romanian rhetoric, probably because not even the angriest local national-ist dares touch the freedom of abortion. It has been reassuring to see many women taking advantage of the recent entrepreneurial freedom; they are now running businesses without stirring disapproval or surprise. The new emphasis on individual rights, values, and achievement and the collectivist mentality proper to the traditional patriarchal society are in open contradiction, but for the time being both enjoy equal prestige and equally large audiences. The immediate consequence is a contradictory social environment in which neither men nor women feel at ease. The real problem is how to match the accepted modern norms with the revival of the powerful and respected patriarchal norms, subjects people are not accustomed to discussing openly. There is hope that, with more openness and diversity, in the long term, women will start recognizing the usefulness of organizing themselves and forming groups for social and professional support. But the hardships of everyday life make such prospects improbable in the short term.

Another obstacle encountered by grassroots groups are the activities of the previous corrupt and hypocritical organization for women. Like all former nomenklatura, members are now doing all they can to further enjoy their previous privileges. They insist on representing Romanian women, secure their jobs by all means, and keep funds and international contacts under their control. A recent investigation discovered that donations from abroad were not distributed free but sold at very high prices. These alleged "representatives" cover for each other and use their positions for personal benefits.[22]

The whole society needs to come to terms with the idealized prewar past, with the messy legacy of socialism, and with the uncertain values of the present. In this process women will undoubtedly have an important role to play.

Notes

1. Virgil Nemoianu, "The Biedermeier Culture in Transylvania," paper presented at the 1990 MLA Convention.

2. Hannah Pakula, *The Last Romantic: A Biography of Queen Maria of Romania* (New York: Simon & Schuster, 1984).

3. William Bacon, Jr., as quoted in Mary Ellen Fischer, "Women in Romanian Politics: Elena Ceausescu, Pronatalism and the Promotion of Women," in, *Women, State, and Party in Eastern Europe* Alfred G. Meyer and Sharon L. Wolchik, eds., (Durham: Duke University Press, 1985).

4. Vlad Georgescu, *The Romanians: A History,* ed. Matei Calinescu (Columbus: Ohio State University Press, 1991).

5. See Claude Karnoouh, *L'Invention du Peuple: Chroniques de Roumanie* (Paris: Editions Arcantere, 1990); and Trond Gilberg, "Rural Transformation in Romania," in *The Peasantry of Eastern Europe,* ed. Ivan Volgyes (New York: Pergamon, 1979).

6. John Cole, "In a Pig's Eye: Daily Life and Political Economy in southeastern Europe," in *Economy, Society and Culture in Contemporary Romania,* ed. John Cole. Research Report no. 24, Department of Anthropology, University of Mass., Amherst, December 1984.

7. It is true that the Dickensian work conditions in a steel plant could discourage the most ardent feminist pioneer's determination.

8. Such studies were extremely rare, and their results were not published and discussed. Beginning with 1980 all sociological and psychological studies (heavily ideologized until then anyway) had been practically banished and the departments of sociology and psychology closed in all Romanian universities.

9. Francine du Plessix Gray, *Soviet Women Walking the Tightrope* (New York: Anchor, 1990),p. 109.

10. In late 1960 a new party leadership grabbed power, replacing the old Stalinist team. The newcomers allowed more cultural openness and eased a bit the heavy ideological pressure. This came to an end after 1971, when President Ceausescu, after a trip to China, made a decree reinforcing the ideological control over culture and private life, starting what was called "the Romanian mini–cultural revolution."

11. John Cole and Judith A. Nydon, "Class, Gender and Fertility: Contradictions of Social Life in Contemporary Romania," *East European Quarterly* 13, no. 4 (Winter 1989).

12. Ceausescu, as quoted in Charlotte Hord, Henry P. David, France Donnan, and Merril Wolf, "Reproductive Health in Romania: Reversing the Ceausescu Legacy," in *Studies in Family Planning* 22, no. 24 (August 1991): 5.

13. For more information, see ibid., and Doina Pasca Harsanyi, "A Long Awaited Freedom," in *Peace and Democracy News* no. 2 (1990).

14. Report of the SCSE, 1990.

15. Shere Hite, *The Hite Report: Women and Love: A Cultural Revolution in Progress,* (New York: Alfred A. Knopf, 1987); Erich Fromm, *The Art of Loving* (New York: Harper & Row, 1974); Isaac D. Balbus, *Marxism and Domination* (Princeton: Princeton University Press, 1972).

16. Fischer, "Women in Romanian Politics," p. 132.

17. Fischer notes that "the individual could be dropped and replaced. Filling the quota was important." Ibid., p. 134.

18. Chuck Sudetic, "Romania Seeks to Reduce Abortions," *New York Times,* January 17, 1991.

19. Daniel Nelson, *Romanian Politics in the Ceausescu Era* (Gordon and Breach, 1985).

20. Andrei Codrescu, "Big Chills: My High School Reunion in Romania," *Harper's* (November 1990).

21. Smaranda Mezei, "The Romanian Woman," interview by Nicholas Trifon, *Iztok* 1 (June 1991).

22. Marta Cuibus, *Liga Femeii Ionescu & Co., Adevarul,* February 5, 1992.

5

Women in Romania:
Before and After the Collapse

Mariana Hausleitner

Those who watched televised broadcasts of the December 1989 revolution in Romania will remember pictures of women facing a hail of bullets in order to bring bread to the street fighters. One will also have seen the proud faces of young girls with MP1s in their hands who sought to protect the people from attacks by the Securitate (Security Police). A new age seemed to have dawned, but the ensuing developments have shown how little things have changed. In the first quasi-free parliamentary elections in May 1990 the transformed nomenklatura in the National Salvation Front won the absolute majority.[1] During celebrations for the new "state father," Iliescu, the people—and especially the women—acted as they had under the enforced personality cult: simpleminded slogans of the leaders were chanted, and portraits of the new leader were kissed.[2] Fewer women now serve in Parliament than in Ceausescu's day—only 21 out of 397 members.[3] No woman has strayed into the leadership of either the governmental party or any of its diverse opponents. The situation changed somewhat in fall 1990, when a few women joined the newly founded Citizens Alliance, an association of opposition groups whose main objective is not to take power but to create a civil society in Romania. Yet on the whole, women play a totally subordinate role in Romanian political life. Investigating the reasons for this, one must confront the troubling inheritance of the Ceausescu dictatorship, which deformed the people.

I. Ceausescu's Misogynist Politics

Over the last twenty years all of Romanian society was terrorized by party ideologists and the Securitate, but above all through hunger and cold. Forced industrialization led to economic disparities that have no equivalent in any other

---

This is an amended version of a paper read at the East European Institute of the Free University in Berlin, which will be published in an anthology in Germany.

Eastern European country, with the exception perhaps of Albania. Hardly any funds were invested in agriculture, and all that could be grown was exported. This approach was intended to pay off the mountains of debt created by mistaken investment in chemical and heavy industries.[4] Since the beginning of the 1980s, most foodstuffs were available only with ration cards, each family being allowed a restricted amount of sugar, flour, and oil per month. The purchase of anything extra on the black market was punishable by arrest. All this meant a special burden for women, whose work in the home had to accommodate these brutal conditions. Each woman had to plan the month's meals exactly in order to make do with the minimal material available. Additionally burdens resulted from drastic energy-saving measures, causing warm water and gas to be interrupted several times a day. Because the delivery of energy to industry was a priority, women had to cook either in the late evening or before four o'clock in the morning. Refrigerators and household appliances were useless because of the frequent interruptions in electricity, and by the end of the 1980s, the per-person consumption of kilowatts had been established precisely; for example, only one twenty-five-watt bulb was allowed per room.

This general misery was supplemented by special measures directed at women to force them to continue to bring children into the world despite hardship. Unlike political theories, Ceausescu recognized that persons are born to women; as a result, women's bodies were brutally instrumentalized for the sake of population policy, not unlike the way in which nature itself was instrumentalized. In 1966 Ceausescu decreed a total prohibition on abortion, because the birth rate of twenty-five births per thousand inhabitants, high by European standards, was deemed too low. And indeed, in contrast to the 1950s, when Romania's population was predominantly rural, the birth rate was in a steady decline. Between 1958 and 1965 the number of abortions rose tenfold, to 1.15 million.[5] Similar developments took place in other socialist countries, such as East Germany and Hungary, but Romania's ideology of growth viewed the falling birth rate as a threat to future economic development. During this period of expansive industrialization, it was believed that more and more workers would be necessary.[6] While governments in East Germany and Hungary tried to encourage women to work by improving child care and entitlement programs for women, Ceausescu resorted to coercive measures. All forms of contraception were forbidden, and divorce was made difficult. Abortions were permitted only for women older than forty-five and those who already had at least four children. In 1986 the minimum was increased to five children. Medical reasons for abortion were accepted only in the rarest of cases, and many women paid with their lives. At the same time, the number of children with hereditary illnesses grew.

In the beginning, these intrusions into the private sphere seemed to have the desired effect. The birth rate soared from 233,687 in 1966 to 527,764 in 1967. But everything necessary to handle this "baby boom"—baby food, doctors, child care facilities—was missing. Because of increasingly miserable living conditions in the 1980s, the birth rate proposed by the executive committee of the Romanian Communist Party—twenty per one thousand inhabitants—could never be achieved. In the 1970s, when distribution still worked somewhat, the birth rate stood between 18 and 21; it then began to sink rapidly, reaching 14.3 in 1984. When compared to Europe, this was still a relatively high rate, one matched only by Albania, Cypress, and Poland (which sometimes exceeded it), but for Ceausescu women's resistance and continued illegal abortions served as a challenge demanding ever more restrictions. In the 1980s, the legal age of marriage was reduced to fifteen years, and women who were still single at twenty-five were punished with a 5 percent tax. Married couples with no children also had to pay higher taxes. As women's control of their bodies diminished further, so did the very existence of a "private" sphere. In order for the state to keep an eye on pregnancies, all women between twenty-five and thirty were forced to submit to regular gynecological examinations.[7] Despite the threats of a long jail sentence for both the woman and her doctor, one could still get an illegal abortion, if expensively. As is only now becoming known, because of the inadequate hygienic conditions under which such abortions took place, 471 women died from the procedure in 1984. If one extrapolates from this figure the number of women who died during the twenty-three years of the ban on abortion, one reaches a five-digit figure.[8]

In order better to apprehend those who rejected his population policy, Ceausescu used the Securitate. Families with fewer than four children had to fill out questionnaires about their sex lives. Fearing denunciation by the Securitate, women felt it unsafe to speak with each other about means of contraception. An absolute taboo reigned not only in the public sphere but among good friends. This resulted in an atomization and deformation of friendships, for friends could not share their most important concerns.

Furthermore, in order to control the sexuality of foreigners studying or working in Romania, the Securitate served as a pimp for high-class prostitutes. Unlike ordinary Romanians, these women were permitted free access to student housing for foreigners as well as to their meeting places in hotels, restaurants, and nightclubs. There were also a limited number of prostitutes made available to the natives; these shared their income with the district police and Securitate thereby protecting themselves from punishment as "social parasites".

II. The Position of Women in Romania Today

When the National Salvation Front murdered Ceausescu in December 1989 and eliminated his decrees, including the ban on abortion, many women viewed the new leader, Iliescu, as their savior. But what has truly changed for women in the last three years? For a minimal price, they can terminate undesired pregnancies. Yet because there was no preparation for the resulting burden on inadequate medical facilities, abortion continues to take place without anesthesia and with old, often rusty instruments. And there are no beds available for recuperating women.[9]

If women decide to bring children into the world, in only a few cases can they raise these children under humane conditions. Even birth is a risk, and 25 percent of the newborns do not survive. In Ceausescu's time the high mortality rate was hushed up by registering newborns only after six weeks.

To be sure, the rationing system for foodstuffs no longer exists, but want and need have not been eliminated. Baby food is still lacking. Foodstuffs in general are still scarce goods, which can be secured only after searching for hours and standing in lines. Many urban dwellers have begun to plant vegetable gardens or keep chickens and cows on small pieces of land in the outskirts of cities, now that the purchase of such parcels of land has become legal. This makes for an additional burden on women, who have to compensate for all the shortages. The lack of adequate clothing means women must frantically sew, and the lack of medicines requires them to gather herbs. This results in even less time to care for children.

All in all, Romania in no way gives the impression of a country on its way to entering the twenty-first century; it is a strange combination of the premodern and the modern. Despite the huge push toward urbanization in the 1970s and 1980s, a close connection to relatives in the country was attentively maintained in order to compensate for the scarcity of food items in the cities. Thus, the values of a patriarchal rural society were maintained under Ceausescu, in spite of everyone's being required to work, including the women in the cities. That the husband represented the family to the outside world and made the most important decisions was never questioned. Even in highly educated couples, men beat their wives to show their authority. The peasant tradition of bride-money was retained because of the poor economic conditions in the cities. Because young couples could not get an apartment on their own, it was demanded that the woman receive a private apartment as a dowry from her parents, without which her chances of getting married were slim.

In spite of the employment of most women, it was still expected, both formally and informally, that women would first and foremost find their satisfaction in motherhood. This representation of women's role has never been challenged in any of the various news organs that have sprung up since Ceausescu's downfall. The few articles that have appeared at all about the role of women lament the growing rate of abortions. Instead of demanding better contraception, National Salvation Front newspapers brand the freer expression of sexuality among the youth with the damning foreign word "libertinage." The very use of this term indicates Romanians' inability to speak about sexuality in their own language. The vagueness of what is meant is even better for the purposes of sexual repression. Meanwhile, no discussion takes place about the conditions which have led to the decline in birth rates.[10] Instead, one hears nostalgia for the cult of motherhood.[11]

Such efforts to reconstruct traditional moral views will be one result of the immense problems raised by Ceausescu's misogynist politics. His prohibition on abortion brought many unwanted babies into the world, leading parents to put these children on the streets. These unfortunates, popularly called *ceauscei,* were formerly kept in barrackslike orphanages. Since the end of 1989 they have been permitted to leave such supervision, and many now live in train stations and marketplaces, trying to keep their heads above water through begging, petty crime, and prostitution. The number of these street children was estimated at the end of 1991 to be more than 21,000. Thirty percent of crimes in Romania today are committed by youths. Those who are caught are sent to reform schools for minors, where there are no persons with psychological training. At best, they will be sent directly to prisons, where they receive the necessary skills in order to enter a full-blown life of crime.[12]

In addition to these roving bands of children, Ceausescu's misogynist policies have left behind another dark legacy—the homes for supposedly "untreatable" children. Horrible pictures of these institutions circulated through the media in early 1990. Under Ceausescu the death rate in such places was 25 percent, and those who survived lived in indescribable filth and misery. Even more than with other citizens, these children were treated as objects having no subjectivity. While more than 130,000 cases have been taken on by diverse foreign organizations, for some the help comes too late.[13] Especially sad is the fate of AIDS patients, 93 percent of whom are children infected through blood transfusions.[14] In order to alleviate the suffering of these forgotten children, the government of Romania eased adoption restrictions at the beginning of 1990, and many abandoned children were sent to foreign countries. Yet the side effects of such laws soon became apparent as a booming business in children began. Thirty percent of the children adopted worldwide come from Romania.[15] In Romania this trade is legitimized with statements like the following: "My uncle sold his eight-month old baby so that his other children could survive. This is what we have come to. But what should we do, when we cannot feed our children?"[16]

A change in these conditions would require state aid for families with many children, but by the end of 1991 the transformation of the economy was still not in full swing, and subventions continued to flow into exhausted large factories of heavy industry and mining. Since women occupy 40 percent of lower-level positions in industry, they are likely to lose jobs first under a restricted economy. Women fear this, because of the low wages of their husbands. The political consequence is that women are not progressive but rather support those politicians who reject radical change. With a lack of economic innovation, there are scarcely any new jobs in the service sector, and as long as the private sector of the economy does not gear up, the state does not have the tax funds necessary to expand the social institutions. Already it is very unclear where the funds are to come from for the proposed one-year maternity leave announced at the end of 1990.[17] In Romania there are no structures of civil society that could take over some of these tasks, as has occurred in Poland. The Orthodox Church has not yet discovered this area of activity.

III. Women in the Public Sphere

The political parties do not have any special women's representatives or programs for the support of women. That does not mean, however, that there are no politically active women. Three women in particular might be mentioned whose activities shed light on the conditions of life in Romanian society, which made possible only a fight for human dignity and existence. While a forum for a discussion of the role of women was not possible under Ceausescu, a few women stepped forward. Unlike the male dissidents, they did not present a programmatic opposition, but acted pragmatically out of a moral sense of responsibility. Ana Blandiana expressed this sharply in the newspaper 22[18]: As a poet of such an unhappy people she could not avoid its suffering, but had to find a way to give it full expression.[19]

During Ceausescu's lifetime Blandiana represented in her short stories the fluid boundaries between reality and madness in Romanian everyday life. In one poem, which appeared in 1985 in the journal *Amfiteatru,* she turned explicitly against the ban on abortion:

> *The Children's Crusade*
> An entire people
> still unborn,
> but condemned to be born,
> lined up before being born,
> foetus by foetus,
> an entire people
> that cannot see, or hear, or understand,
> but marches on
> through the aching bodies of women,
> through the blood of the mothers
> who are never asked.[20]

This poem circulated from hand to hand, which was rare enough in Romania, given the absence of a samizdat press. In return, Blandiana was for a time prohibited to publish. But even greater rebellion followed her publication of a children's story in 1988, for the hero, a tomcat who grew megalomaniacal, clearly represented the dictator.

After the collapse, Ana Blandiana worked with the National Salvation Front. But she soon realized that she was being used as a front for the newly transformed nomenklatura. After leaving the Front and publicly criticizing its structures, she was bombarded by death threats. This did not prevent her in summer 1990 from speaking up for the opposition, who were involved in a hunger strike at Bucharest University. Iliescu brought the miners to Bucharest to smash the opposition, and several women were badly beaten because of their resemblance to Blandiana, who fortunately was abroad at the time. Upon her return, she actively supported a personal dialogue with the misguided miners. Today, Blandiana is president of the Citizens Alliance and active in its efforts to create a civil society. An interesting difference in the political activity of men and women is developing. While men in the opposition have tried to form a political party, women have engaged in the concrete work of building networks between groups, as the rudiments of a civil society. They intentionally try to break out of the circle of the intellectual elites.

Doina Cornea, lecturer at the University of Cluj/Kolozsvar, is another of the few dissidents of the Ceausescu era. For years she lived under home arrest because of her public protests, especially against Ceausescu's destruction of the rural environment. When she attempted to make outside contact, she was beaten by her guards. After Ceausescu's fall, she too became a member of the National Salvation Front. She left it by January 1990, after the sound was cut during the television broadcast of her speech about the Securitate.[21] Since then, she has supported a transformation in Romania based on basic Christian values.

As a last example, Smaranda Enache should be named. She was director of a puppet theater in Tirgu Mures, Marosvasarhely. In May 1989 her piece "Fables, Fables" was prohibited because of its covert critique of Ceausescu. Enache was active in the local organization of the National Salvation Front at the beginning of 1990. In March of that year she left it under protest, because the Front had not taken a stand against the Romanian nationalists of the "Vatra Românească" ("Romanian Cradle"), who provoked a bloody confrontation between Romanians and Hungarians.[22] Since then, she has continuously received death threats. Her candidacy for the parliamentary elections was disallowed for threadbare reasons. In April 1991 she was fired from her job because an examining committee attested to her "inadequate sense of obligation," even though under her direction the puppet theater had received both domestic and international commendations.[23] Enache has continued to work in a leadership capacity for the Citizens Alliance.

Women are only infrequently represented among the older opposition parties, whose leaders are mostly over sixty. But they do participate in the newer movements, mainly in the *Miscarea ecologistă* (Ecology movement) and the Citizens Alliance. Candidates for the Ecological Party are almost all male, but many women have been active in it in their free time, giving one hope that in the future women may play a more important role. Perhaps these women can help to overcome the more traditional tendencies of the ecology movement by focusing attention on more concrete problems. Such practical concerns provide the best chances for drawing women into politics and out of the long-entrenched web of patriarchal relations.

Translated from the German by Kathleen LaBahn

Notes

1. The monopoly of the transformed nomenklatura and its Front for National Salvation made it possible to manipulate the election campaign. Also, the election law that

allowed a political party to be founded with only 250 signatures necessarily split the opposition.

2. The author of this article was a witness to these scenes at election events in Bucharest.

3. See Doina Pasca Harsanyi in this volume.

4. Romania in the 1970s brought in modern technology to use in refining oil they received at cheap prices from the USSR and Iran. When that source dried up, they were left with heavy debts without the means of producing the products that could pay them off.

5. Marianna Buntenschön, "Die Hilfe blieb oft aus," *Frankfurter Rundschau*, July 13, 1974.

6. John W. Cole and Judith A. Nydon, "Class, Gender and Fertility: Contradictions of Social life in Contemporary Romania," *East European Quarterly*, 13, no. 4 (Winter 1989): 469–476.

7. Harry Schleicher, "Mehr Kinder, damit der Sozialismus blüht," *Frankfurter Rundschau*, March 9, 1984; and Thomas Brey, "Wie Rumäniens Geheimpolizei die Geburtenrate förderte," *Frankfurter Rundschau*, January 18, 1990.

8. Heiko Flottau, "Kinderkriegen—von Agenten überwacht," *Süddeutsche Zeitung*, June 11, 1985.

9. Roland Hofwiler, "Vom Gebärzwang zur Massenabtreibung aus Armut," *Die Tageszeitung*, June 21, 1991.

10. Felicity Barringer, "Birth Rates Plummeting in Some Ex-Communist Regions," *The New York Times*, December 31, 1991.

11. Adina Cojocaru, "Dragoste si ginecologie," *Adevărul*, May 14, 1991.

12. Luise Schifter, "Kleine Vagabunden—wohin?" *Neuer Weg*, November 23, 1991.

13. "Les enfants fantômes de Roumanie," *Le Monde*, September 29, 1990.

14. "Aids-Infektionen in Rumänien," *Der Tagesspiegel*, September 26, 1991.

15. "In Rumänien floriert der gewerbliche Handel mit Kindern," in *Der Tagesspiegel*, November 30, 1990.

16. "Rumänien verbessert die Familienplanung," *Der Tagesspiegel*, November 30, 1990.

17. Quoted by Stephan Müller, "Hier schlagen sich die Menschen um ein paar Hühnerköpfe," *Der Tagesspiegel*, May 18, 1991.

18. December 22, 1989, was the beginning of the Romanian revolution.

19. Ana Blandiana, interview with Pavel Chihaia, "Viitorul cu asupra de măsură," *22*, April 12, 1991.

20. Translated by Chrisula Stefanescu, *Iowa Review*, February 1991.

21. There is a government monopoly on the media. The opposition has demanded a second channel, but that has not been granted; Monica Lovinescu, "Doina Cornea si politicul," *22*, March 15, 1991.

22. The latter present themselves as defenders of the cultural rights of Romanians in Transylvania. It is estimated that in Transylvania 50 percent of the Romanians are

members. In some cases people are required to join, such as in the university, or risk losing their positions. They state in their constitutions that they are not responsible for the acts of their members! Their members have attacked and beaten up Hungarians.

23. Gabriel Andreescu, "Smaranda Enache în regatul competentelor," *22*, May 3, 1991. See also Krisztina Koenen's interview with Enache, "Warum war die rumänische Revolution ein Putsch," *Frankfurter Allgemeine Zeitung*, May 24, 1991.

6

A Few Prefeminist Thoughts

Hana Havelková

> . . . solving the female question means solving the male question as well. Both concern sheer humanity . . .[1]
>
> Yes, learned gentlemen must think by their hearts. Not until they go so will the times become joyful and normal.[2]
>
> —Charlotte Masaryk

Whenever the serious problems of women are debated in the Czech lands, someone, usually a woman, raises the question: "What about the problems of men?" If the talk is of initiating women's studies, proposals to constitute male studies come in its wake. When not long after the "velvet revolution" the bookstalls in the streets were flooded with male pornographic magazines, women reacted by demanding that pornography for women be available as well—which it soon was.

Charlotte Masaryk's statements, made at the beginning of this century, certainly do not testify to either the state of society or the general way of thinking at that time.[3] Nor would it be correct to generalize the above-mentioned contemporary reactions. Yet they can be characterized without hesitation as symptomatic of a particular attitude to the women's question in Czech society.[4] Contemporary theoretical thought evinces a reluctance to treat this problem in isolation, putting general human problems above that of sexed identity, and showing a relatively high degree of acceptance and entrenchment of the idea of the equality of the sexes.

The predominance of these features in the approach to the problem of women can be interpreted in two ways: either as a historically shaped structure for perceiving the problem or as a reduced sensitivity to women's issues and the problem of women's identity. Both interpretations truthfully express the nature of our consciousness in regard to issues with which Western feminist theories are concerned. But each of them testifies to something different. Western feminist literature represents a different and a very rich world of thought which offers to enrich our knowledge and behavior. Learning this has required that we overcome our cultural isolation and develop the relevant disciplines; it is essentially a question of time. In this sense the syndrome of rejecting a specific concentration on women's issues can be seen as deriving from our lack of knowledge of the problem, and thus our reduced sensitivity to it.

But acceptance of Western intellectual advances may lead to theoretical misunderstandings or even errors across such traditional philosophical disciplines as politics, economics, law, and ethics. As a theoretical field practical philosophy is closely connected with what has come to be termed the historical experiment of "really existing socialism." There are many strong arguments that women's experiences in post-totalitarian societies constitute the basis for a different practical-philosophical approach to the women's issue, one that differs considerably from the model of feminism derived from the political context of western societies. In any case, it is advisable to be extremely cautious when directly adopting ready-made concepts.

Objections can be made, supported by well-known arguments, that cultural and practical-political issues cannot be separated from each other. But in order to unravel the tangle of advantages and disadvantages, misunderstandings, multitiered compensations, and other specific phenomena embedded in the traditional relations between men and women under the "really existing socialism," one must distinguish between them methodologically.

There is an essential historical argument in favor of this distinction: that the link with the presocialist tradition was not totally broken, in the same way that contact with the world was not totally lost. Many cultural values and customary practices, including those concerning the man-woman relation, were preserved, especially in areas where social relations were not institutionally regulated. This is the reason why institutional interventions into law, politics, and the economy, which did not evolve organically but were imposed abruptly and artificially, severed these realms from their natural tie to the culture. Therefore, I regard it as legitimate to differentiate between phenomena resulting from the socialist system and those that were not its product. A cognitive advantage of this methodological distinction between the social system and the culture is that it becomes possible to explain both the common and the divergent traits of Eastern European societies, in which noticeable differences arise from different precommunist traditions, especially in the relations between men and women.

The Czech lands can serve as an extreme case of such a hybrid society, composed of both traditional elements and an imposed system. Socialist ideas in their original, ideal form were relatively widespread in these lands even before the declaration of an independent republic, and even more so after the foundation of Czechoslovakia in 1918. Historical sources document a progressive tendency as regards the woman question, with its premise of equality. Women had the right to vote and be elected, and the idea that women should enjoy special protection had already been rejected. "What the women's movement lacks more than anything else is genuine, ruthless criticism. And there is nothing more detrimental to this movement than condescension."[5] There was also the motif of an interest common to men and women that was superior to that of one or the other sex: "The struggle for rights is no longer a conflict between women and men as enemies, but a struggle of progress against reactionary tendencies. Not against men, but with men, shall progressive women oppose the reactionaries, whether these are men or women."[6] After the declaration of an independent republic all modern and antitraditionalist tendencies intensified even further. Educated and emancipated women had no small say in creating a new style of life. But their self-realization was made possible, in part, by the miserable situation of other women, such as servants and domestic help representing relatively cheap labor. The conflicting positions of women and men manifested themselves during the economic crisis of the 1930s, during which strong pressure was exerted on well-paid employed women to leave their jobs for men, the breadwinners, while the employment of women doing the hard and worst-paid jobs increased unprecedentedly.

This historical exposé is meant to show that not all the institutional intervention of the socialist system came out of the blue or was due to sheer arbitrariness aimed against tradition. In the Czech case, the high employment of women characteristic of the socialist system probably was not resented by women as much as is sometimes claimed today in sweeping criticisms made of the totalitarian system. Historical analysis is not the subject of this article, but it is necessary to emphasize the intermingling of historical continuity and discontinuity, in contrast to positions that treat our specific historical experience—which must be the starting point for attempts at a general diagnosis—in an oversimplified manner.

This is all the more important given that the previous ideological regulation requires all attempts at general hypotheses about any social phenomenon to take place in a theoretical vacuum. Not only concepts for a philosophy of society but even medium-range theories are lacking. Materials on problems of women and the family are to be found mostly in sociological data and partial studies, such as in family law. A priceless wealth of experience and information could no doubt be found in all kinds of counseling centers. Yet this reservoir of experience is not used to learn about and diagnose the situation of women. There had been a liquidation of a functioning public sphere, and much of the knowledge that should have been public is only now gropingly looking for a way to become public.

The road toward a diagnosis has so far been taken in quite a different direction. Encouraged by the interest shown by Western countries, and discouraged by the lack of it at home, women theoreticians in the social sciences articulate their attempts at a generalization of the experience of Czechoslovak women for their Western colleagues. The first attempts at more general diagnoses thus emerge from a dialogue with Western feminism—one that has its pitfalls and that may or may not be transitional. For Eastern European women, the developed theoretical apparatus of feminism is conducive to a quick application to our personal experience and to such generalizing, often conflicting diagnoses as "Our society is patriarchal" or, on the contrary, "It is generally matriarchal"; "It is sex-conscious" or, on the contrary, "Equality of the sexes is not a problem that concerns us." The long practical and theoretical feminist experience of our Western colleagues leads to an underestimation of the specific historical experience of women in

Eastern Europe. The difficulty of mediating and communicating our everyday life experience in all its details results in a superficial application of concepts with divergent connotations and a simple distrust of our own different experience.

While this dialogue started developing about a year after the November revolution, the discourse in our society has evolved with considerable diffidence. A certain effect still lingers from women's unpropitious experience with the official institution intended to represent them under the communist regime. While failing to defend the true interests of women, this organ overemphatically supported the regime on behalf of the "female half of the society." Yet the absence of interest in the specifically female view cannot be ascribed solely to this lingering trauma. Another of its causes is the fact that the woman question has not yet become a separate political issue, and that as a consequence, women themselves still do not see any distinct reasons why they should engage in political affairs. The feminization of poverty, of which there are already signs, predicted by experts but as yet unrecognized by the public, is likely to change this.

The lack of interest in women's problems originates in the syndrome of putting general human problems above particular issues of sex-related identity, an attitude strengthened by the prerevolutionary political dissent, which focused on issues of political freedom. An assumption that sexual identity is natural, as well as the conviction that women's emancipation has been accomplished and that no one has really benefited from it, all discourage attention to women's issues.

A few examples from personal discussions and literature illustrate the antifeminist arguments: "What I resent about feminism is precisely the '-ism,' which testifies to ideological onesidedness"; "Women have no need of feminism, because they are at least as high up on the social ladder as men, if not higher"; "It is a luxury of a sort, or there is something petty about concerning oneself with partial female problems—because just like men, women are above all concerned with human rights"; "We have had enough of ideological 'dressing'; what is needed is a change in the real, specific conditions . . ."

What has been said so far reinforces the thesis that the system of "really existing socialism" declared that women were equal to men, entrenching this not only in the official ideology but also in the public consciousness. There was a positive form of equalization enforced through law. But this was voluntaristic, inconsequential and problematic. The negative form of equalization was oppression of all through totalitarian means. Differences were removed by being suspended and ignored, prevented from becoming public, or bought off. Positive, legal equalization also had negative effects not only on women but also on children and the entire society, providing an eloquent example of what happens when law, economics, and politics are not in harmony.

It is necessary to differentiate between two forms of equality, positive and negative, of men and women. This is the indispensable first step toward a philosophical reflection of the problem. Different concepts in practical philosophy are applicable to an analysis of each of these forms. In the first case, the relevant concept is individual subjectivity; in the other, it is the private/public distinction. In either case one can observe how different historical experiences shift the semantic contexts of these concepts in feminist theory.

The negative improvement of the position of women as compared with that of men was accomplished through a degradation of all individuals to objects. The totalitarian government thoroughly suspended individual subjectivity in the form of people's autonomous development as citizens, as owners, as thinking beings, as acting subjects, and as men and women shaping their own lives. In the present-day discussions between supporters of the postmodern and the feminist positions, the value of a positive concept of the subject is typically defended for women, as when Rosi Braidotti states, "The problematic of women as subjects is only just beginning to be explored" or "Women cannot afford to argue for dispersion and fragmentation. . . ."[7] In our situation, this concept needs to be defended for women and men alike. Indeed, it remains unclear whether we can participate in the discourse about postmodernism in general. The continuity of our social development was ruptured precisely at the point when modernism's positive values might have been realized. Considering that this society has not been governed by a democratic order for fifty years, it can be said that both modernism's positive values and its criticism remain underdeveloped.

Hence, the problems of subjectivity and identity are not perceived in this society as specifically female ones. In theoretical terms, identity based on sex is still approached only as a sub-problem. There are thus two reasons for making the "generally human" superior to the "specifically female." First, the problem is not one concerning women more than men; and second, in its emphatic form it is an essential problem of all. This "supra-feminist syndrome" raises the question of the legitimacy of the "two-tier structure" of the female problem. Moreover, the negative equalization produced problematic relations between the sexes, as well as many secondary problems for women. One psychosocial consequence has been the reduced sense of responsibility when marrying and in married life, as well as reduced parental responsibility, as in unplanned pregnancies. The Czech and Slovak Republics have one of the lowest average ages of newlywed couples in Europe. From the ethical aspect this is remarkable, but it is understandable when one considers the generally blunted sense of responsibility, the fact that the weakening of autonomous ethics has not resulted in an expansion of an "ethics of care" or an increased sense of reciprocity, whether in partnerships or in other relations, but rather in the opposite. The extraordinarily high divorce rate has not yet been sufficiently analyzed from this point of view.

This thesis about the general suppression of subjectivity, and the consequent extension of the popular feminist term "oppression" to apply to both sexes, may appear too abstract to bear on the situation of women in any significant manner. It is perhaps a theoretical construct behind which a Western reader can hardly see a real world. Yet this very thesis expresses a feature of the society of really existing socialism that pervaded everyday life. You can only understand the specific situation of Czech women when you understand the common experience and suffering of both the men and women.

When explaining the suppression of subjectivity, one should separate the ideological aspect from the real, institutional one. The very opposite was proclaimed ideologically, where the so-called "general development of personality" was presented as the supreme goal of social development. But in practical policy, which was governed by the totalitarian claim to power of a single party, this goal was subordinated to the means—the sole means, according to the totalitarian ideology—of attaining the supposed "collective interest." The latter was, of course, determined without public discussion and in an absolutely voluntarist manner. This relates to another ideological principle that undermined the autonomy of the individual—people's separation from property. A person's general development was said not to be connected with property.

Suppression of individual autonomy by means of the economic system is an almost inexhaustible topic. Briefly speaking, it involved people's total economic dependence on the state, of which they were all employees. Remuneration depended on individuals or company performance only to some degree. Profits made by the stronger were redistributed to the weaker. The low average wage was made up for by introducing a system of various "bonuses," contributions toward the cost of trade union recreation, weekday lunches, and so forth, which quite logically further strengthened state paternalism. Though company employees depended on the state less than civil servants, the state could not only manipulate people but literally blackmail them. Through economic sanctions, such as a demotion to a lower-paid job, the state extorted civic and political obedience.

The law was based on similar antiindividualist principles. Institutions and collective bodies in general were clearly in a privileged position vis-à-vis the individual. In everyday life this became manifest in the arbitrary rule of the bureaucracy. Arranging for anything was an unpleasant experience that required dealing with authorities and confronting their arrogance, while the number of actions that involved contact with the authorities was constantly growing. An example was traveling abroad: the state decided who would be granted foreign currency, the first condition for foreign travel. For each trip abroad one needed a police permit obtainable only after procuring five different stamped permits from one's employer, another example of blackmail through employment. The impact this had on people's self-confidence and self-respect is obvious.

In general, this practice made the individual subject feel paltry in the public sphere. Unfortunately, but quite logically, this had its parallel in research, where the concept of the citizen, the problem of the public, and the ethical issue of a subject's autonomy disappeared from the topics dealt with by philosophy and social science. It was also typical that the theme of subjectivity, in the form of the vulgar Marxist "philosophical" neologism the "subjective factor," found its way back into these sciences in the late 1970s only because the passivity and reduced responsibility of individuals began gravely to affect the productivity of labor!

There is yet another methodologically significant "supra-feminist" consequence. In Western feminist discourse, the division of power to a considerable extent corresponds with the division between the private and the public spheres, and hence the division between men and women. In really existing socialism the overriding division was drawn between the Communist Party, as the organization from which all subject positions were derived, and all those who were its objects. In spite of the fact that women did not sit on the Party Central Committee, they, like men, were given positions in accordance with the degree of their loyalty, not their abilities.

The suppression of subjectivity through the destruction of citizenship subtly deepened another division, which will probably come to represent the crucial moment in the development of a new democracy. The civic consciousness of a large group of people practically disappeared, their subjectivity linked almost exclusively with their private and material lives. There were others who found it difficult to put up with the degradation of their citizenship. The distance between the civic attitudes of these two groups is growing. Women are on both sides, and the division usually runs through families and other demographic groups.

Orientation toward the private sphere was an essential, psychologically formative consequence of the suppression of public subjectivity. The family assumed a special function as the refuge of moral values. The slogan "He who does not steal from the state robs his own family," which became so widespread in really existing socialism, stopped being perceived as immoral by a large number of people. In at least two senses, the family was the field for substitute economic activity. It was the family, or rather the household, where many people put to use their inventive potential and their desire to do things their own way, without having to observe some official regulations. Because of the poor performance of the state economy, and the service sector in particular, women and men alike were forced to engage in all kinds of do-it-yourself activities. Men practiced male trades and women undertook female ones. This may be one of the reasons, supported by the system, why female and male roles are so clear-cut in this country, as some Western feminists have criticized. On the other hand, the degree to which men do female jobs, husbands helping their wives, varies with generation and is most common in younger families. This seems to testify to the emancipating influence. The family performed yet another compensatory function: it substituted for the public sphere. The family and close friends were the only school of political thought given the absence of any opportunity in the media, the schools, or elsewhere for public discourse.

If moral education and education as a citizen took place in the family, it also provided the model for the relation between men and women and reproduced male and female roles. Like so many other problems that must become topics of public discourse because of their importance for the culture and human relations, and because they embody normative issues of what is desirable in basic social relations and institutions, reflection on relations between the sexes was carried out almost exclusively on the individual level. Therefore, even for those who know the situation in this country well, it is difficult to determine what a particular manifestation of "typical" male or female behavior means, because a more general symbolic language is lacking. This can be illustrated by a very curious example. Many women agree that they themselves deliberately encouraged the patriarchal manners of their husbands so as to boost their husband's self-confidence, which the latter had difficulty maintaining in the public and work spheres. We must therefore be cautious in making our diagnoses!

Whether some traditional norms were preserved due to inertia and an insufficient space for exploring problems (female initiatives did not exist, nor did any other), or for these tragicomic reasons, one thing that is certain is that differentiating between the influence of the system and socialist experience, on the one hand, and the influence of tradition, on the other hand, is not easy. Explaining patriarchy directly by appeal to the paternalism of the totalitarian regime is an all too easy and short-circuited approach.

As a consequence of the practice of really existing socialism, the concepts of private and public have meanings and functions different from those of Western countries. It can be expected that these will survive for a long time, and should be taken into account as structural elements. In quite general terms, the relation of the individual subject to the public sphere is abstract, while the subject's relation to the private one is concrete. The latter is thus uneasily accessible for abstract normative correction. Developments will depend on how public discussion evolves.

As the private sphere became more important, so did the role of women. Even though both women and men were active in the public as well as the private sphere, the latter has remained, more than the former, the domain of women, with the mother's role irreplaceable within it. Generally, it was the woman rather than the man who shaped the compensatory functions of the family and its entire lifestyle. At the same time, she was "competent" in public matters as well. In an overwhelming majority of divorce cases it was the woman who initiated proceedings, perhaps because of her capacity to cope with things with or without her husband.

Where the subject was oppressed in the public sphere, the family represented for the woman, much more than the man, the possibility of choice and escape from political blackmail. Women consciously made use of this opportunity. I have recently heard criticism of the "cult of motherhood" in this country, but its defensive function has not yet been thoroughly analyzed. Political blackmail usually took the form of linking professional advancement with joining the Communist Party. The number of female party members was conspicuously low in comparison to male. Women opted for motherhood, and children provided an "excuse" to not join the party even after the mother resumed employment. Women thus deliberately gave up the chance for any greater job advancement and, above all, the chance of participating in management.

Yet as men were less able to escape state manipulation and oppression, it is understandable that giving priority to women's problems is quite a delicate affair, one that raises the counter-question, "And what about men?" But it also gives substantiation to the thesis that even after the revolution, and for a long time to come, the problem of identity will remain one of both human identity and civic subjectivity. It can even be argued that women's need to fight for their new identity not only "as women" but with men as citizens is more idealistic and liberatory.

Quite paradoxically, the positive fact that women were equal to men[8] had a number of negative consequences. The pre-1989 legislation in countries of Central and Eastern Europe contained no clause that could be regarded as direct discrimination against women. The share of women in the work sphere thus practically equaled that of men, leading to an essential change in the division between public and private labor. This change had many positive effects for women. They had broad access to education and further training, and, consequently, developed their individual consciousness, self-confidence, and personal potential, recognizing their own abilities and their independence from men.

Yet it was precisely in this legally guaranteed area that true equality of women and men was not achieved. Statistics document that women were discriminated against, especially in pay. Women with a university education reached the average wage of men with only elementary education. This discrimination had its roots in the suppression of subjectivity in the public sphere and its transfer to the private sphere. The low prestige of a career in politics and management produced a certain model of female choice; women were not resigned to a profession and performance, but put the family before a politically conditioned career. Because women gave up participation in management, they did not have their lobby in it, and their managers did not defend their interests. This further deepened the masculine character of the power and management structures, which in turn made it difficult for women to adapt themselves to the standard masculine career patterns.[9] In this sense it is true, to some extent, that the division of power was based on sex.

Women could not adapt to these career patterns primarily because of their frequently emphasized double burden. Here we cannot evade the question of to what extent they were forced to accept it, and to what extent they chose it willingly. Married women in Czechoslovakia did not have the duty to be employed, yet practically all of them were. In opinion polls women state that they regarded it as their duty to go to work in order to contribute to the family budget. Yet not all of them were employed purely out of economic need, although the woman's pay always improved the living standard of the family. It should also be remembered that one reason why women did not give up their jobs was that in principle they found both roles to be manageable. They did not have to make a strict choice between professional career and family, but they paid for it by being overburdened. I have already mentioned the function that the family fulfilled for women from the viewpoint of their freedom; few women therefore opted for only a professional career.

The point is, I believe, that this model of solving the question of choice between profession and family was so general in our society that it had the character of a social constant with which the employers calculated and from which they proceeded. Every employed woman, if not a mother already, was regarded as a potential one, whose career ambitions were a priori seen as limited. The discrimination experienced by a certain number of women derived not from their primary, a priori underestimation but from a kind of "silent agreement" between them and their employers. This agreement can be very plastically demonstrated by the example of the large percentage of women who deliberately chose lower-paid jobs that did not require very demanding work and that allowed them to cope quite comfortably with their household duties. Clerical jobs were especially popular, because they enabled women to do their shopping and arrange for many other family needs during working hours. But women in factories were really exploited, especially where the bulk of the work force was female, as in the textile industry. Here again the division between the exploited and those who comfortably "settled" in the system did not precisely coincide with that between men and women.

Some further major issues should be mentioned when speaking about women's life in the work sphere as an essential sector of the public sphere. First, for most women their jobs and work outside the household have become a personal value. It can be observed that even women themselves base their judgment of another woman on her profession and how well she does it. Work in the household has become rationalized and has lost much of its prestigious function. As stated, in Czechoslovakia this trend corresponds with the precommunist trend. Second, the work community fulfilled, in much the same way as the private sphere, some substitutive functions. In most cases it represented the only possibility or opportunity to associate with others. It compensated for the absence of a normal public sphere and offered a space for discussions about public as well as private affairs. Women were very well aware of this value of employment. Those who went to work even after reaching retirement age explained that they did so because they had become accustomed to "being with people." And finally, it was the absence of reflection, and expert and public discussion about the large presence of women in the work sphere, which through inertia helped preserve the masculine character of labor. For these changes, the feminist view is necessary.

The preceding argument was meant as a kind of *plaidoyer* in favor of the necessity of prefeminist reflection on the postsocialist experience if a potential feminist view is not to have, right from the beginning, distorted optics, failing to discriminate between what is as problem of women and what is a problem of all. At the same time it documented the different, two-tier structure of the female problem in this prefeminist theoretical phase. The methodological function of the two-tier character of the issue can be reversed, however. The female problem, if grasped by women, will at last open questions of gender relations, and could become the model for analyzing the general problem of identity in postsocialist society. It could focus attention on the unreflected tangle of social advantages and disadvantages, the apparent choices connected with reduced responsibility, and especially the structure of the solutions arrived at by substituting individualist attitudes, oriented toward the family and the work community, for general consensus.

The point of a diagnosis of the past naturally lies in its formative influence on the future. Those who aspire to transform the society still fail or do not want to understand the profound importance of such self-knowledge. Like their communist predecessors, they believe in the self-redemption of principles, especially economic and legal ones. Thus, they unwittingly reproduce what should have been removed in the first place—the idea of individual solutions still survives, the media still function badly, not knowing what to deal with. If men will find it difficult to build their new identity, women will face the need of real choice between pursuing a professional career or having a family, while those who have families already will probably experience even more severe professional discrimination than before. Nothing has yet happened publicly to show women the importance of their solidarity, their lobbies, and their political representation, and they do not yet think about it themselves. It is up to us to spare them the experience of having to pass through all the *peripeteii* of Western feminism, because at this very moment they are farther along in many respects, but mostly do not realize it.

Notes

1. Charlotte Masaryk, the American wife of the first Czechoslovak president, T. G. Masaryk, shared this conviction with her husband. Cited in *Mrs. Charlotta G. Masaryk,* ed. P. Homolková-Křičková (Brno: Vydavatelský odbor U.S.J.U., 1933), p. 212 (only in Czech).

2. Ibid., p. 94. This was meant as a comment on Goethe's *Faust.*

3. *The Heritage of T. G. Masaryk,* ed. Jasoň Boháč (Prague: Práce, 1990), pp. 93–96 (only in Czech).

4. The historical roots of this attitude are connected with the history of the Czech Lands (the Czech part of Czechoslovakia). The history of Slovakia, which had a history in common with Hungary until 1918, is different.

5. P. Buzková, *The Progressive View on the Women's Question* (Prague: 1909), pp. 8, 9, 12–13 (only in Czech).

6. Ibid.

7. Rosi Braidotti, "Patterns of Dissonance: Women and/in Philosophy," in Herta Nagl-Docekal, ed., *Feministische Philosophie* (Munich: Oldenbourg, 1990) p. 121.

8. A. Kroupová, "The Promotion of Equality for Women in Central and Eastern Europe," Ministry of Labour and Social Affairs CSFR, Prague, August 1991 (in English).

9. M. Čermáková, I. Hradecká, and H. Navarová, *The Social Status of Women in the Czechoslovak Society* (Prague: Czechoslovak Academy of Sciences, 1991) (only in Czech).

7

Are Women in Central and Eastern Europe Conservative?

Jiřina Šiklová

Countries of Central and Eastern Europe that considered themselves socialist were isolated for a very long time, and information was often distorted. Prejudices, myths, and illusions developed, including those about "automatic salvation" by a market economy. Western observers also suffer from a mixture of insights and illusions about women's emancipation in our region. Some believe that the high female employment rate in the so-called socialist countries was an expression of women's emancipation not sufficiently appreciated by the women themselves. It is also argued that women in post-communist countries are not self-reflective or conscious of their female identity—even that they oppose current feminist ideas. There is a feeling that the insignificant engagement of women in East European politics means women will miss their opportunity and uselessly repeat past mistakes.

I am afraid that we will make such mistakes, not only with regard to women's emancipation, but also in the process of reprivatization: returning once nationalized property to descendants of the original owners. We will then painfully try to find some satisfactory solutions to the social problems characteristic of early capitalism, for within a few years we will have to struggle with competition between women and men in the labor force.

It is true that our women are often opposed to feminism, but to state this is not enough, any more than an understanding of the political situation derived from the numbers of women in Parliament. The issues of women's economic and political position need much more reflection, as does the issue of feminism in our country. Women's rights form part of the overall problem of human rights, which have been notably neglected in the so-called socialist lands. Under the socialist regime there was no discussion of feminism; the emancipation of women was reduced to the necessity to have a job.

I. Women's Employment

The socialist countries did not follow the original ideas of Marx, Engels, or Auguste Bebel, but primarily their own interests in state and political power. An extensive state economy, pointless armaments, and industrialization required always cheaper labor. Our women were recruited and acquired the dubious advantage of the double burden. Any stress on gender equality was regarded by the state as "the ploy of the enemy," detracting from class warfare. In 1968, 46.1 percent of the work force were women; by 1989 the number rose to 48.4 percent, or practically 94 percent of all Czech and Slovak women. What was considered by Western feminists as a possibility, our women experienced as a reality, though not always of their own volition. Women's paid employment influenced all aspects of their life; it did not lead to women's equality at work, however, but an asymmetrical gender segmentation. Women earned only 50 percent of male salaries for equal work; some jobs were predominantly women's jobs. The stereotype developed of the man as not the sole but the primary breadwinner. Women did not protest, since such notions agreed with deeply rooted traditional ideas about gender, rarely changed by mere legislative action. State measures were intended to solve women's problems, family problems, and problems of child care, but the very nature of a centrally directed system of planning and control worked to silence women. The socialists' "pseudo-emancipation" lost any originally positive attributes and led to a new "women's fate."[1] Formal equality of rights did not lead to equality in reality; lack of time (and overburdening) meant women were much more stressed than men. Most women had a false sense of equality, resented having to be like men, and dreamt instead of a withdrawal into private life.

Men's closer link to the political system meant their career advanced more quickly and they were more likely to get better paid jobs. A report on research in 1987 showed that women in the companies studied held only 5 percent of leadership positions, while 6 percent of the companies employed no women in leadership positions. Men held the job of director 3.5 times more often. Yet both men and women claimed not to be bothered by this discrimination. Forty-one percent of women stated that they preferred men in leadership positions on the job, while only 9 percent preferred women. Such attitudes typify not only late socialism but the early 1960s, when women's participation in leadership positions was only 4.8 percent. Only 1.6 percent of company directors were women.[2] Even in health care, where 96 percent of specialized workers were women, only 11.9 percent held leadership positions.[3] These data reveal the real process of emancipation, but government and decision-making bodies were not interested.

Marriage and family are still the most attractive option for women. The unmarried mother has an inferior social status or is regarded as odd. Marriage is a symbol to women of security; it is better to be divorced than single. You may think, "Your sisters are living in the last century!" But it is not so simple, for there have been economic reasons. Unmarried women with children had lower incomes than divorced women. Married couples held claim to larger apartments than couples who were not married. One received an extra six square meters for a "household." At present, things are moving so fast that we do not even grasp the notion that such a law might be changed.

Yet women's confidence is generally based on their jobs.[4] Despite the fact that 76 percent of women polled in 1991 stated that they worked primarily to better provide for their families, 40 percent also said that they would not leave their jobs even if their husband had a sufficiently high income.[5] These answers suggest a certain discrepancy in logic, which reflects women's ambivalent stand on employment, politics, and their own identities.

The overburdening of women has led to a high divorce rate and women's poor health. The number of divorces per 100 marriages has grown constantly—in 1960, there were 14.4; in 1970, 19.7; in 1980, 28.7; and by 1985, almost one-third of marriages (32 percent) ended in divorce.[6] Women had to give 62 percent of their time off the job to care for their families, while men only gave 21 percent. Only 1.55 percent of male workers stated that they took vacation time when their child was sick.

Cultural ideas have been changing slowly; in spite of other revolutionary changes, the old myths live on. One is the myth of masculinity and femininity. As the enforced false ideology breaks down, many people welcome the freedom to return to traditions once forbidden. Young girls and boys are becoming nuns and monks; women are opting to stay at home. Freedom takes on different forms. This may give the impression we are returning to patriarchy, but it is more a reaction to our recent past.[7]

II. Women in Politics and the Public Sphere

Since 1948 there has always been at least one woman minister in the Cabinet, usually the Minister for Nutrition or Consumer Industry.[8] Only one-fourth of Parliament members have been women, and the central committee of the Communist Party was only 7 percent women. At the sixteenth Party Congress a few years ago, it was sadly noted that only 29 percent of party members were women and that only 18.2 percent of these held nomenklatura posts.[9] Surveys show that women's already minute political influence continues to decline. Men still dominate in the Federal Assembly and other important corporations and bodies.[10] In the Czech Republic women made up 12.3 percent of candidates for the People's Chambers; in the Slovak Republic the figure was 14.9 percent. Out of 300 deputies in the Federal Assembly of the Czech and Slovak Federal Republic only about 30 are women. In the Czech National Council 13 percent (27 members) are women; in the Slovak National Council there are 9 women, or 12.7 percent. There is one woman in the Federal government.

Despite the fact that there are more than 40 political parties, not one is led by a woman. In October 1991 one woman deputy of the Federal Assembly conducted a poll and discovered that 89 percent of the members of her political party believed they would lose votes if a woman were listed at the head of the ticket. Female members of the party held this opinion more often than did males. No Czech or Slovak political party, with the exception of one that did not take part in the election, lists women's problems in a prominent place on its platform.

But women have never been only passive onlookers, as is clear in dissident politics. There, women have had a high profile since the onset of the totalitarian regime in Czechoslovakia in 1948. It was in this country that the first woman, Dr. Milade Horáková, was sentenced to hang for political activity. Others have followed, collectively being sentenced to perhaps hundreds of years in prison.

Women figured prominently in protest actions and demonstrations even prior to the revolution of November 1989, in which they also played an important role. Eighteen percent of the signatories of Charter 77 and 34 percent of its spokespersons were women.[11] At least half of the members of the Committee for the Unjustly Prosecuted (VONS) were women. There were three women among those tried for their activity on behalf of VONS in 1979.[12] One-fourth of the people sentenced to imprisonment in the next big trial in 1981 were women. Women not only collected clothes and money for those imprisoned, but also courageously stood in the corridors outside the courtroom (they weren't allowed inside), so that their presence would encourage those being led in.

During the forty years of totalitarianism, police conducted tens of thousands of house searches. They turned apartments upside down, tore bedclothes out of closets, overturned rugs, emptied wastepaper baskets into the middle of rooms to search for fragments of documents and letters, and threw books from shelves. It was the women who patiently put their houses back in order. That is a fact out of which political capital could have been made, yet no one has done so.

The group of dissidents is numerically negligible. Czechoslovakia has a population of 15 million, but only 1,864 people signed Charter 77. And even in Summer 1989, with revolts taking place throughout the Warsaw Pact countries, only 39,000 people signed the appeal for democracy entitled "Some sentences. . . ." The list of its signatories was unofficially sent abroad and read on Voice of America and Radio Free Europe.[13]

Only three of the repeatedly persecuted dissident women are today members of the Federal Assembly. Two of them have no intention of running in the next election. The feminists of Western Europe and North America consider this a wasted political and social opportunity. But one needs to look at the situation more closely.

One reason for the negligible role played by former dissident women in current politics is that many dissidents are now old and sick. Some have simply returned to their former professions as reporters, authors, teachers—the professions from which they had been excluded for political reasons. To return to one's former profession is not a sign of inadequate emancipation; these women have not withdrawn from politics, and they haven't run away. They are merely not as visible as some people would like. But they had never been active in political parties, held seats in parliament, or occupied ministerial positions, and they do not have such aspirations today. It is my opinion that these women were interested not so much in political power as in maintaining cultural continuity, in keeping alive already existing values. They were ready to risk a great deal and suffer for the real values of culture and freedom, but not on account of mere ideology, which had been repeatedly discredited. This generation of dissidents never knew political life in the form of civilized encounters and a free democratic search for an optimal solution as well as clarification of one's view. Our current experience has not proven so wonderful either.

In addition, one generation of Czechoslovak political life is missing, both for men and women. The generation of students and those who participated in political life and held political positions during the period of reform in 1968 either emigrated or adjusted during the period of so-called normalization, some joining or rejoining the Communist Party. Young people simply cannot grasp that these people could have believed in socialist ideas; having been members of the Communist Party "compromises" them. The generation characterized in the West by the student movements of 1968, the antiwar resistance, and the New Left is simply absent in Czechoslovakia.

The feminist political aspirations of Western movements therefore do not exist for the moment in Czechoslovakia. The roots of women's lack of interest in politics lie in our history. For many women, politics is repulsive, reminiscent of the totalitarian regime. In our society, not only people, alive and dead, need to be rehabilitated, but certain professions as well. Women's lack of political activity also connects with a deeply rooted idea of polarity between those "on top" and those "on the bottom." Under the totalitarian system women accepted the idea that those on top, those who had political power, were men.

The pseudo-elections under socialism, with party-determined quotas for women, did not strengthen candidates' self-confidence, but led to the development of an inferiority complex and a revulsion toward holding political office. Even dissident women who did much of the subordinate routine dirty work at the copy machines, translated texts, and copied political essays and manuscripts, making it possible for them to appear later in samizdat or exile editions.

The picture of a leader throughout my childhood was that of a man with a mustache and a lock of hair falling onto his forehead, with his right hand upraised for an "arayan" greeting, screaming into microphones. He was responsible for a horrendous war. A few years later, Hitler had been replaced by Stalin, a man with a larger mustache who wrote his name into history with the help of millions of dead. Other international leaders such as Mao Zedong, Ho Chi Minh, Kim il Sung, or Fidel Castro have also failed to evoke enthusiasm among members of my generation. The local and nationalist leaders in the region—Husák, Jakeš, Bilak, Honecker, Ceausescu—also failed to impress. One had to be in the

Communist Party to be in a leadership position. But party members were typified not so much by their Marxist conviction as by their conformity and obedience to orders.[14] All this made politics very unappealing.

Women in socialism never allowed themselves to be manipulated to the extent that men did, which I regard as fortunate. Women took refuge in their "double burden," in motherhood and in care for young children. The former power elite deemed such activities to be acceptable excuses for not joining the party or accepting a party function. As a result, today women are nowhere near as compromised by having collaborated with the previous regime as are men.

Fewer women party members meant not only fewer women functionaries but also fewer women informers for the secret police. The present freely elected government inherited a heavily indebted economy and will be forced to take many unpopular measures. Women, holding fewer leadership positions during this period of transformation, are likely again to emerge less compromised than men. These phenomena could provide important arguments for the later political participation of women.

III. Feminism East and West

In many interviews our women manifest an aversion toward feminism, and men are glad to support them. Words like "emancipation" and "feminism" have a pejorative meaning for many Czech women, who use the words nearly as slander. This is also the heritage of the failure of socialist ideology. Yet in spite of this apparent conservatism and antifeminism, it is quite possible that Eastern European women are more emancipated than the majority of their Western friends, including those who speak more exhibitionistically about their emancipation.

Women from the West often reduce the degree of female emancipation and participation in political life to the number of women members in Parliament or the Cabinet. But political participation does not necessarily require membership or a leadership position in some political party; there are other ways to take part in political life and the development of society, alternatives which have the advantage of full ethical and intellectual independence. In the West political experience is derived from a democratic parliamentary system, where political parties and participation in them have great significance. We, on the other hand, are the product of a system that reduced membership in a party to obedience and the loss of individuality. Through personal experience we know that the establishment of quotas for various social groups or other forms of so-called "positive discrimination," which have been so politically important in the West, often become a tool of oppression of the very groups they were designed to support.[15] It is clear to us from our experience that the interests of women, workers, and farmers do not necessarily have to be defended by women, workers, and farmers.

Thus, similar-sounding political terms and phrases have different meanings and significance for women East and West, rooted in our different historical experiences. This will be a hindrance to our mutual understanding for a long time. In addition, there are ideological currents, philosophical directions, and political conceptions in the West with which we are wholly unfamiliar. The isolation of forty years has produced its results: I personally am only beginning to understand what a difference there is between us! The chasm did not seem as deep while the border was closed and I was unable to travel.

Feminism is the product of a political culture of a particular country and of a particular social system. That's why the feminism of the post-communist states is certain to be of a different hue than West European feminism. Each wave of feminism, wherever and whenever it appears, casts a new light on various symbols. It uses its own political diction and is confronted with various adversaries, political traditions, means of expression, and solutions specific to its culture.

In the communist states the proclaimed, formal support of women was often misused against democracy and freedom of thought. In all such countries, for example, there was only one women's association and it was fully subservient to the interests of the Communist Party. And so it often happened that in these states women placed the fight for a democratic society, for freedom of expression, freedom of religion, and human rights above their own interests and those of other groups. Many Western feminists are unable to this day to understand such attitudes, and they interpret it as lack of a political awareness on the part of our women—as a lack of female identity.[16]

No identity, let alone a feminine one, can be imported. The absence of feminism in theory and practice cannot be corrected by merely accepting the experiences and ideologies of the Western feminist movement. Those of us from the post-communist states had a bad experience with the introduction of a foreign ideology and political education. Our women possess, perhaps, a more realistic experience with emancipation than do Western women. Consequently, we have no need to talk so much about our emancipation. Nor do we constantly need to assert ourselves. The battles of Western feminists and their jargon sometimes seem ridiculous to our women. But quite often Eastern European women do not reflect politically on their own emancipation, and they do not react to it ideologically or politically.

IV. Prognosis

Our pseudo-capitalism, which offers illusory salvation to many, will create large social differences. It will result in a social marginalization that will disproportionately affect women dependent on social and old-age benefits, single women, single mothers, and female heads of household. Gypsy women with many children and little job experience or education will be especially badly hit by inflation and unemployment. Even if the state is willing, it will not be able to support them; consequently, a new social injustice will result from another failure of the socialist experiment.

In my opinion, young women with college and university educations, who will not find corresponding jobs, will be exposed to a strong social pressure and will become politically active. The younger generation of women, especially, has attained on the average a higher level of education than men, perhaps even higher than that of Western industrial states. In 1948–49, female university students constituted only 23.2 percent of the total. In 1989–90 women constituted 45 percent of all university students and represented 56 percent of all specialists with a secondary-school education, as well as 38 percent of specialists with full university education.[17] For women who obtain status, experience, and skills in their jobs, a return to the household is unrealistic, except for a short period of time. Yet it is clear that there will be preferential hiring of men; women, discriminated against, will at first be unable to defend themselves. These factors could produce even greater discrimination which would further debase women.

Women with political interests and aspirations are not very active at the moment; change has been too hectic. The present cautiousness of women and their preference for social consensus rather than the introduction of further conflicts is rational and, I think, will in the future be regarded as correct. Given the negative social changes primarily affecting women and political differentiation in general, it is highly probable that a new political movement will appear among women rather soon, and that it will be more left-oriented than our present political life, which is constructed by men. A women's movement will be motivated in the near future by women's need to defend their own interests, and it will be considerably influenced by Western feminism. Young women and students, already confronted by feminist ideas, will transplant these to local conditions, as I am trying to do. They will not be able, however, to influence the more numerous cohort of older women who are unable to change their thinking. The new generations of women will be living under conditions closer to those of their Western counterparts; therefore, the feminist movement will be more attractive to them. This generation, at present eighteen to twenty-five years old, will form itself as a political community in opposition to silent and passive masses of women brought up under the socialist regime. We must not rebuff this generation with too much ideology, jingoism, fighting for power, or official and bureaucratic organizations that will remind them of totalitarian regimes. Concrete social and political interests should be encouraged in lieu of feminist and emancipation proclamations.

In the near future the immense potential of this demographic group (which holds more than 50 percent of the vote) will emerge. To win this group of young women, we need time and space as well as sufficient knowledge about the experiences of the feminist movement in the West. The emancipation in my country has been internalized, including its negative consequences; yet the emancipation is politically unreflected, anonymous. We have to wait for a politically defined movement, patiently but actively. One problem in the Czech and Slovak

Republics is a lack of basic knowledge of Western feminism and its ideological currents. For these reasons, in August 1991 we founded a resource center and library for gender studies which is part of the Department of Social Work and Applied Sociology at the Faculty of Philosophy in Charles University in Prague, as well as a new field of "gender studies." This center was founded with the assistance and support of the Network of East-West Women, represented by Ann Snitow. We offer library services twice a week, and we are distributing curricula for women's studies and translations of articles for those who are interested. We have a network between our universities. Once a month we organize discussions and seminars for visitors in accordance with their interests. We want to keep discussion within the university and not on the basis of political engagements and partisanship. All these activities have been very successful and well attended. To avoid local prejudice and aversion against such notions as feminism and emancipation, we use the term "gender studies," a new term never before used here and probably not even known.

As the conditions of life in our country become more like those in the West, it is likely that we will grow closer in thought, but women from post-communist states will no doubt differ for a long time in their opinions on such subjects as women in politics or the value of quotas in leadership positions. I hope that our women will develop a different style than that of men, which is oriented toward individual success, consumption, and personal power. If women continue in the same manner as men, our planet will not survive. I believe that our women who have had the experience of living under totalitarian regimes will not merely mimic men but will discover a new form of political participation and leadership with enough space for solidarity, one that will uphold our "traditional" female qualities. I welcome more of such feminine traits in politics and leadership.

Notes

1. H. Navarová, "What Did Socialism Give to Women?" Unpublished study, Sociologický ústav (Praha: ČSAV, 1990).

2. Maria Schwarzová, Zuzana Kostolná and Pospíšil, "Barriers to Increasing Employed Women's Qualifications," Contemporary Volume from the Scientific Conference, Central Committee of the Slovak Union of Women, Bratislava, 1989, pp. 208–210.

3. Maria Schwarzová, Zuzana Kostolná and Pospíšil; Alena Heitlinger, *Women and State Socialism: Sex Inequality in the Soviet Union and Czechoslovakia* (London: Macmillan, 1979); Sharon L. Wolchik, "Women and the Politics of Transition in Central and Eastern Europe," paper for the UNU Wider Research Conference on "Gender and Restructuring: Perestroika, the Revolutions and Women," Helsinki, September 1991.

4. Schwarzová and Zuzana Kostolná, "Women's personality in the socialist society," Contemporary Volume from the Scientific Conference, Central Committee of the Slovak Union of Women, Bratislava, 1989, pp. 107–115.

5. "Women's Employment," in *Report of the Institute for Public Meaning*, ed. V. Kobylková and Jan Michalec (Prague, 1991). Research done in cooperation with the International Labor Organization in Geneva; included both the Czech and Slovak Republics.

    Question: "If the salary of your husband were to be sufficiently increased, would you prefer to stay at home?"

    Definitely   28%
    I would consider it   32%
    Definitely not   40%

    "If wages for your children were higher would you stay at home?"

    Definitely   38%
    Definitely not   22%

6. H. Navarová, "Lives of Young Families in Czechoslovakia." Unpublished study.

7. M. Čermáková and I. Hradecká, "The Social Position of Women in Czechoslovakia," internal edition of Sociologický ústav, 1991.

8. Alena Wagnerová-Kohler, *Die Frau in Sozialismus: Beispiel CSFR* (Hamburg: Hoffman und Campe Verlag, 1974), ch. 3.

9. Helena Kolářová (Pseudonym of A. Wagnerová-Kohler), "Die reale Gleichberechtigung-Frauen in der CSSR fast vierzig Jahre danach—in Ost Europa," INFO, no. 67 (1986): 38–49.

10. M. Čermáková, I. Hradecká, and H. Navarová, "Women and Elections," 1990 (unpublished paper).

11. Vilém Prečan, ed. *Charter 77, 1977–89: From the Moral Revolution to the Democratic One*. Documentation (Bratislava: Archa, 1990) p. 525. List of Charter 77 speakers, p. 477. List of Charter 77 signatories, p. 487.

12. In that same trial President Václav Havel had been sentenced to five years of imprisonment.

13. Jiřina Šiklová, "People Power," in *The Building of a New European Home*, (Gloucestershire, England: Hawthorn, 1991).

14. Jiřina Šiklová, "The Grey Zone and the Future of Dissent in Czechoslovakia," *Social Research* 57, no. 2 (Summer 1990): 347–364.

15. J. Ryba, ed. *Women in Transforming Society* (Prague: SLON, 1992), p. 35.

16. Barbara Einhorn, "Socialist Emancipation: The Women's Movement in the German Democratic Republic," in *Promissory Notes*, ed. Sonia Kruks, Rayna Rapp, and Marilyn B. Young (New York: Monthly Review Press, 1989).

17. M. Čermáková, I. Hradecká, H. Navarová, "To the Position of Women in Czechoslovak Society," internal edition of the Sociological Institute of Czech Academy of Sciences, Prague, 1991, p. 38.

8

The Emancipation of Women:
A Concept That Failed

Zuzana Kiczková and Etela Farkašová

For some time we have asked ourselves why the words "emancipation of women" have become such objects of derision and irony even among women. As the theoretical basis for the state- and party-directed emancipation of women, these words played a significant role in the building of socialism in Czechoslovakia, influencing women's real position. We offer an analysis of the concept and the basic principles upon which it rests, exploring the positive and negative aspects of its application. We rely also on our personal experiences with "emancipation," its practical deformations and misrepresentations. This article is written with a view to articulating our experiences of the past, a past that affects our position as women and that will affect the process of change in our society today. We are aware that many points of view are possible; for this reason, our reflections should not be taken too generally.

The Czech sociologist I. Možný stated that "there exist side by side in social consciousness two concepts of patriarchy: an articulated familiar one and an unarticulated structural one."[1] Our concern is to articulate structural patriarchy, for which, paradoxically, "emancipation" forms the conceptual basis. Those women who aim to move beyond the framework of the family and obtain self-realization and self-expression in creative activity, which demands time and concentration, experience very strongly the limitations and disadvantages of patriarchy. But the ways in which this structure and the conditions that disadvantage women operate has not been visible, and its principles remain unarticulated.

I.

"Sameness" versus "difference" is one of the central problems of feminist philosophy, and the position one takes on this issue forms the starting point for different theoretical concepts and practices. "Equality" in our country has been interpreted as sameness, requiring formal and substantive conditions to avoid discrimination against women. "Emancipation" unambiguously meant that women should be self-sufficient and independent and, importantly, equal to men in the sense that they should have the same opportunities for entry into the public sphere. It was argued that there should be no distinction between a "stronger" and "weaker" sex.

In effect, this socialist conception of emancipation was an androgynous one. Furthermore, the paradigm present in the building of socialism, with which women identified, implied that to be equal meant to participate equally with men in socially organized paid labor. It was thus necessary for women to operate under conditions favorable to such participation. It was felt that women ought to (and, in fact, they wished to) fill positions that would have been unusual for their mothers and totally unattainable for their grandmothers. This entry into work took place on a large scale, supported by official ideology and policy, directed from above. As a result, over 90 percent of Czechoslovak women engaged in paid work.

Some women were willing to become equal to men at any price, in order to win social and personal recognition, acceptance, or authority. This meant letting themselves be judged by male standards of rationality, by men who sat on the decision-making commissions. But even so, the occupational structure was and is unequal. Women have similar levels of skills and qualifications as men but are only marginally represented in planning, decision, and leadership positions; in addition, their remuneration is significantly lower than men's. It is not only that the socialist paradigm of equality through paid work was not in practice realized, but that it carried with it the assumption that the admission of female difference meant female inferiority.

The positive consequence of this emancipation was that women gained personal independence and ceased to derive social identity from men. Women had the opportunity for richer social contacts outside of the private sphere, important in a society not so stratified by wealth. A further advantage was that girls and women had a wide range of professional options, job training, and acceptance at secondary-level vocational schools and universities. Girls who chose to attend technical universities were even given preference, through quota systems established by the Ministry of Education. But the whole process unfolded in a social and political atmosphere in which a myth of unity reigned—not a unity of diversity, differences, and heterogeneity, but rather one of homogeneity, of an undifferentiated mass. The society was thereby made easier to control and manipulate through directives, orders, and punishments. The very concept of the emancipation of women reflected these circumstances, in which fear was made part of the mass psychology and people's overriding desire was not to say or do anything too different. Here one can find the roots of the widespread phenomenon of people acting the same, which strongly determined personal relationships.

There were several negative consequences to this androgynous conception of equality, which women became aware of only later and which they have cautiously expressed in private conversations, but never in movements or in demonstrations. Symbolically expressed, women did not have to fight to gain admittance to the "building"—the factory, school, institute, shop—but were free to enter. When inside, they began to see more clearly how the building was constructed, its plan, and finally who organized life in the building and in which language communication was carried on. In every room they ran into the power of the bureaucratic apparatus, its anonymous and alienating character, which demonstrated its existence by requiring unnecessary activities. It created Mafia-like relationships which made life senselessly complex for everyone and even more difficult for women. Two instances are relevant for our consideration. First, the functionaries, unconcerned with any ideals, were "sexless" because depersonalization came with the job. The consciousness that reigned in general and with regard to one's sexual identity in particular rested on the conviction that these functionaries determined the pace and direction of society. Many women were drawn into such positions within the bureaucracy once they entered the building. They lived a life split between the alienating character of their administrative function and the highly personal individual situation of the private sphere.

Eventually, doubts arose about the content, the conditions, and the forms of women's wage labor. The dissatisfaction was doubly great if the women left the "building" and were also mothers or wives. The two burdens became increasingly difficult to bear with the increasing demands created by hyper-organization and low efficiency, as well as the expectation of additional public and social work and caregiving in the family, for whose well-being women were still responsible. This was exacerbated by the deficiencies in consumer goods and services. A woman confronted a dilemma: either a successful career or a family and children. A successful compromise was more the exception than the rule, and all attempts to reconcile the two realms was accompanied by a desperate sense of a lack of time, constant stress, and haste. This was often expressed laconically in daily conversation as "I just don't have the time."

Women learned that to achieve success in the "building" they had to adapt to various vocational and professional roles. They were not active subjects, but passive carriers of the norms contained in the roles. After living some time in the "building" the women gradually started to realize their dissatisfaction with the gender-undifferentiated nature of work. Sociological research showed that women were more dissatisfied than men in their work, precisely in regard to those aspects that men also value—challenge and diversity, possibilities for realization of one's talents, independence, equal salary, and equal rewards. Men work more often in their chosen occupations, are more able to utilize their qualifications, receive higher salaries for the same work, and achieve faster promotion or advancement than do women.[2]

Already by the mid-1980s some sociologists were warning about the dissonance between the content and conditions of work for women and their special needs.[3] These sociologists demanded a new model of work for women as an important condition of the humanization of labor. In the opinion of the well-known Czech author E. Kantůrková:

> Women here are too emancipated, and the emancipation started with the economic emancipation. Feminism in the sense that women must strive for liberation has been superseded here. The women's question here is not their independence but rather their dignity, because the great emancipation also brought disrespect and degradation with it.[4]

"Emancipation" over the last forty years meant a loss of dignity for women, who were reduced to a cheap source of labor that could be plugged in anywhere without regard to specific capabilities, prerequisites, and ambitions. It meant the loss of women's identity, because women had to adapt themselves to the architecture of the "building" and had no chance to become aware of and determine for themselves what it meant to be a woman and to express it in their lives, their social roles, and their personal expectations. The price to enter the building was too high.

II.

One thus begins to have doubts about the paradigm of catching up and being equal when it has meant adapting to the existing male model. It is only in sociology and women's literature that one begins to find the female contours behind the anonymous, universal work force, a discussion of contemporary women in nontraditional situations, and the necessity of new criteria for assigning value to socially useful work by women.

Several female authors, including V. Hanzová, V. Svenková, E. Farkašová, G. Rothmayerová, L. Hajková, and J. Bodnarová have in short stories, novellas, and poems made the daily struggle against time of their female protagonists the major theme. The lack of time for herself, for the children, for the husband she loves; the lack of deep, quiet, or shared experiences; and the feeling of estrangement are often described as the characteristic themes of our female literature.

Literature written by women has also dealt with the theme of women's identity, contributing to "revealing" that identity and helping thematize the world of women anew. It has been oriented toward private life, toward the emotional sphere, toward the plane of interpersonal relationships in the circle of the family, and has often stayed far away from the "great and heroic themes of the building of socialism." These authors have endeavored to define a social role for women that corresponds to their bio-psychological and sociocultural constitution. They have tried to free themselves from traditional points of view and from masculine aesthetic norms. Instead, they have revealed their own specifically female experience of life. Such literature has often been characterized as "escapist" literature by a literary critical apparatus dominated by men. Yet such authors as M. Halamová, L. Vadkerti-

Gavorniková, M. Haugová, D. Podracká, Z. Szatmaryová, J. Kantorová, and T. Lehenová are searching for a new language for the representation of their specific life experiences.

In the conception of emancipation, the pendulum had swung too far toward "equality," although it is beginning to move now toward the counterpole of difference, individuality, and uniqueness, at least according to sociological studies. The empirical experience came into a conflict with the theoretical principles behind the conception. There has been no language or discourse on this theme. Feminism itself is completely missing in the liberal arts; there is no women's studies or discussion of such issues in books and journals. In the bookstores one finds no books on women, research into women's issues, or feminist philosophy.

Not only ideological and economic factors account for this ignorance of sexual differences, but the conceptual orientation of abstraction from particulars. Tradition posits a humanistic universalism that elevates the universal qualities, rights, and needs of every human being to the greatest importance and posits that a better, more just world and all particular problems will be solved by the resolution of conflict at the universal level. The differences between men and women are regarded as marginal problems. But humanistic universalism veils the important point that the masculine principle is taken as the common human principle. The male value system, male thought patterns, and male ways of action become the patterns for the whole social structure.

The universalization of social roles historically prepared the way for the equality of the sexes, but the latter required a change in traditions and habits that had prescribed distinct gender identities and correspondingly different functions, goals, and positions according to a principle of complementarity. This change required industrial society, with its processes of modernization and its concept of the abstract human being, in which the multidimensionality of the person was reduced to that of labor power. The consequence is a profound devaluation of individuality, uniqueness, and singularity of the personality. This has been harmful to women in two ways.

First, the principle that everyone is interchangeable, the view of a person as *homo economicus,* creates and strengthens the idea that both sexes have the same disposition and capabilities, that they perceive the world in the same way and have the same needs, and that all persons must pursue and realize a common goal that transcends difference.

Second, equality so understood as the absolute opposite of difference, conjoined with a teleological dimension, coexists in our society with the one-sided emphasis on the person as a social being. This is conjoined with the claim that changes in the social conditions and forms of organization will change the person. Methodologically, this has the same basis as behaviorism.

Jointly, this has led to the concept of the sexual universality of many roles originally assigned solely to men or to women, first and foremost in the sphere of wage labor. It was forgotten that almost all the roles with decision-making power over persons were created by men. In their content and structures one finds that they implicitly contain the norms of masculine interaction, masculine thought, and an orientation toward masculine needs and values. There are only a few professional roles in which a female structure, norms, and patterns of action are entrenched. Women who take on those roles declared universal—sexually neutral—must almost always adapt themselves to the roles. Only by doing so will women become integrated and accepted into the world of their male coworkers. For those courageous women who rejected this forced adaptation and tried to find a role commensurate with their feelings and value systems, one with more moral resonance, the result was often a deep professional and personal isolation. There was an absence of a pluralistic public sphere and instead a unity of social institutions and organizations in which social and leisure-time activities for women were directed by one central women's organization. In a non-pluralist society, the greater the conformity, the fewer the conflicts. But with this conformity went the loss of a female view of the world, of one's own femaleness, of a "female identity." Any such identity was driven back into the private sphere.

The integration of social roles into the concept of emancipation means methodologically the application of a functionalism, because, as I. Možný claims, one's social roles rather than one's individuality were most important for a social system that had overridden essentialism.[5] The woman became the bearer of many roles in both the public and private spheres. In contrast to men, the spectrum of social roles for women widened considerably. In literary works by some women authors[6] the "superwoman" appears: the woman who is at once a caring mother, loving wife, exemplary worker and scientist, and enthusiastic functionary. These figures, which served originally as ideals or models, have more recently been represented as parodies. Behind these masks usually stands an exhausted, distracted, inauthentic creature. No miracle of emancipation occurred; the woman was not able to transcend the human limitations of physical and psychic energy or the rigid male structures of jobs.

The technological paradigm of unlimitedness predominates—unlimited manipulation of nature and of persons, radical transformation of social conditions, and inexhaustible possibilities for transforming the self. This unlimitedness, together with seemingly sex-neutral roles, has had far-reaching consequences for women. It has overshadowed their specifically female nature and has led, paradoxically, to the creation of a new inequality.

Možný maintains further that "humanizing of work in our society would result fairly substantially in its feminization." A woman brings a more informal atmosphere to work, more collegial relations, especially given our society's weak performance principle in the absence of a market mechanism. Conversely, the woman brings home nervousness, exhaustion, and turbulence born of the fear and tension over whether she accomplished all that was expected of her. Even if she sees the source of her discontent in a husband who helps her very little with the household chores, she still blames society primarily for her discontent. The chief conflict for her is "woman versus society," not "woman versus man."[7]

III.

The concept of the emancipation of women in our society was linked not to liberal individualism but to collectivism and patriarchy in the socialist tradition, which explained the subjugation of women in terms of the social system. This is anchored in the philosophical thesis that the nature of the human being is the sum total of its social conditions. The individual is seen as part of the collective; the individual's development depends on the quality of the social conditions, and the final goal is not the individual's development but the advancement of society. The development of the woman is not to be directed primarily toward her personal interests and dimensions; rather, she should contribute to the well-being of the socialist society through her work, her public engagement, and the education of her children. The idea of individual independence is replaced by one of social dependence.

Holism creates the theoretical-methodological background for this principle of collectivism: the whole is greater and dominates the parts. In the social sciences, the concept of the whole lay in the foreground, while its parts were little attended to, assumed to have lesser value. In daily consciousness an atmosphere was created that did not support individualism, although in the last few years it has become clear that we lack outstanding personalities. The woman was doubly "veiled," once as a component of society and again as a female component.

It is in the question of relationships (Woman/Individual to Society) that the concept of emancipation differs most from that of current Western European and American feminism. The following thesis expresses the views against which women reacted in the creation of a woman's philosophy in Western Europe and the United States: If everything goes well in my family, then everything goes well for me personally. The man's philosophy started with the conviction: If I am in order, then it will also go well for my family. According to I. Možný, the basic change which Western feminism wrought was:

(1) A philosophy that had previously been valid only for men became a legitimate and rational starting point for women;

(2) the basic frame of reference of women's identity and life-project did not necessarily have to be the family; and

(3) personal advancement became culturally legitimate for both sexes.

What sort of answers to these three theses could one expect from a representative of the concept of emancipation in our society? One could expect agreement with the first thesis. The success of the family depends upon the well-being of the man and the woman. The second thesis would be a stronger version: the frame of reference *must* extend beyond the family; the woman must enter into the "building." But with the third thesis there would be absolute dissent. Individualism and individual development is the goal for neither sex, but instead a means for the advancement of the whole. We could formulate the following philosophy behind the concept of emancipation, which would be the same for both sexes: man, wife and family are all right if everything goes well for the whole of society. The thesis may seem too abstract, but it could be documented by the experiences of everyday life. In several spheres the socialist state took on the responsibility for welfare—the establishment and complete financing of day-care centers and kindergartens, of special schools and homes for pensioners and the handicapped, etc. This welfare system especially unburdened women and made possible their higher rate of paid employment, their further education, and their high degree of occupational training.

Collectivism existed not only as a theoretical principle but also as a real form of social organization in which our whole lives played themselves out from childhood to old age. This naturally left behind very specific traces in the individual and in the social consciousness of our people. The idea of historical progress and of an objective historical necessity is deeply embedded in this consciousness. It expressed itself in people's conviction that society was moving toward a better, more perfect and just form. The linear concept of historical progress was evident in daily consciousness. The small, even the gigantic injustices did not break the basic faith that it must someday get better, although one did not know how, when, or where. And anything that was part of that process was itself good.

The concept of the emancipation of women contains all the elements of the idea of historical necessity and historical progress: linearity, evolution, and objective laws of development. In addition, it includes the idea of surpassing oneself through one's children and their children, and the deep conviction that things will go better for each generation. Women are ready to make sacrifices and to renounce their own selves toward this end. Living for the future formed one of the important aspects of identity in our society for both men and women. Women related this to their children; they became the concrete bearers of this good. What was impossible for oneself would be possible for one's children.

On a sociopolitical level, the private sphere provided an asylum from the many senseless aspects of the totalitarian system. In its extreme form, the psychological attitude was that our children have meaning for us even if nothing else here does. Correspondingly, repressive political power was often directed toward the dissenting parents via their children, who served as potential hostages to ensure the obedience and loyalty of the parents. Officials could recommend against the child's admission to specialized training or to the university, and no appeal was possible against such measures.

The holistic approach that gives precedence to the interests and goals of the whole and that considers individual interests as derivative is easily united with a temporal orientation toward the future. For the older generation the orientation was not to the here-and-now, but toward a future hoped-for experience. After World War II the enthusiasm and strong faith in the creation of a more just society, the sacrifices for a greater ideal, and the belief in the strength of the collective were all deeply built into the system of values. For the young women of that time, who are now grandmothers, the imperative "everything for our children" seemed obvious. Everything for our children so that they could study, learn a trade, have an apartment. But they were nevertheless saved one anxiety—that their children would be unemployed.

Later, another imperative, "everything for our grandchildren," came almost automatically. The figure of the grandmother became symbolic of that generation, a person who personified the orientation toward the future. This is the grandmother who hardly finished raising her own children when she began to help care for her grandchildren; the grandmother who had no time for herself, who became not a world-traveling tourist but a caregiver and teacher. The concern for others, especially for the children, grandchildren, the aged, and the weak, became for her the determining moral value, a value closely connected to the meaning of her life, but seldom articulated. This self sacrifice was not always appreciated by those close to her, but even this was not regarded as a significant negative value for her. The responsibility to show the way dominated, "through others I will find myself." The women-grandmothers perceived more negatively the loneliness and isolation of daily life, the segregation in old age, and the removal into an old-age home. Their participation in the family was not only as a pragmatic, material, and financial aid, but also had a direct personal meaning; the grandmother was not only a guest in the young family but a member of it.

Living for the present is more a preference of women in the younger generation. It entails the direct experience of things of value, the effort to live more for oneself, but also being more utilitarian in regard to consumption. There is less use of the future tense in their language. There is a generational change in values and goals, more directed toward individualism than to collectivism. From an orientation toward the future it moves to an orientation toward the present, from enthusiasm to skepticism, from self-sacrifice to self-advancement.

Self-sacrifice is now frequently regarded negatively, as a loss, a regrettable situation, an inability to do otherwise. The one small exception is self-sacrifice for one's children. Self-sacrifice and self-advancement are interpreted as opposites. Women find themselves in a middle position, and which pole they tend toward depends upon their concrete conditions, their preferences, their age, and their individual ambition. Many hide their self-sacrifice so as not to be pitied or seen as inadequate. The tension between self-sacrifice and self-advancement is reflected in the conflict between the private and public spheres, although the tension exists within each sphere as well. In marriage women find their situation to be increasingly difficult when their partner obstructs their self-advancement and self-development. The woman often counters with an argument about the "fate" of her mother, aunt, or other woman in the family. The wife demands from her husband not only his noninterference in her self-advancement but also his direct support. Not fulfilling this demand is interpreted by most women as a lack of understanding, as a deficiency on the part of the husband, and it is often given as grounds for divorce.

IV.

It is relevant to distinguish between the formal and the real emancipation when considering the concept of the emancipation of women. Formal equality appeared in the form of the sexual neutrality of many social roles and in the form of universalism. Real equality must start with sexual difference as a given; it should articulate the specific nature of female subjectivity and identity. Formal equality always brings with it the possibility of real disadvantages and discrimination veiled behind data, numbers, charts, and blinding statistics, thereby legitimizing and legalizing purely formal equality. Those who saw through this game of formal emancipation turned all their criticism against the concept of emancipation. Women know the practical results and the positive side, but they also know the other side and the price women paid–a hectic existence, a permanent lack of time, conformity to the existing social structures, failure due to the double burden of wage labor and labor in the home. In this sense, the concept of emancipation has failed, and it is dismissed in daily consciousness.

We have tried to examine this practical area and indicate on what pillars the concept stood. In our opinion, the most important things are: the principle of sameness of the sexes and the reductionism and interchangeability that accompany the principle; the principle of collectivism and the holistic procedure; functionalism in social roles; the principle of historic necessity, and the temporal and future-oriented dimensions of the concept that result from this; and, finally, the principle of formal equality, with the quantitative arguments that accompany it.

From our own experience and from the reported experiences of our female contemporaries we know that the women in our society do not want to give up the positive ends they have attained. They do not want to leave "the building" en masse to return to the private sphere. At the same time they do not wish to be subjected to the limitations and deformations that make up the "false" emancipation. They would like to enter and work and live in the building not as formal equals but as real others. But that will require a revision of the structure and the architecture of the existing building. We hope that with the global changes in our society this can be partially realized.

Translated by Mark Shaffer

Notes

1. I. Možný, *Moderní rodina* (Brno: Block, 1990), p. 125.
2. Ibid., p. 113.
3. O. Plavková, "K sociologickej identifikácii životných drah žien v našej spoločnosti" *Sociólogia*, no. 4 (1989): 399–409.
4. E. Kantůrková, "Som antifeministka" (I'm Antifeminist), *Literárny týždennik*, March 1, 1991.
5. Možný, p. 115.
6. V. Stýblová, *Zlatá rybka* (Praha: 1988).
7. Možný, p. 122.

9

The Impact of the Transition from Communism on the Status of Women in the Czech and Slovak Republics

Alena Heitlinger

The November 1989 velvet revolution ended more than forty years of communist rule in Czechoslovakia. This paper examines continuities and discontinuities in the changes that have affected Czech and Slovak women since that time.

Women's Equality and Gainful Employment

Women's equality can be defined either as a formal equality of opportunity or as a substantive equality of outcome. The egalitarian standard against which persons are to be measured can entail equal, differential, or pluralistic treatment. Women's equality can take the form of assimilation (women becoming like men), androgyny (enlargement of the common ground on which women and men share their lives together), or maternal feminism, which rests on the complementarity of sex differences and the special moral qualities and needs of women. Insofar as the implementation of women's equality requires significant state intervention, it can increase state power over women's lives.[1]

Throughout the communist period, women's role was defined as a unity of economic, maternal, and political functions; a counterpart to this threefold role has never been spelled out for men. The special treatment of women was also embodied in such state measures as protective labor legislation, health care provisions for pregnancy and maternity, short-term and long-term maternity leaves, and earlier eligibility for retirement. Family legislation and juridical practice simultaneously reflected principles of equal and special treatment. Each marriage partner was obliged to maintain the other to ensure that each had the same living standard; property acquired during marriage was treated as common property of the couple. The duty of mutual maintenance expired after divorce, but if one of the divorced partners could not be gainfully employed (relatively rare in the state socialist economy), the court could order alimony payments for up to five years after the divorce. With respect to custody of children, however, in 90 percent of cases children were placed in the custody of their mothers; fathers were ordered to pay child support.[2]

A significant shift from an exclusively maternal to a more androgynous definition of parenting is therefore quite unlikely to occur in the near future. For example, Pavel Říčan, the director of the Psychological Institute of the Czechoslovak Academy of Science, strongly supports the ideology of "mothercare," though he would like to see it more flexibly applied. He would also lessen the social stigma currently attached to the small minority of women who either do not apply for or do not obtain child custody.[3]

Over the course of the socialist transformation there have been important shifts in emphasis within the special threefold role of women, primarily in response to the declining birth rate.[4] The formerly unitary model of the "ideal" socialist woman gave way to a broader, more graduated model, one that recognized the contribution women make to society by having and raising children, and that took into account age and life-cycle differences among women. Women were no longer expected to fulfill all roles simultaneously.[5]

With the arrival of socialist pronatalism in the late 1960s, many facilities and measures adopted in the 1950s on egalitarian grounds (paid maternity leave, family allowances, subsidized supplies of baby clothes and goods) were expanded to meet explicitly demographic objectives. Most new measures adopted in the early 1970s to help women with their multiple roles (mothers' allowances, low-interest loans for young couples with children) were designed to encourage young couples to have more children rather than to advance women's equality.

While popular with many young women, the pronatalist measures, especially the extended maternity leaves, had a predictably negative impact on women's careers and the domestic division of labor. Another outcome was the reinforcement of the notion, already prevalent among many groups of the population, that paid work was a secondary concern for women with domestic and maternal responsibilities.[6] The ongoing conflict between the demands of home and work led many to reject the goal of women's equality.[7] Many women would like to stay at home, which is one reason why the idea of a "family wage" for male breadwinners is currently so popular in both republics.[8] The communist past has been so utterly rejected that many political leaders and ordinary people in Czechoslovakia today reject women's equality as a goal, oppose reproductive freedom, and advocate a significant reduction in women's labor force participation.

Several new independent family and women's groups define their main task in terms of a moral reevaluation of women's roles. They offer conservative interpretations of women's position in society and stress women's distinctive qualities and interests (such as nurturing motherhood and down-to-earth "practical" common sense), the need to strengthen the father-breadwinner/stay-at-home mother model of the family, and the acceptability of a political system in which men defend women's rights and interests. Among the proponents of these views are several prominent communist dissidents and some newly elected members of Parliament.[9] The emphasis on woman's need to realize her "feminine essence" as the major women's issue is a continuation of the argument put forward by reformers during the Prague Spring, when sending women home and saving on day care was considered a progressive demand.

The ideological push to keep women at home is unlikely to succeed, however, because it will collide with the continuing economic need for women to contribute to the family income. It will also run into conflict with international organizations and international instruments promoting the advancement of women. Just as no overtly restrictive measures against women's employment were taken in the 1960s, it is hard to imagine that the new democratic government would enact discriminatory legislation that directly contradicts the U.N. Convention on the Elimination of All Forms of Discrimination Against Women (which Czechoslovakia signed and ratified) or the several directives and recommendations on equal treatment of women in the labor market adopted during 1976–86 by the European Community, an institution Czechoslovakia would dearly love to join as a full member.

At the same time, the post-communist government is unlikely to pay much attention to indirect and systemic discrimination against women, especially mothers with small children, at the enterprise or institutional level. An adoption of equal opportunity and affirmative action programs, or equal pay for equal work legislation, will be difficult to achieve.

As in the communist period, and as in the market economies in the West, women will continue to enter and remain in the work force due to economic necessity. It is highly unlikely that the elusive "family wage" would be high enough to allow male workers to support their families on their incomes alone. Moreover, increases in the cost of many necessities of life previously subsidized by the state (housing and utilities, food, child care) have increased economic pressures on families to have two earners. So, too, has the threat of mass unemployment.

Women with post-secondary education in professional and managerial occupations can be expected to derive greater satisfaction from work than their less skilled sisters, and for that reason alone are less likely to withdraw voluntarily from the work force. In 1989, however, only 14 percent of all employed women in Czechoslovakia held managerial positions. Of those, 65 percent were in lower-level management, 25 percent in mid-level management, and only 10 percent in top management.[10]

The move to a market economy will produce a pay structure favoring middle-class rather than working-class occupations. While the proportion of women in managerial and professional occupations is unlikely to significantly increase, the earnings of those who remain employed may rise. Higher incomes would then create another incentive to stay employed, and like their Western counterparts, Czech women may resolve the ongoing conflict between career and domestic responsibilities either by remaining childless or by hiring domestic help from the new "reserve army" of the unemployed.

Some estimates suggest that unemployment among women may rise as high as 30 percent as industrial restructuring brings about the closure of entire industries and clerical sectors. The shedding of "uneconomic" female labor is occurring mainly in industries that cannot compete on the world market and in the discredited, overstaffed state bureaucracy.[11] The female-dominated textile industry was one of the most profitable sources of export earnings, mainly from the USSR. Now, antiquated technology has rendered this industry uncompetitive with Third World manufacturers using modernized technology. Moreover, the huge Soviet export market has collapsed, making massive layoffs highly probable.

Any substantial withdrawal of women from the labor force will therefore be a result more of economic restructuring and involuntary unemployment than of successful ideological pressures on women to retreat into domesticity. There is no doubt that female labor force participation will decline, though it is impossible to predict at what level it will eventually stabilize. Much will depend on the availability of part-time work. In the mid-1980s, only 7 percent of women worked part-time, compared to 35 percent in Canada, 44 percent in the United Kingdom, 53 percent in the Netherlands, and 30 percent in West Germany. However, 23–27 percent of all women workers and 40 percent of women returning to work after maternity leave stated they would prefer to work part-time.[12]

Part-time employment may seem a sensible solution to combining the roles of caring parent and breadwinner, but in most capitalist and socialist economies, the income available from part-time employment would not finance independence for a single person, let alone for single-parent families, nor would it better the income available from welfare assistance. The majority of single parents will therefore soon be caught in welfare-poverty traps.[13]

Social Provisions for Maternity and Child Care

By the late 1970s, the Czechoslovak government was spending almost 4 percent of its annual budget on direct cash benefits (family allowances, birth grants, paid maternity leaves, and allowances) and an additional 7 percent on services and subsidies in kind (subsidized day care, kindergartens, school meals, afterschool care, children's goods, tax and rent deductions based on number of children). These levels exceeded comparable expenditures in any other major developed country.[14] However, others have pointed out the low value of cash and tax benefits relative to the average wage and actual costs of raising children. Critics have also noted the poor quality of many child-care facilities, manifested in high child/carer ratios, excessive regimentation, and authoritarian and impersonal attitudes toward children of the staff. Gender-specific protective legislation contributed to the concentration of female workers in low-paid jobs in services and light industries, thus reinforcing wage disparity between the sexes. The pronatalist emphasis on motherhood offered another legitimation for the traditional sexual division of labor within the home.[15]

Welfare provision provided the Communist party-state with its most potent and pervasive instrument of social and political control, and its principal guarantee of political stability and legitimacy. Thus, the "social protection of motherhood" was generally welcomed and taken for granted by women, who have become quite accustomed to a range of family-oriented services and allowances provided by the state. The very existence and the flexibility of some of these benefits gave women a certain degree of choice as to how to combine paid work with maternity.

A significant minority of mothers chose not to apply for the flat-rate maternity allowance, thus taking less than the full two years of partially paid leave to which they were entitled. Moreover, many women chose full-time motherhood more because of lack of alternatives than because of a desire to stay home—despite the work of many influential psychologists who, since the 1960s, have openly criticized institutional child care for its presumed detrimental effect on children's physical, intellectual, and emotional development. The dominant view of these experts has been that maternal upbringing is essential in the early years of a child's life. Public child-care facilities were also found too expensive, although such economic arguments took into account only public, and not private, costs of care.

No more than 22 percent of children under the age of three attended day-care facilities in Czechoslovakia. Since the introduction of maternity allowances in 1970, paying mothers to stay at home to care for their children has been regarded as cheaper and more socially acceptable than formal day care.

As both the Czech and Slovak Republics face pressures to cut their comparatively high expenditures on social welfare for families with children, many subsidies in kind and direct cash grants are bound to disappear. While family and maternity allowances may survive, either in the current universalist form or as a selective program to alleviate poverty, such programs as rent deductions for families with dependent children and low-interest loans for young couples are likely to be discontinued. Supply subsidies for child-care services have been reduced already, with the result that in the third quarter of 1990, fees for day care increased by 36.5 percent and fees for kindergartens by 86.3 percent.[16]

The reduction of subsidies for day-care facilities has sparked little controversy, in part because of the stigma attached to those facilities, and in part because relatively few families used them. The situation is very different, however, with respect to full-day kindergartens, which cater to children aged 3 to 5. Regarded as both educational and child-care institutions, and supported by experts as beneficial for children, they have been also popular among mothers returning to work after the expiration of their extended three-year maternity leave. Until quite recently, almost 95 percent of eligible children attended kindergartens, which were typically located in nice confiscated villas or newly built bright pavilions. While parents paid 200 crowns monthly, the actual operating cost was 1,500 to 2,000 crowns per child.

Both the nature and the magnitude of the subsidy are currently viewed as problems, as are many of the facilities housing the kindergartens. Some of the villas have been reclaimed by former owners, while some municipalities have served notice that they would like to put the attractive kindergarten buildings to more profitable use and rent them out to commercial firms. Some activists have urged parents to defend kindergartens and exercise their electoral power in all localities where officials attempt to close down kindergartens. Instead of rejecting kindergartens as "uneconomical communist institutions," Radka Kvačková and others like her would like to use the pressures of the market economy to improve their quality.[17] During the summer of 1991, the Czech National Council was considering a proposal from the Czech Ministry of Education, Youth, and Physical Education to transform the current supply subsidy into a demand subsidy.[18] While the existing subsidy involves direct public funding of *services,* one that is being proposed would involve public subsidy of *parents*—to give them more choice, to help them increase resources with which to buy child-care services in the open market, and to make service providers more responsive to parents as consumers.

However, Canadian experience suggests that providing demand subsidy as a way of stimulating private provision of child care does not work. Child care is simply not profitable for the private sector without very large demand subsidies, or unless some ongoing operating funding is provided directly to child-care centers. It is very hard to operate a self-sustaining quality day care center or kindergarten if parental fees are to be kept affordable, and as Kate Fillion argues, private entrepreneurs are not lining up to open day-care centers.[19] Moreover, such direct operational grants involve significant state intervention in a supposedly free market.

The 1990 law governing maternity allowances extended payments to previously excluded women (such as mothers with only one child or women who have never been employed) and for the first time made them available to fathers as well. A further extension of unpaid maternity leave is also being considered.[20] Making parental leaves and payments gender-neutral is an important step toward gender equality. However, one should not expect parental-leave schemes to achieve quick results. As long as child-care allowances are set at a flat rate lower than the minimum wage, fathers, who have higher salaries, are unlikely to take advantage of the program.

The transformation of maternity allowances into parental allowances was followed by revisions in old-age social security, which substituted uniform retirement age for a gender-specific one.[21] Revisions of protectionist labor policies directed only at women are likely to be the next step in the transformation of policies directed at women. Making labor legislation more gender-neutral would become mandatory should the Czech and Slovak Republics succeed with their applications to become full members of the European Community. The European Commission takes the view that protective legislation should in principle be consistent "across sexes and occupational areas," and that the only exception to this principle are measures "strictly necessary to protect the special biological condition of women." All EEC member states will eventually have to repeal or extend to all workers provisions that have been based on women's traditional domestic responsibilities and that are in conflict with the 1976 equal treatment directive.[22]

Abortion

Unlike other women's issues, abortion—the most commonly used method of fertility regulation in Czechoslovakia—has figured prominently on the political agenda. Abortion was fully legalized in Czechoslovakia in December 1957, following the lead of the Soviet Union in 1955.

Since abortion availability was widely thought to have played a direct causal role in the rapid decline of fertility (Czechoslovak demographers estimated that abortions and their negative health aftereffects accounted for 30–35 percent of the annual decline of the birth rate), communist policy planners began to look to restrictions on abortion as a possible policy remedy. Various restrictions for granting abortion on nonmedical grounds, supported by some experts and opposed by others, were adopted in the 1970s. However, few women who persisted in their requests were denied termination of unwanted pregnancies in these cases. Nonetheless, freely available abortion "on demand" was adopted only in 1987, when abortion commissions, to which each woman requesting an abortion had to apply, were abolished.[23]

It is estimated that every third pregnancy (every second in large urban areas) is aborted in the Czech Republic. This ratio is very high by Western standards, though it is fairly typical for Eastern and Central Europe. The official goal has always been to reduce the incidence of abortion, but in the context of rudimentary sex education, erratic supply of contraceptives, and the largely unsuccessful implementation of legal-administrative restrictions, the achievement of this goal has remained elusive. Thus, abortion remained easily available throughout most of the communist period. Significantly, debates surrounding the issue were couched in medical and demographic rather than moral terms.[24]

Since the fall of communism, however, the abortion debate has been broadened, increasingly resembling debates in North America, which pit "a woman's right to choose" against "protection of the unborn child."[25] Czech and Slovak mass media have been full of heated exchanges between "pro-choice" and "pro-life" advocates, involving both lay persons and medical experts.[26] An April 1990 public opinion survey revealed a sharply divided public opinion on public policy on abortion. The majority of respondents (56 percent) thought women should have the right to decide whether or not to have an abortion. Only 6 percent of respondents wanted to make abortion illegal under any circumstances. However, 27 percent felt that abortion should be permitted only if justified by health considerations or the child's unfavorable social prospects; another 11 percent supported abortion only if the continuation of the pregnancy threatened the woman's life. Women were significantly more likely than men (61 percent compared to 51 percent) to support women's right to choose.[27]

Not surprisingly, Catholic activists, including some of the new Christian women's groups established after the velvet revolution, have emerged as the leaders of those who want to see women's right to abortion restricted.[28] On the other side of the polarized spectrum is the newly formed Association for Family Planning and Sex Education, which is affiliated with the International Federation for Family Planning (IPPF). The Association (*Společnost pro plánování rodiny a sexuální výchovy*) regards reproductive freedom as a basic human right. While agreeing that the current abortion rate is much too high, it proposes such solutions as improved sex education and availability of contraception. The Association regards any attempts to restrict women's access to abortion as state-sanctioned violence against women.[29]

The government's response to these debates has been to establish a special advisory committee on questions concerning abortion, with a mandate to draft new legislation. The committee consists of representatives from women's and church groups, professional medical and legal organizations, and relevant ministries and parliamentary committees, who all hold widely diverse views on the subject. It has nonetheless managed to agree that the new law must not conflict with the universal declaration of human rights and that it must meet the concerns of both proponents and opponents of abortion rights.[30]

This compromise may not be as difficult to achieve as it may seem, because even the Catholic Czech Conference of Bishops agrees that in a situation when there are 180,000 abortions performed annually, it would be impossible suddenly to reduce the number to zero. While the Czech Conference is not very enthusiastic about the promotion of contraception, it is seen as a lesser "evil" than abortion. Thus, the Conference is in broad agreement with the Czech Ministry of Health's proposal not to tamper with the existing liberal law but to increase substantially the fee for obtaining an abortion. As an incentive to encourage contraception, the Ministry is also proposing to make contraceptives available at no cost.[31]

This kind of compromise may be harder to achieve in Slovakia, where the opposition to abortion is stronger than in the Czech Republic, among both the general public and Catholic organizations. Officials at the Czech Ministry of Health interviewed in Prague in May 1991 indicated that their Slovak counterparts are caught between conflicting political, medical, and religious pressures to outlaw abortion, not tamper with existing liberal provisions, or keep the income from abortion in Slovakia. One can be fairly certain that if abortion is outlawed in Slovakia but permitted in the Czech Republic, many Slovak women would travel across the border rather than choose forced motherhood. In that case, the fees they would be charged for abortion would help to subsidize the Czech rather than the Slovak health-care system.

Commercial Exploitation of Sexuality and Childbearing

With the brief exception of the Prague Spring, there was under communism no visible commercial exploitation of women as sex symbols in advertising, strip-clubs or topless beauty contests. While there was a black market in prostitution and pornography, and routine sexual harassment of women in the workplace, explicit sexual material concerning women was regarded by most men as a "forbidden Western fruit."

Debates on sexuality during the communist period reflected strong norms of conventional heterosexuality and parenthood. Experts (for the most part physicians) writing on these issues in the mass media, school textbooks, and personal advice books went to great lengths to subordinate sex education to parental education. Factual, clinical knowledge about the anatomy and physiology of male and female sexual organs, processes of coitus and conception, causes of sterility and infertility, and the various birth control methods was dispensed far more freely and in greater abundance than was information about bisexuality, lesbianism, or other "deviant," nonprocreative sexual practices. If homosexuality was mentioned at all in personal advice books, it was dealt with either very briefly or as something exotic that "occurred" only to eccentric artists or in "decadent" societies such as ancient Rome. Masturbation was similarly downplayed; if discussed at all, it was only in the context of male sexuality.[32]

This has, of course, changed since the velvet revolution. Prague's privately run newspaper and book stands are nowadays full of cheaply produced pornographic material; one can now go to a gay bar, place an advertisement in newspapers seeking or offering group sex, attend topless beauty contests or strip shows, or even join the Independent Erotic Initiative, which in February 1990 became registered as a regular political party.[33]

While most professionals regard pornography as an unwelcome side effect of full freedom of expression and democracy, but not something to be dealt with by the reimposition of state censorship, the successor group to the discredited communist women's organization, the Czech Union of Women, took a stronger stand. It claims to have successfully pressured Prague's municipal government to restrict sales of pornographic material in the center of the city. Some women in the Union have addressed this issue, as well as prostitution, in feminist terms as violence against women.[34]

Surrogacy presents another potential means of commercial exploitation of women. Current law in both republics permits no private adoption agencies and no surrogate agencies, public or private. Moreover, all private agreements between a would-be surrogate mother and another person (or couple) would be invalid under the Civil Code, as *contra bonos mores,* and unenforceable. While the Czechoslovak legal system makes no explicit provision for the determination or denial of maternity, judicial practice is quite clear on this issue. The legal mother of the child in all cases is the woman who has delivered the child. She is free to give the child up for adoption, but it is highly unlikely that the contracting couple would be selected by the state authorities as the most suitable adoptive parents.[35]

However, the opening of state frontiers and the freedom of travel has made it possible to contract surrogate parents in Czechoslovakia from abroad. Experts tend to believe that advertisements such as the one placed in *Mladá fronta dnes* on November 10, 1990, which offered to pay for surrogacy by financing a holiday in France, was placed by a contracting couple from Austria or some other Western European country close to the republics. If the surrogate child is born abroad, and surrogacy is legal in the country concerned, then the government in Czechoslovakia can do very little about such international forms of commercial exploitation of women's sexual and childbearing capacity.

Women and Autonomous Politics

One of the three rotating spokespersons of the main dissident organization, Charter 77, was always a woman. The documents of Charter 77 reveal that they did not devote much attention to women's issues, but to the extent that they did, they reaffirmed the principles of women's equality and women's right to work. However, the dissident writer Eva Kantůrková urged women to reject the Marxist ideal of emancipation, which in her view communism transformed into a new form of women's slavery: obligatory employment. Instead of seeking emancipation through paid work, Kantůrková urged women to rediscover their "authentic" traditional feminine qualities of compassion, love, and tolerance. Like most other dissidents who took some interest in women's issues, Kantůrková found the universalist concepts of human rights and human liberty more relevant to women's circumstances than the ideas of Western feminism.

Since the fall of communism, seventy-odd new local women's groups have been established, but they have found it extremely difficult to attract members, attention from the government, or funding. Many have folded, while the thirty to forty groups that continue to operate, mainly at the local level as clubs or special-interest groups (such as the Club of Single Mothers, Club of Modern Women, Association of Business Women and Managers, Gypsy Women, or Union of Catholic Women) are very small. Their leaders are not always trusted (sometimes with good reason), their programs lack clear definition, and they often act as adversaries among themselves.[36]

The former official women's organization, the Czech Union of Women, remains the largest women's organization in the Czech Republic. Although it has lost more than half of its membership, it still has more members than any other group, especially in rural areas. It also has more funds than other groups, since it continues to receive subsidies from the Czech government for its organizational, educational, and publishing activities. The women's weekly *Vlasta,* as well as numerous popular women's books published by the Union-owned publishing house, *Mona,* bring in some money directly.

The Political Party of Women and Mothers of Czechoslovakia operates at the federal level. It was created almost singlehandedly by Alena Valterová, a housewife who was on maternity leave during the 1990 preelection period. She appeared on the TV program "Opinions, Viewpoints" on January 15, 1990, to talk about the need to found a political party that would exert pressure on the government, trade unions, and employers to end discrimination against women and to improve the situation of the socially disadvantaged. In response, Valterová received 850 letters from across the country.

Valterová used the respondents and their letters as a basis to establish a network of 250 party activists across the country, and to formulate, with her five closest collaborators and friends, a political program for the party. The party's mandate is to represent the interests of the "socially weak and disadvantaged." To this end, the manifesto of the party made concrete suggestions for changes in family law (especially in regulations governing child support payments and custody), social security, health care, education, availability of part-time work, minimum wage, protective labor legislation, and more rigorous implementation of international instruments for the advancement of the status of women.[37] However, nobody in the government or the general public has paid much attention to this well-thought-out program, and it is by no means certain that the party will survive. Thus, Valterová's hope that the establishment of a grassroots women's political party would offer the quickest means of placing women's issues on the political agenda may remain unfulfilled. Without more support from the federal and national governments, or from Western feminist groups, Valterová and her party will soon collapse from exhaustion, lack of funds, and personal burnout.

What may end up as a more successful approach toward creating a political climate more favorable toward feminism is working through the established political parties. The low proportion of women elected to the federal and Czech and Slovak parliaments has been noted abroad, and this has in turn caused some political embarrassment. Some political parties, especially those in opposition, have begun to pay greater attention to women as a potentially significant political constituency. The Social Democrats and the Communists are well ahead of the other parties in this respect. The Czech Social Democrats are preparing a special women's platform, which includes demands for more flexible and shorter work hours, extension of paid maternity leave and annual adjustments of family cash benefits to reflect the rising cost of living.[38] At the same time, the Social Democrats have developed a special program, entitled "Women Can Do It" (*Zeny to dokazi*), to recruit more women into their party and into electoral politics. In preparing this program, the Social Democratic Party was able to rely on some external help from Social Democrats in Norway and the second International.[39]

Conclusion

The current emotional debates about abortion, reproductive freedom, and women's political participation, along with debates about whether mothers of small children should stay at home and not work for wages, are the first indications of emerging broader debates about women's roles in society, and about feminism in general. Gloomy as things are economically and politically, there is nonetheless a strong potential for the development of serious feminist scholarship and political activism. Much will depend on international feminist networking and support.

Acknowledgments

Research for this paper was carried out with the assistance of grants from Trent University and the Social Sciences and Humanities Research Council of Canada.

Notes

1. Alena Heitlinger, "Marxism, Feminism and Sex Equality," in Tova Yedlin, ed., *Women in Eastern Europe and the Soviet Union* (New York: Praeger, 1980), pp. 9–20.

2. Alena Heitlinger, *Reproduction, Medicine and the Socialist State* (London: Macmillan, 1987), pp. 55–56.

3. Pavel Říčan, interview. "Dítě po rozvodu," *Lidové noviny*, March 16, 1991.

4. Heitlinger, *Women and State Socialism. Sex Inequality in the Soviet Union and Czechoslovakia* (London: Macmillan, 1979), p. 192.

5. Sharon Wolchik, "Elite Strategy Toward Women in Czechoslovakia: Liberation or Mobilization?" *Studies in Comparative Communism* 15, nos. 2–3 (Summer/Autumn, 1981): 140–141.

6. Ibid.; and Heitlinger, *Reproduction, Medicine and the Socialist State*, pp. 64–70.

7. Sharon Wolchik, "Women and Work in Communist and Post-Communist Central and Eastern Europe," in Hilda Kahne and Janet Giele, eds., *Women's Work in Modernizing and Industrial Countries* (Boulder, Colo.: Westview, 1991).

8. Slavenka Drakulić, "In Their Own Words: Women of Eastern Europe," *Ms.* (July/August 1990); Hana Navarová, "Žena a rodina; žena v rodině," in Marie Čermáková, Irena Hradecká, and Hana Navarová, *K postavení žen v československé společnosti* (Praha: Sociologický ústav, Československá akademie věd, 1991), pp. 23–26.

9. Vlasta Parkanová, interview, "Co podle vás znamená 'ženská otázka'?" *Lidové noviny*, November 20, 1990; Ivan Klíma, "Čtyřicet let v nás. Pstavení žen," *Lidové noviny*, March 14, 1991; "Programové prohlášení Hnutí československá rodina," *Žena '91*, no. 2 (1991).

10. Barbara Einhorn and Swasti Mitter, "A Comparative Analysis of Women's Industrial Participation During the Transition From Centrally Planned to Market Economics in

East Central Europe." Paper presented for UN Division for the Advancement of Women, Eastern Europe Expert Group Meeting, Vienna, April 8–12, 1991.

11. Marie Čermáková, "Ženy a politický systém," in Čermáková et al., pp. 17–22.

12. Einhorn and Mitter.

13. Blanka Kovaříková, "Matky," *Tvorba*, no. 46 (1990).

14. Heitlinger, *Reproduction, Medicine and the Socialist State*, p. 35.

15. Alena Heitlinger, "Women in Eastern Europe: Survey of Literature," *Women's Studies International Forum*, 8, no. 2 (1985): 147–152; Heitlinger, *Reproduction, Medicine and the Socialist State*.

16. Wolchik, "Women and Work."

17. Radka Kvačková, "Přežijí mateřské školy? I rodič je volič," *Lidové noviny*, May 29, 1991.

18. Jan Koucký, interview, "Je už jasné, jak to bude s mateřskymi školkami pro něž chystáte radikálni žměnu převedeni dotací prímo na rodiče?" *Mladá fronta dnes*, May 23, 1991.

19. Kate Fillion, "The Daycare Decision," *Saturday Night* (January 1989), pp. 23–30.

20. Wolchik, "Women and Work."

21. Zuzana Šubertová, "Změny v sociálním zabezpečení. Rovnoprávnost mužům!" *Lidové noviny*, May 18, 1991.

22. Commission of the European Communities, *Protective Legislation for Women in Member States of the European Community* (Brussels: Commission of the European Communities, 1987).

23. Heitlinger, *Women and State Socialism*, pp. 186–189; Heitlinger, *Reproduction, Medicine and the Socialist State*, pp. 146–174; Henry P. David and Robert McIntyre, *Reproductive Behavior: Central and Eastern European Experience* (New York: Springer, 1981).

24. Heitlinger, *Reproduction, Medicine and the Socialist State*, pp. 146–174.

25. Martin Zajíček, "Interrupce—diskuse začíná," *Květy*, May 10, 1990.

26. Emíla Boldišová, "Interrupcia áno, či nie . . ." *Smena*, July 26, 1990; Jana Kolářová, "Zabíjení dětí nebo oprávněný lékařský zákrok?" *Forum*, June 27, 1990; Blanka Kutilková and Petra Procházková, "Hrozí invaze těhotných ze Slovenska do Českých zemí? Andělé a hrdlorežové," *Lidové noviny*, January 25, 1991.

27. Sharon Wolchik, "Women's Issues in Czechoslovakia in the Communist and Post-Communist Periods," in Barbara Nelson and Najma Chowdry, eds., *Women and Politics Worldwide* (forthcoming).

28. Ibid.

29. Jaroslav Zvěřina, "Platforma pro všechny, kteří chtějí pomoci. Rodina, výchova a sex," *Večerní Praha*, May 22, 1991.

30. "Nový zákon o interrupcích: Vyhoví všem?" *Lidové noviny*, May 13, 1991.

31. Slavomil Hubálek, "Není to trest," *Lidové noviny*, March 20, 1991.

32. Heitlinger, *Reproduction, Medicine and the Socialist State*, pp. 37–53, 127–145.

33. Slavomil Hubálek, interview, "Erotika a věda," *Forum*, no. 28 (1990): "Morálka, demokracie a pražský striptýz," *Sociologické aktuality*, no. 10 (1990): Rudolf Šmíd, "Nahoře bez," *Květy*, May 10, 1990.

34. "Ženy české proti zkáze . . . a pornografii," *Lidové noviny*, May 28, 1991.

35. Alena Heitlinger, "Current Medical, Legal and Demographic Perspectives on Artificial Reproduction in Czechoslovakia," *American Journal of Public Health* 79, no. 1 (1989): 57–61; Marta Prokešová, "Etici váhají nad zkumavkou," *Mladá fronta dnes*, November 10, 1990.

36. Olga Kučerová-Podkolodnaya. *Report on the Situation of Women in ČSFR*. Presented at the European Forum Conference "Women and Citizenship," Norwick, U.K., June 28–30, 1991.

37. "Program politické strany žen a matek Československa," 1990. Unpublished document.

38. "Žena, rodina—a jak dál," *Právo lidu*, July 4, 1990.

39. Petra Buzková, Czech Social Democratic Women, personal interview, May 29, 1991.

10

Women and Nationalism in the Former Yugoslavia

Andjelka Milić

> Nationalism is primarily negativity . . . because nationalism lives on denial
> and off of denial . . . We aren't what they are . . . Others even have the
> right to catch up with, to overtake us; that doesn't concern us.
> —Danilo Kis
> *The Anatomy Lesson*

I. Nationalism in the Former Yugoslavia

The dawn of new democracies in Eastern Europe following the downfall of communist regimes witnessed two disturbing phenomena: first, nationalism, national separatism, and secessionism, coupled with chauvinistic reactions against the minority population and minority groups in one's own country or neighboring states; second, openly aggressive, discriminatory acts against the civil and social rights of women, rights that were guaranteed by the old communist regime.

While manifestations of nationalism and xenophobia have received notable attention, the subject of women and "the women's question" have been confined to feminist circles in the social sciences and to feminist activists. Epistemological categorization is used to justify giving a more important status to categories such as nationalism on the grounds that they are general, while the treatment of women, and gender, is considered specific.[1]

Instead of worrying about nationalism while treating the conservative restoration of women's status as a marginal issue, we would do better to ask ourselves about the relationship of the two: why and how nationalism degrades women, whether this is always the case, and how and whether women are involved. This is especially pertinent in light of Europe's experience with fascism, which conjoined these two phenomena.

At first glance, national heterogeneity seems to provide the explanation for nationalist conflicts, division, and war in Yugoslavia. This cannot be the main reason, however, because these same nations and peoples were capable of living harmoniously over long stretches of time. Our proposition is that the explanation lies in the connection between the heterogeneous ethnic/national structure and the inadequate political structure. The problem, at least in part, lies in the Yugoslav state's and society's chronic lack of a democratic constitution, and a political and democratic model inadequate to the significant differences in history, language, culture, religion, economy, and politics that multinationality implies.

The combination of national, political, and state components has been crucial for the existence and progressive disintegration of Yugoslavia, and it has emerged in various institutional forms and with various internal combinations of the three. Considering only Yugoslavia's more recent sociopolitical history dating back to World War II, we can talk about two types of nationalism.

The first type is "nationalism from below": patriotism, which spontaneously emerged as resistance to foreign fascist occupation, but also as a result of the working majority's discontent with their previous social status in society. The energy of national resistance and social revolt was successfully channeled by the Communist Party of Yugoslavia, which resolved the ever-present, active national element by shifting it to a higher level of universalist, egalitarian communist ideology. This made it possible to unite heterogeneous national forces in joint resistance against fascism and to create the second Yugoslavia along the communist principles of brotherhood and unity among nations. The political solution to the national enigma was to give political legitimacy to the national interest through a federal state with territorial autonomies, while trying on the social level to reduce, suppress, and overcome this legitimate national interest by shaping society along the lines of egalitarianism and the ideology of a "workers' " society.

The more inefficient the communist regime became on the social level, the more the political-national syndrome of divisions and infighting among the federal members grew. The system reacted heavy-handedly and aggressively to mounting nationalism, which only further activated its insidious energies toward destroying the system.

During the phase of reconstituting Yugoslavia and its federal units on the ruins of communism, we find something different, a state nationalism, which bore down with all its might on the vacated social, ideological, and political arena. Reformed republican communist parties took the lead in this reorientation toward nationalism, but they were soon joined by new parties, some of which quickly surged ahead in their rush to protect the national interest of their people.

Although unexpected, the switch to nationalism by former communist parties seems logical because the distance between the communist collectivist ideology, based on such concepts as "the working class," "the class interest," and "the class enemy," and the nationalistic collective ideology, based on such concepts as "nation," "the national interest," and "the national enemy" is much shorter than the distance between communism and democracy.[2]

Nationally oriented parties representing the interests of the majority nation in their respective republics scored landslide victories in the first free multiparty elections. The ultimate outcome was paradoxical: pluralistic elections resulted in single-party parliamentary structures that rushed to establish sovereign national power-structures "to which the establishment of a democratic and civil society was subordinated, whereas the establishment of a social or welfare state fell into oblivion."[3] In the power struggle between communism and anticommunism, nationalism won out and democracy was again the loser.

II. Women's Patriotism and Emancipation in Yugoslavia During World War II

Yugoslavia's 1941–1945 national liberation war against fascist occupation, like many anticolonial liberation wars in Third World countries following World War II, was the springwell for women's spontaneous emancipation from their traditional patriarchal subordination in the family. As in these countries, in Yugoslavia women acted as support for the male-dominated resistance groups.[4] The Anti-Fascist Women's Front of Yugoslavia, an autonomous women's organization of resistance to the enemy and support for the revolt, was basically initiated by the Yugoslav Communist Party, which coordinated and steered all its activities until it was abolished by that same party in 1950.

However, irrespective of its subsidiary position vis-à-vis the leading political force in the national and liberation war, the Anti-Fascist Women's Front boasted massive participation. It brought together some 2,000,000 women during the war; approximately 100,000 took part in regular partisan military units, and of that number 25,000 were killed and 40,000 badly wounded. There were also many women who, through their veterans' and political activities, came to hold leading posts in the party and in local bodies of administration, as well as those who became national heroes.[5]

Considering just the number who were active during the war, especially militarily, there can be no doubt that women shouldered as much of the burden of war and liberation as did men. The civil, political, and social rights that women acquired and that were given legal shape after the war were not presented on a silver platter by the communist authorities but had been won and earned. There resulted a formal legal equation of genders. Even more importantly, through the national liberation movement, many women experienced the country's liberation as their own spontaneous, unexpected, direct emancipation from the closed world of their traditional patriarchal families and rural backwaters, where their only fate had been to marry and serve the family.

They could no longer go back to this previous world, even if the new authorities had wanted them to. They went to the city, the factory, a job, education, and to all the contradictions of the newly emerging system. While this system generously meted out social justice on the one side, however, it reduced civil and political rights and liberties on the other. The rest of the story is well known. Despite the rights and liberties they won under communism, women remained subordinated and segregated in all walks of life.

Women reacted to the later erosion of their acquired rights and liberties by returning to the family, to children, and to the home, focusing more on their private lives and less on political and public life. In these last crisis-ridden decades of the Yugoslav system, the gender gap became visible in all walks of life.[6]

The reversal of women's emancipation, along with the disappearance of women from the political sphere, provided fertile ground for the onsurge of nationalism. With its conservative but militant attitude toward women it was determined to return women to their proper place and role—home, family, and motherhood. At this point the ideologies of state nationalism stepped onto the political scene.

III. State Nationalistic Projects As Reflected in Gender Relations

What has been the contribution, attitude, and role of women to state nationalistic projects? All these aspects are important for explaining and understanding the dramatic events that led to war, but also created room for an alternative solution in the future. The analysis presented here will show both the manichean logic of ruling by means of destruction, a logic applied by state nationalism and also the birth of resistance to the subordination of the individual's civil, political, and social rights to the abstract collectivity of the nation. Although unequal, this interaction between women and nationalism emerged not only as a new sphere of women's subjugation but also as the beginning of women's own authentic alternative social and political activities. A new, fresh, strong feminist awareness and activity has been making its way into the former Yugoslavia.

This analysis of events and the relationship between women and nationalism will rely on the somewhat revised classification offered for observing the women/ nationalism relationship by Anthias and Yuval-Davis. To wit: 1) woman as the biological regenerator of the nation; 2) woman as the ideological focus of symbolization for defining the traits of one's nation; 3) woman as a participant in national-political discourse and practice; and 4) woman as a participant in the national-military conflict.

1. Woman as the Biological Regenerator of the Nation

There is no question that woman's biological role of motherhood has been of crucial importance for carrying out the state national project, whatever national group it represents. Its logic of totalizing the nation with a view to leveling out internal social differentiation and suppressing internal social antagonisms always targeting women first—specifically, their biological function of reproduction. This boils down to an attempt to have this function, and hence women themselves, serve the state, instrumentalizing reproduction and women's bodies to numerically increase the nation.

Attempts to confine women's reproductive rights go back to the days of the communist system. The lead was taken by Serbia in the latent conflict between the Serbian-Montenegrin minority and the Albanian majority in Kosovo over Kosovo's status. At the end of the 1980s, Serbia raised the question of an imbalance in the population's demographic reproduction, with a declining fertility rate for Vojvodina and Serbia proper of 1.8 and a very high total 4.3 fertility rate for Kosovo with its Albanian majority. This issue was raised belatedly and against a backdrop of antagonistic ethnic relations, and solutions were proposed on the basis of the national and state interests of the Serbian majority in the Republic.

The draft Law on Serbia's Population Policy (1990), submitted for public debate, envisaged the revision of certain previous rights and the introduction of new measures and sanctions, some of which were quite unusual. For instance, it punished families with more than three children by divesting them of all the social benefits they had held under previous regulations, and rewarded families with three children by giving them additional benefits. This not only denied the principle of social assistance to large families, but also constituted discrimination in social assistance, because the families with three and more children were mostly Albanian, seldom Serbian. The planned measures were clearly meant to stimulate Serbian growth. The draft law also provided for added taxes on childless couples on the grounds that they too must pay their debt to the nation, investing economically in its reproduction. The sponsors of the law did not dare openly touch the right of women to decide freely about childbirth, but they did try indirectly to confine this right by making the administrative procedures for abortions more complicated. They thus threatened the right to privacy in this very intimate sphere of a woman's life, which forms an integral part of one's civil rights.[7]

All the proposed measures were essentially of a restrictive rather than stimulatory character, clearly intended to impose new reproductive norms on women and families, without paying the slightest attention to the possibility of carrying out such norms. Not surprisingly, the proposal met with widespread public disapproval among women. Numerous measures of protest were sent to its sponsors, and feminist groups organized a public petition against adoption of the resolution, bearing the signatures of thousands of women in Belgrade. Thus, this assault on women's rights was successfully foiled, but others soon followed.

The Law on Social Care for Children, adopted by the Assembly of the Republic of Serbia on January 26, 1990, places the accent on fulfilling the aims of population policy and on increasing the population's reproduction, instead of on protecting and assisting families and children to ensure the best possible conditions and environment for child development. The newly constituted multiparty Assembly continued this policy, now directly threatening the social rights of women. The proposed Law on Labor Relations used a double yardstick for women—what it gave with one hand, it took away with the other, the result being discrimination in the labor market. Under the proposal, paid maternity leave is granted for a period of up to one year for the first and second child, but for three full years for the third child. It ensures, therefore, that a woman who has three children is excluded from the workplace for five years. It does not take great foresight to recognize the economic unfeasibility of such a proposal, or the covert intention to eliminate women from the labor market, or disfavor them by making them lose their competitive ability. Under the new economic conditions, the labor market is highly selective and brutal, and under the conditions proposed by the draft law the employment of women becomes almost illusory.

Whereas in the case of reproduction, women are generously "rewarded" for conscientiously performing their "national duty," when it comes to retirement they are punished. The previous law allowed women to choose whether to retire after thirty-five or forty years of service, but the new proposal fixed compulsory retirement at thirty-five years of service for women and forty years for men. The elimination of choice becomes all the more paradoxical given that this proposed law is the result of an earlier independent women's initiative that was accepted by the then communist authorities after protracting haggling. Thus, the socialist majority Assembly abolished the communist-passed laws, which honored the initiative and self-determination of women. Serbia is no exception in this respect. The new authorities in Slovenia and Croatia have openly stated in their constitutional documents what they expect of their female subjects.[8]

These bills make it clear that legislation on reproduction is oriented not toward women's interests but toward the nationalist interest in increasing the population of Croatia. An equal, emancipated woman does not suit such a policy, and women need to be either forced legally to improve the performance of their reproductive function or eliminated indirectly from the public sphere. Such acts of oppression against women prompted the awakening of women, of their feminist consciousness and resistance to official policy. The election campaign in all the republics served as propitious ground for women to organize themselves and step more energetically onto the public stage.

In Croatia and Slovenia, democratic women's alliances were formed with a view to bringing women together on a nonpartisan basis. Women became more politically involved by joining numerous new parties, especially democratic-liberal ones and smaller parties open to women's problems. Some parties even ran separate women's tickets at the elections, although without any effect on the outcome. The most interesting and turbulent election scene took place in Serbia, where numerous feminist groups were active, as were women from the former Communist Party, who saw a chance to form their own organizations and step independently onto the political scene. The Women's Party (ZEST) was founded as the first and only party of women; there was also the Women's Lobby, which was to coordinate the activity of women from different parties, and a Women's Preliminary Parliament, an institution representing and protecting women's civil, political, and social rights and liberties. These newly formed institutions soon became the stage for vigorous activity, propaganda, assembly, and discussion among women concerning all aspects of the political scene, determining the main thrust of their action. The idea was to create a communication network that could later be used for more organized action. Yet this proved to be farsighted, given the harder times that followed.

Nevertheless, this quick, timely reaction by women had its effect. Soon many of the newly formed parties had women in their executive bodies, trying, if only symbolically, to attract the women's vote.[9] Of course, these women disappeared from the political scene once the elections were over.

2. Women As the Focus of National Symbolism and Homogenization

The woman-mother symbol is also ideal for homogenizing the otherwise differentiated national being and producing a feeling of national communality, or national antagonism against the other side. Thus, woman, as the mother of the nation, on the one hand, and as a sex object in the possession of the male national collectivity, on the other hand, was given top media attention. The growing, frequent use of women in these symbolic images assumed a very important role in preparing the nation to fight the enemy: first, this symbolism was meant to homogenize the nation into experiencing its own sense of danger or superiority; then, this homogenized energy of national discontent was to be reflected at a high level until the proper situation arose when it could erupt against the rival side.

In examining this (ab)use of women by the politics of state nationalism, it is extremely useful to analyze the breach created between the majority Albanian nation in Kosovo and the majority Serbo-Montenegrin population in Serbia. Both sides used women as symbols, albeit for opposite purposes. The importance of women's symbolic function in arousing a feeling of being nationally at risk can perhaps best be illustrated by a photograph taken at the height of the clash in Kosovo pitting Albanians against Serbs and Montenegrins. The photograph showed a mother patrolling a long village road, holding a child in one arm and a gun in the other. It brought together and symbolized all the salient aspects of national identity and what threatened it: the nation's sense of jeopardy was clearly depicted by the mother and child defending themselves, by her readiness to defend her identity by means of arms but also her readiness to persevere as perhaps the last member of the nation. This photograph helped galvanize Serbian public opinion around the threat to the Serbian minority in Kosovo and to create the resolve to settle this situation in favor of the Serbian minority by force if need be.

Another illustration of the use of women is the way the mass media exploited cases of Serbian and Montenegrin women being raped by Albanians in Kosovo to charge the emotional atmosphere on the conflicting sides.[10] Women as sex object, in the context of the ethnic conflict in Kosovo and the patriarchal masculine ideology, becomes the property of the national collective, and hence its sacred, inviolable borders. Violation of this common property by rape meant symbolically trespassing upon the enemy's territory and brutally destroying its physical integrity.

Frequent media references to these incidents had an effect on both sides. For the Serbian-Montenegrin population in Kosovo, and the Serbian population in

Serbia, the rape of Serbian women signaled not only an extreme threat to the Serbs as a minority population but that it was time for state retaliation against an enemy that dared to overstep the borders of national territory and property. It can be presumed that this had an effect, albeit in the opposite sense, on the Albanian side as well, symbolically confirming the expansionist strivings of the Albanian nation and its power to achieve them.

At the same time, the media conceals the devastation that war perpetrates against a nationally mixed population comprised of couples and children from ethnically mixed marriages. The family dramas, agonizing divisions, stress, and trauma experienced by this large group of people are not the subject of mass media interest. According to statistical data, the war-torn regions of Croatia have the highest concentration of children from mixed Serbian-Croatian marriages, accounting for 25 to 35 percent of the youth population in the most afflicted communities.[11] Such family tragedies in the war-torn regions are being suppressed for the same reasons that rape across ethnic lines is highlighted. Mixed marriages symbolize the possibility of mutual assimilation and integration between different nations, the possibility of transcending the borders of national collectivity with no taboos attached.

3. Women and Nationalist Policy in the Former Yugoslavia

In the above cases, nationalism treated women as passive objects, as victims of legal instrumentalization and media manipulation. But in political participation even nationalism cannot reject the role of women as active subjects, as in the free multiparty elections held in all the Yugoslav republics by the end of 1990. However, elements of the preelection environment negatively affected women's participation. For a good part of the population, the multiparty elections were more confusing than anything else, because people lacked the necessary experience and understanding; women were offered limited electoral options with which to articulate the demands and needs of the times and their own interests; they had limited possibilities for presenting and organizing themselves independently in the political environment, and the leading national parties confined the space for them to engage in decisionmaking and action. Women did not have a proper chance to express themselves as active political subjects or to have their needs and interests properly represented. Let us examine this situation more closely.

The process of constituting political parties was fraught with nationalism. According to an analysis embracing the program documents of some eighty parties in Yugoslavia, "the national supradeterminant [was] stronger than the democratic" in shaping the parties' political views.[12] There was an insufficient elaboration and poor grasp of social and developmental problems, including questions loosely connected to women's spheres of concern, such as the family, employment, social welfare, child care, health care, etc. If it is true that women are oriented more locally and less nationalistically than are men,[13] such an election platform would have an inhibiting effect on women's joining parties, and later the election process. The extremely aggressive come-on of some party leaders[14] and the strongly masculine image projected by some parties only made this worse, effectively reducing women's participation in the election process and distorting its results.

The few facts available on electoral conduct allow one to piece together a mosaic of women's political views and conduct in the preelection, election, and post-election period, and to draw some conclusions about the party establishment's attitude toward including women in the election process.

The preelection polls in Serbia, which sporadically included the gender variable, indicate that women accounted for a substantial part of the undecided electorate.[15] Asked whether they would go to the polls, 35 percent of the women and 64 percent of the men said, "Yes"; 26 percent of the women and 12.5 percent of the men said, "No"; and 35 percent of the women and 22 percent of the men were undecided. The main reason women gave for their reservations about voting were doubts about the elections being democratic and their view that most of the options offered were unacceptable.[16] According to the same poll, only 13 percent of the women in Serbia had joined political parties, while as many as 70 percent said they did not want to join any party.[17] Younger, better educated women favored democratic-liberal parties, while older women, housewives, and peasant women massively supported the reformed Communist Party in Serbia.[18]

The gender variable is also missing from figures on poll attendance, which shows how interested the parties and researchers are in the female electorate. The fact that voter turnout was high, ranging from 71 to 80 percent in all the republics, indicates that most women did not abstain from going to the polls. The same sources analyzing abstinence at elections point to women as one of the main groups that abstained.[19]

Women were only rarely political protagonists, leaders, and participants in the struggle for power, as shown in the percentage of women nominated as deputies in the republics, which varied between 4.80 percent for Serbia to between 5 and 6 percent for other republics, with the exception of Slovenia, with 18.47 percent of all candidates on multiparty elections. Moreover, there is a strong disproportion between the percentage of women holding top party office and their nomination by these same parties to run on their tickets as candidates for deputy.[20] In Croatia, for instance, women accounted for only 6 percent of the nominations, although their share in various levels of the parties' executive committees ranged from 6 percent to 44 percent.[21] Women ran for deputy more often on the tickets of left-wing, liberal democratic, and generally smaller parties, whereas the leading national parties tended to avoid them.[22]

Limited interest and marginalized presence in the party elections was bound to bring total defeat to the political representation of women. In comparison with the single-party communist system, in which women accounted for 19.1 percent of the membership in all republican assemblies and at the federal level, their share has been reduced to 4.6 percent. There are only three women ministers in all the states of ex-Yugoslavia.

The overall election process and constitution of a new political system confirmed the darkest fears of women who had tried to fight nationalistic propaganda and its protagonists. Not only were women left without corresponding political representation, they were also left without a corresponding protective mechanism at the state level, given the collapse of the federal commission for overseeing the implementation of international declarations and conventions regarding women's rights. The demand of feminist groups and organizations for setting up a Ministry for Women was soundly rejected. But the worst was yet to come, and it came with the militarization of the conflict in Croatia.

4. Militarization of the Conflict and Women

As one turns back the film of the Yugoslav crisis, one sees a thread of escalating ethnic tensions and antagonisms running through it, ultimately leading to the outbreak of armed conflict. Marked by nationalist policies that finally found legitimacy as sovereign state policies, war grew inevitable almost from the outset.

The logic of these developments kept placing women in a defensive position, until they were finally overpowered and became victims. This observation can be tested by analyzing women's participation and conduct in the armed national conflict. A look at the war scene reveals a nuanced array of women's characters and roles, which does not allow them to be viewed as simply victims. Women are seen as a) passive victims of the war, such as refugees and victims of devastation; b) mothers, actively opposed to the war; c) fighters on both sides; and d) initiators of the peace movement in Yugoslavia. Let us look more closely at these different groups.

Women refugees and the victims of war reflect women in their classic role as passive victims powerless to prevent adversity. The answer is to save one's own life and the lives of one's children,[23] or to leave oneself open to the risks of war.[24] Typical of how the mass media dealt with this situation was their abstract, quantitative approach, their stress on the need for caring for the refugees while avoiding the tales of individual fates. The latter accounts would be useless for intensifying militant homogeneous national sentiments, because they would produce the opposite feelings of pity, commiseration, and suffering, with demands to end the war.

The next largest group of women active in the national conflict still work within women's typical role: the spontaneous resistance by mothers (joined by fathers) to having their children recruited and mobilized by the Yugoslav Army.[25] For the first time we find public resistance to the war and to the ruling forces of the regime. But women still come out as mothers trying to protect their own children. Their protests caused unfavorable and highly negative reactions on the part of official policy and the authorities, who adopted a twofold tactic: to suppress resistance and at the same time to transform it into protests and events that played into the hands of official policy. The spontaneous resistance of mothers was soon used in all the republics for different political purposes: in some for pro–Yugoslav Army propaganda and the army's protective role toward the Serbian population in Croatia; in others as the "caravan of mothers for Europe" from Zagreb, for propagating abroad the sovereign strivings of the Croatian nation; in others still as a good pretext to refuse to send one's recruits to the Yugoslav Army and thus stress the right to one's own sovereignty (as in Macedonia and Bosnia-Herzegovina). Thus, this spontaneous protest by mothers was not only suppressed; it began to have an entirely different, unplanned effect on the troubled political scene.

Women fighters on both sides remained the most hidden phenomenon of women's participation in the war. There were no figures on the number on either side, and no account of what motivated them to go to war.[26] The mass media were obviously loath to promote this category of women participating in the national conflict. While a woman holding a gun in one hand and a child in the other could be a valuable symbol of national homogenization, in a real war situation the winning logic seems to be that war is a man's affair, with no room for women.

The participation of women as active fighters reflected the same degree of engagement as did pacifist resistance to war, except with a different connotation. In this case, as one might presume, women rallied together from all feminist groups, the Women's Party, and other alternative women's organizations, crowning their numerous protests by forming the Center for Anti-War Action in Belgrade. The peace movement and its antiwar protest actions were greeted by the ruling regime, party officials, and intellectuals, who support the national project with unconcealed hostility. Participants in these drives were openly and from the highest places called "traitors," "cowards," "unpatriotic," and "un-Serbian." Such condemnation led some women who had joined the movement spontaneously to pull back, but it also helped to reinforce the nucleus of feminist actions.

Although this antiwar nucleus was a marked minority on the public scene, the public opinion polls in September 1991 showed that 80 percent of the population in Serbia favored peace—75 percent of men and 86.4 percent of women.[27] This is a sure sign that the future will present a very different picture of participants in antiwar drives.

In Lieu of a Conclusion

To end, let us go back to the two questions we started with: to what extent can patriotism and nationalism be delineated by their attitude toward women, and what is the attitude of women toward them?

On the basis of Yugoslavia's experience with nationalism, we would be prone to say that patriotism is the minimum framework for the collective identity experience; it legitimates the collective in time and space, while giving the individual a sense of belonging. It is based on ethnic identity and traditions, and it emerges largely in relation to perceiving an external threat to the collective. Patriotism gets its energy from inner ethical resistance and individual choice under imposed circumstances. Hence, it is a form of solidarity rather than exclusiveness; it is socially expansive, it integrates rather than segregates, it is not discriminatory vis-à-vis the particularities that constitute the national collective. This explains why women joined the armed resistance en masse, despite their subordinate position in society and the patriarchal society's many socio-psychological barriers to their presence in society and the public sphere.

State nationalism, on the other hand, is a political ideology created by society's elite, and it is efficiently spread by the mass media controlled by these ruling forces. This ideology is internalized by the individual when times are confusing and society is in crisis, when alternative choices and new social projections are obfuscated, and when propaganda can play on an individual's emotions by evoking the past. Behind this euphoric romanticization of the national past is a message to the individual that any behavior to the contrary can incur various sanctions. Hence, this type of nationalism is based on the individual's emotional reactions and fear.

Since nationalism in this case is subordinated to the will and sovereignty of the state, it approaches individuals as objects. It instrumentalizes their feelings with a view to homogenization and in an attempt to achieve its own goals. Women are given a strictly limited sphere of action—to reproduce the nation—and men are instructed to defend it. Plurality both within society and within each individual is reduced, but only temporarily and symbolically. Women, among whom there are many differences, including national ones, reflect these differences in their reactions to the role state nationalism assigns to them. But there is a thread running through women's attitude to nationalism—one of inner resistance, suspicion, and doubt. This is seen externally in women's traditionally apolitical attitude and daily concern for the family. However, this may actually conceal a woman's specific gender rationality, which operates in the form of a silent criticism of men's rhetoric and readiness to be aggressive.

The ruling ideological-political order wants women to abstain from political participation, and in this respect one of its goals has been achieved. But such abstention does not mean that women are ready to take the roles assigned to them. There seems to be an unwillingness that could conceivably turn into open resistance as social and economic conditions deteriorate.

Notes

1. Sylvia Walby, "Women, Citizen, Nation." Presented at the Conference of the European Network for Women's Studies, The Hague, 1990.

2. Vladimir Goati, *Jugoslavija na prekretnici. Od monizma do Gradjanskog rata* (Belgrade: Jugoslovenski institut za Novinarstvo, 1991), p. 33.

3. Srdjan Vrcan, "Izbori u Hrvatskoj" (Zagreb: Revija za Sociologiju, 1991).

4. Kumari Jayawardena, *Feminism and Nationalism in the Third World* (London: Zen Press, 1986), p. 259.

5. Lidija Sklevitsky, "Organized Activity of Women from Croatia in NOB from 1941–45," *Povjesni Prvlozi,* No. 3 1984:97.

6. Anuška Ferligoj, Tanja Rener, and Mirjana Ole, *Zenska, Zasebno, Političn o* (Ljubljana: Znanstveno in Publicistično središte, 1990).

7. Alida Brill, *Nobody's Business: The Paradoxes of Privacy* (Reading, Mass.: Addison-Wesley, 1990).

8. In response to the women's protests and petitions, the President of the Republic, in keeping with his constitutional powers, asked the Assembly to have the new law retain the old laws regarding women's retirement, and it did.

9. In its election campaign the Socialist Party of Serbia fielded a poster depicting a modern young woman standing next to a man, seen from behind, with the slogan, "The Future Lies with Us."

10. For objective data and analysis, see Ruža Petrović and Marina Blagojević, *Seobe Srba sa Kosova* (Belgrade: SANU, 1988); *Kosovski čvor: drešiti ili seći,* report of the Independent Commission (Titograd, 1990).

11. "Nesreća porodičnog rata," *Borba,* September 30, 1991.

12. Miroslav Pečujlić and Vladimir Milić, *Političke stranke u Jugoslaviji* (Belgrade: Stručna Knjiga, 1990), p. 504.

13. Walby, p. 15.

14. At election rallies, the leaders of some aggressive national parties in Serbia called on women to "multiply and renew the Serbian nation"; others observed that the "legal equation of marital and extramarital unions is a method of special warfare against Serbia." Statement by Women's Lobby, September, 1990.

15. Aleksandra Milićević, "Wise and Cautious," *NADA,* November 24, 1990.

16. Ibid.

17. Ibid.

18. Public opinion poll conducted in Serbia, November 1990, by the Institute for Political Studies, Belgrade, December, 1990.

19. Goati, p. 19.

20. Vesna Pešić, "The Impact of Reforms on the Status of Women in Yugoslavia," Regional Seminar on the Impact of Economic and Political Reform on the Status of Women in Eastern Europe and USSR: The Role of National Machinery, Vienna, April 1991, Table 10, p. 31.

21. S. Leinert-Novosel, *Zene-Politička Manjina* (Zagreb: 1990).

22. Pešić, p. 19.

23. According to existing figures as of October, 1991, there are about 300,000 refugees in the entire country, the majority of whom are women and children.

24. Most often mentioned is the suffering of old women who could not, or dared not, be evacuated from the war zones.

25. See Slavenka Drakulić, this volume.

26. A Belgrade television show features a woman who had gone to the battle front to be with her son, who had been recruited by the Yugoslav army.

27. Public opinion poll conducted in Serbia, August 1991, by the Institute for Political Studies, Belgrade, September 1991.

11

Women and the New Democracy in the Former Yugoslavia

Slavenka Drakulić

When the changes began in Yugoslavia in 1989, women were in the streets along with men, demonstrating, meeting, holding flags and banners, shouting, singing, and voting. But when it came to forming new governments, when it came to direct participation in power, they disappeared, became invisible again. Why? What relation do women have to the new governments?

We have to take into account that because of cultural and historical differences, standards of life, natality, and employment, and, finally, war and national divisions, there is no single Yugoslavia, and there are no "Yugoslav women." During 1989 and 1990, a wave of political changes and elections swept over six Yugoslav republics. In Croatia, the Croatian Democratic Union (HDZ), a right-wing nationalist party, won overwhelmingly, as did the similarly oriented Demos, a coalition of six central-right parties, in Slovenia. The Serbian socialist party (SPS), communists converted into socialists, won in both Serbia and Montenegro. In Bosnia and Herzegovina the Muslim nationalist party, SDA, won in coalition with HDZ and the Serbian nationalist party, SDS. And in Macedonia, a coalition of nationalists (VMRO-DPMNO), communists, and federal reformist forces took power. In June 1991 the noncommunist governments of Croatia and Slovenia announced their independence, and in the same month war broke out, first in Slovenia, then in Croatia, and later in Bosnia and Herzogovina. All of this makes it very difficult to analyze the situation of women separately. In addition, most demographic data come from the 1981 census. Yet the trends and tendencies of the new governments toward women remain apparent.

There is a constant pressure from the church and prolife organizations to ban abortion. The concept of the "fruitful virgin-mother" (whatever that means) is used in any HDZ public speeches addressing women as a group. Prohibitions on abortions took hold in Zagreb in November 1991, when the largest hospital there prohibited its doctors from performing abortions, despite there being no antiabortion law.

The first and most obvious fact is that, since the elections of 1990, very few women have participated directly in politics. Under the communist system of the past forty-five years, there was generally a 30 percent quota for women's participation, but these women were tokens, without power, and unable to make their own decisions. The fact that the percentage dropped to only 5 to 10 percent after the new elections (depending on the republic) may reflect the real political culture and patriarchal system. But these numbers may also indicate the strong influence of the conservative nationalist parties' propaganda, especially in Croatia and Slovenia, where the new parties have promoted a very traditional image of women. The HDZ party in Croatia promised subsidies for women with more than three children, expressing their concern about overworked mothers. They explicitly stated that the primary and "sacred" duty of every woman was to stay at home, take care of her family and be a "lady," instead of being exposed to the market or participating in politics. Indeed, most of the new parties in Slovenia and Croatia, including Demos, confined women to the role of childbearer and housewife. Women cannot be encouraged by the presence in the Slovenian government, in 1991, of only one woman minister (of health), while none served in the Croatian government. Meanwhile, a mere 10 percent of the representatives in the Slovenian Parliament are women, although this dwarfs the figure of 4.8 percent (with only 6 percent even as candidates) in the Croatian Parliament—14 out of 270 representatives.

Another expression of the new governments' policies toward women are the new constitutions. Consider the Slovenian constitution, passed in December 1990. Problems with the initial draft constitution began in the very first sentence, which read: "The Constitution originates from the sanctity of life." The prolife cast of this statement is quite explicit; the minister of culture, a Christian Democrat, even explained that the sentence referred directly to the prohibition of abortion. Women were mentioned explicitly in only two articles of the draft (51 and 75), and there only as mothers, in which capacity they were considered to be under special protection of the Republic.

Apart from this obvious reduction of women to the role of mother, there were several other problematic articles. Article 52 stated: "Everyone has the right to decide freely about bearing a child. This right can be limited only for reasons of health." It was not clear what this meant: that a woman could have an abortion only if her health is jeopardized? Or conversely that a gynecologist could refuse to perform an abortion on the grounds that the procedure itself endangers a woman's health? Article 45, called the "conscientious objection" article, also bore on women, since a proposal was made to extend this article beyond military service to include all other professions as well. Thus, a gynecologist might be able to refuse to perform an abortion because of a "conscientious objection." Slovenian women's groups proposed amendments to this article, but to no avail. There was great concern that the new constitution would provide a strong basis for an antiabortion law.

The Croatian constitution was still more conservative than the Slovenian one. Its general characteristic was a systematic limitation of every citizen's right. A right may be granted in one article but limited in the next, with utterly vague criteria offered for such limitations, such as public morals, health, and the security of the republic. Because these categories are not defined in the constitution and because they are essentially nonlegal categories, there is a real danger that the state will define them according to its needs. No reference was made to the sanctity of life, but Article 21 did state that "Every human being has the right to life." Although this article dealt with the abolition of the death penalty, there was a fear that it could be applied to the right to life of a fetus.

The most problematic article in the draft constitution was Article 63, which spoke of providing the conditions for promoting the right to life of every unborn child. This article opened the possibility for the state to forbid contraception and abortion and therefore to violate the human right to decide about bearing a child. This was in explicit contradiction to Article 65 in the draft, which granted the freedom to decide about having children. Because Article 63 was so problematic, women's organizations held a protest conference in November 1990, just before voting took place. The article was dropped in the final text, where it was reformulated and included in Article 62, which reads: "The Republic protects motherhood, children, and youths, and creates social, cultural, educational, material, and other conditions to promote realization of the right to a dignified life." This meant that the constitution left the whole issue of abortion to regulation by law.

Another problematic part of Article 63 had been paragraph 4, which spoke about children's duty to "take care of their old and helpless parents." At first sight, this appears very innocent, of no concern to women as such. But it contradicts the very first article of this draft, defining Croatia as a "welfare state." If Croatia is to be a welfare state, then the state, and not the children, is obliged to take care of the "old and helpless" parents. The question is whether the state in this article absolves itself from its responsibility. Since women are the caretakers, this article would have significant effects on women. The Slovenian draft and the new Croatian constitution thus opened up rather conservative possibilities for women.

In general, the parties in power are putting women back in the home, recognizing them only as mothers and caretakers. Prolife positions were very clearly stated in the party platforms constituting Demos, as well as in the HDZ preelection party programs. One cannot expect that such a nationalist party, worried that the Croatian nation is soon going to disappear because Croatian women aren't giving birth to more than 1.8 children, is going to promote anything progressive for women. Only impending war prevented the government from putting forward a population policy. And tremendous attention was paid to the family, such as constant television coverage of baptisms where the godfather was a member of the government. Taking into account further the strong ties of the Croatian government to the Catholic church, the picture does not look good for women.

The population policy in Slovenia has been much the same, with a general tendency of protectionism concerning the nation's identity. Women in Slovenia are afraid that the new prolife government might propose restrictions on abortion to serve their ethnic nationalism, since the birth rate of Bosnian immigrants is almost double that of Slovenians. Serbia has a similar problem of wanting its Serbian population to increase (its birth rate currently stands at 11.7 per thousand) and wanting the Albanian population in the province of Kosovo to decrease, since it has the highest birth rate in Europe (27.8 per thousand). The question is how to accomplish this, when all citizens are equal under the law? Some years ago Macedonia tried to "solve" this problem of the high birth rate of the Albanian minority in the republic with special, though unconstitutional, measures. For example, schooling as well as medical care was made free for only the first four children in a family; people with fewer children were given a priority in employment and got credits for apartments. These discriminatory measures were implemented in the district of Tetovo, where 70 percent of the population is Albanian, and it was clear that these measures were directed against them. There is a fear that such measures might be taken in all of Macedonia and in Serbia proper.

The lack of political visibility of women and their position as defined in the constitutions pose very serious problems, but economic conditions, especially unemployment, will be more serious still. The average income of women is 20 to 40 percent lower than that of men; the structure of their unemployment is unfavorable; and they are concentrated at the lower levels of the occupational hierarchy, as well as in certain sectors such as textiles and social services. The economic picture varies tremendously from republic to republic, with Slovenia in 1989 having only a very small part of its population—2.9 percent—below the poverty level, while virtually the entire population of Kosovo—81.9 percent— stood below that line. The largest part of the unemployed, between 50 to 60 percent, have traditionally been women. There can be no women's emancipation without a strong economic basis, and given the serious economic situation, women's situation is in serious jeopardy.

The fourth important indicator of the position of women is their public image and the way it is shaped by the media. Under the Communist Party all media were more or less under government control. Sometimes, as in the 1950s, this control was direct, while later it took the form of self-censorship. Although it became legally possible after the election of 1990 to establish an independent newspaper (and many have been established), these are not independent or objective, but connected to and influenced by the ruling political parties. The new governments replaced all the top executives at the TV and radio stations in Slovenia and Croatia. The Serbian Socialist Party and its leader, Slobodan Milošević, controlled and directly appointed the heads of radio and TV. In Serbia, outraged at this situation, opposition parties organized 100,000 people in March 1990 in bloody demonstrations, demanding changes at the top levels of radio and

TV. In general, people working in the media adhere to government policy and conservative positions.

Women are praised in the media as mothers, but there are no articles or discussions about the facts that they form the largest percentage of the unemployed, that they are underpaid, and that they are in a very difficult position if they are single mothers. Women's problems, such as the feminization of poverty, are not "interesting" to the new government.

The media representation of women is in general very conservative. In Croatia in 1990 there was a story that the first brothel had opened. The article was written in rather amused terms, blaming women and emancipation. Sex shops, porno magazines, sex on TV, and telephone sex have blossomed, and the media presents this as evidence of having achieved the hallowed fruits of Western civilization. Women are not reported on at all, unless such reportage serves a political aim. For example, in 1990 when, politically manipulated by the communists' Movement for Yugoslavia party, women demonstrated in Belgrade in front of the National Assembly and demanded a military coup, it was widely publicized. Had women gathered to defend their rights, there would have been virtually no coverage.

It is difficult to confront this manipulation of women. The opposition both inside and outside of Parliament is weak; women's organizations are small and without money or institutional support. The atmosphere of nationalism everywhere prevents women, or anyone else, from engaging in any kind of antigovernment activity.

Furthermore, for many women emancipation is a dirty word. There has been no flex-time offered in employment, no laundries, cleaners, takeout food, or babysitters, and insufficient day care. The negative image of women's organizations during the communist regime makes women's organizing difficult today. During World War II, the Antifascist Women's Front (AWF) did liberate women, and they were treated as equals rather than as sex objects or household property for the first time in their lives. But in the immediate postwar period, the Communist Party built emancipatory policy into the legislation, and the "woman question" ceased to exist. Soon after the war the AWF became a bureaucratic women's organization serving to ensure the transmission of Communist power over women. No spontaneous grass-roots organization (peace, ecological, feminist, workers, etc.) was permitted; if an organization was not institutionalized, it could not be efficiently controlled.

At the end of the 1970s, a new generation of women, born and raised in communist Yugoslavia, were ready to challenge the official view of the status of women and the gap between Marxist theory and social reality. The first public articulation of feminism in 1978 took place at the nongovernmental international conference of women in Belgrade, which invited feminists from France, Italy, West Germany, the United Kingdom, Poland, and Hungary. The conference was a great shock in several ways. The general public was disturbed by the prospect of feminism, which, the media claimed, amounted to a declaration of war between the sexes. For women war veterans, feminism was synonymous with disloyalty to Yugoslavia. Official women's organizations accused the conference members of importing decadent ideology from the West, and the Communist Party accused them of "the weakening of women as potential builders of contemporary socialist society" and of "negating the leading role of the working class and the Communist League." Feminists were ridiculed, trivialized, and aggressively attacked, for in Yugoslavia they challenged something very deep—the patriarchal structure of the society, distinguishing between a real and merely formal emancipation and equality of women, and addressing the as yet unquestioned private sphere. By the end of 1979 the group Women and Society was formed in Zagreb, the capital of the republic of Croatia. This group of about thirty women and some men met regularly, promoted public discussions and lectures on many previous unquestionable matters, and became an open platform, sometimes very political, which was a rarity at the time. Many of its members wrote articles for newspapers and magazines, awakening consciousness about women's problems. Over the next ten years, many new, but small, groups, including lobbies, political parties, SOS hotlines, umbrella organizations, and lesbian groups, appeared in Ljubljana, Belgrade, Sarajevo, and Novi Sad. But feminism in Yugoslavia has not become a mass movement.

Women's organizing is sorely needed, but there are several major obstacles. The first is the very concept of feminism as it was and still is presented in the mass media, reduced to the stereotype of "women who hate men." Very few women will dare say, "I am a feminist," even if they live out many feminist principles. Second, women are mistrustful of women's organizations, which remind them of the official women's organizations. The third obstacle is that women need to learn to take active roles rather than passively waiting for the government to act, as they were trained to do by a system in which everything came from above. For forty years, women knew only the "committee for women." We may find ourselves, as women, in the position of having to emancipate once again. Finally, women are once again being told that something else is more important than their rights: this time, it is democracy. This is especially ironic since democracy is about citizen's, human, and women's rights. Women need to learn that their rights are a litmus test for democracy.

But in spite of everything, women are still capable of organizing, as the events of fall 1991 proved. While their husbands' politics sent their sons to war, mothers on all sides were trying to bring them home. On July 2, 1991, hundreds of Serbian mothers broke into the Serbian Parliament in Belgrade. They were moved to action by the federal army attack on Slovenia when it declared its independence. Seeing their sons fighting in an army that was attacking its own people, the Serbian women were the first to demand the immediate return of the soldiers. "We don't want our sons to die for generals! Generals are killers!" cried the women as they surged through the Serbian parliament building. Hundreds of Serbian women went the next day to Ljubljana, the capital of Slovenia, to bring their sons home from the front line. In Zagreb they were joined by Croatian mothers and in Ljubljana by Slovenian mothers (whose sons were fighting both for the federal army and the Slovenian territorial defense) who were prepared to welcome them. By the time they arrived in Ljubljana, however, the women were no longer simply mothers, but Serbian and Croatian mothers, who wouldn't accept the Slovenian mothers. Divided, they were defeated, and although the Serbian mothers went to the barracks, they never managed to get their sons out.

When full-scale war broke out in Croatia, Croatian women circulated antiwar petitions and organized silent demonstrations to protest the fact that their sons, serving in the federal army, were being sent to fight against their own people. With the failure of ceasefire agreements in August 1991, women's activism intensified. Serbian, Croatian, and Muslim women of Bosnia and Herzogovina stormed the Parliament in Sarajevo, the capital of the republic of Bosnia and Herzegovina, interrupting the session in progress, and took over, imitating the Serbian women. They demanded the immediate discharge of their sons, who were being kept in the federal army long after their military service was over, accusing the federal army generals of using their children as cannon fodder. Two days later, on August 29, 1991, 100,000 people gathered in Zagreb, Croatia's capital, in answer to the women's call to "surround the generals with the wall of our love." At the same time about thirty buses with women from Croatia, joined by buses with women from Macedonia and Bosnia and Herzegovina (women from Kosovo and Montenegro had been stopped by the police) went to Belgrade to take their "Wall of Love" campaign to the federal army.

From the beginning, women insisted their actions were not political, that they only wanted their sons back. But with the country at the brink of war, it was naive to believe that their actions could be anything but political. If the women had succeeded in organizing across ethnic/nationality lines by pulling their sons out, the federal army would have been destroyed. However, this wouldn't have kept the republics from forming their own armies, as occurred in Slovenia and Croatia. The women's uprising was doomed because the generals and politicians—not the women—understood the potential power of their movement, and therefore it was supported and manipulated by their respective governments, to serve each republic's interests. It was Milošević, who needed the federal army for his plans and realized the danger of women's organizations, who called upon Serbian women to boycott the protests.

This historic, spontaneous women's action failed to unite women and all who were against the war. The women needed to define their political aims for themselves. Their common denominator should have been more than their shared desire to take their sons home; it should have been a call for peace. Then Serbian mothers, as well as all of those sick of the fighting, might have joined them. The women fell victim, not only to their nationalism, but to their spontaneity, and to their lack of organization and political vision, itself the product of their alienation from politics over the past forty years.

Women must begin to see themselves as political actors. They need to define emancipation in their own terms, defend their already existing rights, prevent the manipulation of women's bodies. Otherwise, democracy will retain its male face, and men will not be the only ones to blame.

12

Women's Time in the Former Yugoslavia

Daša Duhaček

The following text does not have pretentions to being anything more than a sketch. Written during the process of the disintegration of Yugoslavia, such a theoretical statement must remain uncertain. Following and paraphrasing Julia Kristeva, an attempt will be made "to situate the problematic of women in Europe within an inquiry on time: that time which the feminist movement both inherits and modifies."[1]

In order to make adequate use of Kristeva's stimulating text, some clarifications are necessary. Her work is grounded on an assumption that any movement, including feminism and its organizations, can and does represent the interests of a larger group. Making an effort not to slip into the trap of discussing the avant garde, the question still remains whether feminists convey the standpoint of women, and whether they represent women's interests. The situation is further complicated by the disintegration of the feminist movement in the making, leaving feminist groups marginalized and feminist theorists isolated. What role did women and feminists play in this process? Were they aware of it? Did it serve their interests? If not, whose interests were served?

Although the sequence of major events in the disintegration of Yugoslavia is well known, it will be briefly outlined here in order to relate it to the opening statement of Kristeva's *Women's Time:* "The nation—dream and reality of the nineteenth century—seems to have reached both its apogee and its limits [in] 1929 . . . and [with the] National-Socialist apocalypse . . ."[2]

Yugoslavia, as a state, had a seventy-year history beginning at the end of World War I. Between the wars three constitutive nations were recognized. In the period after World War II three more nations were recognized within a federal state. Although each republic was basically organized on a national basis, none except Slovenia has a homogeneous national population. The Constitution of 1974 gave the republics state prerogatives. After the death of Tito in 1980 the weakening of the economy became evident. After 1987 Slobodan Milošević homogenized Serbia on a national basis. In 1990 Franjo Tudjman, reviving the aspirations to the national state strongly reminiscent of NDH,[3] came to power in Croatia. In June 1991, after long preparations, by an act of its assembly, the Republic of Slovenia entered the phase of national independence. The federation, or what was left of it, complied. The war over the remaining territories began.

The optimistic view of Europe in Kristeva's article proved to be painfully wrong as far as Yugoslavia is concerned, because the nation still functions as a dream on the threshold of the twenty-first century. Using Nietzsche's terminology freely, Kristeva recognizes "monumental" and "cursive" time. Cursive time can either flow aimlessly or be teleologically conceived. It can be cyclical or linear and historical. Although the temporal order is the prerogative of the Father, as is the sign and speech,[4] and "nourishing," "unnameable" space is better suited for the construction of female subjectivity, the latter also retains eternity and repetition as modalities of time and is consequently inclusive of monumental and cyclical time. Linear time or, as Kristeva puts it, "the time of history,"[5] excluded women.

The history of our civilization, well represented by the history of philosophy, has flowed in one direction: the history of ancient philosophy being that of the story of One, the history of medieval philosophy being that of the story of God, and the history of modern philosophy being that of the construction of the modern male subject. Descartes and his claim of rationality, Locke and his claim to liberty, the Enlightenment and its claim to knowledge, Hegel claiming progress, Marx claiming the deed—all shared in the construction of the modern gendered subject with his will to truth and right to freedom. In a modern world, the subject still has access to power, which includes the possibility to renounce it. This is represented by a right to control (some)one's body, a right to (some)one's means of existence, a right to speak, write, and hence vote and sign a contract. For the purpose of this text the accent will be on that particular political right that the individual of the modern world won for himself.

The main assumption of modern political theory is precisely an individual who, as a rational being, deserves to be free. The only way he may enter a community is by forming one of his own free will, therefore by contract, which turns out to be a sexual contract also.[6]

The theories of Hobbes, Locke, and Rousseau are based on those assumptions. The historical events of the English and in part the French and American revolutions revolve around the same aspiration, and the documents of the Act of Habeas Corpus, the Bill of Rights, and the Declaration of the Rights of Man and the Citizen certify those historic promises. Thus, the modern man came of age.

Parallel to this interest in dignity and freedom on which the natural right was founded was another interest—in righteousness and justice. That concern was the underpinning of social utopias from Plato to Thomas More to Marx, and the events, slogans, and documents of the October and in part the French revolutions testify to that. Yet in a brief sketch, one can see that both interests played a role in the creation of the individual agent who set the aim, making history and linear time.

The first-wave feminists, according to Kristeva, demanded that woman be recognized as an equal to man, as a rational human being, who among other things can enter a community only of her own free will, by contract. Liberal feminists, theoretically supported by Wollstonecraft, Mill, and others, argued for and supported the acquisition, in phases, of the right to education and work, one of the highlights being the enfranchisement of women in Western Europe and the United States.

At the same historical time in one part of Eastern Europe, women were also declared equal when their political maturity and the need for economic independence were proclaimed. Those, however, did not stem from the principle of freedom, which at that particular historical instance in the USSR was not stressed as much as the principle of justice, under which the equality of women was subsumed. These rights were theoretically supported by what was later known as Marxist/socialist feminism (Engels, Kollontai).

Kristeva regards socialism, along with Freudianism, as a doctrine that prepared the way for the second generation of feminists, which may well be true. But one may also interpret socialism as a corrective of liberal feminism. Although both liberal and Marxist/socialist feminism conceive of women's subjectivity within linear time, aim at women's inclusion into history, and see women as having both agency and power, there are significant differences between them. Marxist socialist feminism* includes women in history and awards them equality only as part of a system of "higher" priorities, such as class struggle. This is quite different from an autonomous struggle for equality, for recognition of oneself as a subject, and for freedom and political authorship. If freedom and recognition is to be won and not donated it must include a struggle and a risk of life, as has been ably elaborated by Marx's predecessor Hegel.

It is necessary to situate Yugoslav women within a historical context to understand how these distinctions apply to them. Prior to World War II women in Yugoslavia were generally restricted to the domestic sphere, and the society openly adhered to a patriarchal value system. The legislation that followed World War II granted women the right to vote, equal pay for equal work, a right to abortion, etc. Women in Yugoslavia thus entered history and linear time only on the basis of socialism. Currently we are facing the withdrawal of socialist ideology, which risks the withdrawal of everything socialism has brought with it.

In 1989, during this period of change and confusion, in a discussion of multi-party elections in Serbia at the eleventh Congress of the Serbian Communist Party a delegate made the following comment: "It [multiparty elections] would be as if I were to bring another husband to my wife, while I'm still alive!"[7] This

---

* Ed. This use of this term differs from that in the West.

unintentional overriding of the public/private dichotomy is only on the surface a story of the rejection of polygamy, since the underpinning is that the decision lies with one interested party only. The analogy includes the following points of comparison: a husband is likened to a party in power and a wife to a country, a social entity over which the party in question is exercising the said power. The latter (woman/country) may have a choice, but it can only be *given* by the former (man/party) in power. Therefore, the woman, like the social entity, is totally dependent. The woman and the country, or, to explicate one step further, the people of the country in question, are subjects only in the sense of being subjected to, of not having a will of her/their own. This presupposition reveals a strong "patriarchy."[8]

Yet 1990 brought many changes, among them multiparty elections, to all parts of Yugoslavia. As a result, a new assembly was constituted in each republic. Women were pushed to the very margins of public life.

Almost immediately after the multiparty elections in Serbia in 1990, an organization called the Women's Movement for Yugoslavia entered the public scene. Their main activity was the organization of mass gatherings of women in different cities under the main slogan "Yugoslavia, peace, and bread." Other slogans pointed to the "only" enemy of Yugoslavia and peace: "Down with Tudjman, Kučan . . ."; "Mesić out!; "Ante [Marković], you're a thief!" Women carried pictures of Milošević as a defender of peace. The demonstrations were covered by major TV stations and newspapers;[9] the organizers were received by Serbian government officials and Socialist Party leaders. In public offices in Belgrade and in factories women were encouraged to leave their work and take part in demonstrations. The photographs in the papers showed "the women in mink coats" (as they were referred to later) giving speeches to women in factory coats. The unofficial feminist organizations, whose demands and arguments had gained no public support before and especially during the election campaign, renounced the Women's Movement for Yugoslavia.

Similarly, almost analogously, in Croatia when the war operations had already started, an organization called the Rampart of Love formed, undoubtedly by concerned, "caring"[10] women, mothers in particular. Among other activities, they attempted to draw the attention of Europe by organizing visits and trips to plead their case. On returning from one of those trips, at a mass gathering organized for that purpose, they were welcomed by Franjo Tudjman. In response, they chanted slogans in his support.

The abovementioned examples of recent women's inclusion in political life—in historical, linear time—seem to lead to only one, closely controlled, result. At the end of this path, sadly enough, a quite recognizable image emerges of an ideal of a woman, proclaimed equal to men on masculine criteria, and therefore fighting like a man (!) for her nation.

To that effect the leading Serbian paper has started publishing a comic strip entitled *Kninja*.[11] One of the leading characters is Milica, a woman warrior with a traditional Serbian name, looking like a model, possessing the highest combat skills. She declares she "can do anything the men can" and the story proves her right. She is recognized as an equal, is almost allowed to enter historical linear time, and become a subject by subjecting herself to a patriarchal value system and a national (therefore "just") cause. The "nation" is an ideal convergence of a patriarchal and an egalitarian value system and as such serves as an intersection of a modern system and a traditional one defending traditional values in a modern way. This ideal began to materialize as women volunteered for the front.

Parallel to those intersections and inclusions, feminist groups, as participants in antiwar movements, are making an effort not to slip into that particular trap of historical inclusion. If successful, they would meet one of Kristeva's criteria for the second generation of feminists, namely, "the radical *refusal* of the subjective limitations imposed by this history's time."[12]

After the first feminist gathering in Yugoslavia feminist groups formed in Zagreb and Ljubljana. They engaged in many activities but were marginalized by the officials and supported only by likewise marginalized feminist theorists. These theorists met another criteria for the second generation of feminists according to Kristeva: "these women seek to give language to the intrasubjective and corporeal experiences left mute by culture in the past."[13]

In Yugoslavia thematizing the exclusion of women (as postmodernism suggests) is complex. In trying to disentangle this problem, what should be kept in mind are the differences between women theorists, women activists, unofficial and official women's groups, and the majority of women floating between proclaimed equality and a strong patriarchy.

The postmodern story of the "death of man" or the "death of the author" is the second part of a story that began with his birth, the event that marked modern times. The deconstruction of the subject, the question of difference, of the Other, and then the question of differences—all this was preceded by the construction of the subject. "The truth of the matter is: one cannot deconstruct the subjectivity one has never been fully granted."[14] In the West the suffragettes, the first generation of feminists, passed the tests of citizenship by winning political subjectivity within history and linear time. Only after that did the second generation aspire to tell the story of differences. There is a question of the order of things: Is it not more likely, even necessary, that the woman be first recognized as an equal, so that the equality (the equal quality, so to speak) of difference/s she will introduce into the postmodern world will never be questioned as to its/their value? Taking a shortcut by insisting on differences where equality has not been previously established as a self-understood assumption may have a boomerang effect, heading straight to the reinforcement of the patriarchal presumption of the inequality between man and woman.

The women in Yugoslavia did not learn the lesson in citizenship as a way of constructing political subjectivity. Instead, a thin layer of ideologically based egalitarianism was superimposed on a stable patriarchy. Time did make it grow thicker, especially at certain points, as at the level of legislation. Perhaps, given more time, women in Yugoslavia would have won political subjectivity, making use of the legislation that was to their advantage. History took another course. The imposed ideology started withdrawing; the egalitarian layer cracked and revealed an almost untouched patriarchy. What happened? Instead of upholding what they could make use of, what had nominally been guaranteed, women renounced ideology and egalitarianism, and in doing so renounced themselves and fell, with rare exceptions, into the nationalist trap. The Women's Movement for Yugoslavia and to a lesser extent the Rampart of Love are obvious examples of that process.

Sadly, on some occasions, the unofficial feminist groups also walked into the nationalist trap, perhaps in a roundabout way. The third gathering of the feminists of Yugoslavia in March 1990 was illustrative. The feminists from Ljubljana absolutely refused to form any kind of a movement at the Yugoslav level—it was out of the question, not even a loose umbrella organization, if it was under a "Yu" sign. The feminists from Zagreb did not agree among themselves whether or not to join. The feminists from Belgrade would have been consistent in their antinationalist position if they had labeled any nationalism as such. However, they were only critical of their own and refused to react to nationalism in other feminist groups. Ultimately, the feminist groups, by yielding to the calls of their respective nations, became just a part of the mainstream course of events. Women, with some exceptions, thus recognized and respected their national interests over women's issues.

A modern subject entails agency, a postmodern perspective retains resistance,[15] and both could benefit from bracketing some differences (national and ethnic, for example) so as not, in the long run, to do away with differences completely. The alternative is our present reality: the obliteration of all but national differences, of the differences among political options, generational attitudes, educational levels, and professional stands, and, consequently, between men and women. Was it hard to foresee that the national unification on a solid patriarchal ground and with its ideological pretext was the most dangerous unification, one that would annihilate all other differences? Do we not have historical experience of where national homogenization leads?

For women it was logical to draw conclusions of differences among themselves from recognizing their own difference. However, by putting ethnic and national differences forward in a Yugoslav context, women and feminists submitted to a much more unifying mode of existence, which suppressed all other differences in a passionate and exclusive way.

Notes

1. Julia Kristeva, "Women's Time," in *The Kristeva Reader*, ed. Toril Moi (New York: Columbia UP, 1986), p. 190.

2. Ibid., p. 188.

3. NDH (Nevavisna Drava Hrvatska) refers to the Independent State of Croatia, the World War II puppet state of the Third Reich.

4. Julia Kristeva, "Chinese Women," in *The Kristeva Reader*, p. 153.

5. Kristeva, "Women's Time," p. 192.

6. See C. Pateman, *The Sexual Contract* (Stanford: Stanford UP, 1988).

7. *Politika*, December 17, 1989, p. 4.

8. Sir R. Filmer, *Patriarch, or the Natural Powers of the Kings of England Asserted*, ed. P. Laslett (Oxford: Basil Blackwell, 1949).

9. *Nedjelja*, February 17, 1991, pp. 12–13; *Vreme*, February 11, 1991, pp. 33–35; *Borba*, February 9, 1991, p. 1; *Politika*, February 5, 1991, p. 1.

10. See N. Noddings, *Caring: A Feminist Approach to Ethics and Moral Education* (Berkeley: University of California Press, 1984).

11. *Kninja: Knights of the Serbian Krajina*, comic, *Politika*, September 1991.

12. Kristeva, "Women's Time," p. 195.

13. Ibid.

14. R. Braidotti, "Envy: or With Your Brains and My Looks," in Alice A. Jardine and P. Smith, eds., *Men in Feminism* (New York: Methuen, 1987), p. 237.

15. S. Hekman, *Gender and Knowledge* (Boston: Northeastern UP, 1990), p. 189.

13

Women in the German Democratic Republic and in the New Federal States: Looking Backward and Forward (Five Theses)

Hildegard Maria Nickel

I. Division of Labor Under State Socialism: Women's Work in the GDR

In all the developed industrial countries, labor markets are segmented according to gender. But we find a great deal of variety and flexibility when it comes to which labor is actually defined as female and allocated to women. The German Democratic Republic is a case in point. The sheer fact that women and men engage in different labor does not automatically imply discrimination or social inequality. However, where the social division of labor implies power relations between the genders, structures of domination and subjugation, and the division of forms of life and spheres of action, it becomes a constituent factor in patriarchal relations and a guarantor of their reproduction.

In the former GDR, there were three dimensions to the division of labor in this sense. The first concerned the vertical[1] and horizontal[2] differences in the gender division of labor in socialized work—that is, work outside the home. These reflected not only gender differences in the temporal, economic, social, and cultural resources at a person's disposal but also differential decision-making powers and positions in the power relations at work. This constituted the *structural gender hierarchy,* which structured the other two aspects I will describe.

The second aspect related to the particular way of ascribing responsibility for productive, or reproductive, tasks according to gender, or what we call *socialization,* which implies that there is a "natural" allocation of duties, responsibilities, and behavior patterns according to sex. This was the dimension whereby gender stereotypes were *subjectively* anchored in individuals. It concerned the internalization of the structural hierarchy in gender character.

Thirdly, the customary division of labor was structured through the everyday *practices* of men and women, habits associated with the reproduction of human life in both the public and the private spheres. This dimension of daily practice unquestioningly reproduced the gender hierarchy over and over again in the unintentional consequences of everyday activities.

Each one of these dimensions would merit its own analysis in relation to East German history. But the asymmetry of gender power was reflected in all three dimensions, with women enjoying a pervasive "natural" second-class status compared with men.

In the late 1980s, 91 percent of working-age women in the GDR were engaged in paid employment, and 87 percent of these had completed some kind of vocational training. These are signs of equal rights and self-determination for women, but they are also expressions of ideology and distortion. "Hard" statistical facts disguised, concealed, even mystified the everyday disadvantages and discriminations with which women were confronted. This contradiction expresses the totally ambivalent normalization of girls and women of the former GDR.

On the one hand, "women's work" in the GDR meant the pursuit of a career, or at least paid employment. Women had not only the right but, as a rule, the duty to hold a job.[3] On the other hand, women's work meant an unquestioning, self-evident, "natural" responsibility for children, family, and housework. Indeed, it was the ability to have children that "essentially" defined the working woman and mother.[4] Women's work in the GDR was structured not merely by these two sets of demands but by their very "essence" East German women were always responsible for reproduction. In this respect the fabric of female life was clearly distinguished from that of male life. Family life was not insignificant for East German men; in fact, it supplied a vital, if not irreplaceable, framework for male regeneration.[5] But it rarely meant as much work for men as it did for women. Just as the family clearly diminished the appeal of female labor power as a commodity in the market economy, so it boosted the value of male labor power and denied equality of opportunity to the sexes in the labor market. As German unification proceeds, women start with a handicap in organizing a life oriented toward employment.

II. Career choices: Feeding into an Occupational and Economic Structure Founded on Polarized Genders

Prior to unification, fifteen- to sixteen-year-olds gained their first work experience both from vacation jobs and from "Productive Labor," a compulsory school subject that included practical industrial classes such as "shop." This, coupled with what they learned from home, gave them a fairly realistic idea of their future employment. They knew what choices were open to them, and they were also familiar with the narrow limitations of a carefully balanced vocational training system planned by the state.

Research by educational sociologists showed for years that girls performed just as well as boys in shop classes, and that their grades were at least as good. Girls also took vacation jobs as often as boys. However, there was a clear gender distinction in the type of vacation work they did: boys favored industry, while girls chose educational jobs or the retail trade. There were significant differentiations learned from an "invisible hand" with a "secret syllabus" on gender specialization, and these culminated in gender-specific career hopes and choices. As far as formal qualifications were concerned, girls and boys alike were eager to complete a sound vocational training. But their choice of career took them into separate sectors of the economy and occupational categories. When graduates chose their jobs, they exhibited a clear gender polarization that was intensively fostered in the GDR from the late 1960s onward, with over 60 percent of girls who left school in 1987 opting for the same 16 skilled jobs out of 259 possible jobs.[6]

Several of these jobs were virtually exclusively women's: stenotypist, specialized salesperson in economics and finance, skilled worker in textiles. These fields have in common a low wage. Yet some such jobs—hairdresser or financial clerk—were regarded as the "dream career" for girls. As a result, there was a greater demand for these positions than there were jobs. In about twenty-three other skilled jobs, such as precision mechanic and automated plant operator, about 50 percent of those hired were female. There were about forty-eight jobs for which girls made up only 1 to 5 percent of apprentices, including plumber, fitter, and control panel operative. Women held 40 percent of the better-paid jobs, but then only in specific spheres, such as textile and clothing industries and electronics and electrotechnical industries.

These gender patterns of career choice, which also implied entry into a specific context for action with all its related conditions (such as income), was rooted not so much in individual likes and dislikes as in the objective structures of the GDR economy. The allocation of training places was centrally planned, with the majority of girls earmarked from the outset for those jobs in which there was already a high percentage of women, as in the nonproductive sector. This meant that the girls had to fight harder for lucrative positions and were often compelled to fall back on "contingency" or "provisional" solutions. In other words, they trained for a job knowing all the time that they would not get it once they had qualified.[7] Companies preferred males as applicants and as apprentices for technical occupations important to the future of the enterprise. They gave several reasons for this: a high dropout rate among women (the result of social policies with the one-sided goal of enabling women to combine motherhood with employment, rather than offering incentives for responsible parenthood that would also encourage men to take an active role in parenting); conditions and tasks with physical demands ill-suited to women; high rates of work force fluctuation; inadequate technical interest and motivation among girls; and lack of appropriate social facilities for women at their place of work.[8]

From 1975 on there was a particular decline in jobs for girls at the core of technical work: maintenance mechanics for data processing and office machines (from 30.1 percent in 1975 to 18.4 percent in 1987), skilled electronics workers (from 49.7 percent to 20.1 percent), electricians (from 7.9 percent to 3.7 percent), control panel operatives (from 25.9 percent to 8.4 percent). Meanwhile, the proportion of women on the periphery and in operations sectors increased: silicon chip manufacturing, data processing operatives[9] (73.5 percent in 1988), and chemical manufacturing operatives (79.1 percent).

College and university entry reflected a similar polarization. Women constituted 96 percent of new technical college entrants who, after ten years of schooling, were admitted to sources in health (nurse, paramedical technician, physiotherapist), education (nursery worker, day-care or primary school teacher) or the arts. Eighty-two percent of technical college students enrolled in full-time courses were women.[10]

At the university, women were a majority in 1989 in the following subjects:[11]

Economics	66.7%
Education	73.0%
Language, Literature	62.2%
Medicine	55.2%

By comparison, the following statistics show where women were least represented among university entrants in 1989:

Technical sciences	25.3%
Culture, Art, Sport	41.7%
Math, Natural Science	46.0%
Philosophy, Law, Political Science	39.8%

In all the disciplines, almost half the academic staff are women, but in none of the departments does the percentage of women lecturers, professors, or heads of institutes and departments exceed 1 percent. In the whole college and university system women account for between 2 and 3 percent of those at the highest levels—presidents, deans, department heads.

Although the training gap between men and women had been eliminated, there remained important social inequalities and unequal power relations between the sexes. Not all jobs or branches of work were open to men and women equally. Work was gender-defined; women continued to do the reproductive and service work both in paid employment and in the family. This patriarchal equal-rights policy, so deeply rooted in the social democratic and communist labor movements, was not only adopted wholesale by the SED (Sozialistische Einheitspartei Deutschland—Socialist Unity Party, the GDR Communist Party) but was enforced ideologically and practically as well. It was the structural condition for the continuing social inequality between men and women, in spite of the apparently irreversible improvement of women's position in the GDR. While there is no doubt that GDR family and social policy was immeasurably better disposed toward women, at least on the rudimentary level, than the current legislation of the united Germany,[12] it was based on paternalistic and patriarchal premises. Father State "made moms happy" primarily by ensuring that women could give birth in security and combine motherhood with employment. In the context of this loudly proclaimed gender equality it was possible for men to ignore the social inequalities and power relations arising from their adherence to the traditional division of labor between men and women. Even more disturbing, men were almost entirely relieved of their responsibilities as fathers and husbands. They no longer had many duties toward the younger generation or toward the mothers of their children.[13]

In the new market economy, this patriarchal equal-rights policy is now exerting a substantial structural influence. Female labor, even if equal or superior in terms of skill,[14] is at a disadvantage, if not excluded, from a labor market with huge regional imbalances, demanding the ultimate in mobility and flexibility. East German women have comparatively poor chances of tackling the situation, because 90 percent of them are mothers and about 30 percent of these are raising children on their own.

III. Domestic Harmony is Women's Business

Even in the GDR, paid work did not suffice to cater to society's reproductive needs; it had to be supplemented by individual reproductive labor in the family. Although public facilities and services were visibly expanded in the later years,[15] housework was the inevitable sister of paid employment. Despite a growth in household technology, the time invested in housework has remained more or less constant over the last twenty-five years.[16] The headache of combining paid employment with individual reproductive labor has been solved in the traditional manner: three-quarters of it was performed by women (most of whom held full-time jobs).[17] Women were also responsible for the domestic climate, an achievement difficult to quantify in terms of hours. At least a quarter of women in paid employment worked part-time, but the demand for part-time jobs and more flexible working hours was far higher.[18] Regardless of a woman's qualifications or social standing, the family division of labor followed a certain gender-related pattern: women were usually responsible for the caring aspects, routine elements, and tasks that tied them to the family within a certain time or space; men's tasks tended to be instrumental and object-related, tying the man physically to the home with less regularity—tasks such as repairing the car. Although nearly all women worked, men were usually the "main breadwinners," and for all the material independence of working women in the GDR, fathers made a greater contribution than mothers to the family budget. This was reproduced as a stereotype in the values and attitudes of teenagers: boys were keener than girls to find a job with very good pay. Girls could "afford" in this situation to attach less importance to pay and more to finding a job that catered to their "taste" or "interest."

Given this particular gender division of labor (a structural effect of the social division of labor between the sexes), opportunities, resources, and dependencies have again and again been distributed unequally. The old patriarchal structures of social labor are reproduced, as is demonstrated by comparing how men and women spend their time,[19] how much they earn,[20] what rung they occupy on the social ladder,[21] their share of leadership positions, and the content of their employment. Women (girls) developed subjective structures (attitudes, skills) that made their objective dilemma tolerable. They isolated themselves from certain spheres of career development.

It has been demonstrated often enough that paid labor and family labor each observe their own distinct laws and internal logic. In a patriarchal social construction, women's particular skills and orientations place them again and again at a disadvantage in the world of employment. In the GDR, women displayed "poor assertion skills, fear of responsibility, sometimes even a commitment to evading success; they tend to seek a certain 'personalization' of their work situation, i.e., their job satisfaction is determined by social considerations (opportunities for communication, company atmosphere, direct personal acknowledgment) rather than by so-called 'objective' conditions (income, leverage in collective bargaining, promotion prospects). Women experience their occupational labor in terms of content and task-related considerations rather than in terms of relevance to promotion. In their subjective value hierarchy they balance career against family, and career does not necessarily or continually emerge victorious."[22]

Marx says in *Das Kapital*: "As the molder of use values, as useful work, labor is . . . a very condition of human existence whatever form society assumes, a natural necessity which mediates the exchange of man and nature as human life."[23] In this sense, as "useful work," women's work is a component of society's reproduction, both when it is performed within the family, privately, individually, and when it takes the form of paid employment. It is labor that molds (exchange) value, however, by producing commodities, so that the use-value-oriented service work to which women are largely bound appears inferior from the start. It is therefore poorly paid, if not taken for granted, as in the case of domestic labor, as the "natural" gift of loving moms.[24]

IV. A Case in Point: The State Insurance Company[25]

In 1989, the great majority of people working in the insurance industry in the GDR were still women. Of the 851 employees in one sample, 688, or about 80 percent, were women. Of course, the gender-skewed pyramid applied here, too: top management was almost exclusively male. Now that the firm Allianz has bought up the former state monopoly, it is evident that these proportions will shift further against women. The trend was set even before the political changes: women not only lack assertive strategies when their interests are under attack, but they are also starting with a handicap in the extremely harsh tussle for survival.

An analysis of the qualification structure in 1989 showed that 8 percent of insurance employees had completed university, 14 percent technical college, and 63 percent training at a skilled worker's level. A majority came to insurance from other, often entirely different, occupations: dressmakers, shop assistants, laboratory technicians, nursery attendants or day-care workers, factory workers, hospital nurses, or waitresses. They came from jobs that, according to the women themselves, were hard to reconcile with family responsibilities. Sometimes they had been working shifts or had earned even less than they were paid by the insurance company.

One peculiar feature of the service, or clerical work, performed in this company was that it was not linked to a particular qualification, and quite possibly could not have been taught primarily by means of a training course. Apart from a certain amount of specialist knowledge acquired with relative ease, it called above all for experience of a fairly general nature, referred to as "social skills." Employees had to form judgments by pulling together diverse pieces of information, solve problems, and—in most cases—carry out routine tasks that were hardly demanding mentally. The women needed communicative skills. They had to be reassuring and friendly. This meant being sensitive to the needs and wishes of the customer, and so interpretative skills were also needed. And these employees were expected to look "neat and pretty" for their clients. The state insurance company, in other words, drew not only on a specialized skill learned relatively quickly, but also on Everywoman's training, that social competence seemingly acquired quite casually in the course of female life. Now, in the market economy, the demands are changing, requiring the *expert,* on duty round the clock for the sake of his client, highly specialized, brimming with experience and clever tricks in matters of money, competent in the field, assertive, dynamic, athletic: in short, male.

Joining the market economy seems to have lent an enormous impetus to those lines of differentiation that had already emerged and been reinforced by the introduction of computers in the offices.[26] The fear is that women will lose out even in those sectors where they had carved out a firm niche for themselves over the last forty years.[27]

V. In the Lap of the Family: Socialization

The GDR was famed for the extent of its child care. In 1989, 80.2 percent of children up until three years old attended nurseries, along with 95.1 percent of three- to six-year-olds. Of schoolchildren in the first four years, 81.2 percent stayed on for afterschool care.

Although ideologically praised, no study was done of the socialization effects of this institutionalization of child care on the younger generation. Before the "Wende" (the political changes of 1989), the fact that extensive day care did not necessarily mean high-quality care was passed over in silence. At present, however, we are witnessing a complete reversal in the ideological climate. Social child-care facilities are now being redefined in a blanket fashion as a contingency arrangement or as an aid to the working mothers, while childrearing within the family with traditional maternal responsibility is being automatically understood as necessary for the healthy child's development, even by the mothers affected.[28]

The younger generation in eastern Germany is distinguished from its counterparts in the West, in that socialization took place amidst the distinctive tensions between private and public childrearing, between family and school. The socialization process was a balancing act between the family "niche" and formalized public education, which held very different and even contradictory values. This integration of fragmented structures in the heads of growing youngsters led to the schizophrenia of living with two belief systems, one official and one private. It also meant that the younger generation of East Germans was aware of these discrepancies and was able to develop a pragmatic detachment from official "socialist" values—in fact to any kind of official pronouncement. They discovered mechanisms for evading the onslaught of ideological infiltration.

By the mid-1980s, there was a different kind of teenager in the schools than had attended in the middle or late 1970s, even if this escaped the attention of the Education Ministry.[29] The new youth were distinguished particularly by their different values. They were more openly dedicated to individualist forms of happiness and to the kind of pragmatism that everyday life in the GDR had generated as a survival strategy. Pupils and young people in general were less interested in the "great" social values than in health, physical fitness, and a happy family life. Over 80 percent of the students questioned rated these as very important life goals while only 7 percent rated political commitment equally important. They already had practical experience of the fact that "good connections" were essential under state socialism, certainly more reliable than an all-round education or personal achievement. This generation also staked much less on the satisfaction of fulfilling employment.

Eighty percent of the students questioned in the mid-1980s had discovered that one did not say what one really thought in school without suffering reprisals of one kind or another, and half of them said that their own experience clearly contradicted the theories taught in school, especially in the social sciences. The teachers were often aware of this contradiction, but their syllabus prevented them from taking seriously the authentic knowledge of socialist reality in the GDR that their students had gained.

Everyday experience and the theories propounded in school existed side by side without bearing on one another. The conflict was not discussed at school. On the contrary, it was pushed outside into semi- or unofficial realms: private conversations between pupil and teacher or parent and teacher, the twinkle in a teacher's eye that communicated a meaning not contained in the syllabus. A symbolism rich in nuance sometimes imparted to the pupils a subtext beneath the code of official rhetoric.

As a rule, school life was determined by formalism and routine, an ignorance of students' knowledge, and a classroom layout with the teacher up front and in charge. Bureaucratic regulations governed relations between students and teachers. The "guardian" state was thus able to extend its long arm into the tissue of school life, waving pupils into the dunce's corner, deprived of rights, dependent, subordinate—a position they had long since ceased to accept without resistance. For many, the family offered a secure alternative. It was the (only) counter-structure.

In spite of its high divorce rate, the GDR was a closed, traditionalist society with a strong family orientation. The family became a symbol of a political culture without a public face. East Germans are very attached to the "holy bonds" of the family.

VI. Segmenting the Labor Market: Mental Ruptures and Their Ambivalent Consequences

The change of system, or the process of integrating East German society into the market economy of what used to be West Germany, poses demands of a completely new type. Suddenly, that part of Germany which for forty years had a central steering mechanism permeated by dependability and run by means of paternalistic provision, is being subjected to the institutional pressures of a labor market that functions according to the laws of a capitalist economy. Whereas institutional pressure to adapt is being applied rapidly and radically, everyday behavior and consciousness will change only slowly and gradually. It is hard to imagine the mental acrobatics that those concerned must undergo each day as old institutions collapse or are fundamentally reorganized. It is impossible to predict definitively to what extent cultural values of benefit to women can be maintained under these conditions, notably women's right to paid employment. No doubt there will be a diffusion of lifestyles and habit formation in the unified Germany, but these will be structured by an imbalanced hegemony. We are more likely to witness a shift toward the longstanding federal German criteria than pressure to adapt in the opposite direction, although this will change somewhat once the lack of women's movements "from below" has been overcome in the new federal states. This is especially true because the labor power of East German women is not without its market appeal, as certain sectors have demonstrated—social services, health, commerce.

The new demands provoke fear, and not only among women, not least because nobody quite knows where they are leading. In place of *curricula vitae* founded on a centralized state will be "the individualized achievement principle with all its pressures to stage manage."[30] Individuals have to "clear themselves a path through the thicket of options, each concealing its own coercions, and paste together a personal biography."[31] The great thrust of modernization is taking place as a mass "biographical rupture"[32] that affects generations and genders variously, splitting and realigning them, certainly rechanneling the traditional lines of social inequality (classes, social strata). One possibility is that institutionalized biographies might, in this context, acquire new attributes of personal choice and self-determination. In that case, modernization would mean acquiring a greater plurality of individual scope for action, a differentiation of lifestyles, and an individualization of life stories. There are hurdles, however, in the structural pressures, such as labor market trends, social policies, and formalized qualifications for careers. These will result in countercurrents, limiting individual options and even marginalizing certain social groups. In this case, modernization will mean developing strategies to compromise with an increasingly narrow structural framework more strictly oriented to principles of efficiency. It will mean experiencing a social division of opportunity and public resources (economic, political, cultural, and social). There is much evidence that the dominant trend will be toward greater plurality and individualization of options. For East Germans, this trend could assert itself relatively unhampered because—it is my thesis—administrative socialism has already laid the structural and mental foundations.

Why? Regardless of all the official propaganda, a specific value paradigm had emerged by the late 1970s or early 1980s: the private "niche" rather than work for the public good; personal and family well-being rather than political commitment. What might that mean for the future of female paid employment and gender relations in the new Germany? To begin with, we must recognize the ambivalent structural pressures that mold mentalities in this respect, and we must take them seriously. On the one hand, the labor market is growing narrower for women; on the other hand, there is an existential need to ensure a livelihood. Domestic "labors of love" are expected and can gratify, while competition is increasing at work. Certificates of qualification have been devalued by the millions, while "motherhood" and "femininity" are being upgraded. Nurseries and day care are closing down as East German mothers suffer from a latent bad conscience about their children.

Ruptures in women's strategies are inevitable. The ambivalence on which their objectives are based is all too obvious. True, only 3 percent of East German women can imagine being "only a housewife," but 46 percent envisage a temporary employment break and then a return to their careers after a period spent looking after small children: the "three-phase model,"[33] which casts women into the occupational side streets. It would be easy to interpret this process as a conservative relapse. It is a model for coping with the devaluation of female employment and the threat of job loss. It is also an element in the generation conflict. Above all, this process infects daughters seeking "emancipation" from their mothers, all too often sapped by patriarchal equal rights. The daughters—and in this they would seem to agree with the sons—are hoping for a different life they assume will be easier, and to achieve it they are resorting to traditional gender patterns. Paid employment is one factor in their lives, but by no means the only one.

Notes

1. This refers to the career pyramid: the higher a post, the less it is likely to be occupied by a woman. See *Frauenreport 90* (Berlin: Die Wirtschaft, 1990), pp. 93–96.

2. This refers to gender distribution in the various sectors of the economy and specific occupations. Ibid., pp. 37ff.

3. Whatever other reasons a woman may have had for taking paid employment, it was essential to family livelihood. Although women were disadvantaged by the wage and salary structure, earning about 25 to 30 percent less than men, the men's income was in itself too small to keep a family. Besides, about 30 percent of women had no partner and were wholly dependent on their own earnings.

4. U. Scheurer, "Der Preis für einig Vaterland . . ." *Streit* (March 1990).

5. This is reflected, for example, in the fact that divorced men usually married again quickly or if married, did not relinquish a firm relationship until the next had already been established.

6. After ten years of compulsory education, graduates in the GDR could choose to train for any of the 289 skilled jobs, 30 of which were closed to women by law.

7. Every graduate had to enter training.

8. Taken from a study on the career orientation of girls and women under conditions of intensification, published by the Zentralinstitut für Berufsbildung (1989).

9. It may be of interest that in German, these jobs are designated "skilled worker for . . ." in the masculine form, even if almost 100 percent of those concerned are female, as in the case of typists.

10. Although these courses took longer than skilled worker training (four years as opposed to two), subsequent income was relatively low. These courses offered little attraction to men, whereas for women they were often the only alternative to the low-paid skilled jobs open to them.

11. *Frauenreport 1990*, p. 47.

12. Scheuer.

13. It is no accident that 20,000 fathers were missing by late 1989, having gone into hiding in western Germany in order to escape their maintenance commitments.

14. The generation, now about forty years old, has nominally overcome the gap in education and skills between men and women. In spite of this, women's prospects in the labor market are worse than those of men with similar or poorer qualifications. See S. Schenk, "Neue Chancen und Risiken für Frauenerwerbsarbeit auf dem Berliner Arbeitsmarkt in den 90er Jahren," special report commissioned by the Equality Officer, East Berlin Council, October 1990.

15. One example of this trend is that 94 percent of children aged 3 to 6 went to day care, and 73 percent of those under three went to nurseries.

16. The GDR's Institute of Market Research assumed forty-five to forty-seven hours per week for an average family. Other sociological studies placed their estimate at about thirty-eight hours per week (see also *Frauenreport 1990*).

17. An average working week was forty-three and three-quarters hours. Mothers of two children under sixteen in full-time jobs worked forty hours on full wages.

18. Permission had to be granted for part-time work, and was only granted on certain grounds. In many jobs or sectors it simply was not possible.

19. On average women had six hours a week less free time than men.

20. The average monthly income of women is about 25 to 30 percent lower than that of men (see *Frauenreport 90*).

21. The higher the rung, the smaller the percentage of women. In 1989 the upper echelons of politics were occupied as follows:

    Politbureau and SED Secretariat: 26 m, 2 w;
    SED Central Committee: 148 m, 16 w;
    Central Committee candidates: 77 m, 10 w;
    Government ministers: 25 m, 3 w.

22. E. Beck-Gernsheim, "Männerrolle-Frauenrolle-und was steckt dahinter?" *Geschlechtertrolle und Arbeitsteilung,* ed. R. Eckert (Munich: 1979), p. 181.

23. Karl Marx, Marx-Engels Werke, vol. 23 (Berlin: Dietz Verlag, 1972), p. 57.

24. March 8, International Women's Day, was a symptom of the way women's labor was understood in the GDR. It increasingly degraded into a kind of Mother's Day.

25. This case study is drawn from a survey carried out by the Humboldt University's Sociology Institute in Berlin at the end of the 1980s. For more details see Kreher and Hildegard Maria Nickel, "Anfänge moderner Informations—und Kommunikationstechnik im Versicherungswesen . . ." in *Research Report: Die Soziale Realität der Einführung neuer Technologien—Vier Fallstudien in Berliner Betrieben,* Sociology Institute, Humboldt University, Berlin, 1988; Nickel and Schenk, "Angestellteninteressen und Partizipation," in *Research Report: Computerisierung der Büros . . .,* Sociology Institute, Humboldt University, Berlin, 1989.

26. Ibid.

27. In September 1989, before the political changes, there were almost 9.2 million people in the East German work force, about 4.2 million of them women. In November 1990 there were still about 8 million registered as working. In other words, the employment rate dropped by about 1.2 million in absolute terms. Of these 1.2 million, only 50 percent were registered as jobless; about 25 percent had left the work force (e.g., taken early retirement), while 25 percent had left the former GDR. Whereas women were proportionately represented among the unemployed in mid-1990, by June 1992 they accounted for 63.6 percent of the registered jobless. 10 percent of men were unemployed, compared with 18.9 percent of women.

28. INFAS survey, "Frauen in den neuen Bundesländern" (Women in the New Federal States), October 1990.

29. The empirical findings described here are taken from major sociological studies carried out between 1975 and 1986 by the GDR's Academy of Educational Sciences. I worked on these projects from 1977 to 1987. Use is also made of the following Research Reports drawn up by the Academy's Education Sociology Department: "Zur Lebensweise älterer Schüller," Berlin, March 1978, vols. 1–3 (unpublished

ms.); "Lebensbedingungen und Lebensweise von Schuljugendlichen, mit einem partiellen Vergleich zu Lehrlingen," Berlin, October 1980 (unpublished ms.); "Soziale Erfahrungen der Schuljugend in ihrer Bedeutung für deren Bewusstseinsentwicklung und Erziehung," Berlin, October 1983 (unpublished ms.).

30. U. Beck, "Ein Deutschland der Ungleichzeitigkeiten," *Die Tagezeitung*, December 24, 1990, East German edition.

31. Ibid.

32. Ibid.

33. "Frauen in den neuen Bundesländern."

14

The Women's Question as a Democratic Question: In Search of Civil Society

Tatiana Böhm

The revolutionary changes in Eastern and Middle Europe would not have been possible without the widespread participation of women. As different as the opposition movements were in the individual countries, the central demands that mobilized millions of people were for democratization and the guarantee of human rights. Yet the relationship between the gender question and human rights was virtually ignored.

In the former German Democratic Republic (GDR), an explicit women's movement arose in fall 1989, and an attempt was made to illustrate women's political demands as questions of human rights. The essential starting point of the newly developed women's movement was the critique of the women's policy of the old Socialist Unity Party (SED)[1] government. Women's issues were brought into the public sphere not only as problems of a particular group but as a general social problem arising out of domination. There was also an attempt to articulate a concept of political participation outside the patriarchal model of representation. The other new political organizations hardly addressed the role of women in their organization, or viewed women's issues as issues of human rights.

I. Rupture of Myths: A Critique of the Traditional GDR Women's Policy

Women's policy in the GDR was a showpiece of the "successful state" that had "solved the woman question." The high level of women in the work force and women's high level of job qualifications were uttered over and over again like a mantra. If formal equal rights and the social policy of combining motherhood and work was a model of integration long accepted by women, it was nevertheless a model that in the long run *prevented* the emancipation of women, questioning neither the traditional structural division of work at home and in the workplace nor the question of domination. The power relationship between the sexes was a taboo topic. Social differences were thought to require only individual solutions. The price paid for this was the almost complete exclusion of women from the central decision-making process in the economy, politics, and academia. This patriarchal construction of a politics of equal rights led to the so-called "natural" second-class status of women. Moreover, this administrative equal-rights policy was organized for—not by—women, reinforcing the myth of equality for many women and blinding them to their real disadvantages. Economic independence, however important, did not change the fact that over the last twenty years women were treated primarily as objects; no one was interested in them as subjects in complex life conditions, but only as labor power, bearers of functions, and or mothers. The dependence on "father state," the taboo on any discussion of the real problems, blocked the development of a critical consciousness about gender issues.

The Independent Women's Association (Unabhängige Frauen Verband-UFV), formed in fall 1989, focused its criticism on these points by turning away from the state-imposed policy on women. When the process of radical political transformation began at the same time, that heretofore unspoken critique turned into an outspoken protest by active political women. The many different women's groups that had formed since the beginning of the 1980s had already discussed urgent domestic questions under the protection of the church and in each other's homes. The critiques made by these groups were far-reaching, differing from the discussion in other oppositional groups by focusing on the equal-rights policy of the SED party-state without thereby ignoring the themes of ecology and peace.

The political demands of the suddenly visible women's movement of the GDR can best be described by their demand for political participation. The other oppositional groups either did not include the women's question as part of their demands for a democratic public sphere and a guarantee of human rights, or did so only in very rudimentary form. The women's groups focused on this point, making public the question, "Geht die Erneuerung an den Frauen vorbei?" ("Is the renewal bypassing women?")[2] The women researchers in the groups raised the theoretical question of whether society had presented a false picture of the situation of women, ignoring that women had been excluded from the spheres of decision making and from state and political power. They argued that a real renewal and democratic reform could succeed only by taking seriously the interests of the female half of society.

II. The Nearness to Things: Political Involvement and the Question of Autonomy

The surge of protests and the thrust of mobilization in fall 1989 expressed itself in demonstrations demanding democracy, freedom of the press, freedom to travel and of association, the elimination of the power monopoly of the SED, free elections, and a change in the constitution. The women's question, as a general social democratic question, seemed to have a chance only in the presence of a corresponding women's movement.

The UFV, at this point the only representative of an autonomous women's movement, focused on such issues. An essential problem was that the women's movement faced the difficult and almost completely irreconcilable job of developing both an autonomous grass-roots democratic structure and implementing political demands for a fundamental change in gender relations. With the opening of the borders on November 9, 1989, a speedy German unification became the central question, but this fact, obvious today, wasn't transparent then.

Many of the issues that had been the focus of the West German women's movement had a different and complex meaning in the East. In the turbulent times of fall 1989, central questions such as the important relationship between equality and autonomy were not considered; instead these were regarded as two distinct moments in an ongoing process of democratization. For the UFV democratization meant not only the creation of rule by law and the division of power but also the transformation of the political structures and the hierarchy of gender relations. At the head of UFV's list of demands were calls for quotas and affirmative action in all spheres of society, as the only neutral means of breaking down the privilege of men and the second-class status of women. A recommendation was made for the creation of a Ministry for Equality of Women, which would evaluate all laws, measures, and orders from the perspective of the interests of women and develop programs to advance women. "Quotas" meant concretely that qualified women should hold half of all positions, including positions of power. At the same time the UFV demanded a fundamental change in the division of labor in the private sphere of the family. This meant creating legal regulations to which women with access to high positions in politics and the economy would give priority. The Office of Equality for Women had the responsibility to eliminate discrimination against women and to set up affirmative action programs for women. That body was to have veto power against laws or measures unfriendly to women. Analogously, networks between Offices for the Equality of Women were to be developed on a regional and local level. There were to be Officers for the Equality of Women in workplaces and offices, and appropriate facilities for them were to be made available.

Thus, the UFV made use of the experiences of Western European women. Yet the model was not so much West Germany as the Swedish, something almost completely forgotten after unification. The possibilities for intervention, the right to take the initiative, and the right to veto were constituted as fundamentally broader than what had existed in the West German version of this office. By these measures the women's movement hoped to make their demands operative and change gender power structures through political interventions that would strengthen and better control the ban on discrimination. Initiatives for the equality of women would be made a primary state responsibility. To bring these demands into the public sphere and to have a chance to implement them, the women's movement had to constitute itself as an autonomous and independent movement. Gender issues had never been understood by the other opposition groups as issues of democratic theory and political power.

One important reason for an independent women's movement was women's experience of the patriarchal structures of the other opposition groups. For example, the opposition civil rights group Neues Forum (New Forum) rejected quotas both at the level of political demands and within the group. For that reason, at the end of 1989 many women in Leipzig left Neues Forum. Women also had to organize themselves in order to recognize their own problems and articulate them. They had to represent their own interests and develop the relevant strategies and tactics to gain more democratic rights and political and social influence, and to demolish economic prejudices. The autonomous women's movement of fall 1989 put in question not only the totalitarian socialist structures of domination but also the patriarchal mechanisms of power.

The previous system had hindered the creation of a separate women's culture. Women's projects as forms of an oppositional feminist counterculture were regarded as antistate and were prevented through repression. Violence against women was not thematized and was kept under wraps. The closed society of the GDR had prevented a women's public sphere as well as women's projects, but a far reaching need was clear. When it became possible many women's centers, cafés, women's houses, and self-help groups were founded, alongside newspapers such as *Ypsilon* and *Zauenreiterin*. Within a very short time there was a multitude of projects and grass-roots activities. The radical political demands of the women's movement were a presupposition for the development of these projects in so short a time. The women's projects themselves created a public sphere that affected political activity.

III. The Round Table: A School for Democracy

With its founding as a political movement, the women's movement raised its demand to take part, as an independent citizen's movement, in the dealings between the opposition and the government. The model of the Round Table, developed by the Polish opposition, required equal representation of both the opposition and established parties and power groups. This model was installed in practically every Eastern and Central European country in the time between the collapse of the power structures and the holding of free democratic elections. In the GDR the model of the Round Table was particularly characteristic in that it was adopted not only at the national level but at the district and the smallest neighborhood level. The reason for this was the massive election fraud in the local elections of May 1989, the collapse of the old system, and, most centrally, the democratic demand for participation at all levels by the citizens' movements and the newly founded parties. These Round Tables changed from mere means of control of the government to organs of political decision making. No law made by the nondemocratically elected Parliament became effective without the agreement of the Round Table.

In its first meeting on December 7, 1989, the Round Table demanded an accounting of the situation in the country from the government. Decisive laws such as the election law and the law about parties were initiated and defined by the Round Table. As the Modrow government (the GDR Government headed by Hans Modrow in 1989–90) went into deep crisis in January 1990, governability only became possible because each opposition movement and party placed one minister into the government. Among these seven ministers without portfolio was only one woman, the representative of the UFV. Without this participation of the ministers from the Round Table the transition and free elections would not have been possible.

Among the main themes of the Round Table was the dissolution of the State Security Service (*Stasi*), the discussion of a new democratic constitution, and monetary, economic, and social unification. Social unification was first made a theme by the UFV. The representatives of the UFV were responsible for a Social Charter which the Round Table unanimously adopted on March 5, 1990, at its fifteenth session, and which was to lay the foundations for the reform process at the sociopolitical level. In the process of unification, sociopolitical reform had been almost completely forgotten, which proved a negative sign for what would happen to women after the unification.

Very importantly, the Round Table was the decisive school for democracy, a democratic participatory model that was necessary not only for the transitional period but for the future, especially in regard to ecological and human rights problems. The Round Tables were no substitute for a parliamentary form of democracy, but constituted an elaboration of it.

In the time between December 1989 and March/May 1990, all the relevant political groups and parties, including the political movements who were important in bringing about the transformation, were represented in the Round Table. The domination of the Party was broken. In the central Round Table there were thirty-eight voting members.

Of all the citizens' movements, the women's movement had the most difficulty taking part in the Round Table. In the preparatory discussions for the Round Table women were not represented, but by demonstrating in front of the building in which the Round Table was meeting and gaining the support of the other citizens' movements, they won entry. In order to retain the equivalence of seats between the opposition and the established parties, the old unions got a seat at the Round Table along with the women's movement.

This participation of women succeeded only in the ex-GDR, a fact that structured the Round Table and opened another democratic dimension. A place at the central Round Table made it possible for women, if only briefly, to have the possibility of political influence, as in the Social Charter and the draft constitution. The old parties and organizations, but also the new parties and citizens movements, could no longer ignore women's issues. These issues and the gender dimension of power now received enormous publicity. Men had to listen to women and engage in substantive arguments with them.[3]

The perspective of the Round Table was fundamentally different than the authoritarian power structure of the old system, but was also different from a representative parliamentary model. The Round Table was marked by an orientation toward consensus that overrode the power orientation,[4] and in addition there were no constant voting alliances. There were majority decisions, but the minority could clearly present their position by minority votes. The orientation to consensus, to making a common decision, required giving reasons for the decision. This made possible the development of a culture of discussion, an ideology-free discourse in which those confronted, politicians and experts, had to come to a decision in public and stand ready to correct decisions. This opened up new perspectives on democracy.

The working out of the election law shows the democratic preparedness of the Round Table. In its first version, the election of parties was permitted, but not of citizens' movements. Both the old and the new parties had voted against the citizens' movements, enhancing their chances of election at the movements' cost. After protest in the public sphere and qualified minority votes, there was a renewed discussion and attention to the statements of experts. The Round Table was in a position to revise its own decisions. It was marked by a democratic orientation, but one with a difference. The participation, the principle of broad consensus, the possibility of revision and correction of decisions, the broad degree of openness and the rejection of centralized decision making were all principles marked by a strong feminist consciousness.

IV. Women's Rights Are Human Rights

The Round Table set itself the task of working out a new constitution. The years-long lack of democracy and violations of human rights prompted opposition groups to focus on constitutional questions, such as how to incorporate human rights and how to lay the foundations for democratic participation. The formulation of the draft of the constitution showed a new constitutional understanding: representatives of the citizens' movements, including the women's movement, participated alongside the old and new parties. Human rights formulations were thus examined not only from a male perspective but from a feminist one. The very process of discussing the constitution based on mutual understanding was embodied in the formulation of a new constitution itself, as one based on a mutual understanding between the state and its citizens, male and female. The breakdown of the division of the two German states provided the opportunity to reorder relationships among persons both East and West. There was a hope of incorporating the experiences of the women's movement in the new social agreement. The relationship of the sexes was thus seen as a substantive political issue, not a private matter. Participation by women corresponded not only to women's own needs but also to an elementary rule of democracy.

The question was raised: How could women's rights be anchored in a democratic constitution? A simple formulation that men and women have equal rights was already present in the Fundamental Law of the Federal Republic of Germany (FRG), but had by no means brought about substantive equality; women were still systematically disadvantaged. *Gleichstellung* (equality) could not be restricted to equal legal rights.

To better protect the dignity of women, the law against discrimination was expanded to include not only classical forms of discrimination but also discrimination based on sexual orientation and lifestyle. Lesbians in the ex-GDR and FRG had been victims of direct and indirect discrimination. But such state protection wasn't enough; it was also necessary that the constitution state the federal responsibility to create the positive conditions necessary for the substantive equality of the sexes.

The equal rights article was changed from "Men and women have equal rights," to "Women and men have equal rights," thus expressing that it was fundamentally a question of the rights of women. The expansion of Paragraph 2 of the draft constitution said, "The State is obligated to work toward securing the equality of women in work and public life, in education and training, in the family as well as in the social sphere."[5] Equal chances for development of the sexes included all social spheres, and without privileging women this could hardly be accomplished.

The draft constitution also understood women's fundamental right to self-determined abortion. But strengthening women's rights could not be the object of a single isolated article; they needed to depend on the constitution as a whole. The expansion of rights of democratic control and rights of participation in public decisions strengthened women in a heretofore male-dominated political realm.

As a consequence of the quick German unification, this constitutional draft, reflecting the consensus of March 1990, was pushed aside for political reasons. The chances and possibilities to start on the road to civil society, which would have incorporated the democratic order of the FRG, the experiences of the fall revolution of the GDR, and the experiences of the women's movement could not be used. But the questions of legal fundamental rights of women opened up a new discussion in the women's movement in East and West Germany. It provided the possibility for a joint East-West German women's discussion. Innumerable constitutional initiatives by women in the former West Germany show how necessary a discussion of human rights as women's rights are on the long road to a civil society.

V. Results

The actual process of German unification was once again organized exclusively by men, and women's emancipation did not play a role. Since unification, the influence of the citizen's initiatives and especially the women's movement has been very restricted at the parliamentary level; the established parties, in accordance with the structures of the former West Germany, determine politics. It is feared that the united German train will roll over the women's movement. There is much evidence that women stand to lose the most in the German unification. Economic dependency for women is in the cards (women make up more than 60 percent of the unemployed); the destruction of day care affects women more than men; in many spheres access to well-paid work has become incredibly difficult. Competition between the sexes has increased, owing to fewer and fewer jobs. Women who previously felt they had equal rights have come to recognize their disadvantages.

The social collapse in the GDR and the hasty unification has placed many questions and tasks before women, but the development of a strong women's movement in the next few years is hardly to be expected. For women in the East it proved to be an illusion that with the fall of a totalitarian society the fundamentals of a patriarchal society were open to change. Women now stand before the reality of living in a democratic but patriarchal system. At the same time the forty-year reality of gender relations under "really existing socialism" must be researched and understood. Meanwhile, the social problems of women are growing. Concrete action is required in order for women not to lose all rights, particularly the right to a self-determined abortion and the possibility to find and hold onto work.

If the minimal political demands of women from fall 1989 have been realized in the ex-GDR, the diverse new beginnings and projects indicate a differentiated women's movement. Not only are there new women's centers, cafés, counseling offices, etc., but new research libraries with their own documentation centers have been created. Many of these projects create new jobs for women. The state-supported programs that could create new jobs form a jumping-off point for developing a new women's culture. It should not be overlooked that these projects actually do a lot of social work such as counseling women overwhelmed by the transition and the loss of a job. There is a tendency to depoliticize these projects. But the support for self-help going on in these projects is part of an enormous learning process, whereby women learn to articulate their own interests and to transpose them politically. The sphere of politics has changed. The movement has returned to its roots. In these projects lies the chance to discover new and concrete expressions of democracy, to find new ways to a civil society.

Translated by Nanette Funk

Notes

1. "Sozialistische Einheitspartei" was the name of the GDR Communist Party.
2. *Für Dich* (November 6, 1989).

3. Tatiana Böhm, speech on women's issues, June 23, 1990, Barcelona.

4. W. Ullmann, "Speech for the founding congress of the Kuratorium for a democratic union of the German states," June 16, 1990, Berlin.

5. Draft constitution for the GDR, Berlin, April 1990.

15

Lesbians and Their Emancipation in the Former German Democratic Republic: Past and Future

Christina Schenk

I. Homosexuals: Outsiders in GDR Society

The ways in which a society deals with deviation from the norm, with those who are "different" and especially with homosexuality and homosexuals, develop within a historical context and take specific national forms. In the GDR the legal system was sufficiently ambiguous to be used as an instrument of repression. There were no public forums for debate, for the expression and exchange of opinion or a balance of interests. Instead there was a secret service intended to ward off "internal enemies." Yet despite the absence of basic civil liberties, since the GDR was founded in 1949 a liberalization of attitudes toward homosexuality has taken place, albeit very slowly.

At the beginning of the 1970s, gays and lesbians set up the first private gay and lesbian groups in order to make contact with each other, to work through their personal experiences, and to provide support for those who were "coming out." It was also the declared aim of these groups to draw public attention to the situation of homosexuals and to demand changes. Given that at that time homosexuality was generally portrayed not only as a pathological condition but also as a crime, and prejudice against homosexuals continued to be endemic, these activities were of great importance for the self-confidence and self-image of lesbians and gay men.

In view of the restrictive interpretation of civil law, however, public expression and self-organization were out of the question. The Socialist Unity Party of Germany (SED) had not concerned itself with the issue of homosexuality, and as a result there were no clear-cut guidelines for the organs of the state to follow. This led to uncertainty on the part of the authorities, other political parties, and mass organizations when confronted with the demands of homosexual groups. The groups' applications to register as official associations were all rejected.

When specific interests were articulated by lesbian and gay men's groups, they

met with a negative response and were dismissed as demands for unjustified privileges (!) or special conditions. Until the late 1980s, calls for public debate of hitherto taboo social issues and for official recognition of gay liberation groups were seen as implicit criticisms of "socialist society" and were thus rejected outright.

For lesbians and gay men the situation remained unchanged until the late 1970s, when the Protestant church, witnessing the state's repression of dissidents, increasingly offered its protection and the use of its facilities to anyone who challenged "really existing socialism in the GDR," especially on ecology, peace, human rights, and feminist issues. The first church-based opposition groups were formed, from which the opposition movement in the GDR was later to develop. Very few members of these groups were Christians; the Protestant church imposed no such condition upon the groups seeking shelter. This was the major factor enabling an opposition movement to form on church territory in a country where almost three-quarters of the population were atheists.

In Leipzig in 1982 a group of gay men and several lesbian women founded the first (semi-) official homosexual group in the GDR. Admittedly, the official (Protestant) church viewed the establishment of this and subsequent groups with disfavor, and expressed its views with varying degrees of outspokenness; but thanks to the support of clergy and individual parishes it proved possible to set up the group. Similar groups were soon established in other cities. For the first time the groups were able to work autonomously in an atmosphere relatively free of fear. The State Security Service did subsequently attempt to infiltrate but was unable to reduce the groups' newfound effectiveness in drawing public attention to their agenda, or to hamper processes within the groups. The groups were able to make use of the church infrastructure to some extent; the church press could be used for publicity purposes, and the groups were able to raise their profile by participating in well-publicized church events such as the annual rallies, as well as organizing their own events for the public to attend.

Over the next few years, the network of gay and lesbian working groups set up under the auspices of the church continued to expand, providing a forum for self-help, counseling, social activities, and discussion for the first time, and enabling gays and lesbians to initiate campaigns to attract public attention.

The groups exchanged experiences on a fairly regular basis, coordinating their campaign. An annual members' meeting enabled lesbians and gay men from the various working groups to report on their activities and to discuss joint action and objectives. The foundation stone for a lesbian and gay liberation movement in the GDR had thus been laid.

Homosexual groups were not permitted to exist outside the church until the mid- to late 1980s. These groups were founded by lesbians and gay men who did not want to enter into contact with the church on principle, or who did not consider themselves to be in "opposition" to the state. The groups were set up as "clubs for lesbians and gay men" on youth club premises, in municipal cultural centers, or under the auspices of the local "Freethinkers" associations, which had been established in 1988 in response to instructions "from above." Permission to set up these groups was conditional upon members' proving their conformity to state and system. As a result, the approach and aims of the lesbians and gay men who met in these groups differed radically from their counterparts meeting under the auspices of the Protestant church.

The political dimension of being homosexual, combined with criticism of the GDR state, formed the common basis of the church-based groups, which called for the emancipation, democratization, and restructuring of society. The purpose of the homosexual clubs, on the other hand, was to integrate homosexuals into socialist society, without questioning that society or subjecting it to any form of critical analysis. The aim was to become an invisible part of "normal" society. The clubs demanded equal treatment of homosexuals and heterosexuals by the state bureaucracy at a formal level, and expected their members to make a collective effort to conform to heterosexual standards, as by expressing disapproval of promiscuity. The strategy was to conform at all costs and to keep in the government's good graces. As a result they assiduously avoided any contact with the church-based lesbian and gay groups. They even attempted to present themselves to the state as the sole representative of the interests of lesbians and gay men. As a result, relations between the church-based groups and the homosexual clubs became considerably strained.

Despite these activities, traditional homophobia still colored public attitudes toward homosexuality, and archetypical behavior patterns continued, such as, marginalization on the part of the public and voluntary self-segregation on the part of gays themselves.

II. The Lesbian Movement in the GDR: From Female Homosexuality to a Lesbian Identity

Although women in the GDR had the financial security to adopt independent and alternative lifestyles, the model was a monogamous heterosexual relationship and parenthood. In addition, there were no women's centers, cafés, or libraries. For a long time, lesbian personal ads were either forbidden or permitted only in cryptic form in a few newspapers. There was no public recognition that lesbians existed, and absolutely no information provided. In terms of the officially promoted role model for women in the GDR, a lesbian way of life was a deviation from the norm. It was dismissed by the state as a fringe phenomenon, a social irrelevance that could safely be ignored; if taken seriously, it was treated as a potentially subversive phenomenon which had to be dealt with. Joined by the common bond of their homosexuality, lesbians and gay men began to campaign together for improvements in their situation.

The gendered patterns inherent in this situation went virtually unnoticed at first. This was due in part to the nature of the relationship between male and female, which if basically patriarchal was nonetheless less hierarchical and sexist than was the case in West Germany. It was also due to the impact of the official image promoted by the state, which ignored the difference in the situation of men and women in society or at least portrayed it as unproblematic and idealized. It took time for homosexual working groups to confront the divergent and conflicting interests of lesbians and gay men and the elements of traditional sex-role behavior that emerged, particularly in the form of nonverbal dominance and dominant speech patterns.

By its third meeting, the lesbian and gay men's working group in Berlin had already decided to split. From then on (1983) two separate working groups—one for lesbians and another for gay men—existed in Berlin. In the other church-based working groups the lesbians tended to split from the gay men much later, and they did not reject joint action when they felt this was helpful for lesbians.

The separatist trend clearly increased in the late 1980s, and when the GDR ceased to exist, there were eight autonomous lesbian groups in various towns. The close links between the groups justify the term "lesbian movement" in the case of the GDR. An important contribution was made by the lesbian newspaper "frau anders," founded in 1989 and published by women in Jena.

Remarkably, lesbians who joined the "clubs for homosexuals" set up independently of the churches did not establish autonomous lesbian groups. This is perhaps not surprising, given that there was a considerable degree of conformity to state and system within these groups, which made it impossible to discuss the continuing existence of the mechanism of repression, whether traditional or inherent in socialism.

III. Lesbians in Politics

The radical changes that swept GDR society in the autumn of 1989 were brought about by grass-roots movements, some of which had sprung from the church-based opposition movement, while others came into being as the peaceful revolution progressed. Although some women were prominent in these movements, they were underrepresented to a considerable degree, and there was virtually no discussion of women's issues or feminism at the time.

As a result, the Independent Women's Association (UFV) was founded at the beginning of December 1989, soon acquiring a high profile on the political landscape of the GDR. Lesbian women played an important role in setting up and working within the UFV from the start. Even at its constituent meeting, attended by women from all over the GDR, lesbian groups and lesbians from mixed groups voiced their opinions. Their demands to participate on an equal footing were accepted, without discussion, as readily as those of the other women's groups. This was unusual in itself, given that for years lesbianism had been a subject shrouded in silence.

The UFV's program states: "We aim to establish a modern society in which every women and man is free to choose the lifestyle s/he prefers, without suffering marginalization or disadvantage because of his/her gender, origin, nationality, or sexual orientation." The fundamental aims of the UFV are to ensure that all lifestyles that do not encroach on others' rights to self-determination are accepted as equally valid; and that the relationship between the sexes, based as it is upon power, is fundamentally changed. The UFV used its influence at the Round Table to ensure that a ban on discrimination on the basis of "sexual orientation" was incorporated into several fundamental draft laws, including the draft of a new constitution for the GDR (Articles 1 and 22), the Party Law (paragraph 3 [2]), the Unification Law (par. 2 [2]), and the Electoral Law (par. 8 [2]). The working groups on "Equality of Women and Men" and "Education, Upbringing, Youth" issued manifestoes stating specifically that all lifestyles, irrespective of sexual orientation, were equally valid; they also expressed the principle of "respecting the dignity of every person, irrespective of age, sex, sexual orientation, nationality, social and family origin, cultural, political, or religious identity." Yet the UFV was not represented only by lesbians in Round Table talks and its working groups. The principles expressed by the UFV in its policy regarding lifestyles were vigorously supported by the nonlesbian women in the negotiations as well. There was no sign of the "lesbian-straight conflict" that has played such a considerable role in the women's movement in the West.

In mid-1990 representatives of a number of lesbian groups and lesbians from other UFV groups met together for the first time since the political upheavals in the GDR. Their aim was to discuss possible ways of reestablishing the network of contacts that had existed prior to the peaceful revolution in the GDR, and to seek ways to raise the lesbian profile in the UFV. It was decided to issue a declaration to the other women in the UFV, stating that lesbianism was a central aspect of their activities within the women's movement, focusing on the role of lesbian women in the UFV, and urging other UFV women to lend their support to lesbian policy initiatives in the future. They also demanded that "on appropriate occasions the existence and role of lesbians in the UFV should not be ignored or 'overlooked' and that they should play a part commensurate with their numbers in the UFV in building up the association and making it effective." It was proposed that "in accordance with the scale of the problems associated with a lesbian lifestyle in a heterosexist, patriarchal society, one of the spokeswomen of the UFV could be authorized by the lesbian women in the association to speak out on the situation of lesbian women in the area of the GDR." The association accepted the declaration without debate.

The UFV has been represented by two women in the German parliament since December 1990. One of them was elected from the PDS (Partei Demokratischen Sozialismus, the renamed communist party) list, while I myself stood as a candidate for Bündnis 90/Greens (party of civil rights and ecology groups).

I am the only member of the German Bundestag who lives openly as a lesbian. My main fields of work are women's issues and lesbian politics, and—as far as this is possible—gay politics. One achievement in the current electoral term is that the words "lesbian" and "gay" may be used in motions and draft laws by the German Bundestag. Prior to this, only the term "homosexual" was permitted. It is important to use the avenues of parliamentary democracy (plenary debates, motions, draft laws) to make the public aware of these issues in order to combat general ignorance, and if laws are prepared in Parliament that discriminate against lesbians and gays, also to mobilize the lesbian and gay movement.

At the time of this writing in 1992, efforts are being made to abolish section 175 of the West German penal code, which made male homosexual acts with someone under eighteen illegal (in the GDR the age of consent had already been lowered to sixteen in 1989). But it is proposed that it be replaced with a new paragraph 182, being marketed under the name "Sexual abuse of youth." Under this proposed law punishment would be a fine or a maximum of three years' imprisonment. The proposed law makes it punishable to abuse anyone under sixteen by having sex with them or attempting to do so, by exploiting their "immaturity or sexual inexperience." This language was appropriated from the ex-GDR paragraph 149. The terms are vague, opening the door to an interrogation of the purported victim about his or her intimate life, as has often been the case for rape victims. Presumably this new law would eliminate discrimination against gay men, by making the punishment and age of consent independent of gender or sexual orientation. But the previous paragraph 182 had made the age of consent for heterosexuals and lesbians fourteen; here, it would be increased to sixteen. It would also become criminal for an adult woman to have sexual contact with either male or female youths under sixteen, while the age of consent for men would be reduced from eighteen to sixteen. It would become possible, for the first time in the Federal Republic of Germany, to prosecute lesbians under the penal code. In practice this would provide an opportunity for that overwhelming majority of parents hostile to their daughter's or son's emerging homosexuality to control that sexuality with threats of criminal proceedings.[1]

If the real purpose of the proposed law is to prevent sexual abuse, the issue should be sexual activity that takes place "against the will" of the person, whether in or out of marriage, and independent of age, while the punishment for rape should be increased.

IV. GDR Lesbians and German Unification

For the women in the UFV and many other grass-roots activists, the peaceful revolution in autumn 1989 was a euphoric time. We felt that this was the start of the "third way" for the GDR. But issues now on the agenda in 1992 differ radically from those of that period:

—In a capitalist society on the Federal German model, in which economic pragmatism takes priority over the creation of a society in which the needs of individuals (women and men) and the preservation of the ecosphere are paramount, to what extent is it possible to challenge and change the relationship between the sexes as a social, cultural, economic, and sociopsychological problem?

—To what extent is it possible to remove all the various forms of marginalization in society, and in particular, what measures will ensure that all lifestyles are acceptable and that marriage no longer receives privileged status?

—What strategies for success are possible for women in capitalist German society?

The social transformation will be complete in a matter of years. For women, and for lesbians, who lived in the GDR, the graphic differences between the patriarchies of the Federal Republic of Germany and the GDR are becoming only too clear. Consider that:

—Today only about 36 percent of women who are able to work hold a job, in contrast to a figure of more than 80 percent in the GDR. This may change once the East German economy is consolidated, but a number of leading politicians have already made it quite clear that the "excessive level of employment of women in the GDR" should be reduced to "normal" levels. At present, women are steadily being eased out of employment.

—Women's economic independence, which is the prerequisite for an independent lifestyle, is under threat. This thrusts them back into a position of humiliating dependency and makes it particularly difficult for lesbians to find the lifestyle that suits them.

V. The Relationship of the Sexes

The current process of marginalization will lead to a radical change in the relationship between the sexes in East Germany. Society—and women themselves—will attribute a higher status to men, and women's status will decline accordingly. Men will once more be the "breadwinners" and heads of the family, with women primarily assuming responsibility for reproduction. Whereas in the GDR men were increasingly assuming domestic responsibilities, this role will be reassessed, and the main burden will be borne by women once more.

It will no longer be generally accepted, as it was in the GDR, that every woman will have a career as a matter of course, and girls' and women's expectations will therefore change. They will now focus once again on men for their economic security. These processes will make it increasingly difficult for girls and women to come out as lesbians.

The problem of sexism is compounded by the massive attempt now being undertaken by the churches to "re-Christianize" East Germany. Standards and values which became obsolete long ago (value of marriage, abortion) are being revived. As a result, the social status of women is changing dramatically, and these changes directly affect lesbian women.

The fall of the Wall brought many lesbians in East and West Germany into contact for the first time. It very quickly became clear that forty years of separate development in the two German states had resulted in very different mentalities, approaches, and political intentions. The great challenge now facing the lesbian movements in East and West Germany is to ensure that they draw strength and inspiration from their differences and do not allow their dissimilarities to drive a wedge between them. Much will depend on the newly won freedoms being used effectively to make the women's and lesbian movement in both East and West Germany a politically relevant force for the future.

Notes

1. Studies in Hamburg have shown that 41 percent of males and 37 percent of females have sexual intercourse by the age of sixteen. *Die Tagezeitung,* February 19, 1992.

16

"But the Pictures Stay the Same . . ." The Image of Women in the Journal *Für Dich* Before and After the "Turning Point"

Irene Dölling

If one were to take two issues of the women's magazine *Für Dich,* one from 1989 and another from 1991, and place them side by side, one might say: "They are pictures from two different worlds." One set, mostly poor-quality black-and-white prints, could be summarized as stating: "Women work like men and owe their allegiance to a greater unity, as integral parts of a collective 'We.' " The other pictures, in seductively brilliant color, seem dedicated to a different motto: "I am a very feminine woman who relates to the world primarily through my excellent taste for beauty and harmony."

We seem to be dealing with pictures from extremely different worlds. But are these worlds really so far apart?

Pictures *signify* the world in graphically perceptible forms. They are always structured according to specific cultural patterns of meaning and perception, and thus they transmit normative attitudes toward the world. According to Walter Benjamin, photographs, in their "transitoriness and reproducibility," their constant repetition of similar situations, focus the fleeting gaze of the viewer on a "sense of the universal equality of things in the world."[1] Not least among these are stereotypical concepts of "masculinity" and "femininity," which order and structure the wealth of photographs of changing realities into equivalents. They orient perception, the individual assignment of meaning to reality, as well as the practical actions of the viewer.

Proceeding from these basic assumptions, this research project, completed before the "Wende" (the changes of 1989), analyzed photographs from daily life in the GDR,[2] including pictures that appeared in two weekly mass-market magazines. This article concentrates on stereotypical models of "femininity" read from photographs in *Für Dich,* the only women's magazine in the former GDR.[3] The changes this magazine underwent after fall 1989 are discussed, and the analysis concentrates on photographs characteristic of *Für Dich* in the last phase of its existence, from spring 1990 to June 1991, after it had been acquired by the West German publisher Gruner & Jahr. The question will be raised whether pictures that at first glance seem so different do not bear a fatal resemblance to one another.

I. "Our Mommies Work Like Men": A Backward Glance at Images of Women in the Former GDR

The following questions guided the analysis of the magazine photographs in the research project described above:

—How is the double burden of women reflected in the pictures of women and men in their daily relationships?

—What aspects of gender relations are represented in the photographs, and which are not worthy of depiction (and why not)?

—In the photographs of GDR daily life, how are normative models of relationships between men and women and of "femininity" and "masculinity" graphically conveyed?

—Did the previous changes in the life situations of men and women lead to a breakdown in traditional gender stereotypes? Have new stereotypes arisen, or can a largely unbroken effect of traditional models be established?

To anticipate one result of the analysis: No new stereotypes that "molded into a solid form" a qualitatively different relationship of men and women could be found. With a few modifications, hand-me-down, patriarchally formed models of "femininity" and "masculinity" are used to depict graphically actual situations of men and women. Pictures of women, specifically those showing the world of work, illustrate this. Employment was a significant factor in the self-image of women in the GDR, and officially women were recognized primarily as workers. My comments on the image of women in GDR magazines are organized into four thematic aspects.

1. Woman As Productive Worker

Employment was a foregone conclusion for women in the GDR.[4] Accordingly, photographs showing women at work are very frequent in *Für Dich*, outnumbered only by pictures of female models. The unquestioned nature of employment is made graphically vivid through completely unspectacular depictions of competent, productive women routinely and skillfully working while radiating a self-evident confidence in their abilities. A weakening of certain stereotypes of "femininity" can be viewed in the many, usually small-format black-and-white photographs showing women engrossed in their work. Common signifiers of "femininity" play a very subordinate role in these photographs: a woman's dress, hair, figure, and makeup all retreat before her concentration on her work.

What could it mean that women appear not as lovely or weak but as the productive sex in such photos of work life? What contradictory aspects of women's current situation or gender relations in the former GDR do they illustrate?

One level of meaning is that women are indispensable in social production. Women do socially necessary and socially recognized work, just like men. As a result, women are presented less as gendered beings than as professionals displaying nongendered attributes. Given the pronounced gender-specific division of labor, however, this level of meaning presumably plays a subordinate role.

The weakening of stereotypes of femininity transmits predominantly other meanings, which orient individual perception and evaluation of a contradictory reality. This weakening signals that areas of employment are divided between the sexes, and the traditional "order," in which men control crucial activities and positions, is not questioned. This is made graphically concrete in the far more frequent depiction of men *or* women than of both sexes working together.

In addition, the photographs accompanying a report or article use differently sized photographs to show, for example, the director, the men engaged in installing the latest technology, and the women working at an assembly line. Such workers appear nonthreatening to the established hierarchical gender order. Thus, the beauty and sensual seductiveness of the female sex does not have to be emphasized to reduce a real danger or distract from it through displacement.

At the same time, other aspects of "female gender characteristics" are clearly emphasized in the photographs. A large number of pictures of women performing typical "women's" jobs, such as kindergarten teaching, nursing, or finishing and assembling processes in industrial production, do more than describe a gender-specific division of labor. The frequency of such depictions reproduces and confirms stereotypical patterns of the helping, serving, and caring functions of the female sex. Thus, the new, self-evident, competent, and responsible professional employment of women is presented as something that does not basically challenge accepted gender roles. The weakening of stereotypes of femininity in the photographs has a specific meaning in this context, intimately tied to the ability of graphic language to "make the nonhomogeneous identical." By depicting women as efficient producers who are only secondarily "female," these pictures raise formal equality as well as commonality with employed men to the level of conscious perception. This illustrates a truly important change in gender relations and in the social recognition of women, but it also pushes the gender-specific division of labor into the background. Thus, the fact that women remain in the "second rank" and are practically disadvantaged in their "newly conquered" sphere is minimized.

Still another assertion of identity in photographs of working women is graphically conveyed in the contradictory unity of a common status as producers and a second-rank status as female producers. Thus, many photographs show women performing the same work, one after another in apparently endless rows on assembly lines or at check-out counters, identical in posture and movements and individually interchangeable. There are no comparable pictures of men. Men have special assignments and abilities, and the photographs seem to say men are not immediately replaceable or interchangeable. They make visibly clear that female productive labor is "different" from male productive labor, that the former is codetermined by pregnancy, childrearing, and housework.

A certain type of picture appears in both magazines unchanged: man instructing woman. These photographs create a gendered division of labor, a relationship of subordination, a social hierarchy physically obvious in the relationship depicted (boss instructs and checks up on secretary). Many photographs do refer to work interactions in which men and women perform the same tasks. Yet these pictures are also characterized by a visual "language" showing men as more competent, with a broad overview and the final word: *he* is optically enlarged by the choice of perspective, his superiority visible in his calm posture, expert gaze, and confident, explanatory gestures, while *she* looks up at him inquiringly, listening to his explanation—often in a strained posture—or eagerly endeavoring to carry out the instructions and perform well under the critical gaze of the man.

In one photograph [*Photo 1*] two young women are in front of a computer, the man in the foreground appearing more as a shadow but still dominating the scene. The expert, alert gaze of the two women expresses competence and self-assurance. They have little in common with women in photographs from the 1960s, who approached the unfamiliar technology with hesitation and insecurity. Still, the scene is shot at the moment when the man is in action. The postures of the women—sitting or leaning forward on both hands—optically enlarge the man, and the activity of the man (speaking, lively gestures) and the passivity of the women (listening, receptive posture) are contrasted; the cooperation between men and women is made graphically perceptible in accordance with traditional gender stereotypes. The viewer notices primarily the "typical" postures and gestures of women and men in a new context (modern technology), conveying in concrete form: men and women are "this way" (and they should stay this way).

Photographs that "underexpose" traditionally understood femininity in the work sphere reflect employment as a self-evident, everyday experience of women, but also as something that does not yet affect their essential "femaleness." But employment is integrated into the "normal" understanding of "femaleness" in another way as well: some pictures [*Photo 2*] show women in the working sphere as seductive. Captions emphasizing "feminine" qualities or physical characteristics (the "slender, delicate person") have their impact on the model of the professionally active woman: women's professional work becomes "different" from men's professional work. "Our mommies," in a widely used contemptuous expression for working GDR women with children, of course "work like a man," but as mommies they are always second-class workers.

Photographs of working women in which a demonstrative emphasis on "femininity" is noticeable are hardly rare. They convey a picture of the contradictory situation of women in the world of work.

Photo 1

2. The Uses of Beauty

The more highly qualified, responsible, exclusive the woman's professional activity is, the more the picture of an efficient female sex is softened through an emphasis on beauty and a "feminine" body shape.

In accordance with their goal of popularizing the political and professional equality of women in the GDR, *Für Dich* profiled successful women in prominent positions or activities relatively frequently. These "model women" were presented with a demonstrative emphasis on traditional "feminine" stereotypes. This is particularly true of the usually large-format, color lead photographs. Just like the title-page photographs of women, who have managed to be successful in their careers with "determination and charm," with "charm and logic," "determined and understanding," the leads present these women superficially as "feminine" creatures: their hair falls soft and lustrous, the flattering silk blouse harmonizes with the color of their shining eyes, the skin of their face is so pink and glowing that the lines are hardly noticeable, the pinks of the blouse and the lipstick are exactly the same. Subject competence and high position are reduced in importance and the (real or potential) threat to a traditional order is mitigated.

One aspect of the traditional image of "femininity" plays a prominent role in these pictures: feminine beauty and power are made equivalent. This actually refers to sexual power; thus, in the context we are examining, power is transposed to another level, in which the real power of competence becomes the power of beauty. In other words, where a real threat to men's status and privilege is involved, women are depicted as the seductive sex, as the embodiment of sexuality.

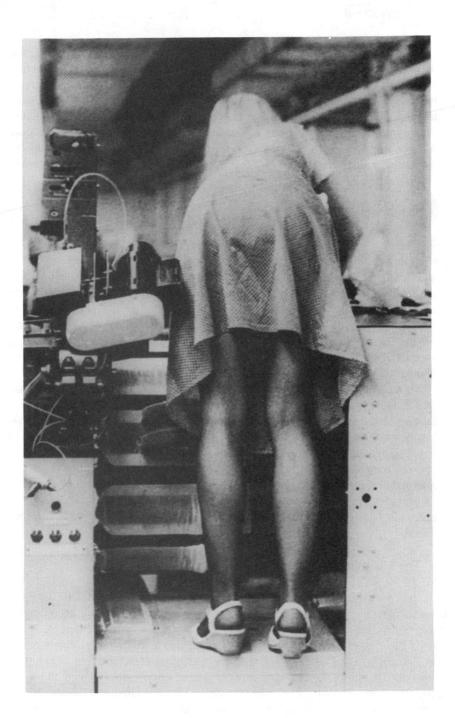

Photo 2

In pictorial "language" arrangements of this type, a subtle form of devaluation of women's work can be seen. In this kind of photograph common stereotypes of femininity diminish the seriousness of the work, as when a woman delicately tests the temperature of grain in a storage silo with her bare feet ("an old peasant method"), her high-heeled shoes lying next to her. The outfit and presentation of the woman more likely triggers associations of "leisure time" or a "stroll on a Sunday afternoon" than "serious" (masculine) work, and also carries the subliminal message that the work of Ms. Agronomist" is not (cannot be) of the quality of that of "Mr. Agronomist."

3. The Double Burden

While the woman is certainly allowed to develop career ambitions, she has to keep things in proportion. Her ambition cannot be allowed to threaten marriage and family. The ever-present stereotypes of motherliness, caring, and selflessness emphasize that women are expected to combine motherhood, housework, and employment. Women with children are far more frequently photographed at caretaking, tending activities than at instructing, teaching, or even playing. Taking care of a husband is also silently conveyed as self-evident. The family appears as the "normal" form of human relationships in the larger context of the photographs.

Yet women's double burden is hardly depicted. In looking through many years of *Für Dich* only one photograph was found that directly—using a photomontage—pointed to the woman performing housework. While photographs criticizing the traditional division of roles in the household by showing men and women engaged in housework appeared in the 1950s and 1960s, such photographs were almost completely absent in the 1980s. Out of the nearly 5400 photographs of men and/or women that appeared in 1986 in the two magazines evaluated, exactly 14 showed women or men engaged in housework. Since housework appears essentially unworthy of depiction, its traditional valuation as nonwork is reproduced.

4. The Masculine Gaze

The "masculine gaze" dominates the image of women in the GDR.

Photographs of the daily life of "normal women" are structured according to traditional models, according to which women are the "other, different, lesser sex." Photographs indicating sensuality or sexuality were found extremely rarely in *Für Dich*. The bodies of the women (and men) depicted were working or reproductive bodies; rare exceptions were limited strictly to very young individuals, who were—presumably—not yet married or still childless. There was no pornography, at least not officially. Photographs that directly used the female body as a screen for the projection of male fantasies or as advertising space for products or ideologies were quite rare in these magazines. Photographs showing marriage as the locus of happiness were also rare, but this says nothing about actual needs or the quality of gender relations. It is an indication of the filtering of reality for reasons of "socialist ideology," according to which women faced neither structural disadvantages nor discrimination, and experienced neither violence nor a sexuality oriented toward individual pleasure rather than propagation.

According to the pictures in *Für Dich,* women are employed and mothers, or, more exactly, employed mothers. Such important areas in the context of their lives as unpaid housework or the relation between sexuality and male violence are filtered out. The context of women's daily lives deemed worthy of portrayal is structured and valued according to traditional gender stereotypes, and the "normality" of social hierarchies, of power and subordination, is casually conveyed as self-evident. These structures were based on the power monopoly of a single party. Like the pater familias in the pre-bourgeois producer-family, the Party assumed for itself the right to act and make decisions in the interest of all, to take responsibility for everything and hold everyone in a tutelary relationship by means of a finely graduated hierarchy. Thus, the patriarchal-paternalistic pattern of differentiation had a directly system-supporting function. In the photographs of working life, therefore, it is not just a matter of the acceptance of a gender-specific division of labor (which is only the result of a momentary situation of economic necessity), structured by traditional gender stereotypes. It simultaneously goes beyond this to involve the acceptance of political, ideological, and cultural structures that anchor the division of the world into the powerful few and the powerless mass, into the responsible and the dependent.

II. The Transformation of *Für Dich* and Its World of Images from Fall 1989 to Its Demise in June 1991

During the short, euphoric phase of rebellion in which everything seemed possible, *Für Dich* changed too. It had been directly administered by the propaganda wing of the Central Committee of the Socialist Unity Party. Now a few of its women editors pushed for change under the pressure of current events. They wanted a magazine that really recognized the interests of women and articulated them as consciously political demands in these times of radical change. For a few months, GDR women could read realistic reports on the actual results of the long propagandized realization of equality in *Für Dich*. They read for the first time about sexual violence in the family, about women in prison, about sexual abuse of children, or the arguments for and against pornography. The magazine gave the Independent Women's Association (UFV) two pages in each issue and thus actively engaged in the construction of a network of women's initiatives throughout the entire GDR. There was no unified editorial concept for the magazine; opinion among the editors was distinctly divided. One lobby within the editorial staff pushed for a more "feminine" orientation, in order to be able to survive the new competition of the media market.

The Volkskammer (GDR Parliament) elections in March 1990 represented a turning point for the magazine. Negotiations were under way with several West German or foreign publishers, and in the end the Hamburg publishing house Gruner & Jahr acquired *Für Dich* along with other newspapers and magazines. The resulting editorial orientation, which only a very few of the members of the old editorial staff refused to accept,[5] was taken from West German women's magazines like *Constanze,* which had failed, and *Tina,* which had become widely read in the East. It went as follows: as little analysis of current politics or women's problems as possible; instead, short, snappy informational reports and aids to action in very concrete matters (writing a job letter or applying for unemployment or child support payments), but above all lots of fashion, recipes, travel tips, cosmetics, and advertising. There was practically no advertising of *Für Dich* in West Germany. Distribution in the New Federal States (ex-GDR) was extremely poorly organized. The sales figures sank rapidly (to 90,000).

The editorial staff took leave of its readers in issue number 24, after forty-five years of uninterrupted publication. The issue was already at press when it became known that this would be the last issue. The "feminist" phase of *Für Dich* was an intermezzo—supported by only a few editors, in any case. The majority of the editorial staff remained faithful to the attitude they had acquired in GDR times: to produce a women's magazine without a critical consciousness of the structural disadvantage of the female sex or the ideological function of the cultural constructions of "femininity" and "masculinity." Thus, the abrupt change in the graphic world after March 1990 was not as decisive as it appeared at first glance. Functionally, it should be seen more as a continuity in the transmission of traditional gender stereotypes during a simultaneous disruption of the reality depicted.

However, in the last phase of *Für Dich* the photographs of working women shown in their daily work lives, which had previously been so numerous on the pages of *Für Dich,* became rare. The reports about the existential suffering of a single mother with three children who had lost her job and was living on welfare were accompanied by photographs that definitely conveyed the hopelessness of her situation.

Photographs depicting women in daily life were in the minority in every issue compared to photographs that—like fashion photography—explicitly presented common images of "femininity" or "masculinity." In this photography, women's bodies represented gender stereotypes more directly than in photographs of daily life. Their normative force was thus also significantly greater. This bright picture world preached to women in the former GDR: to be a woman means to be beautiful. Whether a woman is employed or is a housewife, whether she is professionally highly qualified or has only learned the absolute minimum, whether she has developed more or less successful strategies for the combination of work and motherhood, whether she was interested in things beyond her private horizon or not—all this was peripheral to the central issue, that a woman must be "feminine." Accordingly, there were no longer any "real" or "normal" women to be found on the title pages, but only young models embodying seductive, feminine beauty.

The many fashion pages offered not only an overview of the previously unaccustomed broad array of goods for every size pocketbook; they also hammered in the message: "Clothes make the woman." If working women were depicted, it was not to show them using their abilities, but to aim at their cosmetic beautification. If a woman was mousy to begin with, after cosmetic efforts she was guaranteed to gain personality, self-confidence, and aura, the requirements necessary to win in the competition for the increasingly short supply of jobs. The "before" and "after" was also to be interpreted as before and after the "turning point." The many colorfully pictured ideas for gifts (and their aesthetic packaging), for brightening up the apartment, and for culinary treats for the family made clear what the well-dressed and made-up woman was there for: to consume.

Many things are connected in these photographs: the real, very justified need for improvement in material living conditions, the extolling of a wealth of products, the premise of a "modern," Western lifestyle, the traditional cultural stereotypes of "femininity," and the devaluation of everything that had previously belonged to the daily lives of GDR women, including their external appearance. The lovely, bright pictures were not to be understood as a "return" to traditional stereotypes of "femininity"; they were ever-present in the photographs from the GDR period, too. They were also not merely compensation and escape from a real world of increasing insecurity. With their invitation to become a "new, completely different" woman, they functioned in a larger context to erase the memory of everything which—within the frame of the political-ideological and thereby always virulent patriarchal structures of state socialism—belonged to the experiences of women in the GDR: the pursuit of a (more or less) qualified career, the ability to combine career and motherhood, and the ability to be at least in principle economically independent.

III. The Pictures from the Old and New Worlds: Extremely Different or Astonishingly Similar?

The photographs of women in the world of work or the public political sphere were displaced by photographs in which the bodies of real women became idealized projection screens for traditional stereotypes of "femininity," "feminine beauty and sexual seductiveness." The industrious woman, tirelessly working to fulfill socialist goals, was replaced by a consumer concerned with herself and her appearance. Besides decoding the ideological content of photographs in which the individual professional abilities of women were used for other purposes, the new pictures reveal all too clearly what amount of room to maneuver, what areas of activity are granted to women uncontested. The discrepancy between these photographs and the experiences of women is significantly greater and more obvious than in the daily-life photographs of the working world. The transition from the not consciously registered patriarchy of GDR society to the patriarchy in the new society, which among other things appeared in the form of official recognition of a previously hardly noticed "femininity," is more likely to be seamless. But the similarities in both the "before" and "after" 1989 photographs remain:

—The filtering out of important aspects of female life as unworthy of depiction. Just as in the *Für Dich* of the old days, although the housewife had a significantly higher status within the new image of woman than in the GDR, there were no photographs in the new picture world of women doing housework, shopping, or taking care of children. Unpaid reproductive labor remains invisible in both cases.

—The polar assignment of human characteristics and activities to the male or female sex is confirmed and carried forward in both graphic worlds, and with it the more or less "natural character" of the existing division of labor between the sexes and the second-class status of women. The individual perception of contradictory experience or conflicts between changed conditions and traditional roles are squeezed into the traditional stereotypes.

—Both graphic worlds level out differences, reducing diversity to abstract generalities of gender stereotypes. This triumph of the general over the particular reveals the ideological character of both the old and the new pictures: to use the real experiences and needs of women expressed in this generalized form for the ends of power.

Taking all this into consideration, one can hardly regret the fact that *Für Dich* ceased publication after forty-five years. But with it the only mass-market periodical that provided information to women about the situation of women in the new states (of the former GDR)—even if only in a very limited way—disappeared.

Translated from the German by Dorothy Rosenberg

Notes

1. Walter Benjamin, "Das Kunstwerk im Zeitalter seiner technischen Reproduzierbarkeit" (The Work of Art in the Age of Mechanical Reproduction), in *Walter Benjamin Allegorien kultureller Erfahrung. Ausgewählte Schriften 1920–1940* (Leipzig: Reclam, 1984), p. 413.

2. *Der Mensch und sein Weib: Aktuelle Frauen—und Männerbilder: Geschichtliche Ursprünge und Perspektiven* (Contemporary Images of Men and Women: Historical Origins and Perspectives) (Berlin: Dietz, 1991).

3. *Für Dich* began publication in 1946 under the title "Frau von Heute," which it carried

until 1963. It had a print run of over one million copies at times. In fall 1990 it still printed 950,000 copies.

4. In age cohorts up to forty years, the level of training or starting qualification had reached parity between men and women. In 1988, 87 percent of employed women had completed training and certification. *Sozialreport 1990,* ed. Gunnar Winkler (Berlin: Die Wirtschaft, 1991).

5. Not the least because they were very well paid for GDR or East German conditions and because they received a three-year no-layoff protection agreement, which following the closure of the magazine has been transformed into settlement amounting to two years' salary. Compared with the vast majority of East Germans, who are now losing their jobs, they are in a comparably advantageous position.

17

The Organized Women's Movement in the Collapse of the GDR: The Independent Women's Association (UFV)

Anne Hampele

The Independent Women's Organization (UFV) was founded at a meeting of about 1200 women from the German Democratic Republic (GDR) in the Volks-bühne (People's Theater) in East Berlin on December 3, 1989. It followed upon the growing political crisis of summer and fall 1989 and the formation in September 1989 of several public civil rights organizations that discussed possibilities of common political action. They opened a dialogue between themselves and the state and party leadership, thereby initiating the reform process.

The founders of the UFV wanted to move from a women's policy that treated women as objects to a policy in which women would become subjects. The motto of the provisional manifesto of the UFV, "Ohne Frauen ist kein Staat zu machen" (You can't make a state without women) demanded that emancipation be extended to all fields of society and politics. They explicitly used the concepts of "emancipation" and "feminism." The new women's organization provoked internal, programmatic discussions in other political organizations. Ina Merkel, one of two initial spokespersons, could say with confidence: "Since we came into existence no political group or party in the GDR can avoid the women's question."[1] The December meeting also signaled the start of numerous women's initiatives throughout the country. A whole new women's movement arose, and the UFV appealed to this movement during the election campaign in March 1990 with the slogan: "For women who have the courage to say 'I.' "

What follows is the background and prehistory of the founding of this independent women's organization. Questions will be asked about what these women wanted and why an organization was formed. The work of the organization will also be described. Since the unification of Germany, the conditions of existence for the East German women's organization radically changed. Therefore, the state of the UFV in fall 1991 and its prospects for the future will also be discussed.

I. The Context of Formation

Contradictions in the lives of women contributed to the pressure for change in East Germany. It had become impossible for women to accept traditional or assigned social and cultural roles and to regard them as legitimate parts of a national women's policy.

With Honecker's rise to head of state in 1971, not only did consumer-oriented production improve but a social politics began that brought legal and work improvements for women with children. The policy aimed at increasing the participation of women in production and at counteracting the declining birth rate.

The younger women who were affected by this policy came to regard this improvement as a given. The women's question was regarded as solved. Women and men were officially seen as equal, with both engaged in production; the model for women was an average of two children. Women's conditions of existence were guaranteed by the state. Sociological studies from the 1980s show that women came to make demands for partnership in marriages and ceased regarding marriage as their destiny.[2] The high divorce rate, with two-thirds of proceedings initiated by women, expressed women's willingness to acknowledge conflict as well as their disappointed expectations. "Really existing" social politics created a new form of social integration within the GDR.[3]

The contradictions of this social and labor policy have been one cause of conflict in women's lives, which they tried to solve individually. These policies were also rifts in legitimation. The social policy directed almost exclusively toward mothers—"Muttipolitik" (mommy politics)—strengthened traditional gender roles, limited and worsened career opportunities for women, and saved men from criticism and a change of the power distribution in society. There were, in addition, almost no women in decision-making areas of political life.[4]

Because of their training and the norm of women's employment, women developed expectations about their jobs. Many women experienced sex discrimination in their occupations and in their personal lives, and culturally and politically, without any consciousness of it. The problem of how to reconcile job, child, and family was enormous. While virtually every woman was a mother, many women found that a child disturbed their career. Yet many women in the 1980s took advantage of the "mommy politics" to reduce their burden, turning against the work-centered life of their mothers. That this retreat into private happiness was also flawed is shown not only by the divorce rate but also by women who formed discussion groups during their "baby year" to alleviate the isolation at home. They wanted time for the child, but were unwilling to tolerate the fathers' retreat from responsibility and the official silence about this problem.

The women's movement in the GDR did not begin in 1989; countercultural, ecological, women's, and peace movements had sprung up in West Germany beginning in the 1970s. The language of the mass media on both sides was German. Conversely, the emigration or expulsion of GDR women created new contacts between East and West. Partnership relations between East and West Protestant churches also led to cultural exchange, including the exchange of feminist literature. The GDR's high claims of formal equality for women produced perceptible contradictions, and cultural contacts contributed to women's discussing their experiences and interpreting them in a feminist way.[5]

Women's groups came into being under the protection of the church,[6] which offered a meeting space and modest infrastructure. The homosexual and women's movements were also afforded opportunities by the church for discussions of changing values and morality. The peace movement, within which "Women For Peace" was formed, contributed to the politicization of women's issues.

From the early and mid-1980s women's initiatives began in institutes of higher learning and in research institutes. Within the research council "Woman in Socialist Society" (which had a kind of monopoly on research on women), controversies arose over the official version of the women's question in the GDR, but these stayed mainly behind closed doors. At the universities, women in literary criticism, theology, and the social sciences cautiously started discussions, research, and courses on the theme of women. Latent discontent also existed within the ruling Socialist Unity Party (SED), in which there had been almost no reform efforts. Thus, when the social transformation began, there had been at least a few efforts toward formulating a new women's policy.[7]

These widely separated partial groupings found each other when a public sphere was created in 1989. Since then, they have parted ways somewhat, but have also integrated in new ways. Why did GDR women decide to create a national women's organization? What did they hope to achieve?

II. The Formation and Structure of the UFV

1. The Formation

Women wanted to create a space in society for the different women's groups, to form within the public sphere a possibility for women to become aware of their situation. They also wanted to prepare to enter politics and participate in power.

In the GDR, organizing as a political association seemed the only way to effect social communication without state intervention and without the protection of the church. The nonstate sphere for public debate and engagement first had to be created through the organizations' own work, a development that took shape comparatively late in the GDR, in contrast to Poland. Although women were involved in the general political changes during the intensifying political crisis, the idea of forming a women's organization gained in popularity as women saw that neither women nor themes important to them were convincingly represented in the new political programs. The idea of organizing had already been discussed in the highly industrialized southern GDR. This approach found resonance among women in the new groups and movements who similarly noted the exclusion of women:

> Because of the time pressures no new structures were devised, they just tried to follow the same old models, and that means in principle: patriarchal relations as before. Men accumulated new skills . . . when children were in the office they were the women's job [and about the issue of quotas] they said . . . "Then we would also need quotas for those who wear glasses." There was absolutely no consciousness about these things.[8]

Many women were thereby politicized and learned the reality of sex discrimination, an inequality supposedly nonexistent in the GDR.

Calling the organization "Independent" meant it was not connected to the state. Women thereby disassociated themselves from the official women's organization that had existed since 1947, the Democratic Women's League of Germany (DFD), and refused to be a "mass organization," transmitting Party politics. The new women's organization could have linked up with the DFD; as a quasi-party, the old organization had thirty-two seats in the GDR parliament, the Volkskammer. Instead, one of the slogans of November 1989 was, "We want the *other* women's organization." Women consciously created a new and very different association in order to intervene actively in the tumultuous political process.

The first concrete act of the UFV to share in political power followed immediately upon the creation of the organization, when women demanded, and got, a seat and a voice on the central Round Table. The UFV could thereby participate vigorously in the political, social, and cultural transformation. The Round Tables were "mechanisms for communication" that made possible a nonviolent transition from one-party rule to pluralism. They effected "dialogue between representatives of the old power structure and the new organizations."[9] At first, they were not to be a people's parliament but a public check on the state apparatus until democratic elections could take place.[10] In fact, the central Round Table in Berlin did become a representative body, and the citizens' movements related to it as to a second authority or shadow government. Since their guiding principle was to "carry on politics in the name of the people,"[11] they understood the Round Table mandate as the forum for their participation in political power.

The UFV motto, "You can't make a state without women," fit the citizens' mood of an orientation to fundamental change. It even seemed possible to make a state. The relatively spontaneous form of the Round Table corresponded to women's interest in a pragmatic and directly effective politics, one with little bureaucracy. And, Marxist-Leninist theory had taught that the state was not something external that confronted its citizens, but rather a "social instrument."[12] Both these concepts helped the women achieve a craftspersonlike notion of "making a state." This was also evidenced in the UFV Manifesto, which the congress had promulgated by acclamation as its provisional program. It rested on the premise that in this situation of sudden changing social relationships, new social conditions could be moved around like coordinates on a drawing board to produce a new society.

Until February 1990, the concept of a "society of ecology and solidarity" was in part borrowed by the GDR oppositional groups from the West German Greens, and used to disassociate the movement from the East German and the less understood West German consumer culture. It was understood by GDR parties and movements essentially as a "renewal of socialism," in part because this seemed to be the only path to reform. The independent women advocated a radical reform of socialism, and they had a claim to democracy in the form of their own organization. In contrast to other grass-roots civil rights groups, they did not focus on the democratic reform of political institutions, which was to a certain extent assumed, but on the social order. The manifesto was drafted as a reform program starting with the basic premise of retaining and improving the social and legal standards achieved in East German society. This was also the starting point for the UFV's critique of the society of the old GDR. The equal-rights policy of the GDR and the opportunities it afforded women formed part of their position, and they held that they had advantages in social policy over West German women. The intent of reforming and later *saving* the social legislation of "really existing socialism," along with their critique of consumerism and their demand for socially responsible growth, formed part of the UFV's skepticism toward the West and capitalism. Social policy was conceived as a determinant of women's opportunities. This view became more clearly expressed as the ensuing reform policies began to dismantle the social achievements.[13]

On this point the GDR movement differed from the West German women's movement. In the Federal Republic of Germany (FRG) in the 1970s the discontent about sociopolitical conditions coalesced with the criticism of administrative social policies, starting an intense debate about alternatives within and outside official institutions. Although the GDR movement also started with criticism of existing institutions and rules, it wasn't long before the dismantling of GDR social policy forced the women into the role of defending what already existed. The legal assimilation of East Germany into the FRG completely eliminated the orientation to reform. It brought with it a restructuring of the gender relations of "really existing socialist" patriarchy, down to the smallest details, changes that could hardly begin to be understood then.[14] The loss of legal standards protecting and promoting women worsened conditions for them. This became the basis for glittering, nostalgic memories of the GDR as a "paradise of women's policies" contrasted to "the backward, Third World" state of affairs for women in the Federal Republic. Both statements were mostly, if not completely inaccurate.

This discussion about the relationship to the state, the relevance of alternative projects, the concept of sociopolitical and legal work for women in struggle, and the use of state funding began in some regions only in summer 1991. The controversy about how to rate the GDR social policies affecting women, which had been carried on in various publications during the "Wende" (period of change in 1989–90), could be resumed in a larger framework.[15]

2. The Structure

When it registered as a political body for the elections to the Volkskammer in February 1990, the UFV defined itself as a democratically based political representative of women of the GDR. It conceived of itself as an umbrella organization to facilitate political cooperation between groups and local initiatives, each of which would remain autonomous. This basic idea did and still does characterize the "UFV as an experiment."[16] Of central importance is the idea that through the organization active women would win a place in politics and substantive decision making. Women thereby declared their intent to participate in political power, having seen their exclusion from that process as one cause of the discrimination against them.

The Association wants to remain internally democratic. Its structure conforms to the model of council democracy: the groups are independent of each other in their work. At the county or state level they form delegate bodies for decision making; they are represented by spokeswomen who can be recalled by vote; and their highest decision-making body is the congress, or the full assembly of members. The Association's working committee is the Federal Coordinating Council. The financial policy decided upon at the beginning of 1990 left the major part of members' dues at the state level. The State or Federal Coordinating Council decides about the use of the remaining funds (derived from election grants and from donations from members in federal or state parliaments). Administration and coordination is carried out by state bureaus and a central bureau in Berlin in which employees of the Association work.

For the UFV, as a democratically based political experiment, the effort to find adequate forms of institutionalization is not over, even with its statute of September 1991 making it an organization, not a party. The underlying dilemma has been that the UFV wants to conduct politics in the name of women who at the same time remain independent of the Association. There has been a demand for women with a public profile who combined experience and competence, who could shape policies inside and outside the organization. At the same time there needs to be a close reciprocity between the groups at the base and the plenary discussions, a demand that could easily overtax the time and energy of the women functionaries. The necessary division of work into areas and themes was at times regarded as unwanted bureaucratization and met with criticism.

Guiding this search for cohesiveness was the generally shared rejection of party hierarchy (according to either East or West models), with its autonomous bureaucracies and professional functionaries who would accumulate competency in decision making.[17] From this arose conceptually and also practically a problematic tension between the will to participate in power in a hierarchical and authoritarian state and an aversion toward any strict ordering of the internal decision-making process that could have contributed to greater effectiveness. The demands from the membership for a critique of old policies and the demand for a new order were little reconciled with the requirements of political activity.

By limiting membership in the UFV to women living in the GDR, the UFV defended itself from being taken over by women in the former West Germany and from the "contentiousness" of the West German women's movement. Simultaneously, the UFV became known as the place GDR women could find a common identity in a period when the history and cultural experiences of the GDR were being deprecated.

III. The Work of the Independent Women's Association

The UFV had its greatest political importance in the winter of 1989–90, between the time of its founding and the preparations for elections to the East German Parliament in March 1990. After that, the parties became the real political movers again, and the role of the Round Table eroded.

In the period of transition the women's groups at the local and regional level, just like the other citizens' movements, concerned themselves with the dissolution of the State Security Service (Stasi), personnel changes in the administration, and the redistribution of state and Party property. Through the agency of the decentralized Round Tables, buildings or office space could be obtained for women's groups, or their occupation could be legalized. The first Offices for the Equality of Women [Gleichstellungsstellen] were established.

UFV women worked on various committees of the central Round Table. "The Working Group on Women's Policy" (later called "The Working Group on Equality of the Sexes")[18] handled the demand for substantive, not only formal, equality. The Round Table worked out a document entitled "Basic Principles of a Politics with the Equality of Men and Women as Its Goal."[19] From the copious catalogue of demands the position of Commissioner for the Equality of Women was created at the governmental level. This occurred after the elections to the Volkskammer on March 18, 1990. This was not a separate ministry as demanded, but a Commissioner of the State Council of Ministers, under the Ministry for Women and the Family. The requirement for a corresponding office was also included in the communal laws for the GDR in May 1990, stating that there had to be a Commissioner for the Equality of Women for every town with more than 10,000 inhabitants, something that had not existed in West Germany.

The UFV participated in developing the "Social Charter"[20] which became an important historic document of the opposition during the Wende. It included demands for the right to work, democratic work regulations, humanization of work, the maintenance of social standards that had been achieved, sexual equality, etc. Social policy was supposed to be not only ameliorative but determinative of political and economic decisions.

In February 1990 the last GDR government integrated all social forces into a "government of national responsibility" and affirmed its willingness to take over the responsibility for governing. Both the resolution at the second national meeting of the UFV (on January 2, 1990) to put up candidates for elections to Parliament, and the decision to participate in government show the UFV's interest in political engagement. By the time the official founding convention of the UFV as a political organization took place at the end of February, political conditions had already changed significantly. The citizens' movement and the women's movement as organized in the UFV were hardly equal to the speed of the changes, to the moving of the date of the election from May to March 1990, and to the election campaign, which was structured by the Western members of the large parties and dominated by the theme of "national unity."[21] All this relegated the movements to the fringes of political activity. The women's association formed a coalition with the Green Party, but because of strategic errors in the creation of candidate lists and the inflexibility of the Greens, it obtained no seats in the GDR parliament and thereby suffered a loss of visibility.

From this point on, decentralizing interests of the regional and local women's groups came increasingly into play. The Speakers' Council (which could be called together more readily than the State Coordinating Council) was created as a corrective to the Berlin centrism that had grown up for pragmatic reasons. Since there was no female representative in Parliament during the period of transition, the integrative function of the Association was also missing. The municipal elections were in May 1990. In summer 1990 there were preparations for the October elections to the state parliaments. In coalition with the other citizen's movements—New Forum, Democracy Now, and the Initiative for Peace and Human Rights, as well as the Green Party—it was possible for the UFV to win seats in three state parliaments: in Saxony, Saxony-Anhalt, and, in December, Berlin, as well as about seventy seats in local parliaments.[22] By means of this coalition Christina Schenk entered the German Federal Parliament (Bundestag) in the first all-German elections in December 1990. Nevertheless, these difficult electoral preparations, which ran parallel to the negotiations about the dates and the terms of unification, were unable to generate a mobilization of women like the one brought forth by hopes for reforms during the preliminary elections in February.

What *is* the Independent Women's Association? What does the UFV represent in the last year of the existence of the GDR and the first year of German unity?

While in the period of its origin it was simultaneously and spontaneously an organization and a social movement, the incongruence of these two dimensions became evident after the elections for Parliament. UFV women were now acting in completely different arenas, between which there was not necessarily any communication or cooperation. Women in various activities were linked by their particular concrete engagement, and the Women's Association as a producer of group consciousness lost significance. The conflicting effects of the political "normalization" were apparent, but a perception of the problem or a programmatic discussion did not take place because of the runaway course of events surrounding the reunification. These created enormous demands, both political and personal.

Over the course of 1991, contact and cooperation between women members of Parliament was promoted; these women for the most part had been dependent on their own resources or on the various constellations that had elected them. "Conferences for Women in Parliament" took place, in which women coordinated their experiences and plans for action on such issues as policy toward child care and abortion.

Various Round Tables arose anew, attending again to the experiences of the transition period and acting as forums for dialogue between social groups and politicians. In Saxony UFV women participate in the Round Table on Women's Policy. In Berlin there are Round Tables on women and unemployment, abortion, and violence against women. In other cities and towns similar practices can be found. Regionally such groups are also places for the work of the municipal and state Commissioners for the Equality of Women, of which only a few are still UFV women. This is also true for the sections of ministries that deal with issues of women's policy. These offices for the Equality of Women at the local level sometimes help to direct state monies to women's projects and small businesses. Women who during the winter of 1989–90 were active with the UFV have frequently taken over such functions, but often as members of the large political parties or as independents without political affiliation. After the elections to the Volkskammer and the municipal elections of 1990, UFV women could be replaced by party women (mostly from the Christian Democratic Party or the Social Democratic Party).

Women's groups form the social basis of political and institutional activity in the name of the UFV. Today in the larger cities there are women's centers with meetings on various themes, with cafés, breakfasts for unemployed women, libraries, and opportunities for legal, social, and psychological counseling. Houses for battered women are associated with some of the projects. In some instances continuing education courses, such as in data processing, have been organized by women for women, and financial planning is also discussed. Numerous women have been hired for women's projects and women's centers, usually with government job training funds. In a short time a relative stability has been attained for this new social and cultural milieu. Within, and also independent of, women's centers there exist women's groups for discussion, action, and consciousness raising.

It is not possible to determine how many members there are in the UFV. The new women's groups fluctuate and it is difficult to determine if they are or are not members of the UFV. Groups can cooperate with the UFV without joining it. After the collapse of the GDR many women did not wish to join any organization again out of resentment of the previous overpoliticization of society.

Women in their mid-thirties and forties[23] were decisive in building the UFV and individual women's groups and frequently hold offices in the Offices for the Equality of Women and in the women's sections of ministries. Yet there are some indications that the women's groups are growing younger. University-trained women or graduates initially predominated among UFV representatives since they had the ability to speak publicly and sometimes had professional knowledge that the other women had yet to acquire. "Intellectuals in the leadership" sometimes created tensions in which old conflicts between movement women and women in institutions surfaced.

It is estimated that half of the office work in the UFV is done by lesbians. In June 1990, a plenary of lesbians complained in a declaration to the Coordinating Council that there existed "a disproportion between the part that lesbians have in the existence and working of the UFV and the clarity with which this is communicated to the public."[24] The demands occasionally voiced that a UFV spokeswoman should speak for lesbians have been reduced since the UFV representative in the federal parliament has been a lesbian.

IV. Perspectives

The time which gave rise to the UFV and produced its original raison d'être is past. The two Germanys have been united; spontaneous groups or a political-cultural opposition could no longer hope effectively to influence the political process.

The UFV did not participate with the civil rights groups in the creation of Bündnis 90[25] the political and parliamentary party formed from East German citizen's groups in September 1991. The unfortunate experience in the joint preparations by Bündnis 90 and the UFV for the four elections in 1990 reinforced the conviction that the UFV was not taken seriously by the other groups. At the convention of the Green Party in April 1991, the UFV declared it was ready to cooperate, but would remain autonomous because "women's interests cannot be advanced in male-dominated organizational structures—even in the citizen's movement."[26] Because the West German Greens were not in the federal parliament in 1991, there was no support from them.

The decision in September 1991 that the UFV define itself juridically as a membership organization instead of as a political party was required by the August 1990 unification treaty.[27] It forced the UFV realistically to acknowledge its place in society. The UFV did not represent or mobilize masses of women. "Participation in political power" as it had been understood during the disintegration of the GDR was still an attractive challenge, but it had become an empty abstraction. The debate on whether to opt for the legal status of a party or an organization alienated many women. Of the around 1000 members (in August

1990, there had been about 3000)[28] only some 100 came to the decisive convention in Weimar in September 1991. This confirmed that many felt themselves a part of the Association—they wanted and needed the organization, but did not want to have much to do with its internal workings. Those who participated in the debate took issue most often with what "being political" meant for the Women's Association.

There was general consensus at the congress in September 1991 that electoral candidacies were important and should take place. Since the UFV would fail to meet the hurdle of 5 percent of the vote (needed in order to participate in the proportional distribution of seats), it depended on coalition partners to get candidates on the ballot. Such cooperation depends on the social weight of the UFV and especially on regional and local cooperation. At the end of 1991 there were still UFV candidates in parliaments, but these are only as strong as their extra-parliamentary support. Cornelia Matzke, a UFV representative in Saxony, pointed out that active women were now in many different groups and projects, that this created a problem for the organization, and that the UFV could only effectively continue if it was not "imposed from above" but "filled out by the people at the base."[29]

UFV women were represented in various political positions, but the "base" was formed chiefly of independent groups and projects whose activity consisted to a great extent of social work. Yet the feminist claims of these groups go beyond social work. The future of the UFV may be decided by its success in seizing upon the political content in its work and demands and representing them with the self-confidence of a political lobby in public discussions or in institutions and parliaments, and then organizing them for action, for forums, for Round Tables, for proposals to Parliament, or for whatever concrete goals may be achieved.

The UFV's importance in women's politics grew limited because there developed numerous other possibilities to organize or work around specific problems, and for realizing political ambitions. The UFV found it difficult to conceive the Association as part of a differentiated spectrum of women's politics. It also understood itself, first intuitively, then expressly, as a leftist organization, then became uncertain about its self-definition in the context of pluralism—whether to be left and feminist and thereby specialized and exclusive, or whether to be a "collective movement," a more open umbrella organization with an unspecific profile. This debate flared up again and again, reflecting the group's disappointment at not being an important social or political force.

The second factor that limited the importance of the Association is that the UFV and the women's movement were no longer identical. In the small civil rights groups (Democracy Now, Initiative for Peace and Human Rights) those who formed the base were absorbed into the organizations, creating numerous functionaries and no "movement." In contrast, the UFV faces many self-sufficient women's groups that formed without the UFV's guidance and for whom the UFV had no role to play.

As of September 1991, West German women were permitted to join the Women's Association. Women disappointed with the Green Party are interested in building state associations in West Germany. Whether or not the UFV will succeed in expanding to an all-German organization remained undecided in 1992. The histories of the West and East German women's movements are very different; a political umbrella organization that came about in the East because of the implosion of the socialist state would result in the West in attempts to impose a common political demand on enormously diverse women's activities. The UFV must be primarily concerned with being an important presence in women's politics in the East and a receptive partner for women in the West.

The shaping of political opinion outside the parties continues the critique of the civil rights movements and is a practical beginning for participatory democratization. New social movements are important for cultural innovation, for the creation of alternative milieus, styles of life, orientations, etc. The search for a new understanding of political action and a modus operandi for the organization is really a search for how the original themes—visibility for women, political influence, a society friendly to women and their emancipation—should be transformed to fit the new "normalcy" of the united German state.

Translated by Mark Schaffer

Notes

1. Ina Merkel, "Wie alles anfing," in *Argument extra/ UFV: Ohne Frauen ist kein Staat zu machen* (Berlin: Argument, 1990): pp. 10f.

2. See Jutta Gysi, "Frauen und Familienentwicklung in der DDR, "in *Sozialstruktur und sozialer Wandel in der DDR,* ed. Heiner Timmermann (Saarbrücken: Verlag Rite Dadder, 1989), pp. 93–115.

3. In 1972 abortion during the first three months of pregnancy was legalized. The hours of work for mothers with two children were shortened. The child-oriented policies made it possible for women also to be mothers.

4. Women were without influence in leadership positions of the Socialist Unity Party and the state; they composed a small minority in higher leadership functions; in middle-level leadership functions and in basic activities they accounted for 25 to 40 percent and were regarded as "qualified assistance." Only in the lowest levels of education, vocation, and public life is there equality of opportunity. See Gerd Meyer, "Frauen in den Machthierarchien der DDR," *Deutschland Archiv* (December 1986), pp. 294–311; and G. Meyer, "Frauen und Parteielite nach dem XI. Parteitag der SED: Gründe und Hypothesen zur Kontinuität der Unterrepraesentanz," *Deutschland Archiv* (March 1986), pp. 1296–1321.

5. See Freya Klier, "Die Frau zwischen Kombi und Kreiβsaal," in Freya. Klier, *DDR-Identitäten* (Berlin, 1990).

6. Anne Hampele, "Der UFV: Neue Frauenbewegung im letzten Jahr der DDR," in

Von der Illegalität ins Parlament, eds. Helmut Müller-Enbergs, Marianne Schulz, and Jan Wielgohs (Berlin: Links Druck Verlag, 1991), pp. 221ff.

7. See Gislinde Schwarz and Christine Zenner, eds., *Wir wollen mehr als ein "Vaterland"* (Hamburg; Rowohlt Taschenbuch Verlag, 1990).

8. Hampele, p. 232.

9. Walter Süß, "Mit Unwillen zur Macht: Der Runde Tisch der DDR in der Übergangszeit," *Deutschland Archiv* (May 1990), p. 470.

10. Wolfgang Ullmann, *Demokratie—jetzt oder nie: Perspektiven der Gerechtigkeit* (München: Kyrill & Method Verlag, 1990), p. 162.

11. Marianne Schulz, "Neues Forum: Von der illegal Opposition zur legalen Marginalität," In Mueller-Enbergs, et al., p. 28.

12. Article 1 of the GDR Constitution defined the state as "the political organization of the workers . . . under the leadership of the working class and its Marxist-Leninist party."

13. Reductions in welfare subsidies began with children's clothing in January and February 1990. At the beginning of 1990 there were the first attacks on Paragraph 218, the West German abortion law. "Doctors in Favor of a Financial Contribution by Women Patients," *Berliner Zeitung,* January 27–28, 1990.

14. For example, the laws and rights for the unmarried had long since disappeared in the socialist family law of the GDR. The pay structure of the West German work and wage law rests on the existence of a primary and a secondary wage earner; this continues in the welfare law, where the head of household is entitled to more welfare than the other spouse (usually the wife). A discussion began in 1991 about the pension law, which discriminates against certain women. The basis for calculation of years of work also discriminates against women in regard to security in old age, but in a different way than the rules of the GDR, where the income of the final two years' work served as the base and led to low pensions for women on account of the lower level of their incomes.

15. Since the summer of 1991, there has been a controversy within the UFV about state security, collaboration, and the general responsibility for repressive conditions in the GDR.

16. Christina Schenk, *"Experiment UFV,"* Argument 184 (1990).

17. Ibid.

18. See Helmut Herles and Ewald Rose, eds., *Vom Runden Tisch zum Parlament* (Bonn: Verlag Bouvier, 1990), pp. 30, 76.

19. Ibid., pp. 263ff.

20. At its thirteenth session (February 19, 1990) the Round Table approved the creation a "all-Germany Round Table on sociopolitical issues" and "suggested the drafting of a social charter." It "challenges the government of the GDR to include the social charter as the position of the GDR in the negotiations of the commission on economic, currency and social union." Introduction to the draft in Herles and Rose, pp. 169, 238. Suggestions for the social charter were worked on by a committee at the UFV convention on February 20, 1990.

21. It was assumed in early summer 1990 that all-German elections would not take place within the year, but there was time pressure due to the currency union on July 1, the treaty on unification in June and August, the creation of the five new states, the state elections in October, and the federal elections on December 2, 1990.

22. The citizens' movements and the Green Party put up candidates and campaigned in various coalitions. In Mecklenburg-West Pomerania there was no joint list of candidates, and none of the movements or the Greens got into the state parliament. In Thuringia, where a self-confident women's movement with a longer history existed, the UFV campaigned alone and received 7 percent of the second votes. Berlin elected its city parliament in December instead of in October 1990, at the same time that the federal elections took place.

23. There is some evidence in a study by Daphne Hornig and Irina Meier at Humboldt University in East Berlin that suggests this. The data was collected in summer 1990 by polling a random sample of UFV groups on their social composition. Only twenty questionnaires were returned. Women in this age group were strongly represented. One reason may be the greater vocational and family pressures they experience. The women were equally divided between those with some professional vocational training, vocational school graduates, and university graduates. Industrial and craft occupations were only sporadically represented. Usually women in intellectual jobs, the social sciences, and the service professions were the active members.

24. *frau anders* (May 1990), pp. 4ff.

25. Democracy Now, the Initiative for Peace and Human Rights, and New Forum all participated.

26. Declaration of the Independent Women's Association at the national delegates' conference of the Greens in Neumünster, April 22, 1991.

27. One year after reunification parties and political associations had to adapt their by-laws either to the regulations concerning parties or to the regulations concerning organizations.

28. The status of a member was and is unclear; therefore, the numbers give only trends on classifications.

29. "Ohne Basis bleibt jede Struktur eine leere Hülse," interview with Cornelia Matzke, *Tageszeitung*, October 1, 1991.

18

Abortion and German Unification

Nanette Funk

German unification took place in fall 1990 under Article 23 of the Basic Law of the Federal Republic of Germany, which incorporated the German Democratic Republic into the FRG under its standing laws.[1] The question became: What would happen to the more liberal abortion law of the German Democratic Republic? Would former GDR women lose their abortion rights, which were stronger than those granted by the Federal Republic of Germany?

During the Cold War, competition between East and West Germany had provided an incentive for East Germany to liberalize its abortion laws in 1972, in the middle of a strong but unsuccessful proabortion battle in the FRG. The GDR thereby tried to score ideological points that it was more committed to the rights of women than was West Germany, helping the GDR to legitimate itself among its own citizens.

In 1947–48 in the former GDR the old Paragraph 218 permitted abortion in the first trimester for medical or social reasons or if pregnancy resulted from a criminal act. The law was removed from the jurisdiction of the penal code. In 1950 the "social" grounds for abortion were eliminated, with the consequence, according to Gert Henning, that 60 percent of abortions became illegal.[2] In 1972 abortion on demand in the first trimester (Fristenlösung) was introduced, limited to once every six months.[3] The law also required free contraception for women. Passage of the abortion law was one of the few cases in the GDR in which opposition votes were registered.[4] After the first trimester, abortion was allowed only in cases of danger to the life of the mother, and had to be approved by a gynecological commission.

Abortions in the GDR were done on an in-patient basis, mostly by D & C. But, as reported by Tatiana Böhm, there were still negative attitudes toward abortion in the 1970s; women were encouraged by doctors to continue pregnancies; and women having abortions were often placed in hospital rooms with women trying to save difficult pregnancies. In the 1980s, however, abortions were sometimes urged on women; there was little consistency in attitudes. Information that a woman had had an abortion was passed on through medical forms she had to present to her employer, revealing that denials of personal privacy were not limited to state secret police activity.[5] Although abortion was legal, there was no public discourse about it, and abortion statistics were not included in the statistical yearbook.[6] All this reinforced women's feeling that there was some moral shame about abortion which they could not discuss. Birth control was regarded as women's responsibility, and if a woman needed an abortion, she believed that it was her "fault" because she had been irresponsible.[7] Yet birth control methods were of poor quality, and most women used the pill in spite of concern about its side effects. In the 1980s women in the GDR began some public discourse about abortion; in 1982 Charlotte Wogitzky's book *My Unborn Children* appeared, and there was a discussion in the women's magazine *Für Dich* in 1989.[8]

In the GDR, the rate of abortion had decreased since 1972, from 33.7 per 1000 women to 21.4 in 1989.[9] In 30 percent of cases in 1987 and 1981 abortion was the only means of birth control used.[10] In 1989 in the former GDR there were 73,899 abortions, and it was estimated that there were 200,000 legal and illegal abortions in the same year in the former West Germany, three times as many as there were live births.[11] The numbers are harder to establish for West Germany because of illegal abortions. The birth rate in the GDR per 1000 inhabitants was 13.6, in comparison to 10.3 in the FRG.

In West Germany abortion was regulated by Paragraph 218 of the Basic Law. West German women's abortion demands in 1970 had led to the passage of a law by a close vote in the Bundestag (Parliament) in 1974, referred to as a "periodic model." It permitted first-trimester abortions with compulsory counseling. But the law was overturned by a 5 to 3 decision[12] in 1975 by the Constitutional Court, which declared the law unconstitutional on the grounds that it did not adequately guarantee the legal protection of "becoming life" required by the constitutional principle of safeguarding human dignity and life. The court proposed instead a continuation of the "indications model," in which acceptable reasons had to be given but with an extension of the approved reasons for abortion. This law was put into practice June 2, 1976. First-trimester abortions could be performed if one doctor certified that the woman had a justifiable reason for an abortion; if she was counseled by a state-recognized counselor; and if the abortion was performed by a second doctor. A three-day lapse was required between counseling and abortion. The reasons ("indications") for which doctors could approve an abortion were: danger to the life or health of the mother ("medical indication"), danger that the child would be seriously deformed ("eugenic indication"), a pregnancy resulting from rape or incest ("criminal indication"), and the additional condition proposed by the Constitutional Court, that of difficult social conditions for the mother ("social indication").

The individual states in West Germany had their own local rules about counseling and out-patient abortions; the latter are prohibited in Bavaria. There are several religious counseling organizations, but Pro Familia, a private organization, is the only counseling agency that advocates women's right to self-determination. Since "social indications" were by far the most common grounds for abortion (accounting for 86 percent of all abortions[13]), and this required approval by a counselor, such agencies were especially important. Qualifying for an abortion meant going through a maze, in which one had to know which doctors and counselors gave favorable recommendations. It was sometimes difficult to find doctors who would not use the punitive and painful method of inducing miscarriage. In more conservative and Catholic areas of West Germany it was virtually impossible to get an abortion; in Bavaria, there were only three nonreligious counseling centers out of only forty in total.[14]

All of the GDR parties in spring 1990 supported the GDR abortion policy, and it was overwhelmingly backed by public opinion. With the unification of Germany projected for October 1990, the question loomed large as to which German state's abortion laws would prevail, or whether there would be two different policies for East and West German women. The intense debates in summer 1990 focused on the question of the sphere of application of each law, whether West German women be permitted abortions in the former East Germany, whether the law was to be applied depending on the site of the abortion or on the legal residence of the women having the abortion. It was finally agreed in Article 31 of the Unification agreement that as of unification on October 3, 1990, women in the East retained their right to first-trimester abortions until the end of 1992 while West German women were permitted to have first-trimester abortions on the more liberal terms if they went to the former GDR, but not in the West. By the end of 1992 the Bundestag was required to determine the abortion law for the united Germany. The vote in the Bundestag would be an exceptional vote of conscience, one not bound by party dictates.

The political parties were deeply divided on abortion; intra- and interparty wrangling prevented agreement. In 1990 women in the Bundestag had tried to take the lead, holding nonpartisan meetings to work out an abortion agreement but the Free Democratic Party recalled their member. In spring 1992 the special parliamentary committee to revise Paragraph 218—the "Committee for the protection of unborn life"—remained deadlocked.[15] It hardly heard any women witnesses, or considered the GDR experience with its more liberal abortion policies. Six different bills were proposed. Finally, in May 1992 Uta Würfel of the FDP successfully organized a compromise, joint agreement ("Gruppenantrag") entitled "The law for the protection of potential life, for the promotion of a pro-child society, for help in conflicts concerning abortion and for the regulation of abortion." The very title of the bill indicated the political infighting that led to this compromise. With 32 CDU votes the FDP/SPD agreement was passed in the Bundestag on June 25, 1992, by a vote of 357 to 284.[16] Direct democracy, in the form of a referendum to establish the will of their constituency, was utilized by some eastern German CDU members to shore up their vote for the agreement in spite of heavy CDU pressure to the contrary.[17]

The law allowed first trimester abortions if the woman so decided, but on condition of obligatory counseling. The final decision remained with the woman. She was not obligated to discuss any personal issues or to give reasons for an abortion. There was to be a three-day interval between counseling and abortion. Women who violated the law were subject to criminal prosecution as in the previous FRG law. Showing the influence of the GDR practices, the law also stated that each child from 3 to 6 years old had a right to a kindergarten place and appropriate funds had to be made available for this purpose by 1996. Day care had to be provided to children under three only "in accord with demand," a decidedly vague term. Women under 21 could receive birth-control pills free of charge.[18]

A legal challenge was immediately filed by 248 members of the CSU/CDU asking for a review of the law by the Constitutional Court in Karlsruhe. On August 5 the court decided to suspend the law until the constitutional review took place in November 1992. As of this writing, it is not known whether the law will be declared unconstitutional, as in 1975, on the grounds that it does not sufficiently protect unborn life.

The law required a counseling center for every 40,000 inhabitants and there had to be both religious and nonreligious centers in each state. But the states retained considerable authority in implementing the law. In 1992, the federal government paid 90 percent of the costs for pregnancy counseling centers and the states paid 10 percent. In 1993 the states, all strapped for funds and with varying degrees of financial resources, would bear 90 percent of the costs and local governments, 10 percent. Religious organizations would be much more able to fund their own centers and provide a fuller staff than nonreligious ones.[19] The party governing each state will influence which counseling centers, and how many, are set up.[20] In 1991 51 percent of all counseling centers in eastern Germany were religious although the population was largely nonreligious. Young women, women who are uncertain and women with unexplored guilt feelings will be the most readily influenced by centers which may hope to dissuade women from abortions. Women in the countryside without easy access to such centers will also be affected. Obligatory counseling poses several problems: there is a contradiction in the very concept of "obligatory counseling"; in the cities with under 40,000 inhabitants women will have little meaningful choice in counseling; although counseling centers are mandated by law to enable a woman to carry out her will, their goal is also "the protection of unborn life," without that phrase ever being defined. The hidden assumption behind obligatory counseling is that women are not generally competent or morally to be trusted to decide for themselves whether to have an abortion, or to go for counseling. Many former GDR woman distinguish between the provision of counseling opportunities which they appreciate and did not have in the former GDR, and obligatory counseling, which they do not want.

At the same time that the debate about abortion drags on, there has been an increase in abortions by former GDR women because of the insecurity caused by the transformation with its attendant high unemployment, low salaries, closing day care centers, and contraceptives no longer dispensed freely to women as they had been in the GDR. Some hospitals in the former GDR began to refuse women abortions after unification. The birth rate in the former East Germany has plummeted 50 percent since 1989. There has been a boom in voluntary sterilizations among young women, a move virtually impossible in the former GDR. The reasons for sterilization appear to be similar to those for abortions with the additional reason that some women hope to thereby increase their chances of employment. There are unsubstantiated rumors that some employers have encouraged sterilization.

Although there were some joint efforts by East and West German women for a stronger right to abortion, such as organizing conferences against Paragraph 218, the long debate did not bring the women together. Pro-abortion demonstrations were not very successful. Eastern women were not very activated by the campaign, many feeling that their effective right to abortion would not be seriously jeopardized. Effective action by women in the Bundestag was thwarted by party politics. The law was a liberalization for West German women, formally entitling them for the first time to decide for themselves on a first trimester abortion, but it imposed more constraints on former GDR women, who faced the new requirement of counseling and the reincorporation of the abortion law in the Penal Code. Women in the more conservative western German states such as Bavaria would probably benefit substantively, with effectively greater possibilities for abortion. The tense parliamentary vote in which about half the East CDU party members withstood the pressure of their own party and voted for the compromise showed the serious East/West split in the party system.[21]

Transformation of the abortion laws brought with it correlative normative and moral transformations. The compromise law recognized the unborn fetus as having legal significance, and the language and culture of the debates in 1990–92 changed to make the central issue that of the protection of the unborn fetus and the question which did the job better—restricting abortion or providing daycare. The legal debate over abortion is part of a process of redefining the social role of women in the united Germany, reintroducing religious views in the former socialist system, preserving those views in the West, and retaining state control over women's reproductive capacities. Women's right to abortion, as part of the general women's position in state socialism, one predicated on a nonreligious basis, has become a symbol of state socialism and the confrontation of East and West.

The new public sphere in the former GDR potentially empowers GDR women, but it also empowers the Church and conservative forces. In the former GDR, *Zaunreiterin,* the now defunct *Ypsilon,* created after 1989, and the UFV newsletter *Weib Blick,*[22] created in 1992, regularly discussed the issue of abortion in an attempt to inform women, to create a public discourse about this issue, and to form a women's public sphere, but they have a minuscule readership. East German women's groups have raised issues that West German restrictions on abortion are demeaning to women, that although women are supposed to bear responsibility for caring for children they are not considered responsible enough to decide for themselves whether to have a child. They have argued for broader notions of reproductive rights, including the right of a child to be born into a home in which it is wanted, free contraceptives, counseling on how to use them and information on their effects, and sex education, including sex education in the schools that teaches boys responsibility for preventing pregnancy.

GDR women are overwhelmed by many problems of daily life in the transition, democratic participation is something they are just beginning to learn, and many have yet to unlearn authoritarian attitudes. The East abortion policy is changing, influenced by Western politics, and West German women have benefited somewhat from the influence of the stronger GDR abortion policies. At the same time, the need for federal monies for the general development of eastern Germany, and for women's projects in particular, is being used to justify cutbacks in funds for Western women's projects, pitting West against East German women. One can only hope that Habermas' claim that the "revolution" in the East was a "recuperative" revolution will be mistaken with respect to women, and that the West German position of women will not be simply reconfirmed in the united Germany.

Notes

1. The other alternative would have been unification under Article 146, which would have required writing a new constitution for the united Germany.

2. Gert Henning, *Wieder Paragraph 218? Erfahrungen eines Frauenarztes* (Berlin: 1990), p. 12ff. Cited in Sabine Berghahn and Andrea Fritzsche), *Frauenrecht in Ost und West Deutschland: Bilanz Ausblick* (Berlin: Basis Druck, 1991), pp. 195, 209.

3. Tatiana Böhm, "The Abortion Question: A New Solution in Unified Germany?" *German Politics and Society,* nos. 24–25 (Winter 1991–92): 137.

4. Bergahn and Fritzsche, p. 193.

5. Doctors passed information on to authorities when requested, and those who were reluctant to do so would discourage their patients from discussing problems, so that the doctor would have nothing to reveal. This protected the patient, but could interfere with sound medical practice.

6. Katrin Rohnstock, ed., *Handbuch: Wegweiser für Frauen in den fünf neuen Bundesländern* (Berlin: Frauenbuch bei Basisdruck, 1991), p. 203.

7. Christine Schindler, "Kein Paragraph 218 in Ost and West," *Ypsilon* (May 1991), p. 14.

8. Rohnstock, p. 203.

9. In a study done in 1987 in the former GDR covering eleven gynecological clinics, it was established that 60 percent of the women who had abortions in 1987 were over twenty-five years old; the average age at the time of abortion was 27.3 years old; and women who had abortions had more children than the average for women their age. In 1987, 35 percent of women having abortions had had previous abortions. The study was done by Dr. Gert Henning and referred to in "Frauen im Zwangsfeld-Thema Abtriebung: Zahlen, Fakten, Argumentation, Diskussion," *Ypsilon* 1990, pp. 18–19.

10. The increase in women who had more than one abortion was interpreted as being due to women's reluctance, because of side effects, to take the birth control pill. Ibid., p. 18.

11. From Dr. Marina Beyer, Office for the Equality of Women in the former GDR. Ibid., p. 10.

12. *Der Spiegel,* "Hoffen auf die 'Roten Roben' " May 18, 1992, p. 50.

13. Bergahn and Fritzsche, p. 193.

14. Ursula Nelles, "Abortion, the Special Case: A Constitutional Perspective," in *German Politics and Society,* nos. 24–25 (Winter 1991–92): 114.

15. "Feminismus in Parlament," *Weiblick,* April 3, 1992, pp. 29–32.

16. "Germany Liberalizes Its Abortion Law," *The Week in Germany,* July 3, 1992.

17. Interview with Eva Kunz in Potsdam, July 6, 1992.

18. "Gefährliche Lücken, "Der Spiegel," August 10, 1992, pp. 23–6.

19. *Berliner Zeitung,* July 20, 1992.

20. In the SPD governed state of Brandenburg in the former GDR there are 20 nonreligious, and six religious counselling centers. (Interview with Eva Kunz in July 6, 1992.) In Saxony there are 25 church and 26 non-church centers, including Pro Familia and the Red Cross. (Telephone Interview with Saxony Office for the Equality of Women, July 21, 1992.) In East Berlin in 1991 there were 6 religious (three Catholic and three Lutheran) and 1 non-religious pregnancy counseling center. Answer by the President of the House of Representatives in Berlin to question of Senator Sibyll Klotz, Feb. 4, 1992. Thuringia, Mecklenburg-Vorpommern, and Saxony-Anhalt are more conservative and will be influenced by their governing party, the CDU, in their funding of counseling centers.

21. Polls taken in Brandenburg in October, 1991 by the Institute for Sociology and Social Policy showed that the majority of the citizens there favored the retention of the GDR abortion law. (Cited in Regine Hildebrandt, "Paragraph 218: Strafrecht kann kein werdendes Leben schutzen," *betr:Frauen,* no. 1, Brandenburg. 1992)

22. "Weib Blick" is a play on the German word "weiblich," which means "female." "Weib Blick" means "Woman's View."

19

"Totalitarian Lib": The Legacy of Communism for Hungarian Women

Enikö Bollobás

Hungary has gone through a gradual and peaceful transformation, from the monolithic structure of totalitarianism to a pluralistic democracy, a civil society, and a viable economy. In 1989 Hungary was the first domino, the pioneer of the transition in the Eastern European region, directly influencing changes in East Germany, Czechoslovakia, and Romania.

Hungarians strongly feel part of European, and especially Central European, civilization. They were very much a part of it in the Middle Ages and the nineteenth century; in 1914, Budapest was a European center, and Hungarians lived in a richly articulated European society until the end of World War I. But Hungarians have faced a battered twentieth century, losing half of their country, as well as three to four million ethnic Hungarians to neighboring countries. After 1920 Hungary could not return to her old strength; her illnesses could not be cured. But in spite of that Hungary was in many ways a relatively diverse, pluralistic society, which the Communists managed to turn into a disintegrated, atomized, and thoroughly proletarianized society.

Communism has proved to be a devastating experience, from its disastrous economy, frivolously incurred large debt, wasteful working methods, broken infrastructure, and pollution caused by an unnecessary and loss-creating industry. In addition, housing was appalling and the architecture dreadful. What proved to be a very long-term effect was that the social fiber as a whole became rotten as communism created what was in many ways a morally devastated, materialistic society with an encouragement to dishonesty. One aspect of this destruction was the social injustice this system of "mental cheating," which Orwell called "doublethink," perpetuated on women, forcing them into a subordinate, humiliating, state-controlled position. Only after the fall of communism have women started to do some serious thinking about their role in society.

The phenomenon I would like to describe is complex in two respects. In Hungary, women wishing to live a "self-reflective" life must live with the double legacy of a pre–World War II patriarchal society and the post–World War II communist ideology. The prewar legacy is well-known to feminists of the United States and Western Europe, since similar trends, although in different degrees, marked those societies too: limited choices, traditional feminine ideals, and in general a secondary role for women. But after the war in the eastern part of an artificially divided Europe, communists halted all social development, petrifying certain spheres of social life. Thus, the prewar patriarchal mentalities changed little.

Often the picture of communist Hungary, and especially that of the role women played in the society, was misapprehended by observers. Visitors to Hungary often got the impression that women were very "Western" in Budapest—they dressed well, looked educated, led a semi-Western lifestyle. What could not be visible to short-term tourists, however, was how much time, money, and energy had to be spent in keeping up this Western, but still immensely modest, lifestyle. Furthermore, women were used by those in power when put into Parliament; abortion was often meant to serve as birth control; and maternity leave gave one precarious job security at best, because not even full-paying jobs granted existential security.

Communist propaganda managed to spread the image that the visibility of women in public marked a positive change from the previous state. The rich web of institutions and organizations, including women's organizations that Hungary's civil society had built, at least for a privileged layer of society, until World War II, became part of the past of which the communist system rid itself. Hungarians learned little about prominent role models with which history might have supplied them—women active in the nineteenth century national movement, the European suffrage movement, and the peace movement; women labor organizers of the precommunist era; and women fighting for female education. It never entered common knowledge that women played an important role in the 1956 revolution, not only as nurses and caretakers but as fighters and demonstrators who, for example, organized an anti-Soviet march on the first days of the uprising. In a similar way, the communists banned all thinking and action that challenged the role of the single official women's organization, the Soviet-type National Alliance of Hungarian Women. Thus, they had to silence those feminists in the 1970s who demanded reproductive freedom and the enforcement of the "equal pay for equal work" law.

I have found more gaps between Western and Eastern views on women than exist on most other issues, such as democratic institution building, economic transformation, or environmental protection. Not only did Western leftist romanticism hold that women were better off in the communist countries, there was also the negative prejudice of the silent, anticommunist majority within Hungary, who wholeheartedly rejected the complete set of women's problems as part of communist propaganda, distrusting those who tried to stand up for women's rights.

Neither view is, of course, even close to the truth. The various benefits women enjoyed in the communist societies, such as full employment, free health care, maternity leave, and cheap abortion, only sound appealing to foreign observers, to whom these words have different and much more positive meanings. In Hungarian—as well as Czech, Slovak, Polish, and Russian—these words sound pitiful, cheap, poor, and gloomy, because that is the reality they evoke. When in Hungary we hear about full employment, we know that it has the effect of killing ambition and initiative in millions of people, and that it masked unemployment. When we hear about free health care we do not picture an American hospital but an overcrowded, undermanned, underequipped, underdeveloped Eastern European hospital. When we hear about maternity leave we know how much it pays and that the practice generates underachievement.

Women's position in the paid work force is less advantageous than men's.[1] Yet with the mushrooming of small enterprises, women appear to be active participants in their formation,[2] contributing to the shrinking wage gap. A mobile segment of middle-class women are trying to get rid of their disadvantages. Several very prominent and successful women have emerged recently: the president of the Budapest Stock Exchange, partners at newly launched public relations firms and investment companies, and many successful entrepreneurs, all of whom serve as visible positive role models.

Women in Politics

Although during the forty-three years of communist rule in Hungary women were always present in Parliament (25 to 30 percent), they were supposed to fill—often to overfill—quotas. No woman was ever a member of a body with real political power. This relative absence of women from politics even today has several roots. There is the patriarchal legacy, keeping women in their traditional roles in the family and household even if these roles have changed in some strata of society since World War II. There was the division of household chores necessitated by the inefficient central economy; in a country where moonlighting was widespread, women worked in the household for as many hours as their male counterparts did in their illegal jobs. But perhaps the psychological motive is equally significant: the female functionary has proved to be so repulsive that today women quite understandably want to avoid even the impression of such power aspirations. It will take time for the image of the fanatic, utterly intransigent woman apparatchik to fade into oblivion and allow new female models of autonomous action to emerge.

Women have not yet made a breakthrough in politics: as of 1992 we only had one woman member of the Cabinet at the ministerial level, and only 28 women members of the 386-seat Parliament. Even this number is misleading: of the 28 only 5 were elected by their constituencies (4 in the Hungarian Democratic Forum, 1 from the Agrarian Union). They are the ones who have direct responsibility to their constituency, who can be held accountable for their votes and actions. The other 23 became parliamentarians on party ballots, which means a totally different kind of responsibility and accountability. Yet in spite of these slow beginnings, I see an unmistakable awakening. Women in Parliament, government administration, or political organizations are not puppets moved by some greater power: they act for themselves, as they were elected or appointed for themselves, and can thus be vocal in an unprecedented way.

Control of the Individual

When discussing the women's problem during the totalitarian decades of Hungary, we have to talk about the general control of the individual. When we speak about the oppression of women, we must indeed speak about the oppression of men, children, and not least the environment. We can say that the aggression of history affected women in different ways than it did men, but men in Hungarian society were also not allowed to be autonomous subjects. Hungary became, under Soviet oppression, a country of spiritually and intellectually injured persons, and in such a society men, women, children, and the environment are all instrumentalized and crippled.

Lack of autonomy as an individual or communal value meant that totalitarian control reached the individual, the personal, the "private." Women were forced into early marriages for material well-being and survival, manipulated into early childrearing, overburdened and stressed by housework, made to feel guilty about child care, confronted with deteriorating health resulting from low health consciousness and a poor environment, abused by pornography, and in general, faced with very low self-esteem.

Birth control

During the 1950s abortion was illegal in Hungary; the 1960s brought about an easing of regulations, but the 1962 Criminal Code still made performing an illegal abortion punishable by a maximum sentence of three years. As the practice of abortion became more and more widespread, bringing with it the many side effects of illegality, the legal situation adapted to this practice in a very communist manner: in 1974, a decree introduced by the Council of Ministers contradicted the law in force, allowing abortion under various conditions (single teenagers; single, divorced, separated, or widowed women; married women over thirty-five; those who have undergone three births or "obstetrical events"; conditions of health, rape, incest, or inadequate housing). Legally, the situation has remained confusing.

This easing of regulations had led to a high number of registered "legal" abortions, ranging between 100,000 and 200,000 per year, exceeding the number of live births, adding up to a total of four to six million in twenty-five to thirty years. This number has to be interpreted in the context of a Hungarian population of ten million. There are many reasons for this dreadful number: existential insecurity and hopelessness for the individual in totalitarianism are only partly responsible. The problem of birth control was not handled properly; nonhormonal contraceptives, which are not hazardous to the health of women, have not become widespread. Although condoms are available, many men will not use them, and women mainly use the pill. The mentality that assumes a shared responsibility between the two partners has generally not developed.

Abortion, including interpretations of the higher-than-average number of abortions in most communist countries, was among the taboo topics. Today, after decades of unnatural silence, a heated social debate is going on in Hungary. For the first time, activists can argue for and against abortion, giving voice to their convictions.

Parliament has to clear up the legal confusion by the end of 1992, according to the decision of Hungary's Constitutional Court. Thus, we can expect a heated debate in Parliament as well, where extreme views are going to clash. But I am confident that women themselves are going to put pressure on lawmakers and stand up for something that has been granted to them—even if not constitutionally—for many years.

Pornography and Sexual Abuse

A large percentage of women in Hungary has had to live with various forms of male aggression, from pornography to rape. It seems fair to say that every girl and woman has encountered sexual humiliation, molestation, rape, or abuse in some verbal or physical form—in school, at work, in the family, in the streets. However, no awareness of sexual harassment could develop in the artificially created atmosphere of communism, in which chastity and political orthodoxy were intimately connected. Marital rape was not recognized by law, and only rarely were incidents of assault or wife-beating reported. Even less often were such crimes legally redressed.

Now that Hungarian society has become more open and the ban on pornography has been lifted, we still suffer from the remnants of communist-implanted reflexes. The individual, trying to defend his or her integrity and privacy against uncontrollable offenses, has decided not to notice the harsh sexism of semipornographic posters in taxis, garages, bookstores, and other public places. The violation of one's privacy has not yet become an offense in a region molded by totalitarian ideology, and it is dealt with there by such defense mechanisms as intentional disregard.

Conclusion

No magic cure exists for the long illness of Hungarian society. It would have been difficult enough without the communist intermezzo of about forty years since the Eastern mentality created patriarchal dependence and an exploitation of women.

In totalitarian systems people grew up with the conviction that they were merely acted upon by forces larger than themselves. Women, especially, tend to accept life's "trials"—exhausting housework, abortion as birth control, lower salaries, lack of prestige—as part of a "natural catastrophe." Today, as Hungary slowly but irreversibly returns to the community of European democracies, one of its greatest tasks is to change this, establishing such values as sovereignty, self-reliance, and autonomy, to convince the more passive part of society to become more adventurous, to take the initiative and take risks, even that of failure. The present situation of women is transitional, often incompatible with "Europe-anness," and involves neglect and a lack of awareness and incentives. The builders of Hungary's new democracy are confronting a rigid, immovable mentality toward women, and unlimited devotion, energy, and time will be needed for this fossil's destruction. Parliamentary and constitutional changes, an active foreign policy, and successful economic transformation will drive the country toward Europe, but the present mentality about women must be changed as well.

Notes

1. Women's qualifications for skilled work have increased at a slower rate than have men's. Women's qualifications rose from 4 to 12 percent between 1970 and 1984, but men's training in vocational schools rose from 10 to 28 percent. Women are overrepresented in the least skilled jobs. In 1990, about 37 percent of women in the work force were employed as unskilled and semiskilled workers, although unskilled work has made up a decreasing part of the labor market—31 percent in 1990 as compared to 38 percent ten years earlier. Women have more monotonous jobs, poorer chances of promotion, and job mobility chances that have decreased at a higher rate than that of men. Women work less overtime than men; white-collar women have lower incomes than blue-collar men. See Julia Szalai, "Some Aspects of the Changing Situation of Women in Hungary," *Signs* 17, no. 1 (Autumn 1991): 158–160.

2. Ibid. p. 162. She states that in businesses 32 percent of owners, managers, and employees are women. She cites Agnes Vajda-Tibor Kucki, *The Social Composition of the New Small Entrepreneurs* (Budapest: Institute of Economy, 1990).

20

Feminism and Hungary

Maria Adamik

If you ask males or females in the streets of Hungary what feminism means, the more tolerant would answer "I don't know," while the less tolerant would say it is a strange adjective meaning women who hate men and children, are sexually voracious, don't wear bras, and above all are very unhappy and are lesbians.[1]

If you ask a young female member of the Hungarian Parliament from the Young Democratic Party (the most popular liberal party)[2] how she plans to represent women's interests in Parliament, her response would be that women's issues are not political issues.

When seventeen to eighteen-year old students of both sexes from middle-class families, attending a fairly liberal high school, were asked about self-esteem, gender identity, and the necessity of a women's movement in Hungary, their answers did not differ remarkably from those of adult women. Girls deemed themselves worse off than boys, but they could not explain why. Only 3 percent of girls thought a woman's movement desirable, while boys considered the question crazy. The majority of students thought they would like to pay more attention to their children than their parents had.

When the members of a newly emergent Hungarian women's small entrepreneurs' association were asked why they didn't join the feminist movement, they immediately refused even to think about it, saying they were far from feminism![3] Yet when asked why they didn't join the nationwide association of small entrepreneurs headed by a popular male member of Parliament, they responded that they would never be taken seriously or given attention and that they had many special problems as women: getting loans, raising children, being overworked.

Entering into a somewhat sophisticated debate and referring to the Western women's movement, you are asked, "What have they done? Do they have day care, kindergartens, paid maternity leave until a child is three years old, full employment?" Speaking more precisely, this has been the answer thus far.

Dilemmas of Solidarity, Social Stratification, Cooperation, and Abortion

The present provision of social benefits is fragile. There are powerful attempts to abolish the right to abortion, and one can only hope for the advent of self-confidence, assertiveness, and grass-roots groups. But the past and still persisting culture, the recent political climate, the impoverishment and disappointments in the changes in everyday life jointly mitigate against women or anyone else building grass-roots movements. Women face new challenges without any previous experiences of cooperation, solidarity, lobbying, political self-representation, or grass-roots women's movements.

The mass media has remained as male-oriented as ever, if not worse. In politics there is no pattern of tolerance or liberal openmindedness in the public sphere, much less toward women.

The cornerstone of democracy and solidarity among women will be the current debate on abortion, which has become the big political issue. Hungary, as of this writing in early 1992, has a fairly liberal abortion policy in practice. In 1991 a newly emerged prolife group sought a ruling from the Constitutional Court to declare the abortion laws unconstitutional. In December 1991 the Court refused to decide, but required a new law to be enacted by the Hungarian Parliament by December 31, 1992. The Court has constrained the decision of Parliament, saying that it cannot outlaw abortion altogether, nor can it make abortion freely available. Only the Feminist Network, founded in 1990, has taken action as of 1992, but it is a small group that has to build financial support for such things as photocopying, equipment, or resources for starting campaigns, as well as fund-raising experience. There is no support or representation from women lawyers. Female experts and professionals seem to be reluctant to support the Network or to speak in public about abortion. Since the Constitutional Court's decision, Feminist Network began to get positive media coverage for its forthright pro-woman position.[4]

The majority of international connections with women's organizations, in spite of the fundamental social changes in Hungary, have remained in the hands of the Hungarian Women's Association, the official women's organization that represented the former regime.

The Hungarian Women's Association appears more interested in good connections with the new government (jobs, grants, etc.) than in women's interests. Although cooperation between the Feminist Network and the Association could provide a chance to be effective, at least to defend the right to abortion in Hungary, it is hard to predict the future of that cooperation.[5]

Thus, despite the new political freedoms, there are many phenomena that indicate the transition will do serious violence to the women of Hungary.

Employment as the Remaining Hope

By 1989 Hungarian women's employment reached 80 percent (excluding women studying) of women aged fifteen to fifty-four (retirement age is fifty-five for women, sixty for men). There is virtually no part-time employment. Employment rates are highest for women under forty, where it is a bit more than 90 percent, including those on paid maternity leaves. There was virtually full employment for mothers with young children,[6] and about 90 percent of three to six year olds were in the preschool program.[7]

The total Hungarian population is ten million, half of whom are economically active; of these about 45 percent are women. This proportion has decreased since 1989, partly for demographic reasons, partly due to early retirement, and women at this stage of the transition represent a somewhat smaller proportion of the unemployed than men. Although there was a more than tenfold increase in unemployment from January 1990, as of September 1991 women made up 41.1 percent of those employed and about 42 percent of the unemployed. Six percent of men and 5.5 percent of women were unemployed as of September 1991.[8] Sources estimate 10 to 16 percent unemployment (500,000 persons) by the end of 1992. Among the *registered* unemployed there were more women than men in 1991. In addition, 79 percent of unemployed women in 1991, in comparison to 55 percent of men, received a benefit lower than the official minimum wage. Although the unemployment rate for women in 1991 was less than that for men, Hungary is at the very beginning of a long process of restructuring the economy, and light industry, which is overwhelmingly female, had not been touched as of 1991.[9]

One also cannot predict the behavior of the more than 200,000 women recently on maternity leave whose job protection has virtually disappeared, or the impact of the transition on the fertility pattern. We still do not know the employment pattern of the emerging private sector. In 1991 women in the private sector accounted for roughly 6 percent of the female labor force, whereas according to official figures men's employment doubled. One cannot estimate the hidden employment: those employers who don't pay social insurance contributions for their employees (43 percent of wages). Among the latter group, there are likely to be more women than men.[10]

There is a higher unemployment rate among young, less educated, often Gypsy women. The rigidity of the school system and the increasing size of the cohort entering the labor market in the next four years will make this female population more vulnerable and widen the already existing gap among women in different social strata.[11]

Families with one wage earner are in a very dramatic situation, among the most vulnerable groups of the society. The artificial wage system had been adjusted to the model of families with two wage earners. Presently, with no new wage system, there is more than 30 percent inflation and prices at almost world-market levels. One-seventh of families are single-parent families rearing almost one-sixth of the children under fifteen; 80 percent of these are headed by women. In addition to teenage pregnancies, it is claimed that a majority of single mothers are so by choice.[12] However, this assumes that the conditions of prevailing gender relationships under which they choose does not seriously constrain their options. In addition, there are growing commercial interests, both domestic and foreign, employing young women for various commercial sexual activities.

In general, the transition is likely to widen the gap among different social strata of women. The Hungarian second economy,[13] important both in a narrow economic sense and in a wider political one of preparing citizens for their new role,[14] will have very different effects on women, depending on their class position. The advantages and disadvantages of work and investment in the second economy varied tremendously. One could gain new social connections, recognition, and self-confidence, but one could also become exhausted, isolated, and without any new market skills, which happened especially to women. In spite of their experience in the second economy, women may well be losers under the new market system.

Social and Political Considerations

There are strong political interests calling for official recognition of full-time motherhood as an occupation, thereby reducing female unemployment and the declining birth rate. This is supported by conservative male forces and the reviving Catholic Church, and could also serve the interests of overworked or unemployed women. Furthermore, owing to the lack of resources at both the local and national levels, women will be expected to substitute for the elimination of social services. But neither an ethical campaign on the virtues of motherhood nor coercion by abolishing the right to abortion will ease the fact that women cannot afford to give up their jobs.

Birth rates have followed a European pattern[15] and divorce rates of 11.3 out of 1000 existing marriages exceed those of some EEC countries. Hungary's highest rate was in 1987, with a slight decline since then. Needless to say, women have been blamed for both phenomena. Divorce has been viewed as deviant behavior, rather than the only possibility for individuals to "practice human rights." This is evidenced both by the general public's attitudes and by experts' use of the term "broken family" instead of the neutral "single family" or "one-parent family." It should be noted, using the words of Laura Balbo,[16] that Hungary has never been a children- or women-friendly society.

The decrease in childbirth since 1981 has contributed to the Hungarian negative population growth, which is regarded as a consequence of women's emancipation. Except for some demographic researchers no one takes into account the unfavorable mortality rate (13.2 per 1000 when the birth rate was 11.7 per 1000 in 1988) or the relevance of having the highest suicide rate in the world and a very unfavorable life expectancy for both women and men.[17]

The social legislation concerning maternity provisions still exists, but benefits are devalued and single parents could hardly afford to take advantage of them. In addition, there are attempts to abolish the family allowance, which is the only universal benefit. Families with children are overrepresented in the lowest income percentile. Other than the modestly extended family allowance there is no other special benefit for single parents. Needless to say, this is no accident.[18] In Hungary official sociology paid no attention to poverty until the beginning of the transition, and the field has still not focused on the condition of single mothers.

In another realm, experts have begun to pay attention to the high pollution in the bigger cities, recognizing its very harmful impact on children, and this has been getting some publicity.

Conclusion

When Hungarians decide what kind of society they would like to live in, two basic challenges will have to be met: What is the new consensus between the sexes? and What is the new consensus between the generations? Peter Flora[19] has suggested a third: What is the new consensus between the state and citizens. Can Hungarian society achieve the third without the previous two?

Notes

1. At the same time there are officially recognized associations for homosexual men and divorced fathers, none of which exist for women.

2. The new Hungarian parliament has 7 percent female representatives. For more detail, see Maria Adamik, "A Loss of Rights," *Feminist Review* (Autumn 1991).

3. As far as I know, the association was encouraged by American actors and resources, which helped to organize two conferences in Budapest. There are about three to five thousand members of the association.

4. Zsuzsa Beres of the Feminist Network reports that the media seeks out the Network, asks them to write articles, and is generally interested in what they are doing and in their position on recent events and decisions concerning women.

5. The Feminist Association is a group of less than fifty women, including the author, who was one of the founding members. At this point the majority of the members are white-collar workers. The Network would be pleased to build up contact with representatives of American women's groups.

6. Mothers with children under three who stay home on maternity leave count as employed due to the job-protected nature of this leave. They account for about eight to nine percent of employed women.

7. See refined figures, description of Hungarian parenting policy, and details in Maria Adamik, "Supporting Parenting and Child Rearing: Policy Innovation in Eastern Europe," in S. Kamerman and A. Kahn, *Child Care, Parental Leave and the Under 3s: Policy Innovation in Europe* (New York: Auburn House, 1991).

8. M. Frey, "Nök es a munkánelkuliseg" [Women and unemployment] Munkaügyi Kutató Intézet, manuscript, 1991.

9. M. Lado, M. Adamik, and O. Tóth, "Training for Women Under Conditions of

Crisis and Structural Adjustment (The Case of Hungary)," manuscript prepared for International Labor Organization, 1991.

10. The consequences of this cannot be foreseen. New social legislation just abolished the universal health service, turning instead to a system of insurance. Some proposed social legislation would shrink the basic security of people after decades of compulsory insurance.

11. The "baby boom" was due to the first version of the paid maternity leave introduced in the mid-seventies, and the children of a relatively large cohort of women in their productive years who were born at the beginning of the 1950s under the very strict abortion law.

    Given the worsening labor market, it would be desirable for the schools, especially high schools, to accept more students, but in fact, students need to pass entrance exams just as at the university level. About 70 percent of an age cohort finish high school, while 15 percent finish college.

12. These figures doubled from 1970 to the end of the 1980s.

13. A very thorough and clear evaluation appears in J. Borocz, *Informality in East-Central Europe,* unpublished manuscript, Johns Hopkins University, Baltimore, 1992.

14. Julia Szalai, "Some Aspects of the Changing Situation of Women in Hungary," in *Signs* 17, no. 1 (Autumn 1991).

15. By the end of the 1980s the total fertility rate equaled that of the EEC average: 1.8 births.

16. Laura Balbo, *Time to Care* (Milan: F. Angeli, 1987).

17. Even in comparison with the rest of Eastern Europe, only Romanian women and Soviet men have worse statistics.

18. See the American debates on the possible impact of the AFDC program on marital stability. One has to bear in mind that an increase in benefits wouldn't have led to major welfare dependency on the part of Hungarian mothers, because they are fully employed and therefore have paid social security.

19. Peter Flora, ed., *Growth to Limits: The Western Welfare States Since World War II* (Berlin: W. D. Gruyter, 1986).

21

No Envy, No Pity

Olga Tóth

Western feminists have distorted the situation of women in Eastern and Central Europe in two ways. The first was distortion by envy, expressed in their claim that women in Eastern Europe had, "by some fluke" "gotten it all": education, a trade or profession, full-time work, and an extensive network of low-priced day care that made it all possible. Curiously enough, these feminists' views mirrored the official ideology of the communist state, emphasizing the giftlike character of such facilities, which the "caring state" offered women in exchange, tacitly or not, for their loyalty. Both the communist state and Western feminists emphasized that these possibilities were not available in the West, where women were still fighting for them.

It is important to note that Western feminists held these views only as long as they did not meet women from Eastern and Central Europe. Sociologists with no particular bias on the issue recall the irony of situations that occurred quite frequently at such meetings: the Western experts expressed envy, while Easterners tried to prove that appearances were deceptive. As communist states began relaxing their grip and travel on both sides became more possible, there was a greater exchange of information; the envy gradually disappeared, to be replaced by pity. The present situation, as I have experienced it, is that Western feminists treat Eastern European women with trembling compassion, astonished that women living under such different conditions should look so similar to their Western sisters. Now everything once praised is being questioned—full-time employment of women, child-care allowances, day-care centers—because of economic hard times and our researchers' criticisms of these institutions. When Western feminists learn more about how we lead our daily lives, which are indubitably much more difficult and more complicated to organize than theirs, they wonder how we survive at all. Yet this second view is no less a distortion that the first.

In this paper I try to explain our situation, and our real problems. I do not want readers either to envy or to pity us, but to understand us. The aim of this paper is to eliminate stereotypes and to recognize other ways of thinking, which I am convinced can only benefit feminist thought.

I. The "Private" Sphere

1. The Family, Marriage, and Divorce

While "sexual equality" was an everyday phrase under communist ideology, children continued to be socialized into extremely conservative sex roles. This was indirectly demonstrated by the images of men and women in school textbooks[1] and in the images of women in the daily and weekly papers.[2] Sociological research[3] has shown that parents in the 1970s as well as today have very different aspirations for their sons and daughters. Sons were, and still are, seen as future breadwinners, and daughters—reflecting reality—as only secondary earners. For these reasons working-class and lower middle-class families sent their daughters to secondary schools that did not provide any specialization and vocational skills, while boys were, and still are, mainly sent to schools where they acquire vocational training.[4] Differential socialization was also present at home. Children are generally expected to do very little in the household, and when they are, mainly girls are asked to help.

Role models are very important for children, and time schedule surveys of the early 1970s show that working women spent two and a half hours more per day on household chores than did working men. This situation had changed very little by the late 1980s.[5] Furthermore, childrearing was left entirely to women. Women oriented children toward particular careers, organized their extracurricular activities, and influenced their choice of leisure activities and value system. This gave women a certain type of power in the family. In the hardest years of the 1950s the state suppressed family and individual life, and only institutionalized and heavily regulated education of children was officially permitted. In the 1950s mothers were forced by the economic situation, by ideology, and by political power, to enter paid work, but only a minimum of child-care institutions were introduced, and even today there are not enough. Given this lack, and also social norms, less than 5 percent of children younger than three were in day care in the 1950s, and less than one-third of children three to six years old were in kindergarten and preschool.[6] Maternity leave was only six weeks, and although women were entitled to breastfeeding time after that (one hour a day), this was mostly useless due to the distance between home and workplace.

Worse and worse solutions were tried. Children were sent to their grandparents in the country; they were put into factory nurseries, whose working hours were adapted to the three-shift schedule, so that children of one or two could be left there in the morning, afternoon, or night; they were put in weekly nurseries, from which they were taken home only on weekends, or were simply left at home in the care of older children. Not until the 1970s was a system of childcare facilities implemented that could take in all the children who needed a place. Even then, there was some overcrowding in nurseries, with 104 to 116 children for every 100 places between 1960 and 1980. This situation was even worse in kindergartens and pre-schools for three to six year olds, where from 1970, 51.1 percent of children between the ages of three and six attended, increasing to 85.7 percent in 1989.[7] There were real differences in this respect between kindergartens run by neighborhoods and state- or employer-owned kindergartens. Usually kindergartens supported by employers held to higher standards and were less overcrowded. Educational institutions were extremely hierarchical and rigid, but regulation could not be total, and especially since the 1970s, significant differences developed in kindergartens and schools. School segregation also began between children of different social strata.[8] There was an invisible ranking of schools, and children's place in the system was less a function of the social class or educational background of their fathers than of the educational background, connections, cultural standards and ambitions of their mothers, as well as family connections.[9]

The family unit is extraordinarily important for survival strategies in Hungary. The role of the family is different from that of a society with individualist values. Marriages typically take place early, and there is a low percentage of unmarried people;[10] to be unmarried is not really accepted. Moreover, both men and women enter into their first marriages comparatively early (twenty-four and twenty-one, respectively). An important question is why marriage remained as popular as it did until quite recently.

Ideologically, marriage was considered to be a "petit bourgeois" noncommunist leftover, but at the same time to be the form of cohabitation that made state control easiest and that made the time people spent outside institutions the most transparent.

Until very recently all social policies and the system of social benefits gave people living in families advantages over single individuals. To have even a small chance of obtaining an apartment and to meet everyday needs, one had to marry as early as possible. A single income was not sufficient to live on. Together the man and woman could survive on the combined incomes from their main jobs and the "second economy." Household management, the distribution of resources, and the organization of family life were largely in women's hands, and their work and income were indispensable. Thus, women gained a certain position of power in the family, which became most evident in the case of divorce.

The number of divorces per 1000 citizens has been gradually increasing, reaching 2.8 by the late 1980s. The increase can be partially explained by women's employment, the modernization of society, and a society that *de facto* forces young people to marry too young. Another important factor is that often even two incomes are not sufficient for a couple to get an apartment. Seventy-five percent of young couples start life together in the house of either the wife's or the husband's parents. The conflicts and frustrations this engenders have been significant factors in the breakup of marriages. The particular benefits for women after divorce were also a contributing factor. Divorce courts have awarded custody of the children to the mothers in 95 percent of cases. This meant the women also got the apartments. Men had to pay child maintenance and had very little chance to start a new life. About 70 percent of divorces are now initiated by women. In certain workplaces—primarily those employing a majority of women—"divorce epidemics" broke out.

While divorce proved to be beneficial for some women, there was no real protection for women in need. There were no official houses for battered women or women raped by their husbands. The communist state pretended these problems did not exist or that they were individual problems.

Both men and women were exhausted and full of frustrations. People did not learn how to solve conflicts, and divorce was often seen by women as the only or best way to solve marriage conflicts.

2. Children's Role in Families

Not only are early marriages typical but the first child is usually born within a year of the marriage. Twenty-nine percent of the brides married in 1983 were already pregnant; in other words, one of the immediate reasons for marriage was pregnancy.[11] Although young couples have to wait years for an apartment, a family with children has priority. This is true whether one rents from the state, gets a bank loan, lives in an apartment owned by an employer, or gets a loan from an employer. Another reason for having children early was that for young people reduced to infantile status by communist societies, one of the easiest ways to assert adulthood was to get married and become parents.[12] Children also represented the future, the desires and plans parents were unable to fulfill for themselves. The results of a comparative survey conducted in eight countries in 1988 showed that 90 percent of Hungarians agreed with the view that "A marriage without children is not fully complete."[13]

By the mid-1980s, although the proportion of childless couples had dropped by 5 percent,[14] the population was not reproducing itself. Owing to the low birth rate and a high mortality rate among the middle-aged,[15] the country's population has been decreasing since 1981. The falling birth rate has always been a political issue in Hungary. After World War I, the treaty of Versailles reduced Hungary's territory to one-third of its original area, significantly reducing the population.[16] Economic modernization and industrialization also contributed to a falling birth rate. For conservative nationalist politics these facts gave rise to a vision of the "death of the nation," which has been used to pressure women to have more children ever since.

The natural increase in the birth rate after World War II, and the consequences of the strict antiabortion laws of the 1950s, temporarily laid these concerns to rest. However, the relaxation of the ban on abortion in the absence of up-to-date family planning methods[17] radically increased the number performed. The gradual rise in living standards in the 1960s and a further increase in female employment led to a further reduction in the birth rate.[18] A slow increase in live births started in 1969, but this was not considered sufficient for the communist ideology or for a country undergoing extensive industrial development, where the demand for labor seemed limitless. A heavy attack was launched against the spreading "petit bourgeois" way of life, which gave preference to current consumption as opposed to socially useful "investment": i.e., raising children. These debates did not motivate families to have more children, but they did increase feelings of guilt.

By introducing the Child Care Allowance (Gyermekgondozasi Segely, or GYES) system, the state hoped to achieve an increase in births and a temporary reduction in female participation in the work force. The essence of the system is that mothers of newborn babies can stay home for three years, receiving a fixed monthly sum from the state. At the end of the three-year period, the employer had to reemploy the woman. The popularity of GYES increased rapidly, especially among women with less education or training. Compared to their low wages the fixed amount of 700 forints was not a big financial loss. In the countryside they also could earn money in the second economy from the family garden.

The GYES system came under heavy fire from professionals from the moment it was introduced. Demographers pointed out that in the long term it would not increase births, but would at the most impel couples to hasten the birth of their first child. The age composition of the population would also become more uneven. Another argument raised was that the GYES period would reintroduce a conservative division of labor in families. For young mothers now working exclusively at home, the resultant limited contact with the neighborhood and the absence of other kinds of voluntary organizations would result in a loss of contact with the outside world, diminishing their sense of importance to society and creating serious neuroses. Thus, whether the young mother worked or stayed at home, the child was, and continues to be, a source of conflicts of conscience. There are very few young mothers who enjoy this phase of their life with unambivalent feelings.

3. The Burdens of Generations, or What Are Grandmothers Good For?

In Hungary the generations are very involved with each other. Typically, young couples start their married life in the home of one set of parents, and can expect real financial support from them. Even after they obtain a home of their own, their low earnings at the start of their careers and their more limited participation in the second economy make them unable to survive without parental support. The role of Hungarian grandparents in their grandchildren's lives is several times greater than the equivalent role in the United States. If grandparents live close by, they help out every day, and if they live farther away, they are expected to help at least during school holidays. Feelings of guilt play a certain role in this situation: women who were mothers in the 1950s now feel terribly disappointed that they missed the opportunity to enjoy their children as they were growing up. Their daughters are now raising their own children, and these grandmothers try to give the little ones everything they can—often even more than they can. The children's needs are generally given priority over their own when deciding what to buy.

II. Paid Work: We Insist on It and Suffer from It

One of the most contradictory phenomena in the socialist countries was female employment. As in most Eastern and Central European countries, the post-1945 economic restructuring, with its forced industrialization and collectivization of agriculture, demanded an expansion of the labor force, especially of semiskilled and unskilled labor, which could only be met by integrating large numbers of women into the labor force. Economic needs coincided with the desire of the communist state to keep its citizens under the closest control possible, which could best be done at the workplace. Women's participation in paid labor was not without precedent, since it was the norm for girls from the country, especially the daughters of poor peasants, to work as seasonal laborers in agriculture or as servants in towns from the time they finished (or stopped) primary school-education until they got married.[19] Women had also participated in industrial production, constituting one-third of that work force by the 1930s.[20] However, it was from the 1940s onward that the mass entry of women into the labor market accelerated, and by the late 1980s—the period of so-called full employment—95 percent of women worked full-time. Another incentive to join the work force was that a number of social benefits—health insurance, for example, and later the Child Care Allowance—were tied to employment, not citizenship. Press campaigns were also launched against "idle housewives." Nevertheless, women still played the role of the "safety valve" in employment policy, as they do in Western countries. By the late 1960s, when the first economic reform was being established, it looked as if there would be a labor surplus. It was then that the concept of the Child Care Allowance—the arrangement envied by so many—was born, with the unconcealed objective of pressuring women to withdraw temporarily from the work force.

Despite all this pressure, work had an important place in women's scale of values. An analysis of material sent in for a life history competition in the early 1970s showed clearly that for a large proportion of women being "successful" meant success at work.[21] Interviews carried out in the late 1980s with some of the participants in that competition showed that studying, social mobility, and earning capacity continued to represent the highest values for them. The changes following the communist takeover had made it possible for masses of young women (and men as well) to change their lives in ways they could only have dreamed of before, but also in ways for which they had not been socialized. The women therefore made tremendous efforts to combine their traditional female role with the chance to study and to build the career that the new system offered them.

Until the 1970s the social mobility that started after World War II affected women and men differently.[22] Like men, women had migrated from agricultural jobs to industrial jobs, but in contrast to men they gravitated toward jobs that did not require special skills or training. At the same time women continued to marry "up," while men married "down." This situation changed in the mid-1970s, because women's average educational standard had by that time reached and even surpassed that of men. Since then, men have typically brought the material wealth to a marriage, and women the cultural values and higher average level of education. Women's role in determining the cultural level of the children, and of the whole family, were thus very important. '

Although women participated in paid work to the same extent as men, their income averaged 25 percent less than that of men in all employment categories, being even worse for white-collar than for blue-collar women workers.[23] This was partly due to their lower level of qualifications. Although more highly educated than men, women often lacked specific job qualifications. Another contributing factor was the time women spent away from their jobs raising young children, and absences due to children's illnesses.[24] However, there was also significant discrimination against women at work. Public opinion regarded women unequivocally as the families' secondary earners, and this was especially true from the mid-1970s on, when the second economy started to boom.

Understanding the role of the second economy is an important key to understanding the history of the past few decades.[25] The Kádár regime, which started to loosen up in the mid-1960s, was able to shore up its legitimacy through a relative improvement in living standards, through not the official economy but the second economy. State-owned enterprises, state housing construction, and agricultural production were unable to meet the increasing demand, and a "second economy" started using the state infrastructure. People began to produce, first for their own needs but gradually for the market as well. The welfare and material advancement of the individual and the family were increasingly dependent on the extent to which they were *both* able to take part in the second economy.

However, women played a secondary role in the second economy, participating less than men. This was linked to the strategies around the division of labor within the family. As stated above, after finishing work on their main job men worked in the second economy, while women managed the household and daily life. In so doing, they acquired numerous abilities useful in entrepreneurship, which may help them during the present social changes, and may help explain why their rate of unemployment was lower than men's in 1991.[26] In any case, we cannot view women's situation as entirely negative. Yet compelling women to join the workforce at an unnatural pace and without any social institutions certainly placed a huge burden on several female generations. This may explain the latest public opinion surveys, which show that 35% of women would prefer to stay at home if financial necessity did not force them to work outside it.[27] I am convinced, however, that these attitudes depend on a woman's point in her life cycle: women with small children will want to stay home for extended periods, while other woman will want to work shorter hours. As stated above, Hungarian women understand that their work and earning is very important to the survival of their family. This feeling is stronger in economically hard times. But if we ask women about their desires, they express demands for greater privacy, more leisure time, and less stress.

III. What Is It that We Are Not, or What Is Missing from Our Lives?

1. Civil Society, Voluntary Organizations, Political Movements

The absence of a civil society and its voluntary organizations is well reflected in public attitudes concerning abortion. As noted above, the decrease in the population and the legality of abortion have often been seen as key issues. We now have several prolife organizations that frequently air their views in the press and the legislature, demanding a ban on abortion. They have found a close ally in the Catholic Church. They have no mass support, as they have only a few hundred members, and public opinion polls also show that the Hungarian population is liberal in this respect: 25 percent of the adult population would unconditionally permit abortion; 67 percent would do so in cases where it was justified. Only 7 percent would support a complete ban on abortion. Even of people claiming to follow the teachings of religion, only 17 percent support prohibition of abortion.[28]

Yet there are few signs of the development of a prochoice movement in Hungary. Sociologists and demographers don their academic gowns to list their arguments against the prohibition of abortion, but ordinary women, the "women on the street," make no comment. What can be the reason?

First, we should recall that spontaneous citizens' initiatives were not permitted during even the mildest period of the communist regime. Paradoxically enough in a society that preached the importance of the community, people forgot the techniques of forming and running organizations to defend their real interests. The way organizations that were controlled from the top (such as the official women's organization and the trade unions) operated made people distrust all organizations of this kind. The creation of spontaneous organizations was also inhibited by shortages. People, and women especially, were short of money, time, and human energy. Women did not believe such movements could do anything. The issue of abortion becomes secondary when a woman and her family are struggling to retain their middle-class status and not to sink into poverty.

When weekly work hours were reduced in the 1970s, well-intentioned ideologues hoped that such conditions would give people more time for leisure and recreation. However, the second economy started to boom and people grasped every opportunity to improve their living standards, even if this entailed a significant increase in their working hours. The outside activities that Western women take for granted are almost completely lacking in the lives of average working women with children in Hungary. Then, as now, their little leisure time is spent watching television.

2. Friends and Social Relationships

An issue closely related to the above is the specific nature of social relationships and friendships. Sociological surveys conducted in recent years demonstrate that adult friendships are more instrumental than emotional in character.[29] Although analyses have so far not covered the differences between men's and women's friendships, we can describe some of their characteristics. One of the most urgent social problems of the past forty years was housing. By the 1960s it had become obvious that despite its promises the state would not be able to provide families with homes. There was no rental housing market, and the only option for a large proportion of families was to build their homes themselves. This was done through a form of labor exchange. People helped friends or colleagues build their houses, with the expectation of reciprocity. This type of labor exchange was more typical of men, but women also developed a network to help each other with family arrangements. Hungarian women have many types of contacts, but very few of them are emotionally based relationships of the type Western women experience. When Hungarian women need emotional help, they can expect support mostly from their families. This lack of friendships is felt to be a real lack, and their personalities are poorer because of it.

Not to be envied, not to be pitied . . . People adapt to the societies in which they live. Hungarian women's lives, and those of Eastern European women in general, are certainly more difficult than those of their Western counterparts. We live not only in a poorer country, but in one with a different social and historical background, and different cultural traditions. We would like to have a better, more peaceful life without losing what we have already achieved.

Notes

1. Judit Haber and Judit Sas, *Tankönyvszagu világ* (Budapest: Akadémiai Könyvkiadó, 1980).

2. Olga Tóth, "Kisérlet néhány heti—és napilapbol kirajzolodó nokep elemzésere," doctoral thesis in economics, Budapest University, 1977.

3. Gábor Havas, "A munkásgyerek, a munkásszülö és az iskola," *Szociológia*, no. 4 (1973); and Judit Sas, *Életmód és család: Az emberi viszonyok alakulása a családban* (Budapest: Akadémiai Könyvkiadó, 1976).

4. Until now, three types of secondary schools have existed in Hungary. In 1990 the proportion of girls was 34 percent in vocational schools, 51 percent in those types of secondary schools that provided some vocational training, and 66 percent in classical high schools. See Peter Robert, "Educational Transition in Hungary from the Postwar Period Up to the End of the 1980s," *European Sociological Review* 7, no. 3 (1991); *Oktatási statisztika* (Budapest: CSO, 1991).

5. Alexander Szalai, "The Situation of Women in the Light of Contemporary Time Budget Researches," United Nations Doc. No. E/CONF 66/bp/6, April 15, 1975; and Rudolf Andorka, "The Use of Time Series in International Comparison," in *Comparative Methodology: Theory and Practice in International Social Research*, ed. Else Oyen (London: Sage, 1990).

6. *Situation in Health Care, 1983* (Budapest: CSO, 1985), *Statistical Yearbook of the Ministry of Health and Social Welfare, 1988* (Budapest: CSO, 1989); *Statistical Yearbook, 1989* (Budapest: CSO, 1989); *Statistical Yearbook, 1989* (Budapest: CSO, 1990); *Ministry of Culture, Statistical Reports, 1980, 1989* (Budapest: CSO, 1981, 1990). Cited in Julia Szalai, "Some Aspects of the Changing Situation of Women in Hungary," *Signs* 17, no. 1 (Autumn 1991): 164.

7. Ibid.

8. Janos Ladanyi and Gábor Csanádi, *Szelekció az általános iskolabán* (Budapest: Magvetö Könyvkiadó, 1983).

9. Rudolf Andorka and Rózsa Kulcsár, "Az anya társadalmi helyzetének és iskolai végzettségének hatása a gyermek társadalmi mobilitására," *Szociologia*, no. 4 (1982).

10. Hajnal calls such a pattern "non-European." John Hajnal, "European Marriage Patterns in Perspective," in *Population in History*, eds. D. V. Glass and D. E. C. Eversley (London: Arrnold, 1965).

11. *Családalapitók: A házasságkötés körülményei 1983—ban összehasonlitva az 1966 és 1974 évi helyzettel* (Budapest: CSO, 1983).

12. Peter Robert and Olga Tóth, "Halogatók," *Kritika* no. 7 (1982).

13. Closest to the Hungarians in this respect were the Italians, of whom 68 percent agreed with this statement. The comparative rate for the United States was 46 percent.

14. *Demográfiai évkönyv* (Budapest: CSO, 1990).

15. The mortality of middle-aged men—and to some extent women—is worse than it was in the 1960s.

16. Ivan T. Berend and György Ranki, *The Hungarian Economy in the Twentieth Century* (Sydney: Croom Helm, 1985).

17. Oral contraceptives were introduced in 1967. The number of women using them increased very slowly.

18. The number of abortions reached its peak in 1969.

19. Gábor Gyani, *Család, háztartás és városi cselédséq* (Budapest: Magvetö Könyvkiadó, 1983).

20. Berend and Ranki, p. 90.

21. The life history competition was announced for every woman who felt her life successful. More than 500 autobiographies arrived from all social strata. Most of the competitors were white-collar workers and professionals, but we received a lot of life stories from blue-collar workers and political cadres too. See Olga Tóth, "Life Course and Historical Turning Points," paper presented at the XII World Congress of Sociology, Madrid, 1990.

22. Rózsa Kulcsár, "A nök társadalmi mobilitásának vizsgálata," *Szociologia* no. 2 (1974); and Max Haller, Tamas Kolosi, and Peter Robert, "Social Mobility in Austria, Czechoslovakia and Hungary," in *Class Structure in Europe,* ed. Max Haller (New York: M. E. Sharpe, Inc., 1990).

23. *Employment and Earnings, 1989* (Budapest: CSO, 1990). Cited in Szalai, p. 160.

24. Women with children up to two years old spent 30 to 40 percent of their time on sick leave or unpaid leave because of sick children. Ibid. p. 166.

25. Istvan R. Gabor, "The Second Economy in Socialism: General Lessons of the Hungarian Experience," in L. Feige, ed. *The Unobserved Economy* (London: Oxford University Press, 1984); and Peter Galasi and György Sziráczki, eds. *Labor Market and Second Economy in Hungary* (Frankfurt: Campus, 1985).

26. There were 400,000 unemployed people at the beginning of 1992, 8 percent of active wage earners. The ratio of unemployed women was 40 percent. Source: CSO Budapest.

27. This research was carried out within the framework of ISSP in 1988. The Hungarian part was made by TARKI. The sample was representative for the Hungarian adult population in age, sex and territory. One block of the questionnaire dealt with attitudes toward women's paid work, child care institutions and marriage. See some results in Olga Tóth, "Conservative Gender Roles and Women's Work," paper presented at the 10th EGOS Conference, Vienna, 1991.

28. Mrs. T. Pongracz and Edit S. Molnar, "Az abortuszkérdés Magyarországon, 1991," in *Statisztikai Szemle 1991,* no. 7 (1991).

29. Agnes Utasi, "Az interpreszonális kapcsolatok néhány nemzeti sajátosságáról," in *Társas kapcsolatok,* ed. A. Utasi (Budapest: Gondolat Könyvkiadó, 1991).

22

Gender Politics in Hungary: Autonomy and Antifeminism

Joanna Goven

Soon, if we're not careful, some people will be wanting a matriarchy. God protect us and save us from that!

They liberated [women] far too much in the Kádár system. And since then even more. That's why we can thank [women] for the spoiled, uncontrolled, badly raised young people. For all the divorces and ruined families. . . . They should be satisfied with their homes, their jobs! They should have been the creators of calm, peaceful homes, which now exist only in fairy tales. Women's demands have increased enormously. Soon nothing will satisfy them. Often it is because of them that men turn to dishonesty. (Of course, this doesn't apply to those who live a model family life. They aren't interested in belonging to the matriarchy camp.) Down with matriarchy! . . . At least in Parliament there are only a few of them gabbing uselessly. Some of us still remember the old, women-free Parliament.

If they need to play a role, if they can't bear themselves, let them go on the stage, but not into Parliament.

—Letter, signed "A non-partisan woman," to *Magyar nök lapja* (Hungarian Women's Journal), spring 1990.[1]

In Hungary, the past decade has been marked by an often vituperative public debate over the proper place of women in society. This debate took place in a variety of publications with diverse readerships, from the highbrow *Élet és Irodalom* (Life and Literature) to the more popular *Új Tükör* (New Mirror) and *Nök Lapja* (Women's Journal). What it revealed was not simply the persistence

---

The author wishes to thank the International Research and Exchanges Board and the American Council of Learned Societies for supporting the research upon which this article is based.

of "traditional" attitudes, despite efforts of the Communist Party to transform society, but the development of a misogynistic and explicitly antifeminist discourse resulting from the particular conditions of state socialism. A product of "society" as much as of "the state," this discourse continues to hobble women in Hungary today, particularly in the political sphere.

One way of accounting for this antifeminism is to see it as part of a more general backlash against communist policies—in this case, against the campaign for women's "emancipation," begun and in some sense ended in the 1950s.[2] But an analysis of the discourse shows that this is too one-dimensional an explanation: while the state is certainly criticized for its economic coercion of women into the paid labor force, the primary focus of criticism, and often quite intense animosity, is women. Women are portrayed not as victims of a state-sponsored "emancipation" that overburdened them but rather as powerful agents who have responded to state emancipation by becoming destructive to men and children.

The roots of this antifeminism can be found not only in misguided and coercive state policies but also in the "antipolitics" for which the political opposition in much of Eastern Europe became famous.[3] In the practice of antipolitics, it was recognized that state power is out of reach and that attempts to democratize state politics will be met with effective repression.[4] Antipolitics was the practice of acting outside the state as if one lived in a democratic polity; it was the creation of a private "civil society" as a substitute for democratic politics. As György Konrád puts it:

> There is self-government even under a police state, but only in the sphere of private life. . . . We seek freedom mainly in the areas where we are already freer and can hope to be even more so—where we are our own bosses because we have no superiors, and where we are left most to our own devices: in the area of our free time. . . . At work we have in effect sold ourselves. . . . Small businesses, independent seminars, agricultural societies, and *samizdat* publications are organized in private homes. Official premises belong to the state, homes to "society." Home and free time: these are the spatial and temporal dimensions of civic independence.[5]

As Konrád makes clear, antipolitics brought with it a celebration of the private. In part this can be seen as a reaction to the intrusiveness of the Stalinist state, and to a lesser extent of the post-Stalinist state. But beyond this, antipolitics endowed the family with a key political role in recognizing it as the major locus of autonomy from the state. As the home became the site of democratic strivings, the power distribution within the family and private life also left its mark on the practice of antipolitics: women were expected to provide, where possible, the emotional and material support for men's building of civil society.[6] In Hungary it became characteristic among dissident intellectuals—many of whom, because

of official disapproval, could get only menial jobs, if any, in the official economy—for women to undertake work in the unofficial economy, such as housecleaning, sewing, or dyeing clothes for private boutiques, in order to provide
material support for their male partners' political activity.[7] More basically and
invisibly, women's cooking, cleaning, and child care maintained the private
realm as a functioning and habitable site for antipolitics, and gave men the free
time to engage in it. The idealization of the prewar bourgeois family gave added
ideological support to this tendency and contributed to a nostalgia for a species
of nonconflictual gender relations that had never existed.

Despite its oppositional coloring, this celebration of the private world of the
family in many ways suited the needs of the state as well. As investment in
housing and social services and the level of social-welfare benefits remained
inadequate or deteriorated in the 1970s and 1980s, the regime came more and
more to see family autonomy—that is, self-provision—as a substitute for the
more expensive socialization of such tasks as cooking, laundry, child care, and
care for the sick and elderly. The idealization of the bourgeois mother in a sense
provided ideological legitimacy for these shortcomings of the Kádár regime.
Those who controlled the state therefore had reason to welcome this "resistance"
to it, especially if, as economic necessity required, the popular image of the
bourgeois mother was grafted onto the reality of women's paid employment
outside the household.[8]

The practices of antipolitics and of state socialism itself encouraged a rigid
dichotomization in which "society" was seen as the locus of democracy, while
the state was seen as the ultimate source of all oppression. The focus on the state
as oppressor served to obscure societally centered forms of oppression. As Ottilia
Solt, herself a dissident under the old regime, observed recently: "Jews, Gypsies,
women, and workers have all been faced by the strange phenomenon of the state's
monopoly of oppression yielding to oppression by the stronger in society."[9] This
social oppression is not simply a survival of "traditional" attitudes, but was, in
the case of women, reshaped and reproduced by antipolitics itself. The texts we
are about to examine are by authors who, while critical of state policy, were
employed in professional positions of some responsibility. They expose for us
the darker side of societal antipolitics, namely, a discourse of antifeminism that
blames women for social disorder. By examining this discourse I believe we can
arrive at a better understanding of why it is that women have been unwilling or
unable to defend their interests effectively under the new regime.

The antifeminist discourse was in a sense inaugurated in print in 1982 and
1983.[10] The texts I will be discussing derive from this initial outburst. Although
women had already come under fire for Hungary's declining birth rate,[11] it was
in the early eighties that an elaborated discourse from a variety of sources
appeared, built around similar themes. While many of the allegations made by
these authors may seem farfetched, their themes have been repeated many times
since:[12] women's "emancipation" has led to a reversal of sex roles and of the

sexual hierarchy; women have become aggressive; women and the state have forged an alliance against men; divorce is a part of this alliance; the result is passive, feminized men, a feudal political culture, and the undermining of democratic development. Underlying this pattern is a critique of state socialism as having contravened nature, a critique based on the notion that the bedrock of a healthy society is sexual essentialism.

The similarity of the texts, despite the diversity of authors' backgrounds, occupations, and styles, suggests that the pattern of thinking they reflect is more than idiosyncratic. They allow us to glimpse the underlying currents within Hungarian gender politics and particularly the types of obstacles to full political participation that exist for women in Hungary today.[13]

Miklós Hernádi, a sociologist, links women's alleged "aggressiveness" to role reversal, particularly to sexual role reversal, though the direction of causality is left unclear.[14] According to Hernádi, it isn't women's employment that has "completely reversed the relations between the sexes." Rather, the reversal originated in private life, at the expense of the "age-old model" according to which "the man is a roving hunter who brings down whatever female animal he desires in the heat of the moment" while the woman/wife "stays in one place and waits" for his return:

> Perhaps the greatest change in the history of private life was that women became partners in sexual relations. What kind of partner? The . . . initiating and dictating half . . . If formerly the man went from woman to woman looking for satisfaction, today a great many women, too, see it as their right to keep changing their partners. The men, in order to be able to stay in the competition, more or less renounce their own pleasures and, with new, woman-centered techniques, become slavish manufacturers of female pleasure. . . .
>
> Today it often happens that it is the woman who plays the role of the roving hunter, and the man who sticks by kids and nest, time and again awaiting his wife's return.

> Yet their constant presence in the family nest does not increase men's authority there. On the contrary, though men spend more time with their children, "masculine firmness is increasingly rare. . . . Since they can remain in their 'troop' essentially only as long as the woman wishes, traditional male firmness can be only a pitiful playacting in the heavy shadow of female omnipotence."

For Hernádi, women's sexuality and women's sexual aggressiveness are indistinguishable. Women's sexual desire renders husbands weak, soft, and vulnerable, unable to exercise authority within the family. Real power belongs to women.

As a result society begins to look less than human: "the overall picture before us is one of the relations between the queen bee and her drones."*

The world outside the family collaborates in this subordination and humiliation of men:

> I don't mean to be insinuating, but at the divorce trial the husband is often the only male participant: both lawyers are women, the judge is a woman, the lay members are women and, of course, so is the wife. But even if men were the servants of the law, the law itself is antifather.

And mothers, says Hernádi, in their efforts to get custody of their children and to alienate them from their fathers, are abetted by the still-current myths of women's oppression and of the heroic single mother.

Hernádi sees unleashed sexuality—and divorce laws—at the heart of women's "emancipation" and sees these new women as a destructive social force, unnatural and monstrously powerful, unsuited to the tasks that keep society functioning. He urges the reassertion of male control. Through premarital agreements, he says, men can identify and weed out "the type of woman who needs a man only for his sperm and his name." Men should also start taking responsibility for birth control in order to

> decrease the effectiveness of that weapon which enables the wife to have a child if the husband doesn't want her to, and not to have a child if the husband wants her to. . . . The husband, with his own withheld or released reproductive capacity can become a real partner in having a child.

In addition, women and the courts must stop their antifather practices. Otherwise, if a father feels that

> "he has no more right to his children than to an apartment . . . he will create the next child only halfheartedly. Thus, the whole task of raising the future generation will become women's responsibility, which in the end will logically lead to the widespread use of sperm banks."

Hernádi both charges women with being sexually aggressive and portrays them as being indifferent to men and to sex. Hernádi is not alone in denouncing women for being sexual, but his account shows most clearly the zero-sum, essentialist thinking behind such denunciations: men are desiring and therefore dominating, women are desired and therefore subordinate, men find pleasure in the physical act of sex (and in subordinating women?), women find pleasure in being desired. If women are desiring, they must also be dominating; if women find pleasure in

---

*In Hungarian, *méh* means both "bee" and "womb," and *here* means both "drone" and "testicle."

sex, they have displaced men, who therefore no longer find pleasure there (be-cause women no longer need to be subordinated?). Whether sexually desiring of men or indifferent to them, women are deviant and, apparently, threatening. This fear of women's sexuality is combined with and compounded by reaction to the one area in which women's interests have directly confronted men's interests—and apparently won: the divorce courts. I shall pursue this theme below.

In a reply to Hernádi, Kata Beke takes issue with his description of the "age-old model."[15] Beke is a high-school teacher by profession. Before 1990, she was known as a voice of dissent, criticizing the state's educational policies. In the new regime, she ran for Parliament as a member of the Hungarian Democratic Forum; when it won the elections, she was made State Secretary for Education.[16] In this article, she urges a return to bourgeois family values and practices.

The real man, the classical male, she says, wasn't the "roving hunter," but the patriarchal father:

> The more characteristically masculine a behavior model is, the more it resembles the father. The pater familias is such not only because it was he who sired his children: he is also a responsible head of household, protective and caring.

Similarly, "the more characteristically female a behavior model, the more clearly it resembles the mater familias": "the more emotional, subjective stance, sober practicality, dignity in duty." For Beke, maleness and femaleness are essential and ahistorical. This gender bipolarity is critical to the health and well-being of society.

> In the rich store of historical examples we find that, with all its changes, the European model of marriage has proven to be the most successful and resilient. Because it corresponds to humanity's two-sexed nature, to the set of complementary differences hidden in our genes. Because only here can a new generation grow up in a normal—that is, two-sexed—world . . .

Unfortunately, Hungarian men and women have deviated rather drastically from this model.

> Nowadays, the whole sphere of masculinity has been reduced to a simple biological function. The former brave warriors now set out only on sexual tours, rather than on the great, genuine adventures of human destiny. The Madonna, on the other hand, became a suffragette, a simple biological function became a tool of coercion, and the exalted role of Mater Dolorosa became an attractive veil covering selfishness and aggressiveness.

The children, meanwhile, are left to themselves, or to their teachers and Youth magazine. Their parents have no time for them: both are selfish and obsessed with sex. But the problem doesn't end there. It seems that in approaching the same point from opposite directions, each is in danger of continuing all the way to the opposite pole. What kind of women want sperm banks?

> At most the suffragettes do, and the aggressive, insistent, unfeminine women, depressing examples of whom I am acquainted with; and I am acquainted as well with weak, hysterical, unmasculine men.

She calls, on behalf of Hungary's real women, for Hungarian men to act like real men:

> The normal, healthy-minded woman—and there are still more of them, even if . . . we hear less about them—don't care a whit about matriarchy; they are not accustomed to conquering by force, but to being conquered . . .
> [These women] sorely miss men, and not only in private life. To restore the men—not only to women, but fathers to their children, responsible masters to their households—is the honorable adventure . . . and men's work.

There is no need to punish women; all that is needed are real men, to whom (real) women will gladly subordinate themselves. The restoration of patriarchy is needed to set things right again.

Although Beke is unusual in not assigning women the entire blame for family and social disorder, she avoids doing so by vilifying "emancipated women" and distancing them from "real" Hungarian womanhood. The journalist Magda Gubi, on the other hand, holds women entirely culpable for Hungarian social ills.[17] Gubi's argument gives an unusually explicit rendering of the antifeminist position; it is worth examining in some detail. Gubi contends that while the propaganda of emancipation still sounds the theme of women's exploitation and oppression, the process of "emancipation" has in fact turned the tables: women—working-class women in particular—now treat men (and children) with "violent aggressiveness." Having "woke[n] up to their key position" in society as a result of "social" pressures both to work and to bear children, women realize that, except for their role in conception, men are dispensable:

> In childrearing the man is replaceable; his physical strength is hardly necessary; at most his economic contribution is needed. And the size of his economic contribution is determined by society.[18]

Women's aggressiveness most emphatically includes an aggressive sexuality. Working women have become "consumers of men."[19] On the subject of sex,

> many bizarre manipulative elements color women's equal rights. Thus, women's orgasm . . . became a popular theme, forcing other more important issues into the background . . . wives manipulate this favorite theme of the women's press.*[20]

Women, Gubi claims, use the allegedly socially accepted notion that "sufficient measures have not been taken in the area of women's sexual satisfaction" to humiliate and tyrannize over their husbands.[21]

These women behave no better toward their children. In the relations between mothers and children,

> the dominance of narcissism is increasingly obvious; [mothers] primarily want to receive love, they wish to be loved, and not to give love. . . . They know little and ask little about the development of the children, who are growing up in child-care centers.[22]

While the child-care centers do not threaten a mother's hold on her child's affections, the father, who "directs increasing emotional attention toward his children, from whom he hopes for a more stable and lasting emotional relationship than from his wife," *is* a threat.[23] In response, women become merciless manipulators of family feelings.

> In the exploitation of their advantages, women's ingenuity is inexhaustible. I know young mothers who, when the father is absent, immediately beat their one-year-old child if the child breaks something or gets dirty, but threaten the father with divorce if he should even raise his voice. In this way the mothers try to . . . maintain the image of the father as a threatening figure. . . .**[24]

---

*Neither in my own examination of the "women's press" nor in probing the memories of Hungarian acquaintances did I find any evidence that women's orgasm had ever been a focus of public attention.

**Again, I would like to interject that I found no evidence elsewhere of a tendency for Hungarian women to behave violently; on the contrary, what evidence exists points to considerable domestic violence directed by men at women. (It appears with disturbing frequency, almost casually, in women's written and oral accounts of their lives.) Evidence is hard to come by partly because domestic violence against women has not been recognized as a social, legal, or public-health problem in Hungary, though it is the subject of jokes and folk sayings.

While "public opinion" continues to blame men for family problems, lamenting the fate of divorced mothers and "fighting a vanguard struggle to get men to do the dishes, a significant proportion of young men are fighting a desperate rearguard battle to remain in the family at whatever sacrifice." The working-class fathers Gubi interviewed are, she says, "in a growing panic that their wives will decide to divorce them, in which case, in the spirit of the family law, they [the courts] will award apartment and child to the mother, while for the man there remains little possibility of family involvement apart from his child-support payments." Women, on the other hand, can control access to existing children, and "can decide when and by whom to become pregnant, that is, whether to make fathers of sexual partners who have hardly reached adulthood and who are unprepared for marriage and fatherhood."[25]

Gubi explicitly advances the notion that women have struck an alliance with the state against men.

> Relations between the woman and society are governed by the rules of mutual dependency. Society liberates the woman from family shackles, gives her economic independence, spares her many of the burdens of childrearing, and in exchange asks for an alliance in crushing male obstinacy. The women take on their part in the alliance with their usual violent moods and aggressiveness. This relationship makes it possible for social consciousness to be filled even now with the idea of women's oppression, when the situation has changed greatly.[26]

In the first of the article's two subsections, entitled "The Emancipated Woman," Gubi repeatedly depicts public opinion as being on the side of women. It is "public opinion" that blames men for family problems and the low birth rate (when, according to Gubi, it ought to blame women); that laments the fate of divorced mothers (when it is fathers who are in the lamentable situation); that is concerned with getting men into the kitchen (when men are in fact desperately fighting just to stay in the family home); and that reproaches men for not spending more of their free time studying or doing housework (which produces guilt-ridden men whom women manipulate). Both explicitly and implicitly, Gubi portrays an alliance between women and "society," understood as both state power and public opinion.[27]

It is noteworthy that Gubi uses the word "society" (*társadalom*) here. She is not employing the "civil society" idiom of antipolitics or the state-society dichotomy current in much social-scientific scholarship. It is more like Hannah Arendt's use of "the social"; Arendt contrasts the "conformism" and leaderless despotism of "society" with the courage and individuality of public action.[28] Just as Arendt tended to see "the social" as an undifferentiated, unstoppable force, Gubi's "society" is also undifferentiated, to the point where it is difficult to identify its members at all. Who is society? Not women, because they're the other partner in the alliance. Not men, because they're the victims of the alliance.

Why doesn't Gubi use "the state" in place of "society" in instances such as "society liberates the women from family shackles . . ."? Perhaps she is reflecting the difficulties—and political delicacy or even danger—of extricating state from society when the state and its ruling party monopolize politics and nearly monopolize the economy, and when social organizations independent of this party are prohibited. But others have used "the state" in just this way.[29] And her frequent references to "public opinion" as being on the wrong (women's) side of this alliance indicate that she may also be using society to mean something like "the population," if the population is seen as being eager to conform to official views. But does the population or "public opinion" somehow exclude men? Or are they deludedly thinking against their own best interests? Gubi resorts to the use of "society," I suggest, for two reasons: first, because "women" as the force behind the woman are not powerful enough—it takes the undelimitable, undifferentiatable "society" to convey the force and menace that makes women seem so threatening; and second, because the amorphous, anonymous, engulfing female "society" must stand in contrast to the heroic, embattled actions of male individuals.

By using the term "society" in this way, Gubi constructs an opposition between women/society on one side and men/family on the other, thus reversing the usual, or at least the liberal, identification of women with family and men with society. But this reversal is not as radical as it appears: when the family has come to be seen as the last bastion of autonomy from state control, identifying women with society and men with the family continues to associate women with dependency (this time on the state) and men with autonomy. It is the social—not gender—locations of autonomy and dependency that have changed.

The issue of family autonomy versus women/state/society dominates the article's second subsection, entitled "The Nursery-School Teacher,[30] the family's collective superego." Here Gubi pursues the "alliance" theme to the point of holding women responsible for all that is wrong with Hungarian working-class culture.[31] What (female) teachers and child-care workers want most in children is obedience and tractability. "So it's important [to them] that their instructions be enforced at home as well."[32] Mothers are their agent in the home, whereas "the fathers [whom she interviewed] were more critical of the educational institutions' activities . . . The alliance between mothers and educators to limit individual autonomy develops more easily."[33]

The subordination of the family to those institutions means its subordination to women. The "feminized sphere of teachers"—from whom male students "get the short end of the stick"—displaces the father within the family: "Whereas formerly paternal power represented the societal norms and value system in the family, today the educational institutions fulfill that function."[34] Parents' fear that their resistance will harm the interests of the child "crushes any remaining opposition and brings about the family's utter dependency."[35] According to Gubi, the Hungarian nation as a whole is suffering from this social mothering and a consequent lack of male firmness and authority. Autonomy must be restored to the family and authority (over biological and social mothers) to the father if (male) adults are truly to be adults and children are to be taken care of properly— that is, by mothers dependent on their husbands, not on "society."

Fear of women as sexual beings combines with the threat of divorce practices to men and to the traditional family, and sexual essentialism combines with nostalgia for an imagined bourgeois past to produce a powerful stigmatization of women who act in their own interest, women who "undermine democracy" by not fulfilling their responsibilities on the "home front." While employment outside the home was officially considered the key to women's emancipation, the private sphere was the focus of this antifeminist discourse. The disproportionate power that women have allegedly accrued was exercised not in the public sphere but in private, over the family. Women's virtual absence from positions of political and economic power and leadership, their lower wages, and their disadvantageous position in a markedly sex-segregated economy made it difficult to argue that women had become too publicly powerful. Women were attacked for shirking their duties at home, when in fact, according to a survey carried out by the Central Statistical Office in the mid-1980s, in 80–85 percent of families the wife alone was doing all the cooking and laundry; in 75 percent of families she did all the dishwashing; and in 58–63 percent she did all the housecleaning and daily shopping.[36] Despite all this, women were portrayed as selfish, voracious exploiters of men and as power-hungry destroyers of the family and of democracy.

A look at divorce practices, which directly counterposed men's and women's interests, may help explain the domestic focus of this hostility. The family law of 1952 explicitly rejected the patriarchal code of the past in favor of "egalitarian" marriage. Women were given the same rights to divorce as men, while divorce in general was made easier to obtain.[37] When this was combined with the fact that women's employment outside the home was not accompanied by the appro- priate social infrastructure or changes in the domestic division of labor, that increasing pressures were put on the family for self-provision, and that more and more people turned to second and third jobs in the private economy, it is not surprising that the divorce rate increased rapidly. But the official notion of egalitarian marriage was accompanied by continued essentialist thinking with regard to gender: divorce-court practices were informed by the view that women were naturally better suited to be caretakers of children. This view, combined with Hungary's severe urban housing shortage, helps explain why there are no provisions for joint custody over children in Hungarian law. Official views of women as naturally more suited to parenthood dictated that the children typically be awarded to them; the housing shortage dictated that when the court disposed over a jointly acquired home, whoever had custody of the children should also have the home. And women's generally low salaries made child-support payments from former husbands a financial necessity.

This practice, in which men have in a sense become disadvantaged relative to women, became a central focus of the antifeminist discourse. The potential power of married women with children contained in their ability to initiate a divorce becomes, in this discourse, overweening and monstrous power over all dimensions of family life. This indicates the degree to which the notion of women's interests disengaged from the family's (or men's or children's) remains illegitimate. Women who pursue interests distinct from those of their (actual or potential) family are regarded as selfish, even monstrously so. There has been no feminist movement in Hungary to challenge these assumptions; the state's "emancipation" campaign itself never challenged them, refusing to acknowledge any conflict between women's interests and men's or the family's. And official ideology continued to hold "emancipated" women primarily responsible for the emotional and physical care of the family.[38]

Here again, societal antipolitics were less oppositional than they seemed. Divorce practices represent a *de facto* disengagement of women's interests from men's and from the family's (for although it certainly could be argued that in many cases women seek divorce in order to protect their children, this is not always the motivation), and in that sense they remain illegitimate. Because the family has been seen as the locus of autonomy from the state, it is not surprising that women's "destabilization" of the family is viewed as evidence of their alleged alliance with the state. Yet when the state moved, in its 1974 and 1986 revisions of the family law, to make divorce more difficult to obtain, many of those active in "antipolitics" opposed it: marriage and divorce belonged to the jealously guarded private realm[39] and were to be shielded from increased state interference.[40] Men, too, initiate divorces, though they are not attacked for it, and this was not a freedom they were willing to have constricted.[41] So it was not divorce that was the problem so much as women's propensity to avail themselves of it.

Women, already cast in the role of allies of the state, are seen as playing into the hands of the state when they "weaken" the family. But this is quite revelatory of the nature of the autonomy the family protects: whose autonomy is it? Women's autonomy—their ability to escape abusive or unhappy marriages—clearly could be said to be enhanced over what it was before 1952. It is men's control over their wives that has been eroded. The discussion of divorce indicates that the "autonomy" of the family from the state is being confused with the right of men to control what goes on within the family.

And is there substance to the persistent notion that women have struck an alliance with the state? In fact, in the 1950s the Stalinist state clearly did target women as its entry point into the family. The official women's movement used its propaganda materials to urge women to bring "planned management into the household," raise their children to be good "socialists," and make sure their husbands went to work.[42] Moreover, women were recruited into those sorts of jobs that were most familylike in their function (such as teachers, child-care workers, visiting nurses), had the most direct contact with parents *qua* parents, and thus were responsible for conveying the state's policies and propaganda. As with divorce practices that award children to mothers, women are being stigmatized for official practices that reflect stereotypical and essentialized views of women, views that assume a woman's place is in the home (whether her own or someone else's).

But with the demise of the regime, won't that alleged "alliance" become irrelevant? In one important sense, yes: opposing the state no longer requires one blindly to defend the family. Women can now support women's right to work outside the home or agitate in opposition to sexual discrimination or domestic violence without being accused of playing into the hands of the state or of undermining the one fragile arena of "civic independence." Moreover, with the ending of direct state control over social and political organizations, there is space for Hungarian women to formulate and articulate alternative discourses that take issue with misogynist and antifeminist ideas and practices. But the change in regime that made this possible also makes it much more urgent: not only has women's access to abortion been challenged, but women's ability to work outside the home has also been undermined, by open discrimination and calls for women to return home and by the shutting down of public child-care facilities. And without the acceptance by at least a substantial minority of the population that women have legitimate interests independent of the family, these will be very difficult battles to fight.

Within the antifeminist discourse, blaming women for social disorder stems ultimately from the assumption that women become socially dangerous when they are permitted to leave the private sphere. In other words, women have been stigmatized not only for what they do but for what they are. Given opportunities that expand their autonomy, that limit their subordination within the family, and that allow them to pursue their own interests, women become destructive and aggressive within the family. Thus, the expansion of women's opportunities cripples them for their "true" vocation—motherhood and homemaking. The demise of state socialism will not in itself transform this sort of thinking.

It has no doubt been noted that some of the most virulent attacks on women come from women. How are we to account for this? In a sense they are illustrations of the dilemma politically and professionally active women have faced in Hungary. Those who are critical of the state share in the sense of the family's importance as a locus of autonomy from the state. Yet because they hold professional jobs, they themselves are suspect: they can be seen as beneficiaries of the state's policies of "emancipation" and as irresponsible with regard to their own families. It is perhaps even more important for them to distance themselves from "emancipated women" so as to escape the set of associations contained in the discourse, associations they reflect and feed with their own writings.[43] This need to distance oneself from the taint of "emancipation" continues to influence women in Hungary today. By acting in their own interests, women discredit themselves, confirming the notion that once they leave the role of private caretaker, women become "selfish and aggressive." This is part of the explanation for why feminist organizations have been so slow to develop in Hungary, while antiabortion groups and organizations to defend the interests of divorced men were established quickly.[44] And it may help explain why today's female politicians of even the "liberal" parties have been reluctant to defend women's interests. The current threats to women's reproductive and employment rights may yet incite women to mobilize in their own defense. This analysis of the antifeminist discourse indicates some of the challenges and obstacles, both internal and external, that Hungarian women face.

Notes

1. *Magyar nök lapja*, no. 20 (1990): 9.

2. For more on the "emancipation" campaign, see chapter 2 of my dissertation, "The Anti-Politics of Anti-Feminism: Gender, State and Civil Society in Hungary, 1949–1992" (University of California at Berkeley, 1992).

3. See, e.g., György Konrád, *Antipolitics* (New York: Henry Holt and Co., 1984); Adam Michnik, *Letters from Prison and Other Essays* (Berkeley: University of California Press, 1985), especially pp. 133–198; Václav Havel, "Anti-political Politics," in John Keane, ed., *Civil Society and the State* (London: Verso, 1988); and David Ost, *Solidarity and the Politics of Anti-Politics: Opposition and Reform in Poland Since 1968* (Philadelphia: Temple University Press, 1990).

4. For some as individuals, participation in state power was less out of reach than it was illegitimate and distasteful. Thanks to Martha Lampland for reminding me of this.

5. Konrád, pp. 197–202.

6. This is taken for granted by Konrád in the passage quoted above. He continues: "The evening and the weekend are yours, you can do with them whatever you wish. . . . The working day is theirs, the free time is ours." (pp. 202–203) This can hardly be said to be true for most women, the bulk of whose "free time" is taken up with housework and child care. It is women's assumption of this role that freed men to exercise their "civic independence."

7. See the interview with Róza Hodosán in *Magyar nök lapja*, no. 1 (1900).

8. For more on this, see my "The Anti-Politics of Anti-Feminism." There were times, such as the late 1960s, when fears of unemployment and the consequent wish to get more women to return at least temporarily to the home also fueled state support for such idealizations.

9. From an article originally printed in *Beszélö* (the onetime *samizdat* journal, now legalized and the organ of the SZDSZ), translated and reprinted in *East European Reporter*, Spring/Summer 1991. Solt was one of the founders of SZETA, a private organization that aided the poor. This was considered inflammatory at the time, since it implied that the state was not providing for the less fortunate as it claimed.

10. This is noted by Zsuzsa Ferge, who cites Dávid Bíró's "A 'teremtés koronái' és a

'gyengébb nem' " (*Valóság*, no. 9 [1982]) as having been the first public manifestation of the "men's rebellion" in Hungary. Ferge, "Biologikum és nemek közötti egyenlöség," in *Nök és Férfiak: Hiedelmek, Tények* (Budapest: MNOT/Kossuth, 1985).

11. See, e.g., Ambrus Bor, "Tizenhárom ezrelék," *Kortárs* 7, no. 5 (1963); Árpád Pünkösdi, "Új népbetegség: as abortusz" (The new epidemic: abortion) and Gyula Fekete, "Gyümölcs a korfán," both in *Kortárs* 14, no. 1, 1970; and Gyula Fekete, *Éljünk magunknak?* (Budapest: Szépirodalmi Könyvkiadó 1972).

12. In addition to the sources cited in the text, examples include Bíró; Sándor Berki, "Csaláladban élni: szövetség vaqgy verseny?" [Life in the family: alliance or competition?] in *Mozgó világ*, no. 1 (1983); Gábor Czakó and Judit B. Gáspár, "Egymásra uszulva," *Mozgó világ*, no. 4 (1983); Márta Bakos, "Önkritikusan," *Mozgó világ*, no. 5 (1983); Zoltán Brády, "Apák és fiúk" (Fathers and sons), series in *Új tükör* during the spring and summer of 1986; "Óh, azok a csodálatos férfiak!" (Oh, those wonderful men) series in *Magyar ifjúság* in the summer and fall of 1985; József S. Varga, "Sorstársak vagyunk," *Nök lapja*, no. 10 (1986); "Történelmi felelösséggel" (interview with Gyula Fekete), *Ötlet*, July 30, 1987; and Erzsébet Berkes, "Köszi, köszi" (Thanks, thanks), *Magyar Nemzet*, March 8, 1990.

13. Owing to limitations of space, I analyze only three texts here, although any of those in note 12 could have been included. For more, see my "The Anti-Politics of Anti-Feminism."

14. "Felesleges apák," *Élet és Irodalom*, February 25, 1993. Hernádi went on to develop his views further in a book called *Divorce is Dangerous* (*Válni veszélyes*), published in 1989 (Budapest: Háttér könyvkiadó).

15. "A madonna elment szüfrazsettnek?" (The madonna went off to become a suffragette?), *Élet és Irodalom*, March 25, 1983.

16. She resigned in 1991, criticizing the government for inaction. She had developed a reputation for high-handedness and had lost much of her popularity. Whether or not the reputation was deserved, I cannot say.

17. Magda Gubi, "Szerepcsere" [Role swap], *Mozgó világ*, no. 11 (1982).

18. Ibid., p. 87.

19. Ibid., p. 86.

20. Ibid., p. 88.

21. Ibid.

22. Ibid., p. 87.

23. Ibid.

24. Ibid.

25. Ibid.

26. Ibid.

27. See B. Gáspár: "[Women] are sure that whatever they do, society will support them." (In Czakó and B. Gáspár, p. 88.)

28. Hannah Arendt, *The Human Condition* (Chicago: University of Chicago Press, 1958), especially pp. 38–49.

29. See, e.g., Bíró: "Our state has done much to lighten women's double burden." (p. 68)

30. Literally, the words used (*dadus néni*) mean something like "nursie-auntie" or "nursie-lady" ("*dadus:* (noun, colloquial), nursie": László Országh, *Magyar-Angol Szótár* [Hungarian-English Dictionary] [Budapest: Akadémiai Kiadó, 1985].

31. Why Gubi attributes and limits the phenomenon to the working class is not clear. She sees the parent-teacher relationship as "further develop[ing] that stratum-specific [i.e., working class] attitude in which an individual's lifecourse is experienced fatalistically, as dependent upon unpredictable forces. (The many feudal features of the national character are perhaps in this way further stabilized.)" (p. 91)

32. Ibid., p. 90.

33. Ibid., p. 92.

34. Ibid., pp. 90–92.

35. Ibid., p. 92.

36. Among only those families in which women worked outside the home, the proportions were somewhat, but not much, lower: e.g., 78 percent for cooking, about 80 percent for laundry, about 65 percent for dishwashing. *A nők helyzete a munkahelyen és a családban* (Budapest: Központi Statistikai Hivatal 1988), pp. 21–22.

37. Ferenc Mikos, "Az új családjogi törvény," *Nehéz esztendök kronikája, 1949–1953: Dokumentumok,* ed. Sándor Balogh (Budapest: Gondolat, 1986).

38. On official ideology and "emancipation," see my "The Anti-Politics of Anti-Feminism."

39. As did the reputedly rather wild sexual life for which Budapest intellectuals were known in the 1970s. Sex as a form of political subversion was a notion also embraced elsewhere in Eastern Europe. It seems from my own conversations that in Hungary, as in these works of fiction and not unlike the "Sexual Revolution" of the 1960s and 1970s in the United States, this sexual liberation had more to do with men's sexual freedom and autonomy (vis-à-vis individual women as well as the state) than with women's discovery of sexual pleasure or the ending of the double standard.

40. But perhaps the antipolitical opposition should be disaggregated along these lines: some would have supported (and do now support) state restrictions on divorce and abortion in order to protect "the Hungarian nation" or "Hungarian values." This split is reflected today in the social conservatism of the Hungarian Democratic Forum and its coalition partners versus the libertarianism of the Free Democrats and the Young Democrats.

41. The proportion of divorces officially initiated by women has been increasing: whereas in 1963 50.6 percent of divorces were requested by women and 49.4 percent by men, in 1983, 67.7 percent were requested by women and 32.3 percent by men. These figures should be treated with some caution, however, as they say nothing about precipitating factors: for example, some women initiate divorces only after men have *de facto* left the marriage. Nonetheless, the figures do seem to indicate a

genuine increase in the proportion (and number) of divorces initiated by women. (The number of divorces initiated by men in 1963 was 9,064 and in 1983, 9,482, while those initiated by women increased from 9,290 in 1963 to 19,855 in 1983.) Figures from Erika Rév, *Válóperek krónikája* (Budapest: MNOT-Kossuth Könyvkiadó, 1986), p. 176.

42. See my "The Anti-Politics of Anti-Feminism."

43. This may not be a fully conscious process, and may draw on reservoirs of low self-esteem or self-hatred, themselves in part a product of the state-socialist configuration I've been describing. I thank Anna Szemere for raising this point.

44. One small, embattled explicitly feminist group does exist: the Feminista Hálózat (Feminist Network), established in June 1990. Many members of the former official women's organization established a new organization (Magyar Nök Szövetsége [Hungarian Women's Association]), whose official slogan is "For the advancement of the nation, for equal opportunity, for our children, and for our families." Its leaders have explicitly rejected both feminism and politics.

23

Abortion and the Formation of the Public Sphere in Poland

Małgorzata Fuszara

The draft of a new abortion law submitted to the Sejm (Poland's lower house of Parliament), shortly before the June 1989 parliamentary elections, ignited a fiery and emotional debate about abortion that pervaded the preelection campaign. No recent debate in Poland has been comparable in emotional intensity, pervasiveness of discussions, or the depth of divisions it provoked. There were even attempts to stop the debates for fear they might harm the candidates. The draft, however, proved so controversial that discussions could hardly be stopped. The issue became a difficult problem for political candidates for the June 1989 elections and the presidential campaign in 1990. Candidates were repeatedly asked how they would vote if the draft were examined by the new Parliament. This draft, submitted by seventy-four deputies, was explicitly entitled, "On the protection of a conceived child." It proposed an absolute ban on abortion and criminal penalties for both the woman and doctor. Groups and circles that otherwise shared opinions split sharply on the abortion issue.

These debates must be understood in the context of the formation of a public sphere and new political processes in Poland. Under communism, there were no parliamentary debates, only support for party-sponsored bills. The parliamentary debates on abortion in August and September 1990 and May 16, 1991, with their rhetorical maneuvers, are among the best examples of the recovery of democratic processes, parliamentary life, and the public sphere.

I. The Legal Regulation of Abortion in Poland

In Poland as in many other countries, discussions about abortion developed in the 1920s. New codes were then prepared to replace the legislation still in force in Poland during its first years of independence. The penal code eventually passed in 1932 banned abortion except when pregnancy endangered a woman's health, or if it was a result of a criminal act such as rape, incest, or seduction of a minor.

Discussion about conditions for abortion was resumed almost immediately after World War II, when the voice of antiabortionists prevailed. Their arguments were mainly demographic: the country had suffered a great loss of population which now had to be made up for.

The discussions that developed during the political "thaw" following Stalin's death in the mid-fifties were entirely different in tone. In 1956, a commission was created by the Ministry of Health to examine abortion provisions. The commission was for liberalization of provisions and an extension of the right to abortion. New regulation was proposed and the new act, passed in 1956, was still in force in Poland in 1992.

The aim of the 1956 law is stated clearly in its preamble: to protect women's health from abortions in unsuitable conditions by nonphysicians. Abortion is permitted if there are medical reasons, if the pregnant woman has "difficult living conditions," or if the pregnancy resulted from an offence. The act does not provide for the woman's right to decide but, as stressed in present discussions, in practice it is the woman who decides because of the broad interpretation given to the "difficult living conditions" clause. Physicians base their decision about whether the conditions are "difficult" on the woman's own assessment.

It is uncertain how many abortions are performed in Poland each year, since those performed in private surgeries are probably never disclosed in order to avoid taxes. Such abortions are legal but not registered, and available statistics refer only to registered abortions. In the 1980s about 130,000 or 140,000 abortions a year were registered in Poland—that is, 13.2 per 1000 women aged 15–49, and 18.2 per 100 live births (still birth excluded).[1] Estimates of unregistered abortions vary greatly, ranging between 55,000 and 85,000 per year.[2] Opponents of the draft abortion act estimates the number of women liable to punishment, those who have had an abortion, at 300,000 per year. Church groups quote the highest figure, estimating 600,000 or even a million abortions per year.[3]

II. The Church and the History of Abortion Law

Proposals to restrict abortion in post-1945 Poland have arisen whenever there has been a period of "thaw" and relative freedom, as in 1956 and 1980, years characterized by a greater freedom of speech. In spite of the liberal abortion laws in effect since 1956, there have always been some who wanted that legislation changed. The recent expansion of the public sphere has made possible the articulation of these demands. The 1956 act was repeatedly and fiercely criticized in Catholic circles on the grounds that human life is sacrosanct and should be protected from the moment of conception, that the act's broader impact would be to undermine sexual morality, lead to a cynical attitude toward love, and to hasten overall the physical and moral degradation of the nation.

In 1958, the PAX Catholic Association appealed to the Sejm for annulment of the act and to the faithful, physicians and medical staff in particular, for its sabotage. Discussions grew more heated again in the years 1980–1981 and after 1989, when Catholic groups made another appeal to annul the act.

The Catholic church strongly affects the political process and antiabortion attitudes. Candidates in the presidential and electoral campaigns feared losing the support of the church and often strive to win it. For the same reason, other groups and the press prefer to keep silent on the issue. Such silence suggests disagreement with the bill accompanied by a fear of criticizing it openly.

However, the Church's impact on Polish attitudes and the social backing for the church's standpoint, though very significant, should not be overrated.[4] Admittedly, 95 percent of Poles call themselves Catholics and believers and have a religious upbringing, but sociological investigations reveal that Poles allow for many exceptions to the observance of religious dictates. In one study as many as 57 percent believed one should not keep to those religious dictates which one considers to be wrong.[5] In a nationwide survey taken at the beginning of February 1992, only 11 percent supported the absolute ban on abortion supplemented with penalties, while 22 percent thought abortion should be allowed in strictly specified circumstances, as when the woman's health is endangered or the pregnancy results from rape; 35 percent think that abortion should be allowed but with some restrictions; and as many as 25 percent think that abortion should be offered whenever the woman requests it.[6]

III. The Parliamentary Draft

As stressed by its advocates, the 1989 draft's penal provisions and bans are not its essential part but a consequence of its basic assumptions of the inviolability of human life and the existence of a human life from the very moment of conception. The bill grants legal status to the fetus from the moment of conception.

The bill begins with a declaration of the extensive assistance and care a pregnant woman is to receive. However, as stressed by the bill's opponents, these are general homilies, unrealistic in the present economic situation.

A ban is proposed on all experiments and medical intervention affecting an unborn child, other than those that serve the protection of its life and health. There is a risk that this could be interpreted to prohibit prenatal testing. It contains an absolute, unconditional provision that "Whoever causes the death of an unborn child shall be subject to deprivation of liberty for up to three years." The penalty may be increased if threats or deceit were used toward the mother, or the court may renounce the infliction of punishment if it finds that warranted. The draft also includes penalties for the woman having the abortion, in one of the most criticized sections of the bill. The bill under discussion in the Senate in August 1990, the so-called "Senate draft," no longer provided for the punishment of the woman, but the issue reappeared during the September 1990 discussions. An analysis of the discourse in the August 1990 and September 1990 Senate debates is revealing.

IV. The Senate Debate

The Senate debate started with a one-day debate on August 3, 1990,[7] which senators in favor of an absolute ban on abortion tried to make the sole discussion, hoping to submit the bill immediately to the Sejm. Opponents of the bill, demanding that further discussion was necessary, succeeded in postponing the decision. Further debate was held after the Senate's holidays, on September 28, and 29, 1990.[8] Let us analyze the rhetorical techniques and arguments in the discourse of that first debate.

It is amazing that although only ten persons—seven men and three women—had taken the floor in this first debate on such a highly contested issue, supporters tried to end discussion, revealing little respect for a democratic process. Significantly, no men spoke against the bill, although all the women stated their intention to vote against it. One woman, however, wanted an even stronger bill that would punish the woman as well. One man stressed the harmful effects of creating such a serious split between the many women who had abortions and the rest of society, but not even that senator spoke against the actual bill. Every participant emphatically stated that they were against abortion, but differed fundamentally on the appropriate legal regulations.

Various rhetorical techniques were used, including characterizing one's own position, e.g., that the fetus is a human being from the moment of conception, as "indubitable" or "incontrovertible," or using binary oppositions to describe one's own standpoint and that of one's opponents, e.g., "honest/dishonest," "responsible/irresponsible," "moral/immoral."

Another rhetorical device was the use of temporal and historic signifiers. Those for the bill stressed that the debate concerned the future ("it is the future of Polish civilization," "the debate is a step forward," "it is of fundamental importance for the future"). The "future" was not defined, whether a demographic issue or one of morality. The main point was to associate the draft with a concern for the "future," counting on the favorable associations of any mention of change, the future, and building a new order.

Advocates also appealed to "science," objectivity, and authority. They usually did not quote specific scientific statements, but merely defined their own standpoint as consistent with the latest scientific research, suggesting that their opponents were unscientific. They tried to mask a moral choice as a scientific issue.

Political rhetoric was also used, referring to the duty of parliamentarians, as spokespersons for democracy, to introduce democracy in Poland, which meant the duty to recognize the equal rights and lives of all persons. This was aided by the rhetorical maneuver of calling the fetus a "nasciturus,"[9] first done during the August debate. The concept "nasciturus" suggests that it is a human being from the moment of conception. Jointly, it was argued that this required an absolute ban on abortion.

The opponents of the bill did not generally use such rhetorical devices, although there was one senator who stressed that abortion involves human tears, tragedy, and blood and is a question of moral choice, which those for the bill tried to disguise. He denied that the Senate and Parliament had the right to decide this issue and thereby impose its own moral opinions upon forty million people.

Appeals to authority included those of a senator who introduced herself as "the only specialist in penal law" and another who spoke of himself as being in the natural sciences, implying that he was not influenced by political or ideological concerns. Two senators spoke in the name of a Senate commission, while another said he was taking the floor as both "a citizen" and "a doctor," suggesting that he was speaking not just for himself, but for a specific group. And one senator used the phrase "the right to life" thirty-eight times in her twelve-minute speech.

Let us look at the substantive arguments used by the two parties in the August and September 1990 debates, looking first at the arguments used by advocates of the new act.

These arguments, which appeal to distinct sorts of premises, can be divided accordingly into moral, empirical, and political arguments. Among the *moral arguments* are those that rest on moral claims: that human life is the supreme value and starts at conception, and thus must be protected; that the human being is autonomous from the moment of conception, that it is not part of the mother's body, and that the mother thus does not have the right to decide on its future; and that abortion is immoral, the slaughter of innocent human beings, comparable to killing old or disabled people.

The empirical arguments include *sociological and legal arguments* such as: that the incidence of abortion in Poland is very high, persuasion is not sufficient to control abortion, and legal bans are thus necessary; that legal regulations aim at educating society and changing social consciousness; *demographic arguments* that regions of Poland, especially rural ones, are underpopulated, many people emigrate, so who will work in the future to pay for old-age and disability pensions. One senator stated that Poland could contribute to Europe a value it lacks: a commitment to large families. These arguments reflect the particular concerns of Poland, as is evident in one *historical* argument that Poland would not have conquered the Red Army in the famous battle of 1920 had the Polish women aborted; the 1980 revolution would not have occurred had there been no demographic explosion in the 1950s.

An *"Argument from authority"* refers to an argument containing an empirical premise invoking or endorsing the views of an irrelevant authority. In this debate, they appealed to church doctrines to protect life given by God; to the American Founding Fathers and President Reagan, complete with quotations from his speeches; to the Second Solidarity Congress in 1990, which backed the bill; and to the Hippocratic Oath, the Human Rights Covenants, and other international covenants that oblige the state to protect life, including the life of the unborn fetus.

The *political arguments* included an appeal to democracy, i.e., that the electorate demanded that Parliament should vote for the bill, indicating that the debate on abortion in Poland, in the appeals to democracy, has dimensions not found in the Western abortion debates.

Opponents of the bill rest their empirical arguments on beliefs of the ineffectiveness of penal measures to control abortion; the need to control the causes of abortion by changing women's living conditions, developing care and financial assistance for unmarried mothers; the need to propagate sex education and contraceptives; such unintended negative side effects as illegal abortions performed under unsanitary conditions; or social differentiation into wealthy women who will have abortions in good conditions and the poor doomed to back alleys.

Opponents argue further that the abortion issue is a moral issue and no person has the right to impose his or her moral opinion on others, or to use police to protect that opinion. They appeal to the woman's right to life, claiming that advocates of the bill falsely state that pregnancy poses no serious threats to a woman's life while demanding that she should sacrifice her life in a situation of threat, and that it infringes on her subjectivity to deprive her of the right to choice. They further argue that penalizing abortion is inconsistent with the practice of civilized societies; that the state cannot protect anything from a moment of conception of which it cannot have exact knowledge.

Opponents, too, used political arguments appealing to democracy, claiming that the electorate demanded that Parliament vote against the bill and that the discussion is a substitute for a political debate.

In contrast to the West, arguments for the absolute individual right to control over one's body were infrequent and mostly used in street debates, not in Parliament. This is not surprising in a culture in which the idea of individual rights was systematically censured by official collectivist ideologies. The Senate debaters' attitudes, if they did refer to the right to control over one's body, frequently become extremely patronizing toward women. One senator said, "It isn't classy to say that my stomach is my business, and real ladies never speak this way." At the same time he stated that it was a "confusing slogan, as the Parliament is entitled to debate and decide on that issue."[10]

It was very rare for men participating in the debate ever to mention that they were speaking of a matter that concerned women above all. One who noticed this problem stated that he would have felt better taking the floor on this issue if he had been "a young and attractive girl." Only one man in the Senate took this problem seriously, dramatically describing overburdened women of thirty who looked as old as their own grandmothers. He asked whether senators should become guardians of these women's conscience and judges of their personal tragedies.

Outside of the parliamentary debates, the arguments were more emotional, comparing abortion to "Nazi and Stalinist genocide" and the slaughter of unborn children. There were mass demonstrations and collections of signatures for and against the bill. Opponents of the bill called their adversaries "murderers of women," while banners proclaimed the number of women who had died from illegal abortions.

Differences on abortion reflected general moral and lifestyle disagreements. Advocates of the ban introduced themselves as being for the traditional family, monogamy, sexual moderation, and morality. Significantly, opponents of the bill stressed that they were against abortion as well, but that they wanted to control it through a change of living conditions, better contraception, and sex education while protecting freedom of individual choice.

These pronouncements show that slogans about equal rights of women, unless supported by actions and by a woman's struggle to realize that equality, have little effect The problem about who should decide about abortion has not been settled. Opponents of the abortion law, aware of public sentiment on abortion, asked for a popular referendum, but the Sejm rejected the motion, arguing, contradictorily, that moral problems cannot be settled by voting.

Several other methods were used by opponents of the draft on abortion, including use of the parliamentary procedure of submission of minority motions to submit a competitive draft, "On the right to parenthood, protection of the conceived human life and the conditions of admissibility of abortion." The Parliamentary Women's Club (headed by Barbara Labuda), in order to delay a vote to ban abortion, asked that a very long list of questions be answered before a vote could be taken, especially on the financial consequences if the draft were introduced. The Women's Club demanded that all these questions be answered before the Parliament proceeded to vote on the draft.

A somewhat modified version of the draft was submitted to the Sejm, which decided to refer it, without debate, to an Extraordinary Commission specially created to investigate the parliamentary draft. From the very beginning those who were for a legal ban on abortion outnumbered opponents on the commission by one vote. It was decided that the antiabortion act should provide for no exceptions; also, the plan to punish women for abortion was reincorporated. According to the commission's draft, the only condition under which a doctor trying to save a women's life is not guilty of a crime is if a miscarriage takes place as an unintended effect of his actions.

When no compromise whatsoever seemed possible, the Parliamentary Club of the Democratic Union made a new initiative, announcing its intention to move from a parliamentary resolution suggesting that neither drafts nor the proposal of the referendum should be investigated by the Sejm. This was an attempted compromise. It did stress the evil that results from abortion, the need to include a provision on the protection of life in the Constitution itself, including that life begins from the moment of conception, and the need to abolish the regulations that permit abortions in private surgeries. But it also stated that the government should prepare a program of extended care for the mother, child, and family, and provide for sex education.

The final vote on this resolution took place the day after the debate of May 15, 1991; 208 deputies voted for the resolution, 145 against it, and 14 abstained. Thus, neither the drafts nor the proposal of the referendum was investigated by the Sejm.

This debate reveals the particular contours of the Polish situation: how the creation of a democratic society is reflected in the political arguments about abortion; the importance of stating one's opposition to abortion, whichever side of the debate one is on; the confusion, and even reluctance, to handle public discourse on such issues; and the relative unimportance of the individual rights of the woman, such a major issue in the West.

A further question arises whether positions on the abortion bill reflect divisions into left and right. To discuss this we have to look at the political situation in Poland.

V. The Public Sphere in Poland

The Polish parliamentary elections of June 1989 were the first free elections held in Central and Eastern Europe since 1939. Elections to the Sejm, the lower chamber, were not entirely free, since only 35 percent of the seats were filled in free elections, with the remaining 65 percent kept by the former ruling groups. But elections to the Senate, the superior chamber which was nonexistent under communist rule, were entirely free. When the Polish elections of 1989 were taking place, the political and social changes in the other Soviet bloc countries had not yet begun, and the future of the Polish transformation hardly seemed certain.

Under these conditions, the June 1989 elections presented not so much a choice of positive programs or individual candidates as a chance to vote against the Communists. It was "Walesa's team" who was elected; each member was photographed with Walesa to identify him or her to their constituents as a member of the "team." Opposition candidates had to form such a team to beat the Communists, since the long media monopoly and absence of freedom of expression made it impossible to get to know the candidates individually. The difficulty in creating a public sphere and civil society was enhanced by the lack of a political language to identify positions. The old usage of "left" and "right" was corrupted by the former system, whose abuses and misapplication made those terms lose their original meaning, such that negative connotations were attached to the former term. Communists were identified with a corrupt totalitarian system which the society rejected, rather than spokespersons for a progressive movement. Adam Michnik even stated that he was offended at having been identified with the "secular Left," and responded by calling the authors of the statement "pigs."[11] With the growing stabilization, the former "team" will need to divide according to ideologies, philosophies, opinions, and standpoints. The language in which to accomplish this is in the process of being created.

It is thus difficult to characterize the abortion debate in terms of left and right. If one had to use those terms, one would say that the right and center predominated; voices from the left have been practically absent, except in the communist newspaper *Trybuna*.

The Catholic church plays an important political role, in part because of the past 40 years, the church was the only voice independent of the state and the spokesperson for national traditions and values professed by Poles themselves. It provided the possibility of a minimal civil society, of excluding a limited sphere of one's life from the state, and it supported and employed those who opposed the communist system and who hold power today. Abortion is an issue on which the Catholic church has been unyielding for many decades, aiming at a complete ban on abortion.[12] It is difficult to oppose the church on an issue it finds so important. In addition, the church is an influential power and candidates to political office strive for its backing.

A very interesting situation emerged during the electoral campaign of fall 1991. None of the parties or political groups were outspoken about abortion, its legal regulation, or possible further parliamentary debate. As Foucault has claimed, one method of controlling discourse, especially about politics and sex, is through exclusion of topics, which was precisely the mechanism used by the parties in the parliamentary electoral campaign of fall 1991, only a few months after the fierce discussion about abortion in Parliament. This was the case despite the fact that legal regulation of abortion was generally expected to recur in Parliament.

Those who wanted to ban abortion took other actions as well. One of the church's greatest successes was the passage on December 14, 1991, of a new "Physicians' Code of Ethics." The Chamber of Physicians appointed an extraordinary commission to prepare this new code. The original draft, submitted to the commission on December 14, 1991, permitted abortion by a specialist in the sole case of a threat to the woman's life. The medical community had no opportunity to acquaint themselves with the draft and no chance to express their opinions concerning it. The congress eventually adopted a version that permitted an abortion by a specialist if pregnancy threatened the woman's life or health or if it resulted from a criminal offense. According to this code, a doctor who performed an abortion for other reasons was liable to punishment by the disciplinary court of the Chamber of Physicians, whose penalties included the withdrawal of a medical license. This could have a chilling effect even on doctors' willingness to perform prenatal diagnoses.

In the last week of March 1992, a group of deputies submitted to the Sejm a draft bill almost identical to the previous one. The Women's Parliamentary Club submitted a counterproposal that was much more liberal. In June 1992 the Sejm investigated this draft.

This series of events brought about the unusual legal situation of 1991–92, in which abortion was permitted by law in cases prohibited by this medical moral code. Although a doctor who performed an abortion because of the woman's "difficult living conditions" was not guilty of a legal offense, she or he was nevertheless liable to punishment by the disciplinary court of the Chamber of Physicians.

The function of such actions was also to prepare additional arguments for a limitation on the right to abortion. Should a new abortion act be discussed in Parliament, the antiabortion position was ready with a new argument: even doctors are banning abortion. Surveys have shown that fewer than 7 percent of physicians actually support such a ban,[13] but the adoption of the moral code permits opponents of abortion to present a different interpretation of doctor's opinions.

VI. Women's Political Action

In Poland as in the other post-communist countries, women's movements are weak and poorly organized, and a public discourse about women's issues has to be created. This results from the loss of face of the official communist women's movements and the situation of women. In the years between the two World Wars, 1918–1939, the women's movement developed freely in Poland. Over eighty different women's organizations existed, from professional organizations in cities to women's clubs in towns and villages, church organizations, and the Women's Parliamentary Club.

The women's political situation changed diametrically after World War II, under communist rule. The grass-roots women's movements were replaced by the official Women's League. Like all other social movements and organizations under communism in Poland, independent women's organizations were banned, replaced by organizations established from above. These discredited organizations have made Polish women suspicious of any women's organizations, including those that the new women's movement is trying to organize. The very idea of a political party is discredited, owing to its degeneration and association with the one and only Party that exercised power against the will of society. Groups organizing now seldom call themselves parties, preferring the names "movement," "forum," or "group."

In the 1970s women constituted at least 20 percent of the Polish Parliament. But under communist rule, real power was exercised by the Central Committee of the Polish United Workers' Party (PUWP) and to some extent, by the government. Among these bodies there was only one woman at most. Whenever Parliament gained real power and there was more political freedom—after 1956, in 1989 and 1991—women always found it the most difficult to get elected, and their numbers declined. While women constituted 23 percent of members of the Sejm[14] in 1980–85, they made up only 9 percent of the Sejm after the elections of fall

1991. The absence of grass-roots women's movements that could nominate and promote their leaders exacerbates this situation.

In this difficult context, influential women's groups remain absent. As in other post-communist countries, the lack of a broad representation of women in Parliament and local government is no accident. The official Communist Party women's organizations developed their own elites and are in no position to represent Polish women. At the same time, owing to long years of an absence of democratic process, a public sphere, and genuine social movements, groups representing women's interests could not develop. The discussion on the abortion bill changed this situation, and a number of small groups have been created that aim at defending women's rights: the Movement for Women's Self-Defense, the Association for the Dignity of Women. There are also grass-roots organizations such as the Feminist Association and Pro Femina. All in all there are more than twenty women's organizations in Poland today. Their discussions and activities focus on the abortion bill, but they can be expected to expand to incorporate other women's issues. Representatives of women's movements have no representation whatsoever in Parliament, although they have taken part in numerous street demonstrations and pickets against the bill. In Warsaw there were several street demonstrations in 1991, all ending up in front of the Parliament. Participants demanded that their arguments be heard by representatives in the Senate. If it were not for those insistent demands, nobody would try to learn their opinions on the issue, to say nothing of taking them into consideration. It is therefore clear that the movements representing the interests of women have only started their struggle for recognition, and they have started by entering the public discourse about abortion, demanding that it be part of the parliamentary and democratic discourse. What has so far been the problem of each individual woman will become a problem for society.

Reconstruction of a genuine political sphere is bound to be prolonged.[15] The most interesting effect of the submission of the draft to the Sejm has been the activation of women's groups, the attempt to formulate women's needs, and the establishment of women's organizations. These have been initiated from below, not imposed on women. It can be stated that, paradoxically, the antiabortion draft helped women to create women's organizations and a women's movement in defense of their rights.

Notes

1. E. Zielińska, *Oceny prawnokarne przerywania ciazy: Studium porównawsze* (Warsaw: Wydawnictvo Prawnicze, 1986).

2. S. Klonowicz, "Legalizacja sztucznych poronien a dynamika rozrodczoscjw Polsce," *Studia Demograficzne,* no. 36 (1974).

3. *Prymas Polski w obronie zycia* (Warsaw, 1982).

4. F. Kissling, "The Church's Heavy Hand in Poland," *Conscience* (September/October, 1991).

5. J. Kurczewski, "Carnal Sins and Privatisation of the Body," in *Family, Gender and Body in Law and Society Today* eds. J. Kurczewski and A. Czynczyk (Warsaw: University of Warsaw, 1990).

6. "Aborcja tak, ale z ograniczeniami," *Gazeta Wyborcza,* March 16, 1992.

7. All dates and quotations from the August 3, 1990, debate are from the Senate's own shorthand report of that debate.

8. All data and quotations from the September debate are from the author's own recording, made during a TV digest of the Senate debate of September 29–30, 1990.

9. In Roman law, "nasciturus" denoted a fetus that had certain rights upon its birth, e.g., to inherit the property of its father (even if the father had died before it was born).

10. Recorded by myself.

11. A. Michnik, "Co zostało z komitetu," *Gazeta Wyborcza,* no. 146 (1990): 4.

12. On the Catholic church's standpoint on the abortion issue, see "Declaration on Abortion," Vatican 1974, the Holy Congregation on Faith, approved for publication by Pope Paul VI.

13. J. Supinska, unpublished manuscript.

14. From 1939 to 1989 Poland did not have a Senate at all. The upper chamber had been swallowed by the Communists, since it traditionally represented the upper classes in the Polish parliamentary tradition.

15. On the shaping of the system of power, see M. Fuszara and J. Kurczewski, "Rzad i parlament jako osrodki władzy," *Prace* [journal connected with Solidarność], no. 2 (1990).

24

Political Change in Poland: Cause, Modifier, or Barrier to Gender Equality?[1]

Anna Titkow

For more than 120 years, up to 1918, Poland did not appear on the map of Europe as a state. The period of lost independence and statehood created the model of the heroic Polish woman coping with all sorts of burdens. What was demanded from a woman was endurance and steadfastness in her duties; her importance in bringing up children was also stressed. Women were responsible for maintaining the national language, culture, and religious faith. They were accustomed to performing traditional male roles (keeping the home or running a business when the husband was imprisoned or died). All this created a "social genotype" of a woman coping discreetly with very difficult demands, in accordance with the spirit of self-sacrifice for the homeland and family, not expecting anything other than acknowledgment in return.

That traditional Polish image of woman as protector and preserver of heroic virtues[2], much like the image of woman promoted by the Catholic church, continues to this day. Women's entry into paid work under state socialism amounted to the *loss of a chance* for fundamental changes in the essential social and cultural identity of Polish women, the *loss of a chance* for full and permanent conversion from sex identity to gender identity.

Sociological research shows that under state socialism the main criteria for respect for women were still the proper performance of family responsibilities, effectively combined if possible, with paid work. Even in better-paid sectors, mainly industrial work, women are most often clerks and administrative workers at the lowest ranks or unskilled and semiskilled workers.[3] Women do not make a career, even in the most feminized sectors of the labor market.

It is probably true, however, that coping with the demand of paid work, superimposed on the traditional roles of women, has bettered women's self-evaluation. It has served not only as a source of gratification but as a counterweight to the problems work caused to women's mental and physical health, and also as an asset to women's authority in the family. Having to do the shopping and carry heavy net bags, suffering from lack of sleep and being terribly tired, a woman justifiably felt herself to be an indispensable manager of family life, performing duties and tasks enough for several persons.

I believe that this basic psychological gratification was, and still is, more important for the majority of Polish women than the satisfaction from the job itself, and it can be associated with self-fulfillment, esteem, respect, earnings, and one's position in the social hierarchy. Such gratification may be one of the reasons why women remained and still remain out of the loop of decision making in paid work and politics. For example, in 1986 only 11 percent of the members of the Central Committee of the Polish United Workers' Party (PUWP)[4] were women; of the members of the Consultative Board of President Jaruzelski 5 percent were women. At the Round Table in 1989, among sixty participants there was only one woman. After the election of October 27, 1991, there were no women in the Cabinet; women made up 9.6 percent of the Diet, the Polish Parliament, elected in October, 1991. In local state administration 11 percent of the positions are held by women, but only 6.4 percent of management positions.[5]

However, women's occupational activity was not conducive to the rise of a specific subculture of working women. In general, values and attitudes among working and nonworking women were very similar, including those toward marriage. Some differences could be traced in women's attitudes toward children, sex, and abortion. Working women stressed more strongly that children are the main goal in life. With the same level of education and age, working women were more tolerant of premarital sex and abortion. To some extent, then, having a job breaks the corset of restrictive norms.

Working women did not have their own subculture because they did not create authentic adaptation mechanisms that modified their lifestyle. But work did not threaten their self-image, acting rather as a positive reinforcement of self-evaluation. However, the costs to women were high. In Łodz women have the highest death rates and morbidity from cancer, tuberculosis, and venereal diseases, the highest indicators of absenteeism, and the lowest fertility rates and highest infant mortality in all of Poland.[6]

The Past, the Present, the Future

The Parliamentary elections of June 1989 signaled the escalation of various kinds of threats against women, including threats against their identity, work, and political, public, and personal activities. For example, when the regulation protecting the job of the sole supporter of a family was eliminated from the labor code, the author's intention was to eliminate a regulation that might protect drunkards and loafers.[7] However, this decision produced a situation unfavorable to single mothers. In addition, because of the difficult financial situation, local authorities have shut down kindergartens and infant nurseries. In Łodz, with a textile industry dominated by women, 100 nursery schools have already been closed down. It is estimated that nationwide from 40 percent to 60 percent of such institutions were closed by mid-1991.

Women looking for jobs form half of the unemployed, but the number of offers for them is seven times smaller than that for men.[8] In addition, in the reorganization it is the office staff, primarily women, who are typically first fired. Women are compelled to qualify for new jobs, but they have little chance of finding one. A major group of unemployed women are those from thirty-one to forty years old (31.2 percent)[9] and unemployment is increasing. As of July 31, 1990, there was 5.2 percent unemployment. In December 1991 it was 11.4 percent.[10]

Minimization of women's participation in political life is not surprising given the stereotype that women should play a limited role in public life, which is reinforced by the slogans of National-Christian groups. This goal is exemplified in the legislative activities of the latter group. It was the National Christian Parliamentary Club that sponsored the bill for the complete elimination of abortion. Furthermore, according to confidential instructions, contraceptives are being withdrawn from pharmacies. And even before an antiabortion act was passed, getting an abortion under the state-controlled health care system was difficult. The Surgeon General of Poland induced his colleagues to register women's deaths caused by illegal abortions as due to other causes.

Meanwhile, we witness a phenomenon that may be defined as the beginning of the "Polish women's liberation movement." Provoked by the draft law of the absolute abolition of abortion, it is occurring on several levels: first, on the level of women's mass protest, expressed not in demonstrations but in letters to Parliament and newspapers; second, in the creation of new foundations and new groups established by women themselves, along with programs worked out for women. Female members of Parliament have appointed a women's committee. Some political parties have "women's councils" (ROAD). A women's political party is being organized (Women's Democratic Union), which closely cooperates with the Social Democratic Party.

Although it may appear that we are returning to the situation of women characteristic of the very beginning of the century in Poland, this is only superficially true. An important and positive role will be played by the experience resulting from the politically conditioned "equality" of both sexes since 1945, despite its being authoritatively imposed and very flawed. The political and economic transformation going on in Poland, however negative it may appear for women, should be seen as only a factor modifying the process of achieving gender equality.

Notes

1. An earlier version of this paper was presented at a conference in Berlin at Humboldt University in May 1991, sponsored by IREX and Humboldt University. The proceed-

ings, *Current Problems in the Position of Women* will be published. This article is a revised version.

2. D. Markowska, "Rola kobiety polskiej w rodzinie," *Kobiety polskie* (Warsaw: Ksiazka i Wiedza, 1986).

3. H. Domanski, "Nierownosci zarobkow miedzy mezczyznami i kobietami" (unpublished manuscript); I. Reszke, "Zroznicowanie rynku pracy w Polsce jako zrodlo nierownosci miedzy mezczyznami i kobietami," referat na zjazd Polskiego Towarzystwa Socjologicznego, Wrocław, 1986.

4. This was the name of the Communist Party of Poland.

5. *Report of the Government of the Republic of Poland on the Progress Made in Implementation of the Convention on the Elimination of All Forms of Discrimination Against Women in the period from 1 June 1988 to 31 May 1990.*

6. A. Bujwid, "Profil demograficzny i zdrowotny", *Kobieta polska lat osiemdziesiatych* (Warsaw: Niezalezna Oficyna Wydawnicza, 1988).

7. H. Leśnicka, "Samotne wśród ludzi," *Zycie Warszawy,* no. 105 (1990).

8. E. Olczyk, "Kobiety zorganizowane," *Zycie Warszawy,* April 17, 1991.

9. See ftnote. 4.

10. Chief Central Statistical Office, 9.

25

Feminism in the Interstices of Politics and Culture: Poland in Transition

Ewa Hauser, Barbara Heyns, and Jane Mansbridge

I. A Time of Inarticulation

For women and men, for the working class and the professional class, for every component of Polish society, the language of politics and the understanding of political interests are today in flux. A near-totalitarian order has dissolved; political interests are shifting, along with the perceptions of interests and words for describing such interests.

When potential political coalitions do emerge, they are often orthogonal to traditional Western political patterns. A new political language has to be created in a world of unsettled meaning—a language that serves as a half- or three-quarters-empty vessel, its meaning not fully understood even by its creators. One of the new political parties described its position as "West of center," meaning "more Western European than center," in a political world where most people value "Western Europe" as the opposite of the "communist East" without specifying what they value about Western Europe besides its greater prosperity and distance from communism. The populist demagogue Stanisław Tyminski, whose presidential candidacy eventually frightened the old Solidarity forces into uniting behind Lech Wałęsa in the 1990 election, called his political party the "Party X." The almost empty meaning of the signifier "X" intentionally captures the inchoate character of the emerging political discourse and the potential political coalitions that form and are formed by that discourse.

Our task in this paper is to look for feminism in the interstices of existing language and practices. We predict that the feminisms emerging from such interstices will draw from their own soil and air; they will differ from, while sharing some traits with, American and Western European feminisms; they will arise in unexpected, sometimes unwanted, places; and they will make unexpected contributions to the needs of women in Poland and the rest of the world. The "interstices model" expects forms of feminism to arise in every area of Polish life, including areas now influenced or dominated by the church and the Communist Party as well as areas more recognizable to American feminists, such as battered women's shelters and universities.

In the realm of discourse, the leading role of the Catholic church in Polish political culture distinguishes the problems of Polish feminism from those of other post-communist countries. A politically powerful Catholicism has produced a public discourse that accuses feminism of being both too left and too right, both too close to the remnants of Polish communism (which gave nominal equality to women and granted them rights to abortion) and too much the vanguard of a self-interested capitalism (as in the question of a Catholic Member of Parliament in the abortion debate: "Which Europe do we want to return to? The civilization of death?").[1]

In the organizational realm, the abortion debate has generated some thirty women's organizations—some continuing older structures, but most new and focusing on women's reproductive rights. Like the seventy-two newly registered political parties, these organizations are dramatically fragmented and reluctant to enter alliances or to create a unified front, in part from fear of being associated with the communists.

Much activity that we would call "feminist" does not take place in organizations at all. In Poland, as in the United States and Western Europe, we recognize as a participant in the women's movement every woman who complains to her husband that she should not have to do both her full-time paid job and all the work of the home, including the endless shopping. Every woman is a participant who tries to find a battered women's shelter, even when she fails to find one. Every woman is a participant who in any way makes men and women more equal at her job. In the present situation in Poland, even more than in the United States, we should look for the "women's movement" in the interstices of everyday life, with its unexpected opportunities for what Foucault called *résistance*.

The flux in discourse and the flux in organization interpenetrate one another. Only one of the new women's organizations dares or desires to call itself "feminist"—the Polish Feminist Association—and presently this is an organization of no more than twenty people. As elsewhere in Eastern Europe, the word "feminism" conjures up an array of pejorative associations: one can be accused of being a feminist. A journalist in *Zycie Warszawy* notes that the word "feminism" "causes a smile on the faces of [men]."[2] If "feminism" functions as invective, this is even more true of "homosexuality," which, though legal, is considered a sin, called a "perversion," and silenced. (Asked whether there was in Poland a lesbian movement, or a lesbian strand in the women's movement, all but one of the fifty or so informants we asked in the early stages of our investigations looked at us blankly and said no. One male, university-educated, politically active informant told us seriously, "There are no lesbians in Poland.")

Out of such a fragmented background of discourse and organization, one perhaps temporary coalition has emerged. The threat of a restrictive abortion law led on April 18, 1991, to the creation of the first Women's Parliamentary Circle, drawing its membership from deputies from several political parties, including the former communist party and women from the left groups in Solidarity. Although few journalists attended the Circle's first press conference, the group was instrumental in blocking the passage of the antiabortion law during the May 16, 1991, parliamentary debate. Before the vote, representatives of many women's organizations took part in the demonstrations protesting the law on the streets and in front of Parliament. In the final demonstration on May 15, women chanted, "Fewer churches, more day care!" "This is Poland, not the Vatican!" They waved placards reading, "Law shapes consciousness!" "God save us from the church!" and "God gives a baby, but who will give [pay] for the baby?" One placard read "Onanism is genocide!" (for if, as the church argued, abortion were genocide, masturbation would be too), while one marcher wore a banner reading "Poland *was* enslaved, Polish women *will* be!" [Była niewola Polski, bedzię niewola Polek]. A participant excitedly summed up the event: "Here, the church has just arranged for us a real women's movement!"

The emerging Polish women's movement must be understood against the two major forces of the past in Poland—the church, with its black-robed clerics, and the former Communist Party (the Polish United Workers Party), with its banner of red. These two forces provide the major resources that any social movement needs, but also serve, more forbiddingly, as major sources of oppression. Before the recent transition to democracy, the Community Party provided the ideology as well as the developed practice of all state action; the Catholic church was the only organized force preserving a space for life outside the state's linguistic, cultural, social, and political control. From this confusing compost, in which what a feminist movement needs is sometimes inextricably intertwined with exactly what will kill it, Polish feminism must find a mixture of different soils in which to root.

II. The Red and the Black

1. The Communist Heritage

Under communism, public discourse was always officially "pro-woman," and the state's language and ideology stressed equality between men and women. But Marx's own concept of false consciousness, which led to the Western feminist practice of "consciousness raising," was not thought applicable in an already communist state.

In the realm of organization, day care and other institutions, although inefficient, enabled women to participate in the labor force. With the liberalization in communist doctrine following the thaw of 1956, state policies toward women began to lose their "formal egalitarian" content. As a consequence, Polish women at the end of the communist period had a package of labor laws that placed female employees in a restricted and deeply unequal, though theoretically "privileged," position compared to male workers. The Labor Code,[3] and specifically the 1979 decree,[4] barred women from ninety specific jobs in eighteen branches of industry, including some of the best-paid blue-collar jobs in construction, underground mining, and bus driving. With this decree, the last generation of communists officially outlawed the archetypal Stalinist "happy communist woman on a tractor." The new laws, still in force today, are universally considered "pro-woman" because they are perceived to protect women from physical harm in the workplace. Officials even at the Bureau for Women at the Ministry of Labor and the Ministry for Women, Family, and Youth continue to justify the restrictions on medical grounds, arguing, for example, that driving heavy machinery may cause the uterus to fall.

The reversal in 1956 of the 1932 ban on abortion had a dramatic effect on Polish women's lives, as abortion became the major form of contraception. Only the intelligentsia had easy access to the pill.[5]

Under communist rule, women held few key political offices, a pattern continued in today's democracy. Toward the end of its reign the communist government began to create some women-related offices: in 1982 a Council for Family Matters and a Council for the Elderly and Disabled. In 1986, the government instituted for the first time an office of Government Representative (Pelnomocnik) for Women's Affairs, with the rank of Deputy Secretary of State within the Ministry of Labor, Wages, and Social Affairs. The Representative was to coordinate and oversee the activities of various government ministries to ensure the equal status of women with men in all government, political, economic, social, and cultural spheres and the "bettering of their living conditions."[6] After 1991 the office of the Representative was replaced by an Office of Undersecretary of State for Women and Family within the Council of Ministers (a higher-ranking office), whose portfolio, however, marked a decreased attention to women by including the potentially competing interests of family, children, and youth.[7] The communist Government Representative for Women's Affairs had been charged with, among other things, spreading contraceptive information, developing day-care centers, protecting women at the workplace, and protecting pregnant women. The office of that representative also advocated fathers' participation in childrearing, and sponsored periodic studies of pay structure by gender. No such objectives were stated in the 1991 decree that created the Ministry of Women and Family.

The only communist women's organization, the Women's League, whose head was appointed by the Central Committee, has long been discredited as a façade communist organization with no grassroots support. It had, for example, regularly helped organize International Women's Day in Poland, but since 1968, when women students and faculty of Warsaw University were brutally beaten by the state security forces, this occasion had lost any positive meaning, becoming the epitome of a "façade" holiday. Presently, the Women's League still claims over 150,000 members and offers legal counsel on social, labor, and family law. It also organizes lectures and discussions on such topics as unemployment, and tries to promote retraining in unemployment-prone occupations. Yet its high membership figures do not generate any political weight, for the Party has been almost entirely discredited.

Women had the typical Eastern European experience of high educational levels and, under communism, high employment but lower salaries and authority than men, as well as the "double burden" of responsibility for the home. Barred from certain well-paid blue-collar jobs, women dominated light industries and the poorly paid, feminized professions of medicine and dentistry.[8] It is primarily women who took, and still take time off for infant care and sick children and virtually all women took the permitted sixteen-week maternity leave with 100 percent pay. Many Polish women cannot decide if their employment under communism marked liberation or oppression.

In sum, the Communist Party left a mixed legacy of oppression and potential liberation, both in discourse and in practice. The continuing special relation of the Communist Party to feminism was exemplified in the election of 1990, in which only the Communist presidential candidate, Włodzimierz Cimoszewicz, talked systematically and often with women's groups and had a specific "women's program." Although fewer women than men belonged to the party, a higher proportion of women voters than men supported Cimoszewicz in the election. The candidate, unacceptable to all groups pursuing the (Western) "European" liberatory project, got only about 10 percent of the vote—making him, however, the fourth most favored candidate in the election.

2. The Heritage of Solidarity

In pretransition Poland, as in other communist societies, feminist issues were identified as "leftist," hence communist, hence discredited. Even among women of the intelligentsia active in opposition politics, gender issues were regarded as divisive, likely to undermine group solidarity. In Solidarity, a national movement of opposition with a membership of 10 million and the support of most of the population, the political struggle pitted a unitarily conceived "state" against an equally undifferentiated "society," leaving little space conceptually or organizationally for a specifically feminist consciousness or voice. Since 1989, by which time Solidarity had dwindled to a membership of about 1.5 million and become merely a trade union, women in the union were urged not to introduce issues that could produce even greater divisiveness.

Political action by women could be decisive, although during the communist regime, women workers organized only sporadically within the trade union movement. Strikes by women were often more successful than those of male workers in wringing concessions from the Polish state. In 1970, for example, the textile workers in Łodz, almost all of them women, struck over increases in the price of food. The government representative agreed to meet with the women.

An assembly of militant women, singing patriotic songs, gathered and refused to listen or be placated, crying, "Your children have more to eat than dry bread!" Within a week, food prices had been rolled back, a victory the striking males in other industries had been unable to win.[9]

In the 1980 Gdansk Agreements, Solidarity created a number of special benefits for women, including generous leaves for childbirth and childrearing.[10] These policies met women's real needs but also helped maintain them in traditionally subordinate positions, reinforcing the image of women as secondary wage earners focused on family and home.[11]

Less than 8 percent of delegates to the first Solidarity Congress in 1981 were women, although female workers constituted almost one-half of the union membership. A member of the national executive of the union (ironically a single working mother with a five-year-old child) explained the low percentage of women in the leadership by saying that "for biological and cultural reasons" women bore the primary responsibility for home and family and were therefore reluctant to assume additional political responsibilities.[12]

By not addressing the issue of pay equity, Solidarity in its first stage helped effect a steady decline in the ratio of women's pay to men's. The feminized professions of health (55 percent female) and education (80 percent female) paid 73.59 percent and 82.86 percent of an average monthly wage in 1985, and the ratios remained low in 1990.[13] In 1985, there were three times more women than men registered as unemployed, and three times as many jobs offered to unemployed men as to women.

Solidarity's 1981 program did not call for banning abortion outright, but expressed a hope that with an improving economic situation the economic reasons for terminating pregnancy would be eased. After 1990, it became clear that the economic situation would not improve quickly.[14] Consequently, the Solidarity position on abortion evolved to endorsing, in March 1990, a total ban on abortion, irrespective of economic or even health considerations. This March 1990 decree provoked dissension within Solidarity. The small Women's Section of Solidarity, which had formed in the autumn of 1989, announced a formal "opinion" in June 1990, asserting their strong support for women's right to abortion, and several months later opposed the Polish Senate's new draft bill banishing abortion. The first and only issue of the Women's Section's newspaper, *Kobieta* [Woman], published an open letter to the Polish Episcopate from Barbara Blasinska, an activist and University of Warsaw professor of philosophy, arguing that the Senate's draft bill violated the civil rights of women, discriminated according to gender by placing the entire responsibility for an unwanted pregnancy on the woman, and eroded the church's moral leadership. The newspaper also cited the United Nations position on gender equality in the home, and argued that "Trade unions of the whole world support the position that it is the unequal division of family responsibilities that constitutes the most important barrier keeping women from full participation in employment, trade unions, and political life."[15] The

Solidarity Women's Section also opposed the formation of a cabinet level position for Women and Family, proposing instead a bureau for women's issues alone.

Such views were not welcome in Solidarity, and no second issue of the paper ever appeared. In the spring of 1991 the Women's Section was dissolved. Some of the young women who ran the Section and who had had contact with feminist groups in Western Europe and the United States began thinking of forming a separate women's party, trade union, or modern radical feminist organization. They expressed anger and disappointment in having been silenced in the union because of their feminist stand, objecting that the male Solidarity leadership had not even consulted the female rank and file before endorsing the Senate's draft bill banning abortion.[16]

On April 18, 1991, the Parliamentary Women's Circle was formed, also stemming from the old Solidarity union. Barbara Labuda, a Solidarity activist and now member of Parliament who was instrumental in forming the new group told us with some bitterness, that "democracy is masculine," both in Solidarity, where only men signed the official documents, and now in the Parliament.[17] The main goal of the Parliamentary Women's Circle was to keep any abortion bill from coming to the floor for a vote.

Stefania Szlek-Miller has pointed out that Solidarity did not alter its position much on women's issues during the 1980s. As a male-oriented trade union, Solidarity continued to support family-oriented policies, often closely tied to the Catholic church. The difference is that while in 1981 the women in Solidarity supported the policy of nondivisiveness and even tacitly agreed not to share union leadership on the grounds that their primary responsibility was in the home, by 1991 they had begun to oppose the Solidarity leadership and to think about a women's party. At present, men and women agree on women's special position in the workplace. The women of Solidarity want the maintenance of extended child-related leaves and benefits even more than pay equity, so that abortion is the issue that promises to be most gender-divisive.

3. The Heritage of the Church

Throughout the month of May, every Catholic church in Poland devotes an hour-long evening service entirely to the cult of Mary. The service is well attended and especially favored by women and young people. In August of each year, from almost every Catholic parish in Poland, a pilgrimage sets off on foot to Jasna Góra[18] (Bright Hill) of Czestochowa. From each town as many as 300 to 400 people make this walk (700 kilometers for some) singing songs to the Mother of God as Queen of Poland. Women particularly find comfort in this powerful religious and national symbol within the Polish church.

From a feminist perspective, the Marian tradition in Poland provides meager benefits mingled with heavy costs. The tradition does accord women a special dignity that many feel helps account for the national stereotype of the "strong"

Polish woman. That strength implies independence and self-reliance. But the cult of Mary portrays the center of a woman's life in the home, as a procreator. A woman's vaunted strength is too often the strength of self-sacrifice, as in Janusz Zaorski's famous movie "Mother of Kings," in which a widowed (single) mother handles the struggles of life alone, raising her sons to give their manhood to Poland.[19] Also in the realm of discourse, the Polish Pope has been promoting an international position for the Catholic church which stresses responsibility for others and the dignity of persons over individual gains and profit.

The Catholic church in Poland plays a role different from that in any other formerly communist European country. Ninety-five percent of the Polish population are members of the church. Polish homogeneity, so dramatically different from the other post-communist countries, expresses itself not just in language and to a great degree in ethnicity but also in religion, and in the language and ideals connected with religion.

The Catholic church supported Solidarity, and the present political leadership, with roots in Solidarity, is paying its debts with its present power. The church is also deeply tied to Polish nationalism, defining being a Pole and being a Catholic as indivisible. In 1991, when the church installed Bishop Slawoj Leszek Glodz as a Field Bishop, the chaplain of the Polish Army with the rank of Brigadier-General, he soon issued a statement calling the Polish army the "army of Christ."

The church has succeeded in making Catholic religious instruction an institutionalized part of state education at the elementary and high-school levels; it has had a major impact on the name and personnel of the Ministry responsible for women's affairs;[20] and it has powerfully affected the issue of abortion. Although surveys report that up to 60 percent of the Polish voters oppose the proposed abortion law, the national legislators have found themselves in a position in which the church's ideological, organizational, and political hegemony has created the political necessity for some law restricting abortion.[21] In many parishes, priests distributed cards for their parishioners to sign endorsing the ban on abortion, collected these cards in church, and in some cases threatened the parishioners who did not sign with denial of the sacraments.[22] At the moment, the best tactic for the bill's opponents is to prevent action for as long as possible, since with every month from the end of the communist regime the popularity of the church decreases.[23] Yet Catholic religious discourse still equates abortion with premeditated murder.

In the organizational realm, the church played an important role for women under communism, providing a critical safety net for those who fell through the cracks of a system dependent on employment. The communist state had a limited welfare system. Parts of community life important for women, including the distribution of charity goods and money, centered around churches or parish-based networks of care. When someone died, Catholic nuns often offered the family much-needed clothing, collected from American Poles through the church, and food grown on the church's own farms. The church also acted as a conduit to the West, providing mail and packages forbidden through official channels. However, women's social lives centered on their families and work, not on the church or church circles. Now that the church is no longer the sole link with the West, its community role has diminished. Although the 1990 social assistance legislation, instituting welfare for the first time since 1923, suggested that local social assistance offices to ask the local church to help in setting up services, in practice this form of cooperation has been rare.

Women in Poland, as in most Eastern and Western European countries, have traditionally been more religious than men, a trend strengthened over the last forty years. Many men in the communist party probably did not go to church for fear of losing their positions. With so few women in the party and practically none in its leadership, women could remain closer to the Polish religious heritage and preserve the family church affiliation.

The church in Poland generated many different kinds of organizations for women. For example, in the late 1980s members of the Episcopate Sub-Commission for Women's Matters formed a national organization that assumed the name of an "Association of Ordinary Women." The journalist in *Zycie Warszawy* who reports on Poland's "organized women"[24] placed this organization in direct opposition to the Polish Feminist Association. The Ordinary Women give addresses to women of villages and small towns, stressing the importance of the family and supporting the Senate's draft bill banning abortion.

Like the Communist Party, which did not allow particular interests to organize outside its purview, the church discouraged women from organizing independently. Women's religious groups were an arm of the church, just as communist women's groups were an arm of the party. Both Party and church perceived the world as unitary, with one understanding of the good and one correct interpretation of events. Neither recognized an individual who might have rights, even legitimate interests, that differed from the interests of the whole as defined by the Party or the church. Even Solidarity adopted this unitary collectivist approach, building both its ideology and its organization not on a theory of individual civil rights but on a vision of itself as the representative of all Poland, fighting the imposition of alien rule.

III. The Promise of the West

1. Economic and Educational Inequality

Under the "shock treatment" policies of Polish Finance Minister Leszek Balcerowicz, and even under the less stringent policies of his successors after 1992, unemployment in Poland rose dramatically. The situation of Polish women has worsened more quickly and acutely than that of men. Unemployed women have fewer new jobs offered them than men, and a great many part-time positions, more often filled by women than men, have been canceled on the grounds that such positions are less crucial to the enterprise. With unemployment benefits structured like wage rates, women's lower wages generate smaller unemployment benefits.[25]

Yet most women will still have to work, since at least two salaries are usually necessary for family survival. Under the communist regime, the work ethic was not well-developed, and like men, Polish women often sabotaged economic efficiency for personal or political ends. Polish women are still not strongly committed to the labor force. Full-time homemaking has the romantic allure of an unattainable dream. However, for close to half a century Polish women have been reared to expect full-time work and to value their economic contributions to the household. They will find it difficult to give up nominal equality with men, either in the workplace or in the home.

Women's qualifications for jobs in the "modern" economy, and their educations, are superior to men's, although the labor force is segmented by gender. Women dominate numerically, though not in authority, in the service sector, including in health and education. They hold the bulk of mid-level positions in law, in administration, and in the vast clerical workforce that supports the state, including accountants and personnel advisors in large state firms. Positions like these may come to involve more responsibility, power, and income, as they have in the West. In the new, decentralized, possibly privatized regime there are now great shortages of doctors, dentists, and pharmacists, whose extremely low salaries are likely to increase, as the demand for these services is likely to increase much more quickly than the demand for industrial output from obsolete factories.

Socialist educational policies emphasizing vocational training and technical skills were designed to advance proletarian males. Perversely, these policies, combined with indifference toward traditional educational routes, permitted women to enter and complete elite forms of education in large numbers. The lyceum, which furnishes 80 percent of all university entrants, became feminized. At present, over 70 percent of their enrollments are women. This preparation, far more than socialist ideological commitments to equality, was responsible for the educational achievements of women that produced both early gender equality in universities and high levels of professional training and work among socialist women.[26] The value of women's skills and training will increase in the years ahead.

The logic of socialist societies also supported a way of life that placed a high premium on personal ties, social networks, caring relations, and the capacities to shop, trade, barter, and manage through informal means—the skills the Poles refer to as "załatwiać" (arranging things). Women were responsible for creating and maintaining these patterns of informal exchange, which had become culturally if not economically a way of life.

Capitalism, or the Polish version that emerges, will make these informal networks less important. It will also undoubtedly increase inequality between the rich and the poor, so that inequality among women will increase. Because we can expect that many employers will informally give a preference to men, in the short run Polish women are likely to suffer greater hardship than men. Women will have to fight to keep their positions and the advantages their higher education should bring them in a more capitalist world.

2. Sexual "Freedom"

With Westernization, most post-communist countries are witnessing an increase in sexual experimentation. In Poland, in spite of the Catholic church's trying to strengthen its influence over personal behavior, a modicum of premarital and extramarital sex has been tolerated in all social classes, although the double standard has been strong.

Pornography has been overwhelming the newsstands, with sixty of the new magazines recently published in Poland being explicitly erotic or pornographic,[27] and the Polish version of *Penthouse* becoming a bestseller. These new forms of exploitation build on available strands of misogyny in the traditional Polish culture, exemplified in the long list of sexually debasing insults aimed at women (a woman might be called a "rura" or pipe), while men are insulted only by reference to women, as in "skurwysyn" (son of a bitch).

Public pornography, whether soft- or hardcore, has not become a women's issue in Poland. Private offices, government offices, and grocery stores often sport calendars picturing half-clad or naked women—despite the church's teachings on the sinfulness of the body and the old prohibitions of the "prudish" communists. When we asked a new government official who had been in Solidarity why she put such a calendar on her wall, the official answered, "But these pictures are pretty!" Indeed they are, on glossy paper, sometimes the only colorful spot in a grubby store or office.

Sexual "freedom" is also beginning to assert itself in women's concern with their appearance. Plastic surgeons do a brisk business in nose jobs and breast enlargements, and glossy new magazines feature advertisements for Slim-Fast, the American diet product, now available in Poland.[28] Now that cosmetics are more easily available, Polish women are buying and wearing noticeably more makeup. As one forty-two-year-old woman enrolled in a newly established charm school told an American reporter, "We were told under communism that looks didn't matter, that the bigger goal did, but, of course, that was just a big lie."[29]

Accurate statistics on rape, battering, and incest are unavailable, although one may expect battering to increase dramatically as unemployment soars. A group of women in Krakow proposed the first battered women's shelter in Poland in June 1991; at the time of this writing, space has not been located, and financial support from the state appears dubious.

Women of the Polish intelligentsia have traditionally adopted some of the attitudes of the French intelligentsia toward sex, which include a nonpuritanical approach to the sexual activities of members of their class, so long as those implicitly accept the dominance of men (a weak version of the double standard, allowing men many partners but women only a few). The tolerance is not extended to experimentation with lesbian feelings or the open expression of oneself as a lesbian. There is slightly more tolerance for male homosexuality. In 1991, Kazimierz Kopera, a physician and Deputy Minister of Health, stated in an interview on the much-watched daily television news that what he called the homosexual "problem" was limited to a small group of sexual perverts, and that strict moral conduct would protect anyone sufficiently against AIDS. The next day a deputy Marshal of the Senate, Zofia Kuratowska, herself a physician and professor of medicine, replied on television that Kopera had exhibited both ignorance as a physician and disregard for human rights. The Prime Minister, Jan Krzysztof Bielecki, had the courage to dismiss Kopera from office for making his statement, although several government officials attempted to defend his freedom of speech.[30]

3. Western Culture

On the positive side, the appropriation of American and European culture has included an emphasis on equality, an American media image of women as independent, a tolerance of nonmajority positions, and a concern for "post-material" issues. Among some of the Polish intelligentsia, a distinct and self-conscious class whose members tend to see themselves as the conscience of the nation, a centuries-long intellectual fascination with French culture has produced a serious interest in French feminist writing. If French feminism = avant-garde = attraction to a Francophilic intelligentsia = academic respectability, women trying to set up women's studies programs in universities may find that European high culture opens a chink in an otherwise impenetrable wall of opposition. In mass culture, movies that to some degree assume equality also provide a useful vocabulary for women making new demands. Travel may provide a first wedge into a mentality closed to new behavior. If Green = jeans = hip = feminist = young = Europe, young people may take feminist ideas more seriously.

On the negative side, the popular American culture swamping the cinema programs and music stations also carries an antifeminist message, portraying women as sexual objects and glorifying a crude form of "sexual liberation." "Dynasty" is the top-rated television program, and the movie *Pretty Woman* was a box-office smash. By stressing individual success and a suburban happily-ever-after fairy tale, the American media undermine collective political action and promote a fantasy of pleasurable economic dependence. Western feminism often appears in Poland as rigid and humorless, in the mold of the despised communist dogma, with its prohibitions on certain words and thoughts.

IV. Out of the Flux, Feminism with a Polish Face?

It is too early now to say what forms Polish feminism will evolve, and whether any will have a particularly "Polish face." We can expect the embryonic Polish feminist movement to be torn between a postmodernist recognition of many different kinds of women's and feminist groups and a pull toward the old essentialist emphasis on unity, an emphasis shared not only by the Communist Party but also by Solidarity and the Catholic church.

Feminism will not be imported, but will have to be worked out and fought for by the will of Polish women endangered at work and in their homes by the encroaching male-oriented state and church. Women will continue to organize and surprise men and themselves with swift responses in defense of their established rights. They are also likely to ask for more rights and no doubt for true equality, but they will not do these things in ways American feminists will always like. In some ways, many Polish women are premodern: they pray on their knees, confess their sins to male priests, believe in Satan and hell, let men kiss their hands, and expect doors to be held open while they pass through. All this is part of their cultural legacy. They suffer less from competitive obsessions than do Americans. They expect by right more equality in education and the workplace than do their American or European sisters. It will be hard to consign them to a narrow domestic role, especially when families cannot survive without the present average of 2.6 salaries per household.

It would not be surprising if the most vital and original sources of Polish feminism sprang from women with experience in Solidarity, who have participated in political organizing and often continue to have ties with the Catholic church. While we would also expect organizing among professionals, at the universities, and in forms that do not yet exist—at battered women's shelters and among emerging lesbian organizations—the unique Polish contribution may come indirectly from the two institutions that have dominated the Polish past—the communist party and the Catholic church. From a mixture of these institutions may come an image of a "strong Polish feminist," derived from the "strong Polish woman." From Polish traditions of tenacious opposition to domination against seemingly hopeless odds may come unique strategies of resistance. If Polish feminism can emulate Solidarity in holding together a coalition of very different parts to win important political battles, it will bequeath to feminists everywhere a vital set of understandings to use in our struggle.

Notes

1. In general, however, the term "capitalist" serves as a term of praise, not invective, in present-day Poland.

2. Eliza Olczyk, "Kobiety zorganizowane," *Zycie Warszawy*, April 17, 1991.

3. The Labor Code (Kodeks Pracy) is a book of all labor laws and regulations currently in force. *Kodeks Pracy: Ustawa z dnia June 26, 1974 r. z pozniejszymi poprawkami.*

4. Rozporzadzenie Rady Ministrow z dnia 19 stycznia, 1979 r. w. sprawie prac wzbronionych kobietom (Dr. U. z dn. 27 lutego 1979 r Nr. 4; zm: Dz. U. z 1984 r. Nr. 44 i z 1989 r. Nr. 20).

5. Although some drugstores in major cities continue to sell contraceptives today, they are under attack by the Catholic church. In provincial drugstores, contraceptives are not usually available. For more on abortion see Fuszara (Chap. 23, this volume).

6. Uchwala Rady Ministrow z dnia 1 wrzesnia, 1986 Nr. 134.

7. Uchwala Rady Ministrow z dnia 2 kwietnia, 1991 r. Nr. 53.

8. In early 1991, a pediatrician with fifteen years of practice made 1.3 million zlotys per month, compared to a national average wage of 1.7 million zlotys. (The all-male Warsaw union of bus drivers paralyzed the capital for four days in May 1991, demanding raises from an average wage of two million zlotys per month.)

9. Roman Laba, *The Roots of Solidarity* (Princeton: Princeton University Press, 1991), pp. 86–89.

10. Regarding maternity leave, in 1980 Solidarity made one of its "twenty-one points" a demand for up to three years of paid maternity leave (see Stefania Szlek Miller, "Solidarity Trade Union, Gender Issues and Child Care," *Canadian Slavonic Papers* 30, no. 4 (December 1988): 417–438). Legislation passed since 1981 entitled women, in addition to the prior maternity leave of sixteen weeks on full pay for the first child (eighteen weeks for subsequent children), to receive also a "childrearing leave," with a possibility of a cash allowance based on need, for three years, and up to six if there were two consecutive births (*Dziennik Ustaw* PRL no. 19 [1981]). The Council of Ministers decreed for the first time on July 17, 1981, that the father or another responsible man may receive the childrearing leave if the mother does not use it and supports his application. During this leave, the child carer is protected by law against firing and may be entitled to a cash benefit if the family income qualifies. The period of the leave is also counted toward her or his retirement and job seniority. Since 1989, the cash benefit if the family qualifies is equal to 25 percent of the average monthly wage in Poland for families and 40 percent of this amount for a single parent. A pregnant woman who has tenure in her work contract cannot be fired. If she is employed on a terminal contract and the termination of the employment would take place after her third month of pregnancy, her terminal contract is extended by law up to six months until the birth of the child. Although the law permits men to receive the paid childrearing leave, in practice women are virtually always the ones who use it.

Regarding sick as opposed to newborn children, the first minister of Women and Family, Anna Popowicz (subsequently dismissed from office) recognized that the present law, which allows only women to take extensive leaves to care for sick children, puts women in danger of layoff because it generates high levels of absenteeism among them. There is a tradeoff between preserving employment and allowing absenteeism. The minister wanted to make it possible for men as well as women to take paid leave to care for a sick child. This legal possibility, however, did not guarantee that both genders would use the opportunity equally.

Regarding pensions, the pension and disability law carried over from the communist era differentiates between men and women, women needing only twenty years to be eligible for a pension compared to twenty-five for men, and being eligible for retirement at sixty compared to men's sixty-five. A currently pending and hotly debated new pension law would require a minimum of twenty-five years of work for pension rights for both genders. It is opposed by several women's organizations.

11. Szlek Miller, pp. 417–438.

12. Szlek Miller, quoting "Rozmowa z Elzbieta Potrykus," *Tygodnik Solidarność,* May 29, 1981.

13. See Szlek Miller, after *Statistical Yearbook,* 1985. In 1990, 78 percent of the women employed full-time in the health occupations earned less than the average Polish monthly wage, compared to only 55 percent of the men; in education 60 percent of the women compared to only 38 percent of the men earned less than the average Polish monthly wage. *Maly Rocznik Statystyczny 1991* (Warszawa, GUS: 1991), p. 91. Registered unemployment was only slightly higher for women than for men in 1991, but almost three times as many jobs were available for men than for women p. 151. This trend is likely to continue as Solidarity presses for work structured around a "family wage" for men.

14. Indeed, some of the old regime's new "pro-women" services may have to be cut from the budget subsidies list. Thus, by the fall of 1991, 60 percent of existing day-care centers were threatened with closing down.

15. *Kobieta. Pismo Zwiazkowe,* no. 1 (November 1990), p. 14.

16. Ewa Hauser, interview with Małgorzata Tarasiewicz, former spokesperson of the Solidarity Women's Section, June 27, 1991.

17. Ewa Hauser and Irena Grudzinska-Gross, interview with Barbara Labuda, July 7, 1991.

18. In 1655, during one of the last wars with Sweden, the ill-fated Polish king, Jan Kazimierz, asked the Mother of God for special care for Poland, making her in return Queen of Poland, the black Madonna. In the nineteenth century Henryk Sienkiewicz transformed this event into a national myth in one part of his historical novel trilogy, *Potop* (The Deluge), from which every child in Poland learns the story.

19. The film's director, Janusz Zaorski, was nominated in 1992 to the influential government post of director of Polish radio and television.

20. The Catholic church had suggested that the ministry be entitled Ministry of the Family, but compromised on Ministry of Women and Family. The church further insisted that the first minister be a "believer" (that is, a member of the Polish Catholic church), be married, and have more than one child. The minister chosen according to these criteria, however, seems to have disappointed the church. One of her first acts in office was to attack the provisions in the church-endorsed abortion law that would criminalize abortion in all cases, including fetal deformities and rape. She was dismissed in February 1992.

21. Survey data on Polish voters from Stephen Engelberg, "Abortion Ban Bill is Dividing Poland," *New York Times,* May 16, 1991, p. 14. The disjuncture between religious belief and actual practice on these issues is severe. Survey research using a Polish national sample in 1988 (prior to the antiabortion debate) concluded that although 70 percent of the Polish population considered both using contraceptives and having

an abortion to be sins, almost 70 percent also considered the choice of both contraception and abortion to be "within the right for private choices." Jacek Kurczewski "Grzechy cielesne, a prywatyzacja ciala," *Bog. Szatan Grzech: Socjologia Grzechu,* vol. 1, eds. Jacek Kurczewski and Wojciech Pawlik (Krakow, Uniwersytet Jagiellonski: 1990).

22. Barbara Stanosz, "Dokad zmierzamy?" *Polityka,* May 25, 1991, p. 3.

23. Since 1980, several surveys have asked how much confidence respondents had in a variety of Polish institutions. In 1981–82, 95 percent expressed a "great deal" of confidence in the church; between 1982 and 1989 with some variability, about 85 percent expressed a "great deal" of confidence. In the last two years, however, the percentage expressing a "great deal" of confidence in the church has slipped from 79 percent (November 1990) to 70 percent (April 1991) to 59 percent (June 1991). Tabulations calculated for Barbara Heyns by Albin Kania from Osrodka Badania Opinii Publicznej Polskiego Radia i Telewizju surveys, 1980–1991.

24. Olczyk, April 17, 1991.

25. Unemployment insurance is, of course, wholly new in societies that had claimed to enjoy "full employment." The Polish law on employment of 1989 has been revised four times. Each successive wave has changed the definition of benefits and beneficiaries, specifying different conditions, waiting periods, amounts, and lengths of tenure. The Sejm has debated the merits of entitlements compared to social safety nets at length. At present, Polish law favors entitlements rather than means-tested programs or state-imposed scrutiny of needy families, in sharp contrast to Hungarian and Czechoslovakian policies.

26. Barbara Heyns and Ireneusz Białecki, "Educational Inequality in Poland," in *Persistent Inequality: Changing Educational Stratification in Thirteen Countries,* eds. Yossi Shavit and Hans-Peter Blossfeld (Boulder, Co.: Westview Press, 1992).

27. Bartyzel, p. 9.

28. Gabrielle Glaser, "In Poland, Studying the Fine Art of Chic," *New York Times,* September 11, 1991, p. C9. Polish women also have a long tradition of care for their appearance. Almost every young girl who can afford it learns to put on skin cream and to go for regular herbal skin treatments to a licensed cosmetologist with professional training in dermatology. Polish women who visit or emigrate to the United States complain that the American approach to beauty covers up rather than cleansing the skin.

29. Ibid.

30. Ewa Nowakowska, "Dymisja Wiceministra," *Polityka,* May 20, 1991. A satirical weekly, *Nie,* published what may be the first interview with four gay men and three lesbians who allowed their names and photographs to appear in the press. One of them, Jerzy Maslowski, stated, "We have no political party of our own. There had been various homosexual organizations that disappeared as soon as they were formed. . . . Homosexuals can be found everywhere, in the cultural circles, in the world of business; some of them are very well-known, outstanding personalities. But none wish to be a leader of such an organization in fear of being compromised, subject to ridicule. We can't blame them either, because we are outcasts. Catholic Poland

does not accept us. In this situation, it is difficult to admit to being homosexuals, much less go out on the streets." Another, Anna Lach, doubted the feasibility or usefulness in Poland of actions like the gay pride celebration she had attended in Paris: "Why should we create a separate political program for people who differ from others only in one aspect [as opposed to national or religious minorities]? . . . What kind of a program could it be? To build homes for homosexuals?" "Zwykle szare geje" (Ordinary average gays), *Nie,* January 9, 1992.

26

Soviet Women at the Crossroads of Perestroika

Larissa Lissyutkina

Mutual understanding between Russian and Western women ends where discussion of the women's movement begins. To put it somewhat bluntly, Soviet women are convinced that Western women have no problems and therefore they participate in the women's movement, while Western women are bewildered that Soviet women have so many problems, but no movement.

Soviet women generally note the relative lack of material problems for Western women. This is the focus of contradictions between women's consciousness in the former Soviet Union and in the West. These differences in goals, values, and priorities include the following:

First: Emancipation for Soviet women is not based upon a demand to work. On the contrary, liberation is perceived by many as the right not to work.

Second: Soviet women's ardent desire for consumer goods conflicts with progressive women's criticism of Western consumerism. For Soviet women, the ability to freely select and consume without restrictive provisions has an indisputable value.

Third: Soviet women cannot share the hostility of their Western sisters to the ritualized relationship between men and women. Such gestures as men's kissing a woman's hand, and other ways of emphasizing a woman's weakness, represent a return to feudal chivalrous culture, that is enthusiastically received by Soviet women.

Fourth: Feminism provokes a negative reaction among the majority of Soviet women. As a rule, they do not want to indenture themselves to feminism.

Fifth: The women's movement in the former Soviet Union does not have to fight for free abortion, a common goal in the West. It is, perhaps, the single way in which "socialism" outdid Western democratic societies.

Sixth: There is no unanimity about the problem of quotas in elected political offices. During the communist regime there were quotas in every political body. The first free elections brought a sharp reduction in the number of women deputies in the general union and Russian parliaments. Not one of the female deputies in the new legislature demanded a quota for women.

It is possible to continue the enumeration of points of difference. For example, interviews revealed that Soviet women prefer men to represent their interests in parliament. Writers refer to these well-known facts differently: as backwardness, lack of development of women's consciousness, traditionalism, women's behavior in a totalitarian system, etc.

One cannot explain all this simply by saying that the country survived a crisis—a part of which is the crisis of women's consciousness and identity. The following questions arise: Why did the crisis manifest itself as such, and not otherwise? What characteristics of the crisis are reflected in women's consciousness, and how does this consciousness influence the crisis? What comes from the Russian cultural tradition and what from communist ideology? What is the function and image of woman in the establishment, in the opposition, and in the counterculture?

I.

The societal revolution known as "perestroika" is accompanied by a return to the traditional values of a significant part of the female population. This is part of the wider process of the rebirth of patriotic conservatism: a national self-consciousness, the return to religious beliefs, precommunist idealism and heroism—in essence, the feudal past of the country. The image of women, fully developed within the ideological framework, is a distinctive combination of the traditional and the revolutionary.

Shortly after the disintegration of totalitarian ideology, the open collapse of the image of the working woman as the ideal Soviet woman occurred. Without skipping a beat, the image of the woman worker was overthrown by the ideal of the woman as prostitute or beauty queen (Miss Russia).

Before our eyes, the granddaughters of the commissars, who in the 1980s were Pioneers straining in the kitchen and in the home, willingly posed in bikinis before television cameras. A poll of high-school seniors in Moscow revealed that prostitution was regarded as the most prestigious profession.[1]

What kind of reaction would one expect from people living under forced labor, a hypocritical sexual morality, and impoverishment, and in isolation from the West? The seductive, forbidden fruit turned into an object of blind imitation.

Full employment of the female population in the former Soviet Union never meant the realization of the right to work. It was a compulsory duty that gave the government the ability to use the entire population as cheap labor for the realization of the senseless utopian project of rebuilding society and conquering and exploiting nature. No one has believed in this project for a long time. Labor for the Soviet people has almost completely lost its intellectual challenge and attractiveness, especially for women. In spite of formal equality, women faced discrimination at work that is still intact. They underwent a double exploitation and did not have the right to protest openly against it.

The law making labor compulsory was widely used by the people in power in their fight against the dissident movement, as well as against women who attempted to protest or who expressed dissatisfaction. They were fired, then accused of parasitism, and at any time could be exiled from the city, and deprived of their parental rights. Alternatively, charges of speculation or theft could be fabricated against them. In the period of stagnation there was not only an open reaction against the regime in the form of protest but an escape into private life. This was not possible in the countryside, where people lived into old age in barracks, communal apartments, dormitories, and trailers. The goal of evading control by the "public" was taken as seditious throughout Soviet history.

The house, and especially the kitchen, in the 1960s, 1970s, and 1980s was the only free sphere. In Russia, to aspire to the kitchen does not have the same connotation as in the West. The Russian kitchen was a front of massive resistance to the totalitarian regime and is perceived with sentimental nostalgia today. Here, for the first time in post-revolutionary history, an alternative lifestyle for many Soviet people was formed. Women, who after the beginning of perestroika demanded the right to return to the kitchen, to the family, and to the home, were not only tired from the lack of home life and the senseless expenditure of energy in the workplace, but also feared handing over the rearing of their children to the community organizations and teachers. Most importantly, they by no means perceive their kitchen, which is rarely larger than five square meters, as a narrow corridor cut off from the world. Here, heated arguments about culture and politics take place. From here people go directly to huge meetings in the square with banners and placards. In the kitchen one is surrounded by intimacy, publicity, and intellectual creativity. According to state rules, apartments should have rooms of five square meters per person, but Soviet apartments are always two times smaller than they should be, given the number of family members. In the kitchen life gushes forth. Quite a few more women wish to return to the kitchen in order to be relieved of doing road work, boring office jobs, construction jobs, or factory work.

The shortage of goods and services turned everyday life into torture. Russian women are still unable to distinguish the critical attitude to consumption prevalent in wealthy countries. They want to dress well, use makeup, and travel in cars. To convince them that the profusion of goods in the West represents only a repression of freedom is hardly possible. The asceticism of communist ideology was hypocritically thrust upon Soviet society by its representatives, who usurped privileges and goods for themselves. Those from wealthy countries who advocate the necessity of reasonable, limited consumerism and simple lifestyles appear, in the eyes of the people, similar to the nomenklatura who demanded modesty in consumption from the people while themselves living by Western consumer standards.

Every experience of life during the Soviet regime made the idea of emancipation unacceptable to women. In early communist ideology, soon after the revolution, a woman was accepted as "a comrade of special qualities" (Andrei Platonov). Communist as well as National Socialist ideology oriented women to sports, war games, and party meetings with great enthusiasm. Women comrades differed little from men: short haircuts, pants, cigarettes, a style of behavior that turned them into "their own boys." There were sexless figures in boots as road workers, construction workers, vegetable farmers, etc. The ideal of the woman comrade became famous in literature and in socialist-realist film.

Deritualization of sexual behavior, destruction of its semantics (courtship and wedding norms, norms of intimacy and monogamy) occurred in Russia and persists today. In reaction, women and men are opposed to traditional Soviet stereotypes. A depoliticized cultural opposition oriented to women's roles in the home, the feminine aesthetic, and the symbolism of chivalry, rather than a political women's movement, expresses the opposition to a totalitarian system built on force and the denial of individual differences, including the differences between men and women.

In discussions with Western feminists, it becomes clear that the aims of women in the former Soviet Union challenge not only the past but also the Western women's movement. What are labeled as sexist stereotypes in the West are accepted by Russian women as a return to individuality and to the forcibly wrested feminine "I."

When Soviet women make it known that they like the protection of men, that it pleases them when men kiss their hands, take off their coats, or help them from a car, Western women shriek and whoop with indignation. Of course, women of the former Soviet Union have no illusions concerning the absurdity and hypocrisy of such rituals. Nevertheless, they want them. It is possible to call this a regressive and false consciousness, but there is another reason. It is an expression of a fundamental historical absence, arising from the fact that Russia is a country without a chivalrous culture. Russian women were integrated into social life by means of homemaking—an orthodox charade that now reinforces an exaggerated Russian nationalism. In this context, the attraction of modern women of the former Soviet Union to alien rituals of the Western medieval tradition signifies opposition to Russian conservatism, which rejects chivalrous rituals as decadent, poisonous erotica.

Denial of the remains of feudal chivalry by Western feminists can be regarded as a natural overcoming (Aufhebung) of historical tradition by modern societies, permitting the integration of women into society and ritualizing relationships between men and women until legal regulation steps in. But how can Russian women want this if there is no such thing to "overcome" in their historical consciousness? In addition, in times of disintegration of all norms and values, nostalgia for any form of cultural integration is intensified.

In a country where immature feudalism was followed by immature capitalism and finally by a totalitarian regime founded upon utopian ideals, real social psychology and national consciousness reflects neither the past, not the present, nor the future. This consciousness is transformed by a denial of the past, dissatisfaction with the present, despair concerning the future, and an almost religious rapture united with superstitious fear inherent in a political power verging on nationalism and isolationism. The paradox lies in the fact that while seeking to feminize their social roles, behavior, and appearance, Soviet women justly reject feminism—an attitude they associate with hostile relations with men, coincident with defeminization. In rejecting feminism, the women of the former Soviet Union reject unfeminine behavior and dress, as well as the ever-present conflicts between men and women.

Unfortunately, in Soviet society there are few studies about the real character of this conflict and its reflection in the consciousness of both men and women. Except for the published divorce statistics, the colonization of the lifeworld, the discrimination of women in the workplace and in the home, the primitive sexual upbringing of children and the outward display of disharmony in relationships between men and women are not well documented. Nor is it studied how both sides survive, accept, and interpret this conflict.

If it is possible to call emancipation and independence a condition during which women really cannot count on men to rear the children and provide material well-being, then Soviet women, more than women in any other country, are emancipated against their will. It is natural that women as well as men suffered from the social catastrophe which lingered seventy-five years and became a daily occurrence. But the conscious striving for equality with men hardly appears attractive or reasonable to women. What would be better: possessing equal rights with those who humble us or being free to do nothing? Within the dissident movement, only a small group of women in Leningrad in the 1970s advocated women's emancipation. After they were exiled, dissidents made no efforts to fight for the rights of women. The paramount task was general political and individual emancipation.

Attempts by women to organize themselves became acceptable only a few years after the beginning of perestroika. Since this revival of women's self-consciousness, women's cooperatives and economic associations, women's magazines, single women's groups, and women's studies specialists have come into existence. In practice, the women's movement in Russia lags behind the democratic movement and the emancipation movement of sexual minorities who have formed a party and advertise in the mass media.[2] Numerous publications critical of the situation of women in the Soviet Union appeared in the course of glasnost, but these have thus far had little success.

One of the most significant examples of "negative emancipation" is the problem of abortion. Soviet women cannot even remotely understand the problematics and arguments of Western abortion politics. During Stalin's era, abortion was prohibited, reflecting the State's nonrecognition of women as individuals. Control of reproductive functions was motivated by state interests, analogous to Hitler's Germany. But the ban was lifted in the 1950s, coinciding with the broader political change from the totalitarian Stalinist system to the Khrushchev-type authoritarianism.

Complete prohibition has been replaced however, by complete indifference: doctors generally ceased to intervene in the decision process. No consultation or social work with pregnant women is undertaken. Abortions are conducted without anesthesia under unsanitary conditions. In order to receive anesthesia, women must bribe the doctor. Often clinics that perform abortions devise hurdles for those who want them. The central television station reported that in Yaroslav this operation is, by law, performed only if the husband or a parent or friend of the woman agrees to act as a blood donor. Therefore in the mornings lines of pregnant women form at the Yaroslav clinic along with the men who initiated the pregnancy, or simply supporters. In a country where any surgical laxness is fraught with the risk of AIDS infection this is no small sacrifice. It is simpler to get an abortion at one of the hospitals in Siberia. There women are instructed to arrive at the clinic at about five o'clock in the morning, at which time they are given slop pails and rags. There are no cleaning people in hospitals; the pregnant women must clean the entire building before the operations begin. Many of them suffer from severe morning sickness. The process is dragged out endlessly: one cleans where another has been sick, then gets sick herself, and so on.

Another limitation on abortion is the system of internal passports. A woman who is not registered in a given city or village does not have the right to have this operation. In order to get around this absurd limitation, a woman must deceive the state: she uses a friend's passport, gives a bribe to the doctor, or obtains an abortion secretly. On my medical card in the regional clinic, sixteen abortions are registered; not one of them was mine. I am registered at the departmental and regional clinics. I gave my regional medical card to some friends who live with their graduate-student husbands in Moscow but are not registered there, and therefore do not have access to medical assistance.

Russian women thus have more than enough problems with abortion, in spite of its being free. They do not have to fight for free abortion but for its humanization.

When Soviet women hear that in the West it is argued that abortion should be prohibited as an infringement of the life of the fetus, they either do not understand the discussion or they laugh. Only a few believers can understand the Christian motives for prohibiting abortions. In a country where the living person is turned into, as Stalin said, "concentration camp dust," the protection of unborn life is absolutely unfathomable. The commentary I heard concerning this was the same as that concerning the women's movement: "They can afford it because they live too well."

Soviet women also do not support the concept of quotas in the democratic elections. Many see quotas as the continuation of the communist regime's prac-tices and privileges. Appearing in front of the Congress of People's Deputies (this body was dissolved with the fall of the Union), Galina Starovojtova, one of the shining stars on the political horizon of the past years. harshly criticized the principle of quotas, articulating her famous phrase, "a woman's sex should not become her ceiling."[3]

There is now no discourse about quotas for women. None of the political leaders during perestroika formed a program for women. Anatoly Sobchak, the mayor of St. Petersburg, in a radio interview (the German Wave) on November 20, 1991, said that his fundamental electorate was women. Yet Sobchak does not have a special program for the improvement of the situation of women, who make up 53 percent of the population.

II.

As Ernst Bloch wrote, in "The blindness of the moment" we can know much more about ourselves in the past than in the present. One needs to understand some of the cultural and historical traditions that intersect in the lives and identities of the modern Russian woman.

Enlightened Russian women already took active social stands at the beginning of last century. They became Decembrists, nihilists, populists, socialists, and terrorists. Now, at the end of the present century, they want, for the most part, material prosperity, and their social ideals are apparently embodied in the lifestyle of a middle-class woman from the West. According to sociological surveys, Soviet girls are ready to become prostitutes, but do not want to be feminists. They like to stay in the kitchen or take part in beauty pageants, but do not want to go to work each day. All of this arouses sincere horror among Western feminists.

Those who carried out the Soviet putsch on August 19, 1991, immediately declared a struggle against pornography in its programmatic political statement. Except for that tormented demand and a ban on the publication of newspapers and on television broadcasts, they made no other clear declarations.

Clearly the problem of prostitution, pornography, and the commercialization of the female body has a great symbolic significance for Russia, out of line with the gravity of the problem in this period of transition. What are the cultural semantics of this phenomenon, placed in both historical and contemporary perspective? Where does the border between conservatism and modernity lie in the aims of women with respect to society and of society with respect to women?

The Soviet people have found themselves at the epicenter of a social cataclysm known as "perestroika." They are attempting to restore their crumbled world view and identity with the help of a minimum of three cultural value systems, all refracted through the prism of current experience. The first system is the remains of the communist ideology: as disillusion, chaos, and famine grow, these remains became the object of nostalgic idealization. Second, there is an appeal to the traditional conceptions and values of prerevolutionary Russia, as an attempt to tie together the broken thread and connect to the past over a period of seventy-five years. And third, there are Western values based on the ideas of democracy, individualism, private enterprise, and private property.

All three value systems are compromised in one way or another by their previous history, and each has its critics. All three stand in conflict with one another, and none is capable of becoming the dominant orientation. Under the banner of the ideal of social justice, even in the last century, Russian women rejected traditionalism and actively involved themselves in the life of the community. But social justice does not constitute a generally significant value uniting Russian society today, when the only prevailing aspiration is to survive.

In Russian society there are no "new utopias" now—no image of the enemy, no common goals, and no social ideals of the kind that the revolution and victory in the war represented for the preceding generations. All three value systems are to varying degrees archaic. All three are devoid of romantic charm and of the ideal of sacrifice. They are not even ideals, but mechanisms for the mobilization of various social groups and strata and their pragmatic interests. In the former Soviet society motives of this kind were by definition considered immoral. In its transition from totalitarianism to freedom, the former Soviet society has found itself in a state of anomie. There are no generally significant ideals, norms, or values. Communist propaganda made demagogic use of altruistic ideals—the same ones under whose banner the revolutionary/emancipatory movement first unfolded in Russia. This is one of the reasons for the crisis of ideals and the vacuum of spiritual values in this period of transition.

The present choice of values is subjective and arbitrary. It does not always correspond to the real interests of social groups. Motives such as the settling of accounts with those beliefs that had been forcibly imposed on society, and subjective notions about what is "progressive" in the modern world, have turned out to be crucial. Since Russia was practically cut off from the twentieth century by the "iron curtain," the notions of her citizenry about what was to be found at the cutting edge of social development can be completely fantastical. Western capitalism and domestic feudalism are beyond the limits of their life experience. The emancipation of Western feminism is partly (and maybe wholly) associated with communist rhetoric and is unacceptable among those social groups that take an active stand against totalitarianism and for the modernization of the country in accordance with the Western model.

Commercialization of the female body is perceived as an element of the transition to market relations in which the society sees its salvation. The crusade against prostitution is led for the most part by the same political forces that stand for the return of the country to its precommunist state and by those who nostalgically praise the "ascetic habits" of the communists.

However, hostility toward sensuality, the erotic, and women is not just the heritage of the communist regime. Its roots go much deeper, into the fundamental religious values of Russian culture. In orthodoxy the cult of Mary, the Mother of

God, the savior and defender, is widely prevalent. But the aesthetization and eroticization of the cult of the Virgin Mary that characterized the chivalric knightly culture of the Western Middle Ages was largely absent. The Russian Mother of God is neither a virgin nor a fair lady. She never borders on the erotic. She is most akin to the tragic figures of Western painting who stand at the foot of the cross upon which the Son of God is crucified.

The word "Russia" in the Russian language is feminine. It is usual to call the homeland "mother." For the idealized image of the eternal feminine in Russian culture at the turn of the century a different image was used—Sophia. In the concept of "Sophia-ness," femininity is expressed more abstractly than in the visual, sensual cult of the Virgin Mary developed in Western chivalric poetry and aesthetics. The tragic nature of Russia's historical fate, her people's lack of freedom, her men's lack of freedom—all have imposed upon women the symbolic mission of salvation. The Decembrist women—the wives of the rebellious aristocrats exiled to Siberia for trying in 1825 to overthrow the autocracy—became archetypes of the selflessly devoted woman. They followed their husbands to Siberia, sacrificing wealth and high social positions. There they lived out their remaining lives. The tsar's court declared that the children born in Siberia were considered serfs.

The great exploits of the Decembrist wives created the moral scale applied to women. In precommunist Russia as well, Russian culture was opposed to the pleasure principle. Russian classical literature, being in its essence a "parallel religion," raised the sacrificed and self-sacrificing woman to such a high pedestal that it became impossible to conceive of approaching her. In spite of the wild outburst of pornography on the book market in the last two or three years, the Western sexual revolution, with its ideas of the unfettering of the flesh, has remained deeply alien to Russian culture and Russian women. Neither open readiness to engage in prostitution nor beauty pageants nor the abundance of literature on themes of sexuality have changed anything in actuality.

The image of the woman-savior continued in the Russian Revolutionary movement, characterized by the active participation of educated women. But it underwent a substantive change: while the Decembrist wives were noted for their moral principles and their sacrifice, the women acting in the name of the "People's Will" were noted for their acts of violence as a means of achieving the utopian ideal of justice—regicide, terrorism, death on the scaffold, and torture in prison. The Decembrist model reappears in the dissident movement with its central ideas of nonviolence and human rights; from the second tradition it stretches to the Revolution of 1917 and the totalitarian regime, arising from the idea of revolutionary violence.

It is perhaps only in the poetry of Pushkin that Russian classical literature of the nineteenth century was not hostile to woman as the bearer of the erotic principle. For Russian writers the beautiful heroines were almost always morally or spiritually deficient (Nastasia Filipovna in Dostoevsky's *The Idiot,* Helene Bezukhova in Tolstoy's *War and Peace*).

In the image of the prostitute, Russian culture found a convenient opportunity to combine both deifying and disparaging attitudes toward women. In the works of Dostoyevsky and Tolstoy the prostitute-savior is poeticized and presented as the female equivalent of Christ.

The communist revolutionary ethic, to an even greater degree than the traditional one, opposed the "pleasure principle." It required sacrifices from women in the name of the collective ideal of the "general good." She had to serve the party right up to the renunciation of her own female self. Totalitarian ideology strove in principle to liquidate private life. In the fall of 1989 the Rigan journal *Rodnik* [The Source] published an article by a little-known author, Zalkind, called "The Twelve Sexual Commandments of the Revolutionary," which first appeared in the Soviet press in 1922. In the "Commandments" the principles of class regulations regarding love, marriage, and women are formulated. Full subordination of a person's private life to class interests, the control of society over marriage and procreation, and the "minimization" of sexual activity as useless for the historical mission of the proletariat were all demanded.

If one judges by the book market, cinema, and television, one might get the impression that this statement has been completely refuted. People in Russia have no food, no normal living conditions, no social stability. The family is in crisis; political parties cannot constitute themselves; and there is no women's movement. But maybe now there is at least sex.

The abundance in print and on the screen of sex (or "polovukhi" as contemporary uninhibited young people say) represents a sad symptom of the fact that in real life people have neither the time nor energy for pleasure. There is direct evidence of a deep crisis in sexual relations, in the understanding of one's own social role, as well as of misunderstandings in the realm of mutual expectations and demands between men and women.

In today's society it is difficult for a woman to meet a man whose identity has not been destroyed. Instead of equality between men and women, there has been a lowering of both sexes to poverty and the deprivation of political rights. While economically oppressed and spiritually crushed, Soviet men are forced to conform to the traditional roles of the head of the family and master of his wife. In the face of this challenge from women and society the capitulation of men took many forms: rejection of marriage and family, the role of the "buffoon," and homosexuality. If Russian women of the postwar generation were doomed to be single because the war has physically destroyed men, then contemporary young women are doomed to an even more burdensome solitude without any halo of tragedy. There are men, but they are ghostly and fictitious. They are, as a rule, not real people or comrades in misfortune, capable of sharing with women the burdens of everyday life, poverty, and endless uncertainty. Men in Russia today need salvation as never before, for they cannot deal with life, freedom, or their relationships with women.

But Russian women, despite all their sympathy with traditionalism, do not aspire to "bear their cross" and save their husbands and lovers. Along with the attempts at modernization and westernization of the country, the pleasure principle has begun to "break through the shell" of a society of which it is not characteristic. In the conservative camp this has caused a shock. The village writers, the guardians of traditional feminine virtuousness, almost beside themselves, anathematize beauty pageants, rock culture, jeans, pornography, personal ads, and prostitution. They perceive their gravediggers to be modern Western society in the image of the foreign-currency prostitute, the universal whore.

Public furor surrounding Russian sex is even more confused by the circumstance that at the beginning the erotic boom had, in addition to its glaring lack of taste, an entirely concrete and positive meaning. This was the emancipation from the desexualization of life under communism, the recognition of one's bodily self as an inseparable part of one's identity. Whether we like it or not, this was the beginning of the overcoming of the totalitarian identity. From there visible threads extended to forced registration, to the norm of five square meters for a living space, to public health, to education, to legislation, and to all the other fetters on the body in a sick society.

The persistent public show of foreign-currency prostitutes in the mass media clearly contains a challenge to the totalitarian communist code of morals. In numerous television programs, Moscow prostitutes have behaved with an apparent shade of "dissidence." If Western prostitutes belong to "the underworld," then Moscow prostitutes form instead a "counterculture"—so much has their professional activity been ideologized.

The prostitute, the lone entrepreneur breaking taboos, is the pioneer of the market economy, from which is supposed to come universal salvation. This salvation is personified by the male foreigner—the new totem—who fills the vacuum, replacing the cast-out idols of the communist pantheon. The age of the transition to a free market in post-communist Russia may be graphically symbolized by the grotesque marriage of the hard-currency "intourist girl" to the foreign businessmen.

And how do Russian women value Russian men? This probably sounds harsh, but the exchange value of Russian men on the internal market does not exceed the exchange rate of the ruble against the dollar. Social conflict between men and women in Russia is spreading. In progressive Russian literature oriented to an ideal of modernization and Westernization of the country, another cliché is persistently projected onto women—that of the female traitor.

At least three significant Russian writers—A. Solzhenitsyn, V. Aksenov, and A. Sinyavsky—have written basically the same thing. Solzhenitsyn wrote about the betrayal by the Motherland, which in popular consciousness is connected to the image of the mother. Sinyavsky, in his essay "Strolls with Pushkin,"[4] used the expression "Russia-Bitch," which provoked a literary scandal. And Aksenov, in his novel *The Island of the Crimea*[5] created the image of the contemporary Russian woman who betrays her lover, agrees to become a KGB agent, and informs on him. In addition, she has the first name Tatyana, like the heroine of Pushkin's novel *Eugene Onegin*—the model of fidelity to one's duty and husband—and the last name Lunina—the name of one of the Decembrists exiled to Siberia. Significantly, Aksenov's heroine betrays both her husband and her lover for the chance to live in the West, but in the end she herself dies. A young American woman becomes the guardian angel of the Russian hero, betrayed by Tatyana Lunina, and his family line continues outside of Russia. His grandson is also born to a foreign woman, selflessly devoted to his son. The tendency to debunk the image of Russian women can also be found in many national works of lesser stature.

Thus, one can state that male writers reproach contemporary Soviet women for having allegedly betrayed their own ideal self, for having thrown themselves off the pedestal. In present-day Russia women no longer embody the spiritual and moral ideal. They have been demoted from "Mother Russia" to "Miss Russia."

If Russian women had something to lose in their communist past, they would undoubtedly have found a way to fight for it. The absence of any fight means no special values were left. This includes men: warrior—bureaucrat—workhorse—dissident—convict—alcoholic. Men in all these incarnations have been found unsuitable for the home, family, and normal cohabitance with women. In the aftermath of the great experiment in the creation of "the new man," the male factory worker and the female collective farmer have come down from the movie screen and from the pedestal, bashed each other over the head with the hammer and sickle, and ended in divorce. The worker whiles away his days in alcoholism, the collective farmer her nights near the "Intourist" hotel, and both are sure that they have ruined each other's life.

Who in this case has betrayed whom becomes a purely academic question. Russian men have quick-temperedly charged their women with reproaches which themselves appear to be a result of the stress of the transitional period—the sharp change in social roles, the breakdown of stereotypes, the lack of correspondence to the ideal sexual type. Men are confused and dismayed and need the woman-savior and defender more than ever. But women categorically refuse to remain on their elevated pedestal. They expect from men a normal everyday life, material well-being, and even, to the indescribable horror of the patriotic nationalists, good sex. As the Russian philosopher Boris Groys, living now in Cologne, states, "For the Russian thinker, a woman stands only as a deceptive symbol of Russia. She arouses and at the same time diverts his erotic energy. The Russian intellectual as a "Russian European" is essentially androgynous. His very Russianness is his anima, his femininity."[6]

A paradoxical situation has been created: on the one hand, Russian women are breaking radically from the past, and men condemn this as a "betrayal." On the other hand, women openly declare adherence to traditional feminine roles, from housekeeping to prostitution. At the one extreme, an active role in the creation of commercial and creative associations; at the other, indifference to politics. Feminism has found no place in contemporary Russian women's consciousness. Will the developments in Russia proceed along the path of rapprochement with Western feminism?

Hardly. Western feminism itself has dried up. It is too politicized. And the crisis of Russian women's consciousness is unfolding mainly in the cultural sphere. It is relatively autonomous and only partly influenced by political strategies. Many of the ideas and demands of Western feminism have turned into dogma and have no relation to reality. It does not react to new phenomena. It's possible that the paths of Western and Russian women will come closer at some point in the future, to which both sides will arrive changed.

But now I can say only one thing: Among my contemporaries, I have not met a single one who would have willingly chosen her involuntary fate: to be a Russian woman in the age of perestroika. Perhaps there are such women somewhere, but I personally have not met them.

Part I translated from the Russian by Kimberly Boltz. Thanks to Adele Nikolsky for revisions.
Part II translated from the Russian by Maude Meisel and Nicole Svobodny.

Notes

1. In Western newspapers and magazines, many people refer to this study. However, the source cannot be located at this time.

2. Sexual minorities include, for example, homosexuals, lesbians, transsexuals, etc. The name of their political party is the Libertarian Party.

3. In Russian, "sex" and "floor" are homonyms. Thus, the floor should not be as high as a woman can rise.

4. Andrei Sinyaysky, "Strolls with Pushkin," *Voprosy Literatyry*, July, August, September, 1990.

5. Vasily Aksyonov, *Ostrov Krym* (Ann Arbor: Ardis, 1981).

6. Boris Groys, "Rossija kak podsoznanie Zapada," *Rodnik*, 1990, p. 52.

27

Finding a Voice: The Emergence of a Women's Movement

Elizabeth Waters

At the end of 1979, an unofficial almanac, *Woman and Russia,* began circulating in Leningrad. The journal was the work of a group of women who were part of the dissident movement but shared a dissatisfaction with what they saw as its failure to acknowledge problems specific to their sex. The members of the group differed in their views on how exactly women were disadvantaged and what precisely should be done about it, and soon went their separate ways. The editor of the almanac, Tatyana Mamonova, subscribed to an analysis of women's position close to that of Western feminists and demanded equality and an end to stereotypes; most other members of the group affirmed their allegiance to Russian Orthodoxy and the central importance of the mothering experience for women. Tatyana Mamonova turned to the West for solutions to the wrongs of women (her editorial in the almanac assumed that in Europe, where women had already won prominent political positions, the "woman question" was largely solved); the majority believed salvation lay rather in the resurgence of Russian orthodox spirituality.[1] Debate in Russia between those looking outward and those looking inward has a history stretching back to the mid-nineteenth century, when Westerners and Slavophils first faced each other in the political arena. Debate about the biological or social origins of sexual identity and roles has an even longer history.

In the USSR in the 1970s, independent political debate of any kind, feminist included, was ruled by the authorities to constitute anti-Soviet activity. Contributors to the almanac were harassed by the KGB and threatened with imprisonment. In the run up to the Olympic games the following year, when the government clamped down heavily on the dissident movement, several were deported.

It was not that the "woman question" was ignored by the Soviet regime. Indeed, during the 1970s, questions of personal life and marriage were given unprecedented coverage in the media. But the government exercised its right to supervise all social analysis, to control all organizational activity. Concern at the inequalities women still suffered, expressed within prescribed limits and tendered in a spirit of loyalty, might be permitted in the pages of the mass-circulation woman's magazine *Rabotnitsa,* but were not to be tolerated in unofficial publications; likewise women were allowed no independent organizations, only the officially sponsored Committee of Soviet Women (CSW). This organization had evolved from an antifascist committee formed in 1941, which in turn had replaced the officially sponsored women's movement active in the 1920s but closed down in 1930 on the grounds that female emancipation was complete. It served an important propaganda purpose, particularly in the years after the emergence of "second-wave feminism": chaired by the first woman astronaut, Valentina Tereshkova, its representatives attended UN and other foreign functions to demonstrate the superior rights enjoyed by women in the USSR.

The election of Mikhail Gorbachev to the position of General Secretary of the CPSU in April 1985 and the climate of glasnost generated by the reforms made it possible to call into question the accuracy of the propaganda portrait of the Soviet way of life. Social problems, such as drug abuse and prostitution, and inequalities became subjects for media comment. Political movements, independent and militant, began to take shape for the first time since the twenties. Yet the public ferment, while extraordinary in its scope, did not encompass a challenge to the gender order. Women featured in public debate as the root of social ills, but not as victims of inequality and subordination. Despite the claims of Soviet ideology to have emancipated the female sex and solved the "woman question," patriarchy was firmly entrenched. Women, burdened by paid and unpaid labor, were not in a position to take advantage of the new opportunities for political and economic initiatives opened up by perestroika, and ideology suggested that they should not try.

When the propaganda claims concerning women's emancipation were eventually challenged, it was less to expose their lack of substance than to deny the validity of the professed objectives. The country was experiencing a crisis of spirituality, it was said, which could be traced to the breakup of the family and to the absence of proper homes and of proper women to organize them. The communist regime was condemned for having uprooted wives and mothers from the family, where they belonged, thereby depriving society of their domestic skills. On this matter conservatives, who subscribed to a Slavophil program, a return to Russian traditionalism,[2] and radicals, who espoused the market economy and Western pluralism, were in agreement. They shared the essentialist view of sexual difference: women's place was in the home.

In his book *Perestroika*, Mikhail Gorbachev had spoken of returning women to their "purely womanly mission" of housework, child care, and homemaking. At the same time, he considered it imperative that women should achieve a higher profile in public life and indicated that this could be achieved through the activity of the women's soviets.[3] Like the CWS, women's soviets had a history: grassroots political organizations had thrived in the 1920s, were abandoned in the Stalinist period, and then revived under Khrushchev. The women's soviets, like their precedessors, were in principle designed to defend women's economic and social interests; like their predecessors they were in practice tightly controlled from above. At the Party's command, the women's soviets multiplied; by the late 1980s there were said to be almost a quarter of a million. But they were not successful at channeling women into public life. The CSW, on the other hand, did win greater visibility under a new chairwoman, Zoya Pukhova, who made strong criticisms of the Soviet system and of women's status within it. In particular, the Committee drew attention to the conditions under which women worked—lack of safety regulations, long hours—and the likelihood of high levels of female unemployment as a result of economic reforms.

Independent women's groups, at a meeting held in summer 1990, also took unemployment and women's right to work as central themes. They carefully confirmed their allegiance to "family values," but insisted these values should not be implemented at the expense of women's economic rights. NEZHDI, the document drawn up at the meeting, went on to outline a nonessentialist view of human nature that went against the grain of the Soviet consensus, a critique of femininity that placed its authors firmly in the mainstream of modern Western feminism.[4]

These independent organizations had developed at the end of the 1980s in different geographic locations, attracting women from a variety of social backgrounds. In Leningrad, Olga Lipovskaya edited a woman's paper, *Zhenskoe chtenie;* in Moscow province, a group had formed on the basis of a local women's soviet. In Moscow itself, LOTUS—the League of Liberation from Stereotypes—was set up by women with jobs in academia and feminist research interests; Olga Voronina's article in the major sociological journal *Sotsiologicheskie issledovaniya* broke new ground by describing the Soviet Union as a man's world and employed non-Marxist analytical terms to substantiate her case[5]; Valentina Konstantinova, a specialist on the women's movement in Britain, and Natalya Zakharova and Anastasya Posadskaya, a sociologist and economist, respectively, were responsible together with Natalya Rimashevskaya, the director of the Institute on the Social and Economic Problems of Demography, for drafting recommendations on the status of Soviet women to the Council of Ministers, a document subsequently published in *Kommunist,* the official journal of the CPSU, under the title, "How We Solve the Women's Question."[6]

In the spring of 1990, the Institute established a Center for Gender Studies, the first of its kind in the Soviet Union, equipped with one small office and a large fund of enthusiasm.[7] Despite its government financing, the Center distanced itself from officialdom, from the party and the CSW, and openly backed the democratic opposition to the right-wing swing of the Gorbachev government. In an address published in January 1991, in response to the deaths of demonstrators in Lithuania and Latvia at the hands of the black berets, the special police task force, the Center appealed to the non-native population of the Baltic republics to dissociate itself from violence and called "on all people to take part in acts of protest and solidarity. Our silence now will mean our permanent silence."[8] While the Center sided with the opposition against the regime, at the same time it was critical of the democrats' tendency to assume politics to be a male domain and to favor the return of women to the home.

The Center took the view that the "woman question" had never been solved in the USSR, that "the patriarchal system of gender relations" was still being reproduced at all levels of society. It aimed to develop "women's perspectives" on academic, political, media, business, and administrative matters. It hoped to influence government policy, "to sensitize policymakers to understand that all decisions they take have a women's/gender dimension." It was committed to encouraging women to find an independent voice.[9]

At the beginning of 1991, a women's movement was still in its early stages; gender as an organizing concept exercised nowhere near the pull of ethnicity. Though women were angered by redundancies and by the endless shortages, rarely did these sentiments translate into action; women were more likely to demand dignified domesticity than independent equality.[10] Feminism was, however, receiving a certain amount of sympathetic media coverage and making some impact on public consciousness. A cartoon in one of the recently founded newspapers used the acronym LOTUS as visual shorthand for "unisex."[11] In an article in *Moscow News,* a businesswoman producing quail eggs for their food value remarks in passing that she is a feminist and concludes, "Mark my words, fellow countrywomen! In the coming five years be prepared to see your husbands, reformed by Russia's feminist movement, serve you morning coffee and a couple of quail eggs . . . in bed!"[12]

The following interview with Anastasya Posadskaya and Valentina Konstantinova of the Center for Gender Studies was recorded in Moscow in February 1991—a couple of months after Eduard Shevardnadze had resigned from the government, predicting a right-wing coup; a few weeks after Soviet troops had fired on demonstrators in Lithuania and Latvia, and Prime Minister Pavlov had introduced deeply unpopular monetary reforms. The situation in the capital was tense. Though hundreds of thousands had turned out to demonstrate against government policies, the conservatives had the upper hand, or so it seemed.

The Center for Gender Studies was in the thick of events. The interview was interrupted by telephone calls and visitors. The energy and enthusiasm of the place were reminiscent of the early days of second-wave feminism, yet the political context could not have been more different—poverty and social disintegration, the ever-present possibility of repression and dictatorship.

Q. Could you explain how the Center is organized and what are its aims?

Posadskaya: The Center is a research unit. We would like to do everything, to be a teaching, methodological, and information center as well. Unfortunately, at the present we have just the one Center and no funding for anything else; what we do extra, we do out of enthusiasm. We are looking for ways to attract funding, so that we can properly support the other activities.

This year we have two main projects. The first is "Woman and the Market." We are analyzing the impact of the present economic reforms—decentralization, the transition to the market—on women and men. It's clear that the women are going to be made redundant, because they are presumed to have another purpose in life, and they cost more in benefits. We pointed this out in our articles. Unfortunately, the process is already in full swing. Research done at the KamAZ Truck Factory shows that over recent months the percentage of women in the labor force has fallen 5 percent, from 53 percent to 48 percent. The factory employs its own sociologists, and our institute has been conducting research over a number of years, so there is an awareness of what's happening, and the situation is causing concern. But if it wasn't for the sociologists the redundancies would not be recognized as having any significance. So in addition to writing recommendations to the Soviet of Ministers and to the Supreme Soviet, we have to make clear to women and society that it is a political problem that requires a strategy.

Q. Are women's lower qualifications also a factor in the redundancies?

Posadskaya: The general educational level of the female work force is slightly higher than that of the male work force. But men have the edge in professional and technical education. And women find it harder to improve their qualifications "on the job." Certainly, this is one of the reasons why they are being made redundant. But the second reason is that they are the recipients of benefits. The belief is widespread that because of the specificities of the female organism women are a particular, peculiar type of worker. Which, mind you, hasn't prevented women from doing very hard work. In the old days factories and offices did not mind how many workers they had and were quite prepared to take on women: the more the merrier. But now they begin to mind, and those workers who are entitled to benefits find themselves outside the gates.

Q. What is the predicted level of unemployment?

Posadskaya: It has been estimated that sixteen million could be unemployed nationwide by the turn of the century.* And, obviously, the majority will be women. According to my calculations, women

---

*(Ed.) This figure is much below the latest projections which are more like 50 million for Russia.

made up over 80 percent of those who were made redundant when the government apparatus was rationalized with a great deal of fuss in the mid-1980s, in the period from 1985 to 1987. The women who lost their jobs were rank-and-file employees, not executives; the men who made up the other 20 percent were no doubt due for retirement anyway. It would be reasonable, I think, to expect that the same percentage of the sixteen million—if this figure proves to be accurate—will be female.

Q. It is often said that because life for Soviet women is so hard they would welcome the opportunity to bow out of the paid labor force. Do you think this is the case?

Posadskaya: This is a very common view. But one has to recognize that life is not easy for men either. The combination of doing a job and coping with the harsh realities of everyday life is difficult for any person. But our patriarchal ideology connects these difficulties with women only, which is not as it should be. Our research at the KamAZ Truck Factory and in Taganrog, and other surveys too, show that less than 10 percent of women—the exact figure varies from survey to survey—would want to give up working, even if their husbands earned enough to provide an acceptable standard of living for their families. Many women say they would like to work part-time, which is understandable. Many men, no doubt, would also be prepared to work less. But for some reason no one seems anxious to offer them the possibility!

Konstantinova: The Center's second research project is entitled "Women and Politics." We are interested in the crisis of the official women's movement and in the development of the unofficial women's movement. In Moscow and Leningrad and possibly in other republics too, an independent women's movement has emerged. Over the first few years of perestroika women sat back without comment and watched men making all the decisions. Now the situation is changing. In our society two incomes are essential to maintain the most basic standard of living, so the fact that women are having to face up to the possibility of losing their jobs creates the conditions for the development of a women's movement and an ideology of equality. But because there is no theory, no methodology, the movement is tending to polarize.

Q. What are the two poles?

Konstantinova: On one side there are the feminists and the democrats, on the other the conservatives. Some women are for economic reforms, for the market, for pluralism, for a multiparty system. Others oppose reforms. In fall 1990 there was a meeting in Kuibyshev of women who demanded a "socialist future for our children": they were in favor of what they called "socialism," but against pluralism and democracy.

The movement was inspired by the hard-line political organizations of the Russian-speaking population in the Baltic republics; ethnic tensions have proved an important catalyst. The democratic tendency is very weak. A women's party was recently set up in Leningrad, the EPZh (United Women's Party); we've received information about a women's political group in Tomsk as well. The percentage of women in the established alternative political organizations and groups is very small. Only 1 to 2 percent of the Social Democratic Party are women. I recently attended a seminar of the Moscow-Helsinki group, the civil rights group organized by Larisa Bogoraz. These sorts of organizations, which are quite new in our country, are attracting women. There isn't really any consciousness of the importance of women being politically active even among women who are active. Patriarchal ideology is still strong. The leaders, being true democrats, will say that "women's place is in the home," even though women like Larisa Bogoraz, for example, demonstrated in Red Square in 1968 [in protest of the invasion of Czechoslovakia], and spent time in prison and in the camps.

The women's movement is still very weak. Women don't yet understand that they're discriminated against; they don't see themselves as a social force.

Q: Is the political participation of women a Russian phenomenon, or are women joining groups and organizations in other republics?

Konstantinova: In Kazakhstan women have a strong presence in the antinuclear and ecological movements. And also in the civil rights movements that emerged after the racial conflicts in December 1986, when about 90 people were imprisoned; the leader of the Alma-Ata Helsinki group is a woman.

Q: Are women engaged in other types of political activity?

Konstantinova: In Moscow prostitutes have organized, have held demonstrations demanding safe sex and the availability of condoms.

Posadskaya: Prostitutes in Leningrad organized a sit-in, or rather they blocked the entrance to one of the hotels, in protest at the policy of refusing them entry.

Konstantinova: A lesbian group was set up recently in Moscow. That's a new development.

Q: Do you have contacts with the women's soviets (zhensovety)?

Konstantinova: Some zhensovety are active on ecological issues.

Posadskaya: We have contacts with these zhensovety that are independent-minded, that don't feel obliged to toe the line, to be at the beck and call of the Committee of Soviet Women. With a few of them we have very good relations. Olga Bessolova's Political Club grew out of a zhensovet. Our forum to be held at the end of March is in fact sponsored by the women's soviet of the Nuclear Physics Institute in Dubna.

Q: Has the Committee of Soviet Women (CSW) been invited to the forum?

Posadskaya: We have sent them information on the same basis as everyone else. If the Committee wants to take part, it must send in "theses," the same as everyone. And if they are judged to be of interest, it will be given the opportunity to present them at the forum. But the CSW doesn't have any special rights.

Q: How has the Committee reacted to the emergence of a women's movement?

Posadskaya: It has tried to bring it into its fold. And that's what we don't want. So there is something of a confrontation. Those of us who are involved in organizing the Dubna forum—the Center, Olga Lipovskaya—don't take part in the get-togethers at the CSW. Valentina Konstantinova and I won't go to the CSW. Let the committee get on with its own work: inviting businesswomen, learning the new vocabulary of feminism, even sexism. That's fine by us.

Q: Are you saying the Committee is changing?

Posadskaya: If it can survive only by changing, it will change. But as soon as the going gets tough it backtracks. And obviously we don't want to cooperate with organizations of this type. The Committee has funds, large premises, access to the media, and could have responded to the Lithuanian events by rallying women against dictatorship. But did we hear anything from them? Absolutely nothing. Or rather we heard reactionary speeches. So I have little faith in their reforms.

Q: How did you respond to the events in Lithuania?

Posadskaya: It was a difficult moment for us. We met here in the Center to decide what to do. We phoned Radio Moscow. We phoned women we knew and invited them to meet here; we composed an "Address to Women." We thought that even if we didn't get many signatures to our petition, at least a different voice would be heard. We didn't want the authorities to be able to say that all women were in favor of the use of force. The Committee for Soviet Women did nothing at all. We went on the big demonstration on January 20, organized by the democratic forces in protest against the events in Lithuania. We collected signatures as we marched. We wanted to have a speaker on the platform, but by the time we got to the square the speeches were over. So the demonstration passed without a single woman speaker. In fact, we didn't know how to go about getting ourselves on the speakers' list. How to make an application, where to send it. Now we do. So it was a useful lesson for us.

Konstantinova: I phoned Radio Moscow several times and talked to young democrat journalists working there. They promised to read out the address in one of their programs, but didn't. Their news bulletins didn't even mention our petition and the number of signatures collected during the demonstration.

Posadskaya: We feel, though, that the address did achieve something. Every single woman and man we approached during the demonstration agreed to sign. If we'd had the time, we could have gotten half a million signatures! A lot of people asked where they could find us, and we've had a number of phone calls since. So women do have something to say; it's a matter of giving direction to that voice.

Q: In the West it was dissatisfaction with the "sexual revolution" that brought many women to the women's movement. Women as sexual objects was initially a more common theme than women as objects of economic exploitation. Is a similar focus likely in the USSR?

Konstantinova: At the moment questions about sexuality are not articulated. For many years this has been a taboo subject, so it is difficult for women to define questions and formulate demands. But I think that matters of personal sexual life are bound to become important. In a patriarchal society like ours it was difficult for men and women to discuss questions of this nature, and personal relationships are definitely an area of discontent and dissatisfaction. Frigidity in women is common, and men have their problems too. Then there's the question of women as sexual objects, though most women don't see it as a problem, don't see themselves as being objectified. The time will come, I would say, but not yet.

Q: The view that the Soviet Union is experiencing a sexual revolution is commonplace in the press today. Do you agree with it?

Konstantinova: Well, it's certainly the case that young people at the moment are extremely interested in sex. Sexual education is at a very primitive level. Abortion is widespread, illegal abortions included. There used to be a great deal of hypocrisy in sexual matters, which is only slowly being overcome. During the first telebridge between the United States and the USSR, one Soviet woman, responding to a question about sex, declared, "In the Soviet Union there is no sex and cannot be." Everyone laughed, of course. Now things are more open.

Q: I see that one of the items on the agenda for the women's forum is "the image of women in the media." What will be discussed under this heading?

Posadskaya: "The image of women in the media" was our starting point. In 1987 and 1988, when Natasha Zakharova, Olga Voronina, Valya Konstantinova, and I began to meet, the press was talking about "cuckoo mothers," women who abandoned their babies to children's homes.[13] Women were seen as responsible for all social ills—both the old people left to fend for themselves and the neglected children. Single women, who were victims of society, were made out to be villains. The Committee of Soviet Women, which has the right to make legislative proposals, drafted a bill to punish the "cuckoo mothers." I have a copy and I preserve it as an important historical document. Without any kind of analysis of who these women were and what their reasons were for acting the way they did, proposals were made to fine them and put an identifying stamp on their internal passports. At the present moment much more humane proposals are being drawn up to provide greater government support for women who have no home and no money.

So under the heading of the "image of women in the media" we will discuss stereotypes and prejudice of this sort. There's also the question of pornography, which has been an issue for several years now and about which we have different opinions.

Q: Could you say something about your disagreements?

Posadskaya: The LOTOS group—the four of us!—spent quite a lot of time debating the subject. One approach was to talk of the "rampant spread" (razgul) of pornography, the use of the female body as an object of consumption. Beauty contests, of course, come into it here. My approach is different. Pornography may be a good or a bad thing; let's say for the sake of argument that it's bad. But what about censorship? If you say erotica is permissible but pornography is not, who is going to decide which is which? We would need some new State Committee to do the job. And that, of course, is what we've got.[14] In my view, censorship is more damaging to democracy than pornography is to women. Society, by and large, will eventually get over pornography. Maybe there will be some people, some women even, for whom pornography will continue to be necessary for various reasons, so for them let there be the "top shelves" or whatever. At the moment we're like children who develop immunity by first contracting the illness. Pornography, in other words, may produce immunity against itself. At any rate, it will be the individual's personal decision to use pornography or not, to participate in its production or not, either as object or subject. It seems to me that the "rampant spread" of pornography is an inevitable stage that society has to go through. Taboos on representations of the naked body and on the public discussion of sex were built into the totalitarian system, but interest in these matters hasn't ceased to exist just because of the silence.

Q: It is noticeable that the focus of representation is the female body, just as it is in the West.

Posadskaya: Men have been represented too, though not with the same regularity. I have seen a reference to a male body-building contest, with a foreign holiday for the winner. But yes, it is by and large the female body that is objectified, and it is possible to put forward a feminist explanation for this. In our society there are inequalities in the relationships between men and women in every sphere, including the sexual. The colossal number of abortions—more in any one year than the number of live births—is one example. Childbirth without the option of anesthetics is another, the absence of contraception, a third. Wherever you look women are getting a raw deal. There is an element of violence in men's relationships with women, and this is reflected in the type of erotica and pornography that our society produces. But I really don't feel comfortable with discussions on this subject. I feel myself a hopeless philistine! I am sure the reasons for pornography are deep and complex, and some of them we don't yet understand. Certainly, this is something that needs studying, that needs fundamental analysis. But I'm not a specialist.

Q: Have women's groups registered protest against pornography?

Posadskaya: In one of our official statements we referred to the "rampant spread" of pornography. I personally was against the use of this phrase because it sounds like official "Sovietspeak" of the worst kind. But I was in the minority.

Konstantinova: I was also unhappy with it. You have to ask yourself, I think, who uses the term. And the answer is: the far right—Pamyat,[15] for example—and those with a patriarchal mentality.

Q: Have women's groups placed abortion on their agenda?

Konstantinova: Our birth rate has been declining over recent decades as it has everywhere. But we have a uniquely high rate of abortion. This is partly because for various reasons women are not prepared to use contraception, and partly because the government fails to offer a proper service—to organize clinics, even to supply contraceptives in sufficient quantities. So far women's groups have not raised the question of abortion. Women who are better off, or at least better educated, find a doctor who will perform the abortion for them, illegally. Though it has to be said that the number of deaths from such illegal abortions is high, especially among young people. So if abortion isn't yet an issue—

and don't forget that a women's movement hardly exists as yet—it is bound to become one in the near future. Women in the past accepted the appalling abortion provisions because they saw them, I think, as a personal ordeal. Now that conditions in the clinics are being written about in the press women can see that they affect thousands of others as well. What was entirely hidden is now coming into the open. Articles have been published in the mass women's magazine *Rabotnitsa* describing the nightmare of abortion and how women felt afterward.[16] And the mailbag of letters from readers has been enormous. Cooperative abortion clinics were operating a couple of years ago in Moscow, offering vacuum suction abortions, but they have been closed down. So I suppose one has to say that the improvements are not linear. It is possible that the Orthodox Church will make a stand and demand criminalization.

Q: Would you say the Communist Party has always paid only lip service to the principle of sexual equality?

Posadskaya: It is possible to find in Lenin's works a lot of statements about the need to change relationships between the sexes, to transform everyday life along communist lines. The Bolsheviks tried to transform everyday life by reducing the size of kitchens! But the emotional relations between men and women did not change. The "great emancipators" from the early period of our history, the civil war period mainly, including Alexandra Kollontai and Inessa Armand, are of course important: these were women who broke new ground, women who were active creators of history. But I wouldn't say that there is that much interest in them at the present time. Kollontai, for example, is remembered as a diplomat rather than as a feminist.

Konstantinova: I think these women are in fact more interesting, more multifaceted than the information we have access to suggests.

Posadskaya: Yes, I think that is true. Though when I read Kollontai, I must admit I was disappointed. On the one hand there was her splendid *Social Basis of the Woman Question,* and on the other, her continual preaching of the importance of motherhood, her insistence that it was a crucial state function, her emphasis on maternity, maternity, and more maternity. Well, motherhood is women's function, there's no getting away from that, so feminists could argue that making it more visible has to be commended, but at the same time Kollontai was laying the foundations of an ideology that recognized motherhood as woman's special sphere. Kollontai is full of contradictions. But that of course doesn't mean that she shouldn't be discussed. Research in this area would be welcome.

Konstantinova: Kollontai did a lot for women. But she was a typical

Bolshevik and lacked tolerance. There were achievements in her day, of course—canteens and kindergartens. But all the reforms were subsequently distorted. In some ways the twenties was a renaissance, though admittedly it's difficult to talk of a renaissance when the terror began right after the revolution. Terror, intolerance, class hatred. It's difficult for us to find out about that era, about Kollontai, for instance. There just isn't the information available. When I read the Western biographies, I realized how much was missing from the Soviet ones.

Q: In the West, particularly in Europe, and particularly in the early stages of the development of the women's movement, the relationship between Marxism and feminism was hotly debated. Do you expect this discussion in the USSR to be less important because Marxism is seen to be discredited?

Konstantinova: It's hard to predict. It's quite true that Marxist and socialist ideas are out of favor. But the ideas themselves will, I think, return to the agenda.

Posadskaya: Western feminism has used Marxist concepts, and there is a mass of such research in this field. Feminism in my view can rule out Marxism as a dogma, but not Marxism as an intellectual approach. Marxism still has something to offer in that sense. If Marxism is understood as a social approach to historical questions, and gender as the social, not biological, determination of sexual difference, then the Marxist approach would seem an entirely appropriate one. But at the same time it is clearly insufficient. Marx did not pay attention, for example, to domestic labor. He saw it as unproductive. In the Soviet Union, relations between women and men within the family have changed less than the relations between the sexes outside the family. Women in the public sphere are still in subordinate positions; they aren't the ones making decisions. I wouldn't want to say that emancipation through participation in social labor has been discredited. It still seems to me that the right of women to work is fundamental, and also strategically vital.

The democrats want to get woman out of the workplace, out of socially productive life, because they associate her being there with the system of totalitarian socialism, because they see her employment as one of the bricks of the system they oppose. They think they are doing women a favor by sending them home. The domestic sphere, isolated from the public, is perceived as being extremely attractive. And so, the argument goes, women should have the privilege of inhabiting it, should have the benefits of a less alienated existence. You hear it said that in our society, only one sex, the male sex, was really oppressed by totalitarianism; women were saved because of their relationship to the domestic sphere. So women were liberated and men were oppressed. Everything was stood on its head!

Well, not quite. Politics in our society were in fact "instrumental" in relation to both women and men.

In February 1992, six months after the attempted coup, I returned to the Center for Gender Studies. Since my last visit, Leningrad had become St. Petersburg and the USSR had ceased to exist, replaced by a loose and troubled Commonwealth of Independent States. The democrats had been bolstered by the defeat of the plotters in August, yet weakened by the further disintegration of the country. The first steps in market reform had been taken, but the economic situation was bleak— inflation, food shortages, plummeting living standards.

I talked to Anastasya Posadskaya and Valentina Konstantinova about political changes since our previous meeting, their impact on women and on the Center. They noted how during the defense of the White House in Moscow, at the time of the coup, women had been in the front row of the "living ring," appealing to soldiers not to shoot, but how the steep decline in activism since August had affected women as well as men.

Women are tired of politics and exhausted. Women in the subway, studying a flyer for a forthcoming demonstration against the "communist-fascist threat," say: who cares, so what if the reds or the browns come to power, life cannot get any worse. Peasant women in Tula province complain of the fall in their living standards and blame the democrats. Even members of the Moscow intelligentsia are less appreciative of their newfound freedoms.

Over the past year the democrats as a whole have not abandoned their view that women's place is in the home, but some of the small political parties have begun to take an interest in feminist ideas. The Labor Party has asked the Center to assist in drafting a program on women. Members of the Social Democrats— a tiny but intellectually influential group, one of whose leaders is author of the Russian constitution—have attended seminars at the Center. So perhaps the democrats will see the light. Already a number of women—including Tatyana Zaslavskaya and Galina Starovoitova—have made a name for themselves in national political life.

The Center has had a busy year. As of the beginning of 1992 new research projects were launched: an oral history project "What was it like to be a Soviet woman?" and "Gender Aspects of Emigration from the Former USSR." It is preparing an alternative submission to the UN Commission on the Convention on the Elimination of All Forms of Discrimination Against Women, just in case the official papers paint too rosy a picture. Data on women's wages are being collected. Business courses are being set up to teach entrepreneurial skills to women. In the grim economic climate, modest battles—such as those to preserve traditional female craft industries—assume importance. The threat of closure hangs over the Center as it does over all academic institutions, but there is optimism that the storm can be weathered.

The Center remains cautiously optimistic about the future of the women's movement. In March 1991, the first independent women's forum was held successfully in Dubna, Russia. The two hundred–odd participants, representing forty-six organizations, discussed a wide range of topics, from participation in the democratic movement and women in the market economy to problems of the creative arts. In its concluding document the delegates recognized the existence of "socioeconomic, political, and cultural discrimination against women" in the country, pointed to the "myth" of women's biological destiny, and set out proposals for equality in politics, economic life, the family, culture, and education.[17] Tentative plans were made to organize a second women's forum in September 1992 in the mining region of Kusbass[18]; there has been discussion about the form the conference should take (whether it should be a festival or perhaps a seminar) once the financial obstacles to holding a conference—travel expenses, the costs of accommodation—have been solved.

The women's movement that emerges over the next few years is unlikely to be monolithic in structure; rather, it will likely consist of different strands and organizations. Women will begin to find a voice and make their own demands.

Notes

1. *Woman and Russia: First Feminist Samizdat* (London: Sheba, 1980). For a discussion of the authors of the almanac and their disagreements, see A. Holt, "The First Soviet Feminists," in *Soviet Sisterhood*, ed. B. Holland (Bloomington: Indiana UP, 1985), pp. 237–365.

2. See, for example, V. Rasputin, "Pravaya, levaya gde storona?" *Nash sovremennik*, no. 11 (1989): 140–149.

3. Mikhail Gorbachev, *Perestroika: New Thinking for our Country and the World* (New York: Harper and Row, 1987), pp. 116–118.

4. For an English translation of the document, see "Feminist Manifesto," *Feminist Review*, no. 39 (1991): 127–132.

5. O. A. Voronina, "Zhenshchina v 'muzhskom obshchestve' ", *Sotsiologicheskie issledovaniya*, no. 2 (1988): 104–110.

6. N. Zakharova, A. Posadskaya, and N. Rimashevskaya, "Kak my reshaem zhenskii vopros," *Kommunist*, no. 4 (1989): 56–65.

7. *Occasional Newsletter* (June 1991), pp. 3–15; "Tsentr gendernykh issledovanii," undated pamphlet, pp. 1–8.

8. *Obrashchenie predstavitel'nits nezavisimykh zhenskikh organizatsii*, January 14, 1991, unpublished address.

9. *Occasional Newsletter*, pp. 3–4.

10. Galina Sillaste, "Zhenshchina v politicheskoi zhizni," *Kommunist,* no. 8 (1991): 7–11.

11. "Sic!" *Nezavisimaya gazeta,* January 17, 1991.

12. V. Orlov, "Quail Eggs for Breakfast," *Moscow News,* no. 2 (1991): p. 7.

13. On this subject, see my " 'Cuckoo-mothers' and 'Apparatchiks': Glasnost and Children's Homes," in *Perestroika and Women,* ed. M. Buckley (Cambridge: Cambridge University Press, 1992), pp. 123–136.

14. A state committee on public morality was set up toward the end of 1990.

15. "Pamyat" (Memory) was set up in the early 1980s, ostensibly to preserve the country's cultural heritage. The organization has become identified with right-wing nationalism and anti-Semitism.

16. *Rabotnitsa,* no. 7 (1987): 12.

17. *Itogovoi otchet o rabote 1 nezavismogo zhenskogo foruma,* Moscow, 1991; "Concluding Document of the First Independent Women's Forum," *Feminist Review,* no. 39 (1991): 146–148. For a report on the conference, see C. Cockburn, "Democracy Without Women is No Democracy," *Feminist Review,* no. 39 (1991): 141–148.

18. Kusbass has become a focus of working class militancy over recent years. A women's group was recently set up in the region.

28

Eastern European Male Democracies: A Problem of Unequal Equality*

Zillah Eisenstein

I begin this query wondering what the relationship between feminism and the Eastern European democratic struggles begun in 1989 might become. Part of the problem for this discussion is that feminism and democracy are terms with multiple and even conflicting meanings. Yet I remain committed to the "imaginings" encompassed in the radical potential of both feminist and democratic politics.

Democratic changes in Eastern Europe include pieces of liberal democracy, capitalism, and socialism. What the exact blend will be will develop out of the specifics of each country. If new ground is to be charted out of the old dilemmas of the individual versus state authority, the insights of feminist theorists, developed since the mid-1970s, must refocus the discussion of democracy to include sex and gender relations and familial structures and their relation to individuality and the economy. This refocusing does not imply the importation of erroneous Western standards, or Western feminism, to Eastern European societies. Rather, it means rethinking how democracy is specifically being formulated, especially for women, through a lens that limits the resolution of the conflict between the individual and the patriarchal, totalitarian state.

Both Western liberal feminism and "communist" enforced statist feminism share an emphasis on women's equality that supposedly treats women like men: entry into the labor market is equated with equal rights. Both models obscure the fact that women are not treated equally in the market, and on the whole occupy second-class citizenship in terms of job opportunities and pay. So neither model can seem liberating to women who already are in the market, at the bottom rungs of it, and are also responsible for the care of children, household chores, and the maintenance of everyday life.

Below, I examine the possibilities of democracy for women in the present context of gender relations within Eastern Europe. I discuss the problem of sexual equality and its relationship to a notion of sexual difference and protectionist legislation. I also discuss the writings of Václav Havel of Czechoslovakia and, briefly, Mikhail Gorbachev of the Soviet Union, as representative of the "new" post-totalitarian state discourses on women's "role" in the new democracies.

The developments in Eastern Europe allow for radically new conceptualizations—though not necessarily implementations—of democratic theory. They demand a renegotiation of the exchange between liberal and socialist theory via a feminist lens. The "ideas" of economic equality taken from socialism, and of individual freedom taken from liberalism, must recognize the notion of individual diversity that derives from a consciousness of gender and racial diversity, taken from "feminists of color" in the United States.

At present the discussion of democracy in Eastern Europe erases liberal feminist theory as well as socialist feminist theory, developed in both the East and the West. And there is something very "old" about theories of democracy premised on a citizenry that is assumed to be male, and a politics reduced to the relations of power within the economy and the market.

What's New and Old in Democratic Theory

The developments in Eastern Europe pose spectacular challenges to the ways in which the histories of liberalism and Marxism have been understood. This is not to say that the critique is entirely new or that the complete opposition between capitalism and socialism is an accurate reading of historical political theory to begin with. The critique of capitalism by liberals for being too inequitable or the critique of socialism by Marxists for not being sufficiently concerned with individual freedom, have frequently been made.

What is new is that the states of Eastern Europe and the former Soviet Union, beginning with Gorbachev, criticized communism's totalitarian past and invoked a private market economy. It is also new that there is no political language set in place to embrace these new developments as Eastern European countries try to find some blend between political liberalism, political pluralism, and individual freedom, with market economies that still embrace a form of social planning. What presently exists is neither completely liberal, nor completely capitalist, nor completely socialist. This uncharted territory should hold out the possibility for dislodging the patriarchal foundation of male gender privilege of *both* capitalism (and with it liberalism) and socialism. Instead, patriarchy, with its hierarchical sexual relations, is being rethreaded.

The fact that gender was insufficiently theorized by Marx and Lenin is problematic for socialist and democratic theory and has been extensively discussed. But the fact that it was insufficiently recognized and theorized by Gorbachev and Havel in 1989–90 is problematic in a different way, given the well-developed feminist critiques of liberalism and socialism made over the past two decades. This makes more glaring a conception of democracy without any recognition of the inequities tied to sex, gender, or race. This is still a part of the legacy of Marxism.

A radicalized notion of democracy—and with it of equality and individuality—must specify that citizens are women and men, that the economy and family structures are the basis for society, that the demand for better consumer goods is as much about people wanting condoms, tampons, and diaphragms that fit as it is about those wanting food and shoes. That sex and gender play a part in the demands for a freer society and gender equality must affect discussions of what freedom means. The crisis of family and alcoholism in the former Soviet Union for example, reflects problems of familial responsibilities and the triple day of labor of Russian women as much as it reflects the problems of a totalitarian state. Reproductive issues intersect with economic choices and options; lack of consumer goods can affect whether one chooses to bear a child or not; contraceptive devices (as consumer items) affect sexual practices. Sexual choices and reproductive issues play back and forth endlessly with the economy—and each realm simultaneously has a life of its own.

Liberalism and Marxism both privilege the economy as the core of society. The world of paid work defines the possibilities. Given this view, Marxists assume that women's entry into paid work defines her equality. And with it the Soviet state, as well as other Eastern European countries, declared that women had equality as they became part of the paid labor force. Liberal theory privileges the economy as well, but does so by distinguishing between the public (market) and private (family) spheres. The liberal democratic state does not declare the equality of women as part of state discourse: her equality is not at issue. Rather she has the freedom either to enter paid work or not to do so.

The difference in the state discourses between supposed economic equality and individual freedom of choice is key here. In neither instance is woman "really" equal or "really" free, because gender equality cannot be equated with the right to work, nor can individual freedom be sufficient when women and men's contributions are not similarly valued to begin with. Rather, women have the freedom to choose to work in the lowest-paying sectors of the economy, which is true for a majority of women in the United States as well as Eastern European countries; and they are so "equal" that they get not only to work on their jobs but to take the major responsibility for childrearing, buying consumer goods, and maintaining the home.

So where are we? Someplace between liberal and socialist visions of patriarchal society, where the tension between individual freedom and gender equality has not been resolved. This place—in between—is where democratic theory presently traverses. This place means that one has to recognize the heterogeneity of power and dislocate the economy as *the* core of democracy. Liberals and Marxists alike assume that the essentials include food, shelter, and clothing, and that these essentials are provided for by the economy. This, then, is the first order of business: get the people what they need. But societies need to sexually reproduce themselves, and this is also a core need. And people like to be sexual as well. So there are at least three cores here.

Of course, Marx and Engels recognized early on in their discussions that the division of labor arising from the sex act is the *first* division of labor.[1] They also then promptly forgot about it. Other Marxists followed suit. Communism, the supposed "positive transcendence of private property,"[2] would emancipate women. Democracy would come to women via the transformation of the economy.

Liberal theory promises less, because liberalism does not promise emancipation to women or men; instead, it promises opportunity. But the privileging of the economy and the denial of a sexual division of labor and gender hierarchy, remain the same. The family, women's labor within it, the activities of sexual reproduction and childrearing are all hidden in the political sense, because liberal theory only theorizes the relations of the market economy. Women are made absent as women in terms of their gendered place in the family. If they appear, they do so as workers, demanding equal pay (in the labor force) or equal rights before the law in the public sphere.

Democratic societies need democratic families *and* democratic economies, and democratic sexual and racial relations. The family, as well as the cultural dimensions of sexual and racial relations, needs restructuring.

The struggle toward democracy must envision the heterogeneity of power. Such a focus helps remind us of diversity in the first place: individuals are diverse, and gender and race diversifies us further. Diversity must underline the concern with democracy by including a concept of individuality that encompasses the differences among people. As such, equality cannot merely mean the sameness of treatment. It must encompass uniqueness and similarity simultaneously. The complete opposition between "the" individual and "the" community that underlines both Marxist and liberal theory is challenged by feminist inquiry.

If individuals are similar and different from each other at one and the same time, then the individual cannot be subsumed into the community. Individual needs may (or may not) be the same as those of the community. An individual will always need freedom of individual expression. "Communist" regimes, as well as socialist theory, have been slow to recognize this. But neither can the individual be seen as totally antagonistic and in competition with all others in the community, as liberal theorists would have it. If individuals are not *only* different, but also similarly human, collectivity is possible. Recognizing gender helps us to negotiate this arena. Identifying woman as both an individual and as a member of a sexual class reminds us of individuality and collectivity simultaneously. Feminism recognizes both the individual woman and the woman defined by her sexual class identity. It gives a different concrete starting point for the dialogue between liberalism and socialism[3] and democracy.

The focus on *sexual* equality specifies a diversity inherent in equality itself. So does a focus on racial and ethnic equality. The universalized notion of equality, though a starting point, simply will not do. Sex equality reminds us that there are two sexes, not one. It reminds us that universal constructions are never sufficient and that the individuality of men and women is not constructed identically. Uniqueness is then theoretically recognized as part of the democratic project.

In order to democratize socialism so it can begin to embrace a "real" equality for women, the construction of equality as the sameness of treatment—either between men, *or* between women and men—must be dislodged. Equal treatment must recognize individuality and sameness. And in order to democratize liberalism to embrace a "real" freedom for women, this reconstructed notion of equality must underpin individual freedom in order for people to be equally free. Radical pluralism and radical individuality have to reinvent the meaning of equality, and with it democracy. Feminist theory, to the degree that it reminds us of diversity— in terms of gender and race—underlines the radicalization of democracy.[4]

As we try to retrieve the importance of individuality or individual diversity from the notion of liberal or possessive individualism,[5] we need to recognize the sex and race of the individual. And as we attempt to reinvent a notion of equality from socialism, we need to reweave it through a concept of gender equality that recognizes racial and ethnic diversity. With this as a starting point, we can then attempt to really think of how to democratize *and* "individualize" the market, as well as family life and with it sexual and racial relations.

"Really" Rethinking Democracy

Problems exist with the rethinking of democracy. But in the mish-mash of ideas lies the distinct possibility that democracy is something more than what either liberal democrats or socialists ever imagined. What is absent in this rethinking are the insights of feminist theory. Both liberal and socialist feminists have long recognized the importance and the inadequacy of each of these systems for creating gender democracy.

Liberal feminists, to the extent that one homogenizes the differences within this category, push the liberal discourse of equality of opportunity and freedom of choice to its outer limits to specify the lives of women. The discourse of rights becomes partially radicalized in this process as the masculine presumption of individual rights is challenged and rearticulated for white women and women of color.[6] When these universal rights are specifically claimed by women, the existing patriarchal order is destabilized. A major limitation of liberalism for feminism is that the concern with sexual equality is often reduced to the economic and legal realm. The specific needs posed by woman's particular physicality— her capacity to bear a child—stand outside this realm or are equated with it. There is no recognition or theorization of this biological reality of a "sexed" body or its gendered meaning. There is no specificity of race. Woman is treated like the universalized man. And to the degree there is no universal man, there is no real sameness of treatment. There is only the promise of it.

Socialist feminists have criticized Marxist and socialist theory for equating women's oppression with her exploitation, for assuming that capitalist wage labor explains the problem of women's inequality. Socialist theory, via Marx and Lenin, assumes that socialism and eventually communism will resolve the "woman question." But feminist critiques argue that there is a semiautonomous hierarchical division of labor and society that derives from the engendered differentiation of woman from man, which cannot be reduced to the problem of bourgeois exploitation of the proletariat. Gender, like race, cuts through economic class divisions. Patriarchy, the political process of hierarchically differentiating woman from man, exists semiautonomously from the economic marketplace. One arena does not automatically clarify the other, although they remain interconnected. But this is not the understanding in Eastern Europe today.

Equality of the Sexes and Eastern Europe

Instead of posing "really existing socialism" against the ideal of socialist equality, let us pose "really existing sex equality" against the ideal of gender and racial or ethnic equality. This means examining the difference between statist doctrine and a more real equality. This involves examining how protective legislation legislates inequality by enforcing women's domestic and secondary wage earner status rather than enhancing equality. Protective legislation in these countries has most often been used to create, as well as justify, the unequal gendered organization of the economy rather than "real" sexual equality. Or special provisions like free day care and maternity leaves have been used to assist women in their gender roles, rather than to reorganize gender responsibilities between men and women. This is why many Eastern European women refer to previous statist polices as "false equality" and "forced emancipation."

The kernel of women's rights in the Soviet Union, Poland, Czechoslovakia, and East Germany has been the right to work for pay.[7] In reality, women's pay is lower than men's, and their domestic responsibilities are not defined as work. There is no problematization of gender differentiation.

Sexual egalitarianism as defined by statist doctrine has two components. It equates women's equality with her entrance into the market, like men. And it singles women out for "protection." This is the "logical" extension of the patriarchal underpinnings of socialist equality for women: the institution of motherhood must be enforced alongside and within the market. Woman is supposed to be treated "equal," like men, *after* this gender differentiation is put in place. It is an equality that presumes inequality in the first place. Woman is engendered as a mother first. Then she is supposedly equal *as* a mother, rather than as an individual.

Protective legislation is carried out in sporadic and suspect ways. Mainly, it sets women apart from men as potential bearers of children, rather than enabling them to be mothers. Protective legislation is contradictory at best, not because treating men and women differently necessarily negates fair treatment, but rather because protective legislation in these instances constrains women's choices as different in order to ensure women's domesticity. It enforces the differentiation of woman from man in order to ensure women's difference from men. This is not the same as recognizing specialness in ways that will allow for a greater freedom of choice in the long run, *after* special provisions are made.

Protective legislation in socialist "statism" creates a complicated and troublesome picture. It is insufficient and problematic, and yet it is sometimes better than nothing. It can provide partial relief in an already bad situation, even while it reinforces gender discrimination. Legislation providing maternity leave—and job tenure during it—and day-care provisions for children has provided much-needed assistance to women in Eastern Europe. And even though there is a big difference between "assistance" and equality, no one wants to give up the former without the assurance of the latter.

To the extent that changes toward the "free" market endanger maternity and child-care provisions, women are hesitant and reluctant about the changes. They fear loss of their jobs. Their particular status—defined by domestic, wage, and consumer labor—defines specific problems for them. The "new" democracies pose a more complicated challenge for women than they do for men: the "free" market will endanger much of what has been guaranteed them "as women" in the past and it is not clear what it can bring them "as women" in the future if it continues the patriarchal stance of "old" socialism and western capitalism. This may be the most complicated for the women of East Germany, where the support systems for women in paid employment with children were among the best offered anywhere.

One wonders whether if women lose their "protection," however partial it is, they will have to fend for themselves and their families even more than they do at present. Will they be relegated to the home in reaction to the excesses of socialist statism? This reflects the dilemma of actually being both a woman (in need of some "specific" rights and policies) *and* an individual (similar to other women and men). When policies assist women *as* women (mothers), they enforce the existing gender code. It is also true that these policies can lessen discrimination, as they can potentially lessen woman's sole responsibilities for children and domestic chores.

The right to first-trimester abortions; shorter work weeks for women with two or more children; one paid day off a month for women over forty, married women, or women with children under sixteen years of age; a paid maternity year off at about 80 percent of one's salary; free day-care and infant-care centers—all bespeak the dilemma for East German women.[8] They are right to fear that new legislation will misrepresent the complicated reality of women's specific needs and their universal human rights.

This is the dilemma that feminist and democratic theory faces. How does one recognize general human rights and needs simultaneously with the specific needs of gender and race when existing "specific" needs in part reflect relations of gender and racial oppression? We supposedly are the most inclusive, and therefore the most democratic, when the rights we speak of are general and universal. I argue instead that a radically inclusive notion of democracy must first recognize the specificity that exists *within* the universal.

The totalitarian past, and with it a notion of "state enforced feminism" that has never been "really" feminist or egalitarian, has discredited the discourse of sexual equality.[9] The recognition of reproductive rights for women remains outside the purview of "formal" equality. If women are treated "like" men, reproductive rights issues are silenced because no man ever needs an abortion, and no man needs contraception to prevent his own pregnancy as a woman does. It should be noted that this standard of "likeness" functions in both liberal democratic and socialist theory. Neither recognize reproductive rights as essential to the complex of democratic rights. Both are constructed with men (and their nonreproductive bodies) in mind. This sets the context for statist notions of equality.

There is no easy resolution to the issue of how special legislation recognizing women's particular responsibilities should be woven into a "neutral," non-sex-specific notion of equality. Or how special legislation can be used in such a way as not to relegate women to a secondary status or a "mommy track." The mistrust of statist rhetoric encompassing sexual equality creates a complicated politics that defines much of the context surrounding "women's" issues. To the extent that abortion has replaced other contraceptive choices as a means of birth control, the demand for condoms or diaphragms is seen as a liberation from excessive numbers of abortions. Reproductive rights would require sex education and the right to contraceptives *before* the right to abortion. To the extent that pornography represents, in part, a denial of state coercion, it is often embraced as a statement of individual freedom. To the extent that the family functioned as a private sphere of resistance against the "communist" state, women were valued in the role they played in this sphere[10] and feel protective of it. An effective feminist politics must thread these concerns through a renewed critique of the patriarchal formulations of socialism *and* capitalism.

There is a singular absence of discussion of gender as part of a revitalized notion of democracy and democratic theory, as well as a singular absence of women in the "new" democracies. There is little new about this absence, just as there is little new in the fact that as unemployment grows, women are the first to lose their jobs.

The Former Soviet Union and the "Woman Question"

The Soviet state was the first government in history to write women's emancipation into law, in 1917, and to make abortion legal on request in 1920. Abortion was then criminalized under Stalin in 1936, and reliberalized in 1955. The 1977 Constitution, article 35, declared equality of rights between women and men. Protective legislation barred women from as many as 460 occupations in order to protect their maternal function and their gender roles. Motherhood rather than parenthood was at issue in this legislation; biologism existed right alongside Soviet egalitarianism.[11] But there is no consistency in this protectionism. Women have always done heavy labor in the countryside and have been the rubbish collectors and street cleaners in the cities.[12]

Soviet society had the largest number of women professionals and specialists on the globe, although few filled the top ranks, and close to 90 percent of its female population was in the work force.[13] There is an average gap of about 30 percent between men's and women's wages; women predominate in low paid "feminized" occupations; and nearly half of the female work force is employed at unskilled manual labor.[14]

The average Soviet woman had six to eight abortions in her lifetime. But it was not unheard of to have as many as eighteen.[15] Women's health care is a key concern for women, particularly the availability of safe abortions. Given waiting lists in hospitals, anywhere from four to eight million abortions are performed illegally each year.[16] More adequate supplies of reliable contraceptives form another major concern. At present, diaphragms come in only three sizes, and it is almost impossible to get condoms and spermicidal cream.

The problem of safe abortions and available contraceptives reflect more than a troubled economy. But little has been made of these sexual and other gendered aspects of consumer problems. Perestroika was limited to the economic side of consumerism, even though many of the problems were derivative of gender issues: the scarcity of labor-saving devices for the household; long queues creating extensive time spent shopping; a shortage of most consumer items; children's nurseries being ill equipped and scarce. Many of these consumer issues directly affect and reflect the sex and gender systems of society. And they in part constitute what Gorbachev called the "decay of family life." But instead of restructuring the economy in terms of the needs of women's lives and their families, the Soviet state wanted to refocus woman on her role at home.[17] Part of the problem here is that as woman is redirected toward the home, the home will not be liberalized or democratized. Whatever restructuring there will be will take place in the economy.

There will most probably be an increase in the gender segregation of the labor force and a renewed interest in woman as mother. Woman will be freed from her "involuntary emancipation" and be allowed to return to her family. But this is the old vision of patriarchal democracy, harkening back to eighteenth-century France and J. J. Rousseau. In the process of newly rejecting totalitarian communism, patriarchal gender relations have been rearticulated in old ways.

In Gorbachev's *Perestroika,* his plan for "restructuring" Soviet society, he stated that women have been given "the same right to work as men, equal pay for equal work, and social security. Women have been given every opportunity to get an education, to have a career, and to participate in social and political activities." He did not compare the theory with Soviet practice. Instead, he said that "we have failed to pay attention to women's 'specific' rights and needs arising from their role as mother and homemaker, and their indispensable educational function as regards children." He said that women do not have enough time for their special domestic and familial roles. He blamed the slackening of family ties on "making woman equal with men in everything." Perestroika meant returning women to "their purely womanly mission."[18] Gorbachev therefore legislated, beginning with the five-year plan in 1991, an extra six months of tenured but unpaid maternity leave.

There seems to be a real variety among former Soviet women in responses to these issues. Surveys have shown that many rural women prefer to work and show little interest in leading domestic lives.[19] Other studies show that professional women find their work, along with their children, to be the most important aspects of their lives. Yet according to Tatyana Tolstaya and Francine du Plessix Gray, women do not want to work.[20] Given the political context one can understand the representation as such. But it is not clear that these authors sort out the issues clearly enough. They lump all Soviet women into one, while lumping Western feminisms together similarly in a homogeneous presentation of early liberal feminism à la Betty Friedan: that women want the right to work and to not be relegated to the home.[21] Actually, there is much more similarity than difference between the two societies today in this realm.

Václav Havel, playwright and former dissident, came to represent as president of Czechoslovakia the "democratic" spirit of the revolutions throughout Eastern Europe. But exactly for "whom" was his democracy intended? He has been a searing critic of the totalitarian state and its destruction of people's inner self. His distrust of the state leads to his "antipolitical" stance on politics: individuals must know and trust themselves rather than political ideology. His critique, however, remains male-defined. Although one is free to extend his radical indictment of totalitarian statism to the realms of patriarchal family and private life, he does not do so. What is needed is not a mere extension of his critiques to the lives of women but a reinvention of democratic theory that does not focus merely on the economy.

Havel argues that today totalitarianism is no longer the enemy. Instead it is "our own bad qualities" that we are left with. His presidential program therefore focused on bringing "spirituality," "moral responsibility," "humaneness," and "humility" into politics and by doing so making clear "that there is something higher above us."[22] His focus is on the individual, as well as a higher order: God alone can serve us.[23] There is an uneasy mix of liberal individualism and religiosity here, and it raises the question of the place of religion in Havel's "antipolitical" politics.

Havel is committed to economic democracy. Capitalism is no simple answer for him: "enormous private multinational corporations are curiously like socialist states."[24] Anonymous unaccountable bureaucracies exist in both economic systems. Rather, economic units must be set up to continually renew their relationships with individuals. Havel subscribes to the open competition for power as the only real guarantee of public control. He prefers "small enterprises that respect the specific nature of different localities and different traditions that resist the pressures of uniformity by maintaining a plurality of modes of ownership and economic decision making."[25] This sounds good too. However, historically, traditional patriarchal families usually exist alongside small business economies. The query remains: are Havel's individuals men and women, or just men?

His construction of post-totalitarian democracy privileges the universal over the specific: the state represented "special interests." But in rejecting state totalitarianism, democratic theory needs to recognize that the universal condition is never just that. Socialist theory assumes that the proletariat represented the universal needs of humanity. Liberal theory assumes the universalist stance of rights. However, there are specific needs that must be recognized within the proletariat, between individuals, between men and women, between ethnic factions and religious groups, between different races. Universalism does not ensure democracy; it merely promises that it is so.

Havel's vision of democracy focused on and privileged the economy as the arena of democracy. Democracy requires that relations "between man and his coworkers, between subordinates and their superiors, between man and his work" do not lose sight of the personal connection.[26] What of women and their work? And what of the relations defining the place of work to the home, and the relations of men and women to these spheres and to each other? Can we assume that Havel's critique of privilege extends to male privilege? Can we assume that when Havel argued that everyone should, as much as possible, have the same chances in life, that he included women in this viewing? Or does the bearing of children, or domestic responsibilities, define her options differently?

Havel calls for democracy in the market. But for whom exactly? And what does he call for in the family? He argues that there is a higher order of religion that should constrain all politics. But religion has hardly been a democratic friend of women, as seen in Poland.

When we explore more carefully the imagery of gender in Havel's writing, his commitment to democracy for women becomes more troublesome. One worries that women are not just forgotten in his "post-totalitarian" thoughts, but that a post-patriarchal construction of democracy is not what Havel had in mind for Czechoslovakia.[27]

In discussing his criticism of the Warsaw Pact and NATO Havel said that United States troops should not be separated from their mothers forever. Why not speak of parents in this instance? When speaking of the difficulty of life, he stated that today the problems cannot be solved by, as it were, "running away from Mommy."[28]

Havel's representation of woman was generally as a mother, not as an individual. He relied on "the" mother as an inevitable construction, and engenders it as such. What about fathers or the non–sexually specified "parent"?

Havel's langauge and imagery remind one that he was not thinking about women as part of his polity. He only wrote about men, naming them as "men." He wrote of moral "impotence" and the "castration" of culture.[29] It is men who can be impotent, or castrated. I do not think he is a post-patriarchal democrat.

Havel's brief thoughts on feminism are unsettling and troubling. When a group of Italian feminists visited Prague seeking women's signatures to a petition claiming "respect of human rights, disarmament, demilitarization, etc.," Havel received them with disdain. He stated that he did not mean to ridicule feminism, because "he knows little about it," and "assumes that it is not merely the invention of a few hysterics, bored housewives, or rejected mistresses." Yet he nonetheless stated, "in our country even though the position of women is incomparably worse than in the West, feminism seems simply 'dada.' "[30]

As long as feminism remains thought of as "dada", the struggle toward "real" democracy will be much harder. Totalitarianism and statism cannot be fully dismantled without addressing the unquestioned patriarchal privileging of men in the state, the economy, and the home. Democracy must be formulated for family life as well as the market if it is to have real meaning for everyday life. Formulations of democratic theory for the 1990s must make this clear: women are individuals with specific rights that require the retheorization of democracy through sexual, racial, religious, and gender relations. Existing liberal democratic and socialist theories of sexual equality are insufficient. Women's specialness must be recognized in a nondiscriminatory context.

Feminism and Eastern Europe

Although there is little agreement about what exactly feminism is or its appropriate role in creating post-patriarchal democracy between women in the Czech and the Slovak Republics, the United Germany, or the former Soviet Union, there are feminist voices to be heard. The feminist challenge now is to address a radicalized democracy that unsettles the gendered structures of statist socialism and "free" markets. The new imaginings involve a critique not merely of socialist theory but of the practice of statist socialism. And the critique of capitalism is threaded through an uneasy embrace of liberal individualist rights discourse. The outcome will not be socialism or capitalism, and it will not be simply "post-totalitarianism," although it will remain defined in part by each.

In this mix of ideas—socialism, capitalism, liberalism, democracy—feminist theory and politics become crucial. Feminist theory, even in its liberal democratic version, recognizes the importance of individual identity within the collectivity. A feminist must recognize the collective category of woman in order to identify an individual woman within it. With feminism as the starting point for democratic theory we start from the tension between individuality and collectivity, instead of from the false starts of one or the other.

I distinguish here between a liberal individualism that pictures an atomized and disconnected person in competition with others from a post-patriarchal individuality that recognizes the capacities and diversity of individuals as a part of a community that can either enhance or constrain their development.[31] The individual is no longer seen as separate and disconnected from others, although the individual is a distinct reality always to be reckoned with in terms of the endless choices at hand, and this is best accomplished when equity exists.

There is an individual character to our social nature, and a social nature to our individual character. The individual and the collectivity need not be seen as oppositions, but they must be seen as distinct. Because liberal Western feminism requires the recognition of woman's life as part of a sexed/gendered class, however implicit and unformulated this understanding may be, feminism lays the basis for the move beyond liberal patriarchal individualism.[32] Conceptually, liberal feminism and with it the feminism of women of color move beyond individualism, because they recognize the collective reality of sexual class and racial oppression. And yet feminism cannot leave the individual behind, or subsume her to the needs of the group, because there will always be at least one woman who will need the right to decide for herself whether to bear a child or not. What better check could there be for ensuring democracy?

Sex equality, specifically for women of color, means treating women like the individuals they are. And this demands the struggle for racial equality as well. It requires that women enjoy their universal human rights, as men shall, but that they also enjoy the capacities that are unique to them. That means that women will have rights that men will not have—like the right to abortion, to prenatal care, to tampons. This necessitates a post-socialist and post-capitalist democracy that is no longer patriarchal or racist. As such, it moves closer to democracy. And this time it would be "new."

Notes

*   I want to thank Miriam Brody, Mary Fainsod Katzenstein, and Rosalind Pollack Petchesky for their helpful reading and commenting on an earlier draft. I also very much want to thank Hilda Scott for her extraordinary generosity in helping me make contact with several Czech feminists and scholars. And I also want to thank Florence Howe, Mariam Chamberlain of the National Council for Research on Women, Debbie Rogow of the International Women's Health Coalition, and Elizabeth L. Gardiner, for all their help in locating information for me.

1.   Karl Marx and Friedrich Engels, *The German Ideology* (New York: International, 1947).

2.   Karl Marx, *The Economic and Philosophic Manuscripts of 1844* (New York: International, 1964).

3. For a more developed discussion of this point, see my *Radical Future of Liberal Feminism* (New York: Longman, 1981) and *The Female Body and the Law* (Berkeley: University of California Press, 1988).

4. Zillah Eisenstein, "Specifying U.S. Feminisms in the Nineties: The Problem of Naming," *Socialist Review* 20, no. 2 (April–June 1990), p. 55. Also see Carol Lee Bacchi, *Same Difference: Feminism and Sexual Difference* (London: Allen & Unwin, 1990); and Diana Fuss, *Essentially Speaking: Feminism, Nature and Difference* (New York: Routledge, 1989).

5. See C. B. MacPherson, *Democratic Theory, Essays in Retrieval* (Oxford: Clarendon, 1973), and his classic *The Political Theory of Possessive Individualism, Hobbes to Locke* (London: Oxford University Press, 1962).

6. See my *Radical Future of Liberal Feminism;* and Carole Pateman, *The Disorder of Women* (Stanford: Stanford University Press, 1989).

7. Hilda Scott, *Does Socialism Liberate Women? Experiences from Eastern Europe* (Boston: Beacon, 1974). Also see her "Why the Economics of 'Real' Socialism," *Women's Studies International Forum* 5, no. 5 (1982): 451–462.

8. Nanette Funk et al., "Dossier on Women in Eastern Europe," *Social Text* 9, no. 2 (1990): 88.

9. Ruth Rosen, "Male Democracies, Female Dissidents," *Tikkun* (November–December 1990), p. 11. Also see Celeste Bohlen, "East Europe's Women Struggle With New Rules, and Old Ones," *New York Times,* November 25, 1990, p. E1; and interviews with Anna Bojarska of Poland, pp. 4–6; Helke Misselwitz of East Germany, pp. 6–7; and Tatiana Shcherbina of the Soviet Union, p. 8; *Women's Review of Books* (July 1990).

10. Rosen, p. 101.

11. Genia Browning, *Women and Politics in the U.S.S.R.* (New York: St. Martin's, 1987).

12. Maxine Molyneux, "The 'Woman Question' in the Age of Perestroika," *New Left Review* (September–October, 1990), p. 29. Also see her "Socialist Societies Old and New: Progress Towards Women's Emancipation," *Feminist Review,* no. 8 (Summer 1981).

13. Katrina vanden Heuvel, "Glasnost for Women," *Nation,* June 4, 1990, p. 773.

14. See Natalya Baranskaya, *A Week Like Any Other: Novellas and Stories* (Seattle: Seal Press, 1989) for a compelling description of everyday life for Soviet women.

15. See A. G. Khomassuridze, "Abortion and Contraception in Georgia," *From Abortion to Contraception,* TBILISI, 10–13, October 1990.

16. Parker, Inside the Collapsing Soviet Economy," *The Atlantic,* June 1990, p. 70.

17. Molyneux, pp. 28–30.

18. Mikhail Gorbachev, *Perestroika: New Thinking for our Country and the World* (New York: Harper & Row, 1987), p. 103.

19. Susan Bridger, *Women in the Soviet Countryside* (New York: Cambridge University Press, 1987), p. 225. Also see Mary Buckley, *Women and Ideology in the Soviet*

Union (Ann Arbor: University of Michigan Press, 1989); and Ellen Carnaghan and Donna Bahry, "Political Attitudes and the Gender Gap in the U.S.S.R.: Evidence from Former Soviet Citizens," *Working Paper #53* (October 1988), Soviet Interview Project, University of Illinois at Urbana-Champaign.

20. Tatyana Tolstaya, "Notes from Underground," *New York Review of Books,* May 31, 1990; and Francine du Plessix Gray, *Soviet Women: Walking the Tightrope* (New York: Doubleday, 1989).

21. Betty Friedan, *The Feminine Mystique* (New York: Dell, 1963). See her later *The Second Stage* (New York: Summit, 1981) for a rebuttal of her earlier stance equating paid work with equality.

22. Václav Havel, "The Future of Central Europe," *New York Review of Books,* March 29, 1990, p. 19. Also see his "History of a Public Enemy," *New York Review of Books,* May 31, 1990, pp. 36–44 and "The New Year in Prague," *New York Review of Books,* March 7, 1991, pp. 19–20. Also see Timothy Garton Ash, "The Revolution of the Magic Lantern," *New York Review of Books,* January 18, 1990, pp. 42–51; Philip Roth, "A Conversation in Prague," *New York Review of Books,* April 12, 1990, pp. 14–22; and Vit Horejs and Bonnie Stein, "The New King of Absurdistan," *Village Voice,* January 16, 1990, pp. 31–35.

23. Václav Havel, *Living in Truth* (Boston: Faber & Faber, 1989), p. 117.

24. Václav Havel, *Disturbing the Peace* (New York: Alfred A. Knopf, 1990), p. 14.

25. Ibid., p. 16.

26. Ibid., p. 13.

27. Alena Heitlinger, in personal correspondence with me, wonders how I can expect Havel to be a feminist within the present cultural context of Czechoslovakia: March 3, 1991.

28. As quoted in Jefferson Morley, "Mr. Havel Goes to Washington," *Nation,* March 19, 1990, p. 375.

29. Havel, *Living in Truth,* p. 23.

30. Ibid., p. 180.

31. See my *The Radical Future of Liberal Feminism,* p. 114.

32. Ibid., pp. 191–192.

29

Feminism East and West[1]

Nanette Funk

Slavenka Drakulić, a writer from Zagreb, recently wrote an essay about an American woman who had interviewed her and later wrote asking Drakulić to submit an article on women in Yugoslavia for an anthology the American was putting together. Drakulić laughed at the topics proposed in the letter, such as an "analysis about women and democracy, the public sphere, civil society, modernization, etc. A kind of Critical Theory approach." Drakulić was asked specifically about "the kinds of interventions women have made in the public discourse, e.g., about abortion, women's control over their bodies, what sorts of influence women have had in the public discourse . . . "[2] Drakulić regarded all these questions as inappropriate, reflecting the typical American misunderstanding of post-communist women. She was also annoyed at the American woman's ease and readiness to publish about post-communist women after she just "spent several weeks in Berlin."[3] And she was critical, if at points grudgingly complimentary, about the American women's persona, clothes, and hair, calling her "surprisingly, [for an American feminist, presumably] dressed with style."[4]

One can only imagine the reactions of that American woman upon reading this account. Well, not quite, since I am that American woman. I wrote that letter and the invitation was to contribute to this volume, which Slavenka Drakulić did. My reaction was only made more bitter by my desire to speak to my past, to my mother and grandmother, and all the women in my family who as Jewish women from Central and Eastern Europe and the former Soviet Union had suffered, as women as well as Jews, in those societies. I was hurt, outraged, and angry, reactions exaggerated by reading the chapter while in a hospital bed in a bitterly cold and drafty room on one of the coldest days of the year, bringing to mind the

---

I want to thank Linda Nicholson and Robert Roth for reading an earlier version of this draft and for their cooperation and many helpful comments and suggestions.

conditions in Moscow hospitals I had read about. Except that I was in one of the "better" hospitals in New York.

Yet I began to reflect on this interaction. Were Slavenka Drakulić's essay and my reaction only individual responses, they would not be significant. But they are symptomatic of the risks, tensions, and difficulties inherent in discourse between Eastern and Western women. In many post-communist countries contact between Eastern and Western women has only been sporadic, and the tensions have arisen only in individual instances and outbursts. But in Germany, where there is a direct confrontation between East and West, these difficulties have become systemic, playing havoc with the possibility of joint action and even dialogue between East and West German women, and causing tremendous bitterness and suspicion on both sides. It is therefore worthwhile to analyze what underlies such tensions.

I.

First, Slavenka Drakulić's comments reflect the tensions arising from the real structural power and economic imbalances between Eastern and Western women and the societies of which they are a part. In this particular case that imbalance means that publishing in the West potentially brings greater recognition and financial benefits than publishing in the East, and that some Western women will have greater access to that publishing world than most Eastern women. Paradoxically, the opposite was true in this case; this publishing project gave a voice to post-communist women, and did not speak for them.[5] Nor is it true that Western women generally, even professional women, have such ready access to publishing.

Second, because the East is being *incorporated* into the West, both the power and status hierarchies as well as an individual's sense of worth, status, and social respect are undergoing severe dislocation. Those who are among the most respected, sometimes deservedly so, as in the case of Slavenka Drakulić, have to insert themselves in a world that plays by somewhat different rules, has different standards, and already comes complete with its own status and power hierarchies. In Germany this has resulted in strong public attacks on the literary merits of the most renowned East German writers, mainly women, including the well-known author Christa Wolf. Resentments toward the West accumulate on the part of post-communist women and form the background for their meetings with Western women.

Power imbalances also exist at the level of discourse, where Western feminist discourse is hegemonic in feminism, risking the suppression and distortion of post-communist women's concerns. Western women, in speaking their own language of feminism, do risk imposing standards of discourse, as I did, provoking intellectual and political resentment, and sometimes shattering the possibilities of political cooperation, as has happened in Germany. Some questions that Western women pose are indeed inappropriate. Yet in this case the questions proposed in that letter to Drakulić became the themes of fascinating essays by post-communist women themselves.[6]

In addition, since Western standards of style, dress, and cosmetics are being imposed on post-communist women, these are the standards that Eastern women aspire to, or are being judged by, not the reverse. Faced with these structural differences Eastern women are at times resentful or self-conscious. Ina Merkel of the former GDR expressed initial feelings of insecurity at being judged by West German standards, seeing herself, her body, and her dress, suddenly quite differently and more critically through a West German lens.[7] This is one of the many reasons that in Berlin, where the confrontation between East and West is so direct, Eastern women prefer not to venture into West Berlin, but stay behind the Wall that once was. Although it is true that Western women may have more wealth, affordable access to Western clothes, and greater experience in dealing with these standards, this is not true for all Western women—not even all professional women. In many cases, defensiveness, resentment, and retaliation are the response by post-communist women, again constrained by the need to accommodate themselves to the new hierarchies into which they are plunged.

Western women can be insensitive and oblivious to all these structural inequalities. They can also be arrogant in assuming that, after twenty years of a Western women's movement, they know best the "real women's issues" or "what is to be done" politically and individually. These are attitudes ex-GDR women frequently confront in West German women.

Discourse between East and West is also pervaded by negative stereotypes on both sides: of American and Western feminists as "man-haters" or of post-communist women as simply having bought into sexism and having subordinated themselves to the family. The reaction by Drakulić, in which she presumed a Western woman's ignorance of Eastern Europe or a certain style of dress for American feminists, reveals the operation of just such stereotypes and how they can be mistaken in a particular case.[8]

In addition, there are tremendous differences in culture,[9] socialization, and personality between Eastern and Western women, and in what Habermas has referred to as the "lifeworld," that stock taken for granted of unreflected beliefs and world views. All these differences create tensions and hostility and harden into prejudices, which have provoked confrontations and fractured meetings between Western and Eastern women, especially in the united Germany. Women in state socialist countries appear to be more oriented than Western feminists toward children and the family, have different attitudes toward the individual and the collective and to authority, are more skeptical of the benefits of paid work, and have different attitudes toward men or toward collective action. Language itself is a contested issue, as illustrated by West German women's resentment of

East German women's use of male grammatical nouns to refer to all persons, a form of speech that West German women had struggled hard to overcome.

In the face of all these differences, there is a tremendous risk of misunderstanding. In particular, there is a risk of Western women's moralistic rejection of post-communist cultural differences. This moralism can be predicated on a lack of understanding of the meaning and origin of these practices[10]—such as the fact that a family orientation in state socialism provided an escape from state control. Western moralism itself risks provoking a resentment and defensiveness and hardened suspicion toward Western women as "know-it-alls."[11]

Post-communist women also do not want to be dominated by the priorities of Western women, or to be swamped by debates among Western feminists that do not resonate for them. East German women already have resentments on such issues as well as toward the ignorance and lack of understanding West German women have of their lives, their daily problems, their present and past.

U.S. women like myself who are particularly concerned about Eastern European women often bring our own agenda, especially the ever-present consciousness of the Holocaust, to our dealings with Eastern Europe. We are often Jewish women confronting our own identity, our families' Eastern European and Russian heritage, and our own experiences of Eastern European patriarchy and the strengths and weaknesses of women in our families. This complex history provides Jewish women with both an empathy and identification with post-communist women and a concern about their relationship to cultures in which there was, and still is, strong anti-Semitism.

As women wanting to work together, our goal should be to lessen our prejudices, ignorance, and mutual suspicions, and to come to judgments in ways that make possible cooperation between women. One cannot enter a dialogue between Eastern and Western women without expecting disagreement, misunderstanding, and mistakes. Drakulić's comments reveal the need for a dialogue regarded as a joint enterprise directed toward understanding each other, rather than a battle to prove the other wrong. Rather than being a threat, our differences should be seen as an opportunity for mutual and collective self-reflection.

II.

However, given all these differences, one is confronted with the question of whether a fruitful and meaningful dialogue is at all possible, whether Western feminism's issues, claims and goals can be anything other than "relative," appropriate in the West but not in the East. An argument that might be made would go roughly as follows: "Eastern women want something different from western women. They want to return to the home and leave the paid work force. Western women cannot engage in an authoritarian form of cultural imperialism telling Eastern women what to desire. Eastern women have different cultural and historical backgrounds and different values from Western women. Paid work may be emancipatory and a goal of feminism in the West, but not in the East. A women's movement in the East will confront different issues, have different values, demands and goals."

In what follows I want to reject such an argument while acknowledging that it contains partial truths. I will argue that in spite of the differences between Eastern and Western women's desires and among Eastern women themselves, Eastern and Western women have much in common and women's movements East and West can share many concerns, values and goals. The preceding argument, I will argue, misinterprets the desires of post-communist women, the relationship between women's desires, and the goals of a woman's movement, as well as the goals of Western feminism. I will begin my examination by first considering the reasons post-communist women give for their desires and the values that underlie those reasons. I will focus particularly on the purported post-communist women's desire not to be in the paid labor force. The goals of women's movements East and West, it will be shown, should be similar in many ways. I will then relate this discussion to the transformation of the public and private spheres in post-communism.

1.

Post-communist women's reasons for not wanting to work in the paid labor force fall into three categories: a cost-benefit analysis in which the price of paid work is too high; a greater concern for the collective family good over their own individual benefit; and an essentialist position that women's nature is different from men's, that women's nature is to be in the home.

In some post-communist countries one set of reasons predominates over others. In the former East Germany the third set of reasons appears to play a rather minor role, while it may play a stronger one in some Slavophil traditions in the former Soviet Union. In all of these rationales we can find various degrees of commonality with Western women's desires and with feminist values, in spite of the differences that may appear on the surface.

Women's desire to leave paid work depends most commonly on an implicit cost-benefit analysis. The reasoning seems to be as follows: the double burden of work and family responsibilities threatens mental and physical health and well-being (by producing exhaustion, fatigue, stress, and sickness); the long work days threaten intersubjective needs by restricting chances to be with one's family;[12] paid work requires "gender alienation," having to be "like a man"; although paid work can be meaningful, it is all too often boring and absurd and provides only limited autonomy, given low salaries. Certainly, paid work provides some benefits and satisfactions, such as friendship, solidarity, relief from boredom at home, some economic goods, and a degree of respect and autonomy. Yet in spite of these benefits, the harm it generates is above any acceptable threshold.

One immediately recognizes that this is a form of reasoning very common in the West. Further, women who reach such a conclusion (and these by no means include the majority of post-communist women) appeal to the very same qualities to which Western feminists appeal: health and well-being, respect and self-respect, dignity, self-realization, self-determination, autonomy, freedom, and justice. Relations with family are one way of trying to satisfy intersubjective needs, even when those relations are distorted by oppressive structures. One can hardly have respect and self-respect if work requires one to be "like a man". But this does not provide justification for claiming that the cost-benefit rationale reveals a *basic* difference in Eastern and Western goals, forms of reasoning, or values. Rather, the assessment of costs and benefits are different, both because of different circumstances and different expectations. This does not justify a claim that Eastern women's movements must be fundamentally different from Western feminist ones.

There are, however, those post-communist women who in such a cost-benefit analysis would give greater priority than do Western women or Western feminists to the intersubjective goal of being with children and activities in the home. But if one considers the reasons for this, it will be seen that this, too, does not provide grounds for assuming irreconcilable differences or fundamentally different priorities.

The emphasis on family pleasures by some Eastern women reflects that under state socialism, women and men had more possibilities to experience some small degree of satisfaction in the home than elsewhere. One couldn't travel; there were limited "leisure-time" activities and virtually no public sphere. Options outside the home were regularly blocked. The home was thus preferable to some women, in spite of the oppression within the home itself. It is not that being with one's family was necessarily of greater *intrinsic* worth than other goods, but that some women's expectations (even if illusory) for realizing *this* good were greater than those for any other good. Women especially turned to their children as a source of meaning.[13] The family also became the substitute arena for activities that in the West might be found in the public sphere. For example, it was here that one could more safely discuss social, cultural, and political issues. Rather than being the antithesis of the public sphere, the family became an ersatz public sphere.[14] Eastern women also used their commitments to the family as a strategy to sidestep participation in the discredited political system.

Jointly, all this vividly shows how fully the public/private distinction is not fixed and ahistorical. The fundamental dichotomy in state socialism was, in fact, between the family and state. The family thus had a very special and powerful status as the primary institution that stood in opposition to the state. Women who wanted to be in the "private" sphere wanted something different than what would be meant by a Western woman's orientation toward the family.

Women's interest in the family under these particular social and political conditions thus does not indicate an intrinsic difference between Eastern and

Western values but a difference in the historically specific social meaning of the family. Under such complex conditions, where there was more possibility for freedom in the family than elsewhere, Western women would also give more attention to the family. In addition, in the United States, there has been an emphasis among feminists in the 1980s on family and children, and on the tensions between work and the family. This renewed emphasis, however problematic, raises questions about whether the difference in actual desires between U.S. women and post-communist women is very great.

Post-communist women cannot, however, always be construed as rejecting paid work on the basis of an implicit cost-benefit analysis, with its presuppositions of weighing individual goods. In some cases they reject an emphasis on their own individual good in favor of a collective end,[15] such as the good of their children and family. But here, too, to draw a conclusion that the goals of post-communist women's movements must be basically different from those in the West or that the form of reasoning is radically different is not warranted.

To the extent that this emphasis on the collective good indicates an undervaluation of the lives of women, this is the very issue the women's movement confronted in the West. It does not indicate any basic difference between the two cultures. An Eastern women's movement would not have to give legitimacy to this underestimation of the worth of women's lives any more than did the Western women's movement.

But the lesser emphasis on the individual good may also be due to a traditional culture and half-modernized state socialist culture that did not place such great value on the individual and individual autonomy. This value, however, as well as the actual individual/collective relationship, is presently undergoing transformation, and reevaluation in the East. For very different reasons, the individual/collective relationship is also under revision, if only gradually, in the West. Greater attention in the West is beginning to be given to collective goods such as the environment and, in the feminist movement, the value of autonomy is being reexamined and greater importance is being attached to relational goods. Even more attention needs to be given to these issues in the future. Neither culture is so inflexible and fixed on this issue that one can conclude they are irrevocably committed to fundamentally different values. It rather suggests that both East and West women would benefit from further reflection on these topics.

Thus, whatever the cause, the emphasis on the collective good does not entail the Eastern and Western women have *fundamentally* different values or that there must be a fundamentally different orientation of Eastern and Western women's movements.

What, then, of post-communist women who reject paid work because of an essentialist belief that it is women's nature to be in the home? Doesn't this provide evidence that there are fundamental differences between East and West? Although it is a problem many women who adopt this form of essentialism often do so to argue that women should not be forced, either politically or economically, to enter paid work. They do not want the role of woman simply to be modeled on the male role; they want the role of homemaker to provide a legitimate alternative for women. Women who offer both essentialist and cost-benefit rationales often express their underlying desire as the desire to have a *choice* of whether to stay in paid work or not, in stark contrast to the situation in many state socialist countries. Clearly, there are strong gender-role presuppositions in speaking of such a "choice" for women. But a women's movement can recognize this desire by acknowledging that, indeed, women's role should not be modeled on men's, and that women who want to return to the home should not be castigated when society offers women only second-class positions in the paid work force, a double burden, and no meaningful position in the political sphere.

In addition, a meaningful "choice" between paid work and remaining in the home requires the social policy and structural conditions—in the home, in gender roles, at the workplace, in the labor market—that would enable women to do *either*, to stay home or not. Such a choice requires adequate day care and the absence of institutional discrimination against women in employment. But these are the same concrete demands made by Western feminism.

However, a post-communist women's movement does not have to adopt this essentialism and incorporate all women's desires into its program and advocate that women should leave the paid work force. In general, one has to distinguish between the desires some women may have, and the desires it would be appropriate for a women's movement in each country to advocate. Not to make this distinction would be to adopt a version of an unacceptable "subjective welfarism," stating that the welfare and emancipation of women is defined as a satisfaction of all women's present subjective desires. Feminism is not committed to such a position and is not necessarily representative of all women's desires, since it recognizes that existing desires have been constituted under problematic conditions. Desires formed under the absence of conditions of free and open discourse, or in the absence of consideration of relevant issues, whether in the West or the East, can hardly have the same status as those desires and beliefs women would be likely to have after fuller discussion. Moreover, a women's movement recognizes that new socioeconomic conditions demand new perspectives,[16] and that women's desires and beliefs are likely to change because of these rapidly changing conditions. To recognize all this is not to dictate to women what their real needs are, creating a "dictatorship over needs." The women's movement instead would create a forum for women and encourage their participation in a discourse to form these new perspectives.

Thus, whatever reason post-communist women have for wanting to leave the paid workforce, it does not reflect an irreconcilable difference between Eastern and Western values; it does not mean Eastern and Western women's movements must have different goals.

2.

It is important to note that women's increasing unemployment has not been a matter of choice.[17] Given recent projections of vast unemployment in the former USSR and projecting from the available data on unemployed women in which women make up almost two-thirds of the unemployed in several countries (such as the former East Germany) unemployment will be overwhelmingly *forced* on women. Removal of women from the labor market is one means post-communist societies are using, whether passively or actively, for the quasi-modernization under way to replace a state patriarchy with a Western form of male domination, to deal with unemployment, and to redefine the social role women. Women themselves, are not being asked.

Women might prefer to be able to choose whether or not to work, but it doesn't follow that they are *now* choosing not to work. To have the choice not to work they would have to be in stable marriages with husbands with stable jobs making a family wage. However, nothing is stable in post-communism, and *none* of these conditions generally hold.[18] The economic necessity to work, the despondency at being unemployed, all form evidence that unemployment is not a choice. Many women are single mothers or are in unstable marriages, given 30 to 40 percent divorce rates. If they have husbands, the husbands are often unemployed or inadequately compensated, and more than two jobs in a family are often necessary for survival, as in Hungary or Poland.

Many women also stay home because day care is closing, conditions are poor, or children are disoriented by the massive social transformation. Since the woman is more likely to be unemployed or making a lower salary than the man, it often makes economic sense for her to stay at home. Here, of course, there is a parallel to the West. Discrimination in hiring plays a major role in women's unemployment.

There is also the simple question of whether women, in any of the senses discussed above, actually want to return to the home. In many countries there is no reliable data about this, and it most likely varies between countries and social classes. Where surveys have been done, as in the former GDR,[19] Soviet Union, and Bulgaria,[20] only a small percentage of women say they would want to return to the home, even if they could afford to do so. In addition, Eastern women often do not want to leave the paid labor force completely, but to work "part-time" when they have children under three, where "part-time" can include a virtually full-time day according to Western standards (since the state socialist work day was typically eight and a half hours a day).[21]

III.

What is clear is that post-communism not only involves a transformation of the public sphere, but also a transformation of the family, the boundaries between the public and private sphere, and the nature of the private sphere. Such transformations require fundamental normative changes. Women's position is central to, and symbolic of, all these changes. As the family loses the special significance it had under state socialism, women are more restricted to the family, and excluded from the new public sphere as it grows in importance. Modernization has, historically, often been harmful to women.[22] One cost of the rationalization and modernization now going on is the sacrifice of women's well-being, much as occurred under communist rationalization.

Any analytic social theory of the transformation in post-communism needs to pay special attention to the family, its changed meaning, the transformation of the role of women and the way in which women's authentic participation in a newly forming public sphere could change the very nature of practices in the public sphere itself. Unfortunately this is not the case in the theory most frequently used to analyze post-communism, the theory of post-communism as the formation of civil society. In contrast to the Eastern European proponents of this theory, Western advocates of civil society theory—John Keane, Klaus Offe, Karl Hinrichs, Helmut Wiesenthal,[24] and Jean Cohen and Andrew Arato—do at least mention the family and include it in civil society. But even here, as exemplified by Cohen and Arato's extensively developed theory of civil society, the transformation of the family plays at best a minor role in the discussion. Although Cohen and Arato include the family in civil society, they discuss it infrequently and say that "we make the public spheres of societal communication and voluntary association the central institutions of civil society."[25] They do not ever raise the issue whether the political forms of the public sphere may themselves be more amenable to men than to women.

Cohen and Arato, and other civil society theorists, distinguish civil society from the economic system. By placing the family within civil society, they thereby distinguish the family from the economy. Although the family is not regulated solely by the economic consequences of actions, such a distinction between civil society and the economy seriously risks underemphasizing the way in which economic processes, considerations, and consequences do significantly regulate actions in civil society and the family in particular. Family and individual decisions—that one must work to have individual goods, or that the heterosexual, two-parent family will live where the man works because of his higher salary and greater job opportunities—are economically regulated decisions fundamental to many other family decisions. The problem of too sharply distinguishing the family from the economic reveals the general problem of the distinction between civil society and the economy.

IV. Conclusion

None of the above discussion should be interpreted as denying real cultural differences East and West and among post-communist countries themselves.

What I have argued is that in spite of the differences in tradition, culture, personality, beliefs and desires there is much in common between Eastern and Western women's issues and goals and in particular, in regard to the issue of paid work. Contemporary women's programs East and West will differ because of economic, political, and cultural differences. What a women's movement will demand will of course depend on the reconstituted socioeconomic system— whether in Romania or Bulgaria it will be an agricultural society, for example. In spite of cultural differences, the problematics are similar: Women's right to abortion, the right to jobs, and prevention of rape and violence against women are becoming important women's issues in post-communist women's movements as they have in the West. The issue of respect for sexual preference is beginning, however tentatively, to be raised in some countries.

Moreover, post-communist women's articulation of their desires and resentments about work can help to strengthen the paradigm of the employed woman for the women's movement in the West. Given the greater participation of women in the work force in the West compared to thirty years ago when the second-wave women's movement started, there is, in fact, similarity between Eastern and Western women's needs. Western women, now overwhelmingly in the work force, confront the same tensions as do post-communist women. Post-communist women's concerns should reinforce for Western feminism that work *simpliciter* is not the goal. Rather, a feminist demand must be for meaningful work in a rationally organized, humane society that reconciles the importance of the collective good and intersubjective needs of all persons with the instrumental needs of society. Work must be organized accordingly, for all persons while preserving justice.

The problems Eastern women confront in the conservative turn in some Eastern countries or the repressive nationalist threats in others, resonate with problems women face in the West. Post-communist women's critical examination of Western feminism can provide us with fresh insights into our own history and theories.

The paradigmatic "woman" is no longer who she once was in the early second-wave women's movement in the 1960s and 1970s, the white upper middle class woman trapped on the "pedestal" or in a domestic prison. Post-communist developments also make vivid the importance of women's participation in the political public sphere. Post-communist women's needs epitomize second wave feminism, stage two.

There will continue to be many differences, and justifiably so, between women's movements in the East and the West, in methods, strategies, and intermediate goals. But none of that should preclude a fruitful, mutually beneficial dialogue or justify a conclusion of fundamental, irreconcilable differences between East and West women's movements. In spite of all the differences that have come to light between women of the West and the East, which must be kept in mind, there is much that we have in common and much that we can learn from each other.

Notes

1. I use the term "East" in this essay to refer to the former USSR and the countries of the former Eastern bloc, of Eastern and South Central Europe.

2. Slavenka Drakulić, "A Letter from the United States: The Critical Theory Approach," in *How We Survived Communism and Even Laughed* (New York: W. W. Norton, 1992), pp. 126–127.

3. Ibid., p. 126.

4. Ibid.

5. Given that Ms. Drakulić has published extensively in the West, it would have been appropriate to temper such resentment in this case.

6. The posing of questions was itself regarded as part of a free and open dialogue in which the questions themselves could be, and were, challenged, revised, and even rejected.

7. Ina Merkel, . . . *und Du, Frau an der Werkbank: Die DDR in den 50er Jahren* (Berlin: Elephanten Press, 1990), p. 7.

8. I had, in fact, not just gone to Berlin for a few weeks, but had had regular contact in Germany and parts of Eastern Europe for the last twenty years.

9. In Germany the differences even extend to how one takes leave of another person. Former GDR women shake hands, which West German women reject as unduly formal and a practice they rejected in 1968.

10. West German women see these family-oriented practices as the very same ones they had rebelled against in 1968, but they ignore the different cultural meaning these practices had under state socialism.

11. In the former GDR West Germans are ironically referred to as "Besserwessis" ("Those-who-know-better-than-the-rest-of-us-Westerners"). East German women are equally critical of West German culture, regarding West German women as anti-children, or too quickly unsettled by the presence of children.

12. The long work day sometimes required sending children to week-long overnight day care, relatives in the countryside, or almost nine hours each day in day care.

13. See Havelková and Goven in this volume.

14. See Havelková and Lissyutkina in this volume.

15. See Havelková in this volume.

16. See Joshua Cohen, "Maximizing Social Welfare or Institutionalizing Democratic Ideals? Commentary on Adam Przeworski's Article," in *Politics and Society* (March 1991), pp. 39–58.

17. See Nickel in this volume.

18. In some cases, husbands leave women because of the shame of not being able to support the family, leaving the women alone with children. There are also many single parents.

19. In the ex-GDR, when asked if they would give up their jobs if their husbands made

more money, only 3 percent of women said they should (see Nickel, Chap. 13, this volume).

20. See Petrova in this volume.

21. See Nickel in this volume.

22. Krisztina Mänicke-Gyöngyösi, "Frauen Osteuropas zwischen Tradition und Moderne: Eine Einführung," introduction to lecture series, 1991–92, *Frauen und Frauenthemen in der Forschung am Osteuropa-Institut,* Free University, Berlin (unpublished program).

23. Karl Hinrichs, Claus Offe, and Helmut Wiesenthal, "Time, Money and Welfare State Capitalism," in *Civil Society and the State,* ed. John Keane (London: Verso, 1988), p. 226. See also Christopher Pierson, "New Theories of State and Civil Society: Recent Developments in Post-Marxist Analysis of the State," *Sociology* 18, no. 4 (1984): 563–571; and Mihaly Vajda, "East Central European Perspectives," in Keane, *Civil Society and the State,* pp. 330–360.

24. Jean L. Cohen and Andrew Arato, *Civil Society and Political Theory* (Cambridge, Mass.: The MIT Press, 1992), p. 411.

Contributors

Maria Adamik is a sociologist at the EFTE University in Budapest. She is cofounder of the Hungarian Feminist Network and has written on women and Hungarian social policy.

Tatiana Böhm was Minister Without Portfolio in the last German Democratic Republic government, headed by Modrow, and represented the Independent Women's Organization in the Round Table in 1990. She has lectured widely on women and is currently working at the Office of Women in Brandenburg, Germany.

Enikö Bollobás was appointed Minister Counselor and Deputy Chief to the Hungarian Embassy in Washington, D.C., in 1990. Dr. Bollobás was Associate Professor of American Studies at Jozsef Attila University of Szeged and Eotvos Lorand University of Budapest from 1977 to 1990. She has published extensively in Hungarian and internationally. Her professional interests include women's studies, American studies, and Judaism. She has been active in Hungarian opposition politics since the early 1990s, was a founding member of the Hungarian Democratic Forum, and founded the political discussion group "Hungarian Feminists" in 1989.

Irene Dölling is Professor of Cultural Studies at Humboldt University in Berlin (East). She was founder of the Interdisciplinary Center of Women's Studies at Humboldt University in 1989 and is the author of many articles on women and several books, the latest being *Der Mensch und Sein Weib*.

Slavenka Drakulić is a well-known novelist, feminist, and cofounder of the first feminist group in the former Yugoslavia, Women in Society in 1974. She is also a cofounder of the Network of East/West Women, founded in 1991. She has published two novels and two books of essays, one of which is *Deadly Sins of Feminism* (1984). *How We Survived Communism and Even Laughed* and her novel *Holograms of Fear* were published in the United States by W. W. Norton in 1992.

Daša Duhaček, from Belgrade, has taught philosophy in a Belgrade high-school senior class since 1977. She edited a special issue of the journal *Feminists' Views.* She coordinates the Women Studies Initiative in Belgrade. She has translated Western feminist and philosophical texts into Serbo-Croatian.

Zillah Eisenstein is Chairperson of the Department of Politics at Ithaca College. Her most recent book is *The Female Body and the Law* (University of California Press, 1989). This article is part of her book *Reclaiming Democracy: Sex, Race and Rights* (University of California Press).

Etele Farkašová studied philosophy and sociology at Comenius University in Bratislava, where she is a lecturer in philosophy. She has published monographs on theory of knowledge and studies on the relationship between art and science, as well as essays in feminist philosophy with Zuzana Kiczková. She published four books of stories and is a member of the Group of Slovakian Writers.

Nanette Funk is Associate Professor of Philosophy at Brooklyn College, City University of New York. She has written on political philosophy, critical theory, aesthetics, and current affairs in Germany. She has recently done research on women in the former GDR and has written several articles on this topic.

Małgorzata Fuszara is at the Institute of Applied Social Sciences and head of the Center for Socio-Legal Studies on the Situation of Women in Warsaw, Poland. She has a Ph.D. in law and lectures on law and gender. She has published about thirty articles in Polish, English, and German. Her major publication in Polish is *Everyday Conflicts and Ceremonial Justice.*

Raina Gavrilova earned her Ph.D. in History from the University of Sofia, Bulgaria, in 1989. She is Chief Assistant Professor in the Department for Cultural Studies there and was visiting researcher at the Annenberg Institute in Philadelphia for the academic year 1991–92.

Joanna Goven is a graduate student at the University of California at Berkeley, where she is completing her dissertation, "The Anti-Politics of Anti-Feminism: Gender, State and Civil Society in Hungary, 1949–1992." She has done research in Hungarian factories, and her current research interests focus on gender and class in the privatization processes of Eastern Europe.

Anne Hampele was born and lives in Germany (West). She is a graduate student at the Central Institute for Social Science Research of the Free University, in Berlin. She is writing her Ph.D. dissertation on women and the transition in the former GDR, focusing on women and unemployment and the women's movement in the former GDR. She has published several articles in Germany on these topics.

Doina Pasca Harsanyi has a B.A. in French and Romanian Languages and Literature and a M.A. in French Language and Literature from the University of

Timisoara in Romania. She is a researcher at the Center for Humanities, at the University of Timisoara. She was on the Editorial Board and wrote frequently for the journal *Timisoara,* one of the first independent newspapers in Romania. She has done many translations and has lectured widely.

Ewa Hauser is a Polish ethnographer (University of Warsaw) and anthropologist (Johns Hopkins), as well as an associate of the Susan B. Anthony Center for Women's Studies at the University of Rochester. During 1990–91 she served as a consultant on Polish legal reform for the World Bank.

Mariana Hausleitner was born in Romania and has lived in Germany since 1966. She has a Ph.D. in Political Science and History, with a thesis on the topic "The Nationalities Problem in Romania." She does research on Soviet and Eastern European politics and presently teaches history at the East European Institute, the Free University, Berlin. She is active in the Human Rights Committee for Romania and has published several articles on Romania and the Soviet Union.

Hana Havelková is a research fellow of the European Center for Human Rights Education and a lecturer in Ethics at Charles University in Prague. She has written on the Frankfurt School, feminism, and ethics and recently edited *Human Rights, Women and Society* (Prague: ESVLP, 1992). Since April 1992 she has been a member of the Board of the International Association of Women Philosophers.

Alena Heitlinger is Professor of Sociology at Trent University in Peterborough, Ontario. She was born in Czechoslovakia, which she left in 1968. She has published extensively on women's issues, health care, the family, and population dynamics in Eastern Central Europe. She is the author of *Women and State Socialism* and *Reproduction, Medicine and the Socialist State.*

Barbara Heyns is a Professor of Sociology at New York University and Director of the Colloquia on Social Change in East Central Europe. She lived in Warsaw from 1990 to 1992.

Zuzana Kiczková studied philosophy and German in Comenius University in Bratislava in the Slovak Republic where she also teaches. She has published several articles on philosophical and methodological problems in biology, particularly in evolutionary theory and genetics, problems of scientific world views, and feminist philosophy.

Valentina Konstantinova is a Senior Research Fellow and Deputy Director of the Center for Gender Studies in Moscow. She is an active feminist, involved in organizing a feminist network in Moscow. Her Ph.D. thesis was on feminism in Great Britain, and she is currently interested in women in politics and new social movements in the former USSR.

Larissa Lissyutkina has a Ph.D. from Moscow University, with a thesis on Max Weber's sociology of religion. Until 1991, when it closed, she was a researcher at the Academy of Sciences in the Institute for the History of the Workers Movement. She has published three books on new social movements in Germany, and articles on new social movements in the West and informal movements in the USSR. She has also written on Raul Wallenberg. She had a fellowship in Germany for the year 1990–1991, and published frequent journalistic articles in Germany during that time.

Jane Mansbridge is Jane W. Long Professor of the Arts and Sciences at Northwestern University in the Department of Political Science, and a Faculty Fellow at the Center for Urban Affairs and Policy Research at Northwestern.

Cornelia Merdzanska graduated from the University of Sofia with a degree in English Language and Literature. She is Assistant Professor in the Department of English Literature at the University of Sofia.

Andjelka Milić received her Ph.D. in Sociology from the University of Belgrade. She is Professor of Family Sociology in the Department of Sociology, Faculty of Philosophy. She has published several books about family, youth, and women and feminism, as well as on political behavior.

Magda Mueller is Assistant Professor of German Studies at Stanford University. She has taught at Columbia University in the German Department and specializes in women and women's issues in Germany, and the philosophy of Ernst Bloch.

Hildegard Maria Nickel is Professor of Sociology at Humboldt University in Berlin (East), Dean of the Social Science Faculty, and cofounder of the Interdisciplinary Center of Women's Studies at Humboldt. She is author of many articles, has lectured widely on women in the former GDR, and has recently coedited a book, *Women in Germany*.

Rossica Panova was born in 1956 in Sofia, Bulgaria. She has a B.A. in History from the University of Sofia and is a researcher at the Institute of History in Sofia.

Anastasya Posadskaya is an economist and a head of the Center for Gender Studies in Moscow. She received her Ph.D. from the Institute of Economics of the former USSR Academy of Sciences on the topic of the employment of women in the former USSR. She has done several sociological surveys on women and has written several articles on women. She is a very active feminist in Moscow.

Dimitrina Petrova has been a Member of Parliament since June 1990 representing the environmental movement ECOGLASNOST, one of the founding members of the Union of Democratic Forces (UDF). She is a Professor of Philosophy at the Kliment Okhridski University of Sofia, Bulgaria, and teaches courses on the philosophy of law in the Department of Law. She has published extensively in the field of philosophy and political science. She is currently working on a critical theory of value rationality. She is a founder of ECOGLASNOST, the most active opposition organization in Bulgaria during the last year of communist rule. She is now affiliated with the Center for the Study of Democracy (CSD), an independent institution for research and policy analyses established in Sofia in 1989. She is starting a women's studies project at the CSD.

Christina Schenk has been a member since 1990 of the all-German Parliament (Bundestag) from the feminist Independent Women's Association (UFV) part of Bündnisgo/Greens. She focuses on women's policy and social policy. She was a co-founder of the UFV. She had previously been a research assistant at the Academy of Sciences of the GDR in physics and had done post-graduate studies in sociology.

Jiřina Šiklová was a member of the Faculty of Philosophy at Charles University until 1970, when she was fired. She then worked as a cleaning woman and social worker in a hospital. She was one of the signatories of Charter 77 and was a dissident, smuggling literature into the country. She was imprisoned in 1981 for a year for this activity, and again in 1988, working as a cleaning woman again until January 1990. In May 1990 she was reappointed to the faculty of philosophy at Charles University. She is a member of the International Committee of the Helsinki Citizens Assembly and helped to found the Center and Library for Gender Studies at Charles University.

Anna Titkow has a Ph.D. in Sociology and works at the Institute for Philosophy and Sociology at the Polish Academy of Sciences. Her major fields of interest are medical sociology, social stress, and gender studies. She is cofounder of the Sisterhood is Global Institute.

Maria Todorova is Professor of History at the University of Florida in Gainsville. She was Professor of Balkan History at the University of Sofia, Bulgaria. She was a Fellow of the Woodrow Wilson International Center for Scholars in 1988, Fulbright Visiting Professor at the University of Maryland, College Park, and the University of California, Irvine (1989–90), and Mellon Distinguished Visiting Professor at Rice University (1990–1992). She works on problems of nineteenth-century Balkan social and political history and is the author of several books. Her most recent book is *Balkan Family History and the European Pattern: Demographic Developments in Ottoman Bulgaria* (American University Press).

Olga Tóth is Professor of Sociology at Estvan University in Budapest, Hungary. She has written many articles on women and the family.

Elizabeth Waters teaches Russian and Soviet history at the Australian National University. She has published articles on the social history of the 1920s and on social issues in the era of perestroika. Her current research project is a study of gender and Soviet society, 1917 to 1991.

Index

Abortion, 2, 11, 55, 57; arguments
against, 101, 195, 198, 242, 244–50,
279; arguments for, 242, 245, 246–8;
attitudes to, 101–2, 196, 200n21, 203,
206, 220, 254; birth rates and, 23,
101; church and, 102, 123, 200n20,
242, 243, 249, 259, 264; conditions,
279; constitution and, 12, 124–5, 126,
157, 208; counseling, 196, 197, 198,
200n20 , 279; gynecological exams,
46, 55; health and, 101; *See* also Catholic Church; Contraception; Demography; Elections, abortions and
Abortion: mortality and; 55, 255, 297; nationalism and, 113, 125, 126; opposition to, 242–3, 246–7, 259, 264; privacy, 195; prochoice, 220; protests,
113, 198, 247, 251, 259; punishment
for, 243, 247; rate of, 195, 198,
200n9, 204–5, 222n18, 242, 297; reasons for, 101–2, 195, 242; restrictions
on, 123, 241–2, 243, 249; rhetoric of,
244–5; rights, 2, 113, 157, 199, 242,
246, 247, 248, 262; Stalin and, 242,
278; *See* also Contraception; Physician's Code of Ethics
Abortion in: Bulgaria, 23–4, 37; Croatia,
123, 125; Czech and Slovak Republics,
101–3; former USSR, 101, 274, 278,
279, 295, 297, 310–11; Germany,
191n3, 192n13, 194–200; Hungary,

204, 208, 216–7, 236; Poland, 241–
52, 254, 258, 260, 262–4, 272n21; Ro-
mania, 6, 49, 50, 54–6; Slovakia,
102–3; Slovenia, 124, 125
Abortion legislation in, 46, 101–2, 113;
Germany, 194, 197, 198; Hungary,
204, 205, 208; Poland, 241, 243, 244–
50, 259, 260, 262, 264; Serbia, 113;
Slovenia, 124; *See* also Parliament and
abortion; Law and legislation
Abuse of women, 40, 56, 103, 205, 267
Adoption, 11, 57, 103
Agriculture, 39, 54
AIDS, 57, 279
Aksenov, Vasily, 284
Albania\Albanians, 2, 55, 112–3, 115,
116, 126
Alcoholism, 285, 305
Androgyny, *See* Emancipation, and an-
drogyny.
Anthias and Yuval-Davis, 112
Antifascist Women's Front(former Yugo-
slavia), 111, 127
Antifeminism, 2, 4, 24, 25, 230, 226–8,
232, 236, 278; as critique of state so-
cialism, 227, 233; blaming women
and, 226, 232, 236; divorce and, 228–
30, 232, 234–5; in Hungary, 225–40;
private sphere and, 234, 236; *See* also
Feminism
Antipolitics, 225–6, 235, 312

337

Anti-semitism, 302n15
Antonescu, Marshal, 141
Arendt, Hannah, 232
Association for Family Planning and Sex
    Education (Czech and Slovak Repub-
    lics), 102
Association for the Dignity of Women,
    251
Association of Business Women and Man-
    agers (Czech and Slovak Republics),
    104
Attitudes towards other women, 25, 27
Autonomy, 67, 204, 226, 233, 235, 236;
    and the individual, 324

Balcerowicz, Leszek, 265
Banat, 39
Bebel, August, 75
Beke, Kata, 229–30
Bessolova, Olga, 294
Biełecki, Jan Krzysztof, 268
Birth control: and antifeminism, 228; in
    Bulgaria, 23; in GDR, 195; in Hun-
    gary, 204–5, 228; in Poland, 255, 270;
    in Romania, 41; See also Abortion;
    Contraception
Birth rate in, 27, 96, 254; Albania, 126;
    former USSR, 297; Hungary, 210,
    215, 216, 217, 226; Romania, 54–6;
    Serbia, 113, 126
Black market, See Underground economy
Blandiana, Ana, 58–9
Blasinska, Barbara, 262
Bogoraz, Larisa, 293
Bolshevik, 39
Bonner, Elena, 30
Bosnia-Herzegovina, 123, 129; immi-
    grants, 126
Braidotti, Rosi, 66
Bulgarian Association of University
    Women, 29n7
Bulgarian Women's Union, 34
Bundestag, 190, 196, 198; See also Par-
    liament
Business, and women, 26, 300

Capitalism, 23, 74, 80, 98, 165, 184,
    312–3; feminism and, 258; former

USSR and, 277, 281; patriarchy and,
    304, 309, 310; socioeconomic transfor-
    mation and, 303, 314; women's in-
    equality and, 308
Catholic Church, 125; in Hungary, 210,
    220; in Poland, 242–3, 249, 258, 259,
    263–5, 269, 270, 271n20, 272n3; poli-
    tics and, 258–9, 271n20; Solidarity
    and, 264; See also Abortion, church
    and; Church; Politics, church and
Catholic Czech Council of Bishops, 102
Ceausescu, Elena and Nicolae, 43, 46,
    48, 49, 50, 51n10, 53, 54–5, 57
Center for Anti-War Action in Belgrade,
    119
Center for the Study of Democracy (Bul-
    garia), 26, 28n5
Chamber of Physicians (Poland), 249,
    250
Charter 77, 77, 104
Chernobyl, 27, 28–9n6
Childbearing: and constitution, 124, 125;
    in Bulgaria, 19, 23, 32; in Croatia,
    124; in Czech and Slovak Republics,
    96, 98, 103, 262; in former USSR, 97;
    in Romania, 46, 56; in Serbia, 113; in
    Slovenia, 124; miscarriages and, 29n6;
    rate of, 19, 32, 210; "surrogate moth-
    ers", 103; See also Maternity benefits
Child care, 231, 233, 270; allowances,
    217; in GDR, 181; in Hungary, 213,
    214, 215, 218, 226, 231; in Poland,
    261; leave, 270n10; See also Day care;
    Family allowances; Maternity leave
Childcare facilities, See Daycare
Childrearing, 145, 214, 230, 270; and
    child custody, 95, 228, 234–5
Children, 22, 45, 55, 57, 99, 124, 254;
    antifeminism and, 24–5, 228, 230,
    231, 232, 233, 235; attitude to, 8, 17,
    91–2, 214, 216, 217, 254; divorce
    and, 234, 235; gender and, 214; in Bul-
    garia, 17; in Hungary, 214, 215, 216,
    227, 230, 231; legislation and, 113,
    270n10; nationalism and, 116, 118,
    119, 125; orphans and, 57; parents
    and, 125; political power and, 91, 233;

poverty, 27; transition and, 145, 326; *See* also Marriage, children; Daycare

Child support payments, 216, 232, 234

Christian Women's Movement (Bulgaria), 35

Church, 9, 14, 166; education and, 264; homosexuality in the GDR and, 161–2, 182; nationalism and, 264; women's groups and, 182, 265; *See* also Abortion, church and; Catholic Church; Politics, church and

Citizen's Alliance (Romania), 53, 59

Civil society, 28, 53, 57, 59, 157, 182, 225, 249; absence of, 220; theory of, 13, 327; *See* also Public sphere

Cimoszewicz, Włodzimierz, 261

Club of Modern Women (Czech and Slovak Republics), 104

Club of Single Mothers (Czech and Slovak Republics), 104

Codrescu, Andrei, 50

Collective (ism), 10, 16, 50, 67, 85, 92, 112, 168; differences East\West, 5, 6, 324; emancipation and, 90–1; individual and, 6, 67, 90, 246, 283, 306, 324; women and, 324; social control and, 85; socialism and, 91; *See* also Holism.

Committee for the Unjustly Persecuted (VONS), 77

Committee of Bulgarian Women, 34

Committee of Soviet Women, 288, 289, 293, 294, 296

Communism, 42, 201–2, 260, 261, 303, 306; feminism and, 259, 261, 303; postcommunism, 25; precommunism, 63; *See* also Work, women's attitude to

Communist party, 68–9, 76, 78–9; church and, 265; in former Yugoslavia, 110–1, 114, 117, 127, 128; in Poland, 248, 254, 261, 265; media and, 126–7; sexual equality and, 298; universalism and, 110; women and, 13, 175, 254, 261, 265, 289

Communist women's organizations, *See* Women's organizations

Consciousness raising, 259

Constitution in, 12, 124–5, 131; Croatia, 124, 125; former USSR, 311; GDR, 156, 157, 164; Poland, 247; Slovenia, 124–5; *See* also Abortion, and constitution

Consumer goods, 86, 274, 276, 305, 311; and consumption, 92, 184

Contraception in, 305; Czech and Slovak Republics, 102; former USSR, 297, 311; GDR, 194; Germany, 198; Hungary, 222n17; Poland, 260, 270n1 0; Romania, 46, 49, 54; *See* also Birth control

Cornea, Doina, 59

Croatia, 114, 116, 117, 118, 119, 123–5, 127, 129

Croatian Democratic Union (HDZ), 123, 124, 125, 132

"Cuckoo mothers," 296

Czech Ministry of Education, Youth and Physical Education, 100

Czech National Council, 100

Czech Social Democrats, 105

Czech Union of Women, 103–4

Daycare: attitudes to, 8, 99, 145; costs, 99, 100; law and, 197; private, 45, 98–9; quality of, 98; subsidies for, 98–100; utilization of, 99–100; *See* also Childcare

Daycare in, 308; Bulgaria, 27; Czech and Slovak Republics, 98–100; GDR, 144, 147, 148n15; Hungary, 209, 214–5, 226, 236; Poland, 254–5, 259; Romania, 43, 54

Decembrists, 282

Democracy, 121–3, 152–4, 155, 191, 251, 263; abortion and, 241, 244, 246, 248; antipolitics and, 226, 312–4; consensus and, 156; diversity and, 306; family and, 12, 306, 311, 314; feminism and, 303, 304, 305, 307, 314; in former USSR, 292, 293, 299, 300; in former Yugoslavia, 109–10; women and, 27, 35, 151, 157, 185, 208, 234, 260, 263, 304, 305, 309, 310; *See* also Round Table in

Democracy Now (GDR), 187, 190
Democratic Union, Parlimentary Club (Poland), 247
Democratic Union of Women (Bulgaria), 28
Democratic Women's League of Germany (DFD), 183
Demography and demographic policy in, 26, 46, 54, 114; Croatia, 114, 124; Poland, 242, 245; Serbia, 113; Slovenia, 126; See also Birthrate in; Pronatalism; Population policy
Demos, 123, 124
DFD, 183
Discrimination: attitudes towards, 97, 181; awareness of, 183; in Bulgaria, 26; in Czech and Slovak Republics, 98; in employment, 7, 23, 70, 75, 140, 181, 192n14, 219, 276; in former USSR, 275–6, 311; in GDR, 140, 141, 148n10; in Hungary, 220, 236; in Poland, 260, 261; in Romania, 44; in social assistance, 113; law and, 113, 157, 192n14, 262
Dissidents and women, 13, 77–8, 226, 229, 278, 287
Division of labor, See Employment, gender division of labor in; Family, division of labor in
Divorce, 9; child custody, 96, 234, 236; in Bulgaria, 20; in Czech and Slovak Republics, 76, 95, 96; in GDR, 181; in Hungary, 210, 215–6, 227–8, 229, 232, 234–5, 236, 239–40n41; in Romania, 54; rate of, 326
Domestic work, 299; affective work and, 44, 142; attitudes to, 299, 312; communism and, 44; division of labor in, 76, 96, 139, 142–3, 215, 217; employment and, 142; in Czech and Slovak Republics, 96, 97–9; in GDR, 139, 142; in Hungary, 203, 217, 234; in Poland, 254; in Romania, 40–4, 50, 54, 56; men and, 142; See also Double Burden
Double burden, 45, 71, 86, 169, 230, 269, 288, 299, 322–3; attitudes toward, 45, 147, 218, 224, 299; career

and, 140; desire to continue working, 45; desire to return to the home, 93, 96, 220, 266, 299, 321, 326; in Bulgaria, 17, 19–20, 23, 33, 36; in Czech and Slovak Republics, 70–1, 75, 87, 93, 96; in former USSR, 276, 298, 299; in GDR, 142, 147, 171, 174–5, 181; in Hungary, 204, 213, 214, 217, 218–9; in Poland, 253–4, 261, 266; in Romania, 44; See also Domestic work; Employment; Motherhood
Drakulić, Slavenka, 318–20
Dual role, See Double burden
Dubna, 12, 294, 295
du Plessix Gray, Francine, 312

East\West women, 319–325; differences, 1, 3–4, 8, 323–5, 327–8; language and, 3–4; misunderstandings, 1, 3; moralism and, 321; values and, 323–4, 328; See also Values
Ecoglasnost, 29
Ecology, 12, 29, 59, 293
Economic transformation, See Socioeconomic transformation; Unemployment
Economy, 8, 75, 140, 304, 305; market, 26, 95, 142, 144, 146, 147, 265, 304; second economy, 215, 219, 221; underground economy, 45, 54; See also Employment; Unemployment
Education, 70, 81, 141, 266; and gender, 141, 145–6 148n14, 182, 214, 266, ; in Bulgaria, 17, 19, 22, 33; in Czech and Slovak Republics, 97; in former USSR, 291; in GDR, 145, 182; in Hungary, 209, 214, 215, 219, 222n4; in Poland, 266
Elections, 110, 114, 116, 124, 133, 248, 254; abortion and, 241, 243, 249; nationalism and, 110, 124; women, 12, 116, 117–20, 134, 188, 193n21, 254, 274; See also Politics, women's participation in; Political parties
Emancipation, 10, 79–80; androgyny and, 85, 277; attitudes toward, 49, 65, 79, 81, 84, 86, 87, 93, 127, 180, 226–8; collectivism and, 91; difference and, 85,

93; dignity and, 87; employment, 85, 91, 274; "forced," 24, 278, 308; in Bulgaria, 19, 22–3, 24, 25; in former USSR, 274, 277, 278, 281, 288, 310; in former Yugoslavia, 127; in Hungary, 237n1; meaning of, 25, 48, 79–80, 85, 89–1, 93, 95; patriarchy and , 7; sexuality and, 228, 277; socialism and, 27, 65, 74, 75, 84–5, 151

Employment, 7, 70–1, 85, 86, 89, 98, 141; attitudes to, 26, 64, 76, 83n5, 98, 148n3, 275, 276, 280; benefits, 7, 20, 291, 309; business and, 26, 50, 203, 206n2, 207, 209

Employment, discrimination in, See Discrimination; Double burden; Socioeconomic transformation

Employment, gender division of labor in, 138–9, 143, 253, 266; Czech and Slovak Republics, 262; GDR, 138–44, 166, 179n4&5, 181; Hungary, 235; Poland, 262

Employment: health and, 253, 254; industrialization and, 126, 218; inequality and, 85–6, 303; job segregation, 26, 71; leadership in, 75, 85, 97; part-time, 98, 142, 149n18, 209, 265–6, 292, 326; pensions, 271n10; protective legislation, 95, 98, 100–1, 148n6, 254, 259–60, 308-, 310, 311; qualifications, 144, 147, 179n4, 206n1, 219, 266, 291; quotas, 4, 48, 78–9, 85, 97, 153, 154; rate of, 139, 209, 218, 311; retirement, 114, 208–9; salaries, 85–6, 97, 48n20, 219, 262, 270, 271n13, 303, 311; single women and, 76, 209, 254; See also Double burden; Maternity leave; Motherhood, single mothers; Motherhood, employment and; Unemployment

Employment in communism in, 64, 75, 261, 275; Bulgaria, 17–8, 22; Czech and Slovak Republics, 64, 75, 85, 97–8; former USSR, 292, 311; GDR, 140–1, 143, 144, 147; Hungary, 203, 206, 208–9, 218; Poland, 260, 261, 266; Romania, 41–2, 45

Enache, Smaranda, 59

Environment, 27, 28–9n6; See also Ecology

Epistemology, 109

Equality, 1, 48, 49, 88, 95–6, 133, 267; androgyny and, 6, 95, 134, 303, 308, 310; attitudes to, 6, 62, 75, 85, 278; differences and, 65, 85, 88, 90, 135, 310; egalitarianism, 27, 41, 70, 136, 308; feminism and, 133; formal equality, 93, 95, 182, 259, 275, 310; gender and, 142, 214, 234, 255, 262, 266, 267, 298, 305, 306–7, 308; inequality, 22–3; meaning of, 6, 25, 47, 65–6, 84, 153, 305, 306, 307, 308; of opportunity, 25, 95, 97; rights and, 34, 75, 152, 157, 184, 247, 278, 310; salary and, 97, 262; socialism and, 63, 75, 80; substantive, 157; work and, 75

Essentialism, 6, 25, 27, 89, 97, 227, 228, 229, 234, 269, 322; antiessentialism, 289; East European women and, 324–5

Ethnic tensions, 23, 39, 105, 201, 293 See also Gypsy; Muslims

European Community, 97, 101

Family, 146, 210, 226, 311, 323, 327; allowances, 98–100, 210, 217, 218, 270n10; antifeminism and, 227–8, 234–5, 288, 296; autonomy and, 233–4, 235; daycare, 226, 261; democracy and, 306; division of labor in, 219, 234, 261; economy and, 68, 69, 70, 72; family wage, 96–7; in contemporary literature, 87; in Czech and Slovak Republics, 64, 75; in former USSR, 288, 289, 296, 299, 305; in Hungary, 233–4, 235; in Poland, 253–4, 265, 270n10; in Romania, 42–4; law, 153, 235; members, 92, 217–8; men in, 142, 148n13; policy, 141–2, 217; public sphere and, 323; school and, 145; single parent and, 9; state and, 226, 233; women's status, 75, 210, 253; See also Child rearing, and child custody; Day care; Gender roles; Mater-

nity leave in; Motherhood; Domestic
work
Federal Republic of Germany (FRG), 184
Feminism, 2, 37, 88, 127–8, 131, 133,
261, 269; attitudes towards, 35–6, 65,
74, 79, 127, 128, 207, 320; church
and, 258, 263; communism and, 258,
259, 287; Communist Party and, 258;
democracy and, 303; difference and,
84, 133, 303, 328; East\West
women, 319–20, 325, 327–8; in former USSR, 274, 278, 280, 286, 289,
290, 292; in Hungary, 235; in Poland,
257, 258, 261, 263, 268, 269; interstices model of, 257–8; family and, 8,
9, 324; liberal, 304, 307; Marxism,
299; paid work, 322; post-communism,
1, 20, 319–325, 327–8, 322, 324; socialism and, 154, 308; socialist, 304,
307–8; See also Antifeminism; East\
West women; Western feminism
Feminist Network (Hungary), 208,
211n5, 240n44
Femininity, See Gender roles, femininity
Fillion, Kate, 100
Foucault, 249
frau anders, 163
Free Democrats (Hungary), 239n40
Free Feminist Association, 29n8
Freedom, 304, 305, 307; and choice,
326; See also Individuals, and freedom
Friendships, 221
Für Dich, 6, 14, 168–79, 195; and UFV,
175
Functionalism, 89

Gay men, See Homosexuality
Gender identity, 8, 47–8; and alienation,
322; and bipolarity, 229
Gender roles, 68–9, 96, 139, 143, 169–
70, 253; antifeminism and, 227, 229–
31, 234; attitudes to, 142, 143, 227,
229, 254, 266, 274; beauty and, 267,
272n28, 275, 280, 296; changes in, 6,
7, 8, 96, 166, 169, 177, 285; choice
and, 325; church and, 265; communism and, 95, 175, 277; division of la-

bor and, 171, 235; domestic work and,
142, 178, 234; education and, 139–40,
141; employment and, 169–72, 174,
176, 235; family and, 142, 181,
239n36, 234, 263; femininity and,
168, 169, 170, 171, 172, 175, 176,
282; gender equality and, 305; images
of, 168–79; in former USSR, 275,
277, 282, 284, 285; in Poland, 266; in
Romania, 39–40; in the home, 276;
marriage, 175, 181; masculinity, 229–
30, 283; mothers and, 171, 175, 181;
Oriental tradition, 16; power, 172; return to home, 45, 81, 97, 99, 326;
self-respect, 253, 254; triple burden,
23, 305; See also Double Burden; Employment, gender division of labor in;
Literature and women; Sexuality
Gender studies, 82
German unification, 157, 194, 196
Gleichstellung, See Office for the Equal-
ity of Women (Germany)
Greens, 184, 189, 191, 193n22
Gorbachev, Mikhail, 288, 289, 303, 304,
311–2
Groys, Boris, 285
Gubi, Magda, 230–4, 239n31
GYES, 217
Gypsy, 23, 80–1, 209, 226
Gypsy Women Association, 104

Havel, Václav, 304, 312–3
HDZ, 123, 124, 125, 132
Health of women, 27, 29, 46, 55, 76,
203, 253, 254, 311
Henning, Gert, 194
Hernádi, Miklós, 227–9
History, 131–3, 201; in former USSR,
277–8, 280, 282, 298–9; in former Yu-
goslavia, 111–2, 133; of abortion in Po-
land, 242; women and, 10, 16, 18,
30–4, 39–41, 62–4, 202
Holism, 90–2
Homosexuality: attitudes toward, 160;
Bulgaria, 20; church and, 161; Czech
and Slovak Republics, 103; former
USSR, 278; GDR, 160–2, 163, 165;

law and, 165; Poland, 268, 272–3n30;
  See also Lesbians; Stasi
Honecker, Erich, 181
Horáková, Milade, 77
Household work, See Domestic work
Housing, 221, 234
Human rights, 156
Hungarian Democratic Forum, 229,
  239n40
Hungarian Women's Association, 208,
  240n44

Identity, 6, 10, 66, 70, 85, 253, 284;
  alienation and, 86; in Bulgaria, 19, 21;
  in literature, 87
Ideology, 27, 80
Iliescu, 53, 55
Independent Erotic Initiative, 103
Independent Women's Association
  (UFV), 152, 153, 154, 155, 180–93;
  elections and, 187, 189, 190; Für
  Dich, 175; lesbians and, 163, 189; par-
  liament and, 185, 187, 190; Round Ta-
  ble, 183, 186, 188; Social Charter,
  186; state and, 180, 183–4, 187
Individual/ism, 5, 67, 88, 92, 132, 145,
  146–7, 204, 277, 278; and emancipa-
  tion, 91; and freedom, 304, 305; See
  also Collective
Industry, 32, 218, 254; forced industrial-
  ization, 53–4; insurance, 143–4; labor
  market and, 75, 218; textile, 98
Initiative for Peace and Human Rights
  (GDR), 187, 190
Instrumental rationality, 5, 89, 300
International Women's Day in, Bulgaria,
  19; Poland, 260
Islam, 16, 19

Jaruzelski, 254
Jewish, 226, 318, 321
Job segregation, See Discrimination, in
  employment; Employment, gender division of labor in

Kádár, Janos, 224, 226
Kantůrková, Eva, 87, 104

Kazakhstan, 293
KGB, 287
Kommunist, 289
Konstantinova, Valentina, 290, 292–9
Kvačková, Rada, 100
Kindergartens, 27, 99, 100; See also Day
  care
Kis, Danilo, 109
Kobieta, 262
Kollontai, Alexandra, 298–9
Konrád, György, 225, 237n6
Konstantinova, Valentina, 289
Kopera, Kasimierz, 268
Kosovo, 112–3, 115
Kristeva, Julia, 131, 132, 133, 134
Kuratowska, Zofia, 268

Labor force, women in, 64, 147; Bulgaria, 22, 32; Czech and Slovak Republics, 75, 98; GDR, 140–1; Hungary,
  209; See also Employment
Labor market, 22, 26, 146, 147, 218; See
  also Discrimination; Employment
Labuda, Barbara, 247, 263
Language, 35, 148n9
Law and legislation, 26, 67, 100; in Bulgaria, 16; in Czech and Slovak Republics, 98, 100–1; in GDR, 160, 184,
  192n14, 194–9; in Hungary, 208; in
  Poland, 241–50, 255; in Serbia, 113;
  socialism and, 70; "surrogate mothers"
  and, 103–4; See also Abortion, legislation in; Children, legislation; Constitution in; Employment, protective legislation; Lesbians, law and
Leadership positions of women in: GDR,
  143; Poland, 262, 263, 265; See also
  Power of women in; Politics, women's
  participation in
Lesbians, 9, 11; in Bulgaria, 20; in former USSR, 293; in GDR, 157, 160–7;
  in Poland, 268; law and, 160, 164,
  165; UFV and, 189
Liberalism, 304, 305, 306, 307; See also
  Feminism, liberal
Lipovskaya, Olga, 289, 294

Literature and women, 87, 282–3, 284, 285
Lithuania, 294–5
Łodz, 254, 261
LOTUS, 289, 290, 296
Luca, Gherasim, 45

Magyar nök Lapja, 224
Mamonova, Tatyana, 287
Marriage, 8, 66; advantages of, 76, 215; children and, 55, 216; economic position and, 76, 215; in Hungary, 204, 215, 219, 232, 234; in Romania, 40, 55; mixed, 116; rate of, 8, 32
Marx, 75, 143, 299, 304, 306, 308
Marxism, 22, 299, 303, 305; and feminism, 299
Marxism-Leninism, 183
Marxist feminism, 35, 133
Masaryk, Charlotte, 62, 72n1
Maternity leave in, 26, 309; Czech and Slovak Republics, 99–100; GDR, 309; former USSR, 312; Hungary, 203, 209, 210–1, 211n6, 212n11, 214, 217; Poland, 261, 270n10; Serbia, 113
Matriarchy, 230
Matzke, Cornelia, 190
Media, 25, 27, 28, 50, 115, 208, 224; abortion and, 199, 249, 298; feminism and, 14, 268; in Croatia, 127; in former USSR, 284, 286–7, 288, 289, 290, 295–6, 297, 298; in former Yugoslavia, 126–7, 134; in Hungary, 208; war, 116, 119; *See* also *Für Dich*
Men: abortion and, 246; attitudes to, 283, 284, 285; domination and, 228, 230; family and, 139, 142, 228, 233; in former USSR, 283–4, 285, 292; in parliament, 76; masculinity, 229–30; totalitarianism and, 299
Merchant, Carolyn, 23
Merkel, Ina, 180, 320
Mibescu, Marta, 41
Michnik, Adam, 248
Military, women in, 118
Milošević, Slobodan, 126, 129, 131–2

Ministry for Women and Family (Poland), 260, 263
Miscarea ecologista, 59
Mlada fronta dnes, 104
Modernism, 10, 66
Modernization, 23, 146–7
Modrow, Hans, 155
Montenegro, 123, 129
Mortality rate of, children, 56, 57, 210, 216, 222, 254; women, 31, 46, 56, 216, 254
Moscow Center for Gender Studies, 289–301
Moscow News, 290
Motherhood, 56, 69, 99–100, 147, 210, 298, 311; constitution and, 125, 311; employment and, 9, 71, 140, 141; media and, 127; mothers, 115, 236; rate of, 142; single mothers, 9, 76, 142, 209; war and, 118–9, 129, 134
Movement for Women's Self-Defense(Poland), 251
Mózny, I., 84, 89, 90
Muslims, 37, 123
Muttipolitik, 181

National Alliance of Hungarian Women, 202
Nationalism, 10, 116; collectivism and, 110, 120; communism and, 110; Communist Party and, 110; democracy and, 109–10; ethnic minorities and, 105, 120; in former USSR, 275, 277, 278; in former Yugoslavia, 109–18, 123, 125, 126, 127; in Hungary, 216; in Poland, 264; in Romania, 50; patriarchy, 135; patriotism, 110; war and, 115, 118–19; women and, 105, 112–20, 121n14, 127, 129–30, 135, 136; *See* also Abortion and nationalism; Children, nationalism; Reproductive freedom, nationalism and
National Organization of Women (Romania), 49
National Salvation Front, 49, 53, 55, 58, 59
Neoconservatism, 36

Network of East-West women, 82
Neues Forum (New Forum), 154, 187
NEZHDI, 289
Nomenklatura 48, 50–1, 53, 59n1

Office for the Equality of Women (Germany), 153, 157, 186, 188, 189
Old age pension, 100; *See also* Retirement
Orthodox Church, 37, 57

Pamyat, 302n15
Parental leave, 20, 100, 270; *See also* Maternity leave in
Parenting, 66, 96, 140
Parliament: and abortion, 196, 242, 244–9, 262; Bundestag, 190, 196, 198; in Croatia, 124; in GDR, 164–5, 183, 185, 186, 195–7; in Hungary, 203–4, 205, 207, 208; in Poland, 241, 243, 244–51, 254, 259, 262; in Slovenia, 124; *See also* Sejm
Parliament, women in, *See* Politics, women in
Parliamentary Women's Club (Poland), 247, 250, 263
Partei Demokratische Sozialismus (PDS), 164
Patriarchy, 84, 135, 304, 305, 308, 313; attitudes to, 230; in Bulgaria, 18, 22; in former USSR, 288, 290, 292; in GDR, 141–2, 143, 158, 163, 169, 175, 178, 184; in Hungary, 229; in Romania, 41, 44, 56; language and, 15; nationalism and, 135; rights and, 307; social structure and, 143, 202
Pauker, Ana, 42
PAX Catholic Association, 242
Peasantry, 8, 32, 39, 41–3, 45, 46, 300
Pension, *See* Retirement
Perestroika, 1, 280
Physician's Code of Ethics, 249
Pleasure principle, 283–4
Polish Feminist Association, 251, 258, 265
Polish United Workers' Party (PUWP), 250, 254

Political parties, 49, 53, 76–8, 105, 114, 115, 116, 117; abortion and, 49, 196, 247, 250; in Bosnia-Herzogovina, 123; in Croatia, 123–5; in former USSR, 300; in GDR, 187, 191n4, 193n22; in Poland, 189, 250, 254, 257, 258, 259; in Serbia, 123; in Slovenia, 124; women's issues and, 49, 77, 104–5, 114, 124–5, 196; women's participation and, 114, 117–8, 158, 188, 250; *See also* Politics, women's participation in
Political Party of Women and Mothers (Czechoslovakia), 105
Politics, attitudes towards in: Czech and Slovak Republics, 70, 78; former USSR, 300; GDR, 182–3, 189, 190; Hungary, 203; Poland, 250, 273n4; Romania, 48, 57
Politics: church and, 249, 258, 264; power of women in, 149n21, 156; quotas, 124, 203, 274, 279, 280; toward women, 181; women's issues, 12, 36, 65, 151, 153, 182, 207, 251, 254; *See also* Abortion, church and; Power of women in, politics; Quotas
Politics, women's participation in, 12–3, 165; Bulgaria, 18, 26, 29n8, 36; communism, 23, 25, 59, 77, 124; Croatia, 124; Czech and Slovak Republics, 65, 76–9, 81; former USSR, 275, 292, 293; former Yugoslavia, 114, 118; GDR, 151–2, 154–5, 182–3, 185–7, 188, 189–91; Hungary, 202, 203, 204, 208, 227, 229; Poland, 247, 250, 251, 254, 255, 257, 259; Romania, 49–50, 53, 58–9; Slovenia, 124; united Germany, 164, 196; *See also* Elections; Political parties; Round Table
Popowicz, Anna, 270n10
Population policy, 113, 126; *See also* Demography
Pornography in, 11, 310; Bulgaria, 27, 36; Czech and Slovak Republics, 62, 103; Croatia, 127; GDR, 174; former USSR, 280, 296, 297; Hungary, 205; Poland, 267
Posadskaya, Anastasya, 290–300

Postcommunism, 2, 12, 14, 327
Postmodernism, 66, 135, 136
Power of women in: economy, 141; family, 215, 227; former Yugoslavia, 117, 123, 124; GDR, 138, 139, 141, 152, 153, 154, 156, 172, 186; Hungary, 203 234, 227, 228; politics, 18, 77, 117, 123, 124, 152, 153, 154, 156, 186, 203; *See* also Leadership positions of women in; Politics, women's participation in
Pregnancy, 66; and prenatal testing, 243
Private sphere: antifeminism and, 227, 234–5, 236; antipolitics and, 225; as asylum, 91, 146; autonomy and, 233; identity and, 69, 89, 225, 235; in literature, 87–8, 89; in socialism, 68–70; meaning of, 321, 323, 327; state and, 226, 310; substitutive function of, 68, 71; women and, 16, 69, 70; *See* also Family; Domestic work
Private sphere in, 133, 225–6, 310, 326–7; Bulgaria, 16; Czech and Slovak Republics, 68–9, 75; former USSR, 276, 283; GDR, 153, 181; Hungary, 225–6, 234–5, 236; Romania, 55–6; *See* also Family
Pro Familia, 196
Pro Femina, 251
Pronatalism in: Czech and Slovak Republics, 96, 99; Romania, 46; Serbia, 113
Prostitution, 12, 55, 103; former USSR, 275, 280, 281, 283–4, 293
Protective legislation, *See* Employment, protective legislation
Public sphere, 12, 13, 16, 18, 27, 58, 76; abortion and, 241–2, 248; absence of, 47, 64, 89, 161, 248, 251; creation of, 151; family and, 323, 326, 327; individual in, 67, 69; subjectivity and, 68, 70; transformation of, 326–7; women in, 71, 152, 154, 182, 234, 289, 328; *See* also Employment; Politics
Public vs. private sphere, 5, 66, 68–70, 92, 276, 305, 323; children and, 145; transition and, 145, 326–7
Pushkin, Alexander, 285

Quotas, *See* Politics, quotas; Employment, quotas

Rabotnitsa, 288, 298
Rakhova, Silvia, 28
Ramparts of Love, 134, 136
Rape, 115, 205, 267
Rationality, 23, 85
Rationalization, 327
Religion, 26, 76, 197, 255, 264, 272n21; women and, 265, 287; *See* also Abortion, church and; Catholic Church; Church
Reproductive freedom, 96, 112, 199, 279, 305; ethnic conflicts and, 112; in Slovenia, 124; legislation and, 114; nationalism and, 114; state policies and, 23; *See* also Abortion; Catholic Church
Retirement, 114, 208–9; pensions, 192, 270–1n10
Říčan, Pavel, 96
Rights, 307, 309; individual, 50, 132, 265; of participation, 157; reproductive, 22, 113, 246, 247, 310; universal, 310; *See* also Abortion
Rights in: Bulgaria, 20, 22; Czech and Slovak Republics, 63; former Yugoslavia, 112, 133; GDR, 151, 156–7; Hungary, 234, 236; Poland, 247, 248; Serbia, 112–3; *See* also Abortion, rights
Rimashevskaya, Natalya, 289
ROAD (Poland), 255
Round Table in, GDR, 154–6, 164, 183, 186, 192n20; Poland, 254

Second economy, 234; *See* also Underground economy
Secret police and women, 79
Securitate, 48, 53, 55, 59
SED (Sozialistische Einheitspartei Deutschland), 141, 175, 182
Sejm, 241, 242, 244, 247–51passim; 272n25
Self-realization, 64, 93; and self-sacrifice, 92

Serbians, 39, 112–4, 116, 117, 119; and Serbo-Montenegrin, 115
Serbian Socialist Party, 126, 133
Service sector, 57, 266
Sex education, 103, 246, 248
Sex equality, *See* Equality, gender and
Sexuality, 40, 47–8, 56, 167n1, 239n39, 249, 267; antifeminism and, 227–8, 231; communism and, 11, 46, 47, 49, 281, 283–4, 295, 297–8; democracy and, 306; double standard, 267, 268; emancipation and, 228, 295, 297; exploitation and, 11–2; functionaries and, 86, 284; in former USSR, 281–2, 283, 284, 295; in Romania, 47; media and, 127, 172, 283, 296–7; religion and, 282; women's, 2, 227–9, 231, 234
Sexual liberation, 45, 267
Sinyavsky, Andrei, 284
Slavophil, 10, 287, 288, 322
Slovak Republic, 72n4, 76
Slovenia, 114, 124, 126, 128, 129, 132
Sobchak, Anatoly, 280
Social Charter (GDR), 155, 186
Socialism, 6, 8, 13, 88, 184, 308, 309, 314; in Bulgaria, 17, 18, 23, 24; in Czech and Slovak Republics, 85; in former USSR, 293; in former Yugoslavia, 113; in Poland, 253, 266; in Romania, 47; "really existing," 63; women and, 5, 63, 79
Socioeconomic transformation, 2, 4, 7, 9, 324, 326, 328; discrimination in, 7, 98, 144, 289, 291, 311; in Bulgaria, 26, 36–7; in Czech and Slovak Republics, 98; in former USSR, 291, 292; in GDR, 143, 146, 166, 175; in Hungary, 210; in Poland, 265; in Romania, 41, 57; *See* also Unemployment
Solidarity (Solidarność), 9, 245, 270n10, 259, 261, 262, 263; and church, 263, 264, 265
Solt, Ottilia, 226, 237n9
Solzhenitsyn, Alexander, 284
SOS Hotlines, 128
Soviets, 288–9, 293–4
Stalinism, 260, 279, 311

Stasi (State Security Service), 155, 161, 186, 192n15
State, 226; civil society and, 249, 261; family and, 226, 232–3, 235, 323; policy toward women, 180, 181, 235, 236; socialism, 4, 227; Stalinist, 226, 235; women in the, 183–4, 235, 261; *See* also Politics, women's participation in; Civil society; Public sphere
Sterilization, 198
Subjectivity, 5, 66–8, 70, 135, 136
"Superwoman," 19, 89
"Surrogate" mothers, 11, 103–4
SZETA, 237n9
Szlek-Miller, Stefania, 263, 271n12&13

Technological paradigm, 89
Teleology, and socialism, 88
Tereshkova, Valentina, 288
Time and women, 5, 86–7, 91–3, 132, 134, 135, 136; in literature, 86–7
Timisoara, 49
Tirgu Mures, 59
Traditional culture: in Bulgaria, 16, 17, 20, 32; in Czech and Slovak Republics, 75, 76, 82, 87–8, 104; in former USSR, 275, 277, 280–2; in former Yugoslavia, 111, 120; in GDR, 146, 163; in Hungary, 225; in Poland, 249, 263–4, 267, 269; in Romania, 39–42, 50, 56–7; patriarchal tradition, 20, 39–42, 50, 76, 111, 267; *See* also Peasantry; Values
Transylvania, 39–40, 60–1n22
Trybuna, 249
Tudjman, Franjo, 131, 134
Turks, 23
Tyminski, Stanislaw, 257

Uj Tüköv, 224
UFV, *See* Independent Women's Association.
U.N. Convention on the Elimination of all Forms of Discrimination, 97
Underground economy, 45, 54
Unemployment of women in, 98, 326; Bulgaria, 26, 27, 35, 36–7; Czech and

Slovak Republics, 98; former USSR, 289, 291–2; GDR, 149n27, 326; Hungary, 203, 209, 237n8; Poland, 225, 262, 265, 271n13; Romania, 57
Unemployment insurance, 272n25
Union of Catholic Women, 104
United Women's Party (Russia), 293
Universalism, 66, 68, 88
Urbanization, 42

Vacarescu, Elena, 41
Valterová, Alena, 105
Values, 7, 68, 204, 206, 218, 254, 278, 282, 289, 322–4, 328; communism and, 283–4; conflict of norms, 50; crisis of, 281; differences East\West in, 322–6; family, 68, 146, 323–4; in GDR, 145, 146–7; perestroika and, 275, 280–1; utopian ideals, 278, 280; See also Collective\ism; Individual\ism; Autonomy
Vatra Romaneasca, 59
Violence against women, 27, 40, 46, 56, 175, 231n, 297
Vlasta, 105
Vojvodina, 113
Volkskammer, 183, 185; See also Parliament, in GDR
Voronina, Olga, 289, 296

Wałesa, Lech, 248, 257
Wall of Love, 129
War, 116; in former Yugoslavia, 109–22, 123, 128–30; peace and, 118, 119; political structure and, 109; reasons for, 109; resistance to, 118–9; women and, 109, 111–6, 118–22, 128–9
Weiblich, 199
Welfare, as social control in communism, 99
Western feminism, 1, 3, 13, 14, 64, 77–8, 82, 202, 213, 262, 303; attitudes to, 207, 268, 277, 286, 320; desire and, 325; differences with East, 5, 6, 80, 82, 90, 318–21, 322–5, 327–8; influence of, 1–2, 6, 81, 263; paid work and, 322, 325, 328; relativism, 5, 14,

321–2; support by, 105; See also Anti-feminism; East\West women; Feminism
Wogitzky, Charlotte, 195
Women and paid work, See Employment; Double Burden; Gender roles, employment and; Unemployment
Woman and Russia, 287
Women and Society (former Yugoslavia), 128
Women for Peace (GDR), 182
Women in Socialist Society (GDR), 182
Women's Democratic Union (Bulgaria), 35, 36
Women's Democratic Union (Poland), 255
Women's journals in, Bulgaria, 35; Romania, 49; Czech and Slovak Republics, 105; GDR, 165–79
Women's League (Poland), 250, 260–1
Women's Lobby (Serbia), 114
Women's movement: contemporary, 151, 153, 180, 181–2, 191, 255; interwar, 250; See also Independent Women's Association
Women's Movement for Yugoslavia, 128–9, 134, 136
Women's organizations, 9, 10, 13, 258; attitudes to, 127, 128, 250; church and, 182, 265; conservative, 96; communist, 13, 34–5, 49, 50–1, 80, 250, 260, 289; feminist, 34, 127, 134–6, 289
Women's organizations in: Bulgaria, 20, 25, 28, 29n8, 33–4, 35–6; Czech and Slovak Republics, 96, 104; former USSR, 278, 288–300; former Yugoslavia, 113, 114, 118, 119, 128–9, 134–5, 136; GDR, 51, 155, 158, 182, 183, 188; Hungary, 202, 208; Poland, 250–1, 255, 258, 259, 260, 265, 267; Romania, 49, 50–1; See also Communist Party; Independent Women's Association
Women's Parliamentary Club, 249, 250, 259
Women's Party (ZEST) (former Yugoslavia), 114, 119

Women's Preliminary Parliament (former Yugoslavia), 114
Women's studies, 28
Work, dual role of women and, *See* Double Burden; Domestic work in; Employment; Motherhood; Unemployment
Work, ethic, 266; paid, 96, 299; values, 266, 325, 326, 328; *See* also Equality, work and
Work: women's attitudes to, 26, 299, 322; in Bulgaria, 26; in Czech and Slovak Republics, 64, 71, 76, 86, 89, 96, 98; in former USSR, 292; in GDR, 143, 147, 181; in Hungary, 220; in Poland, 253, 254; in Romania, 41, 45; *See* also Employment, attitudes to
Worker-mother duality, *See* Domestic labor; Double burden; Employment; Motherhood

Working mothers, *See* Domestic work; Double burden; Employment; Motherhood
World War I, 201, 216
World War II, 111, 127, 131; and women, 111, 133, 242, 250, 283
Würfel, Uta, 196

Young Democratic Party (Hungary), 207
Ypsilon, 154, 199
Youths in GDR, 145
Yugoslav Army, 118, 119

Zakharova, Natalya, 289, 296
Zaunreiterin, 154, 199
Zhenata dnes, 35
Zhensovety, *See* Soviets